CISSP Practice Questions

Third Edition

Michael Gregg

CISSP Practice Questions Exam Cram, Third Edition

ISBN-13: 978-0-7897-4959-8

ISBN-10: 0-7897-4959-9

Library of Congress Cataloging-in-Publication data is on file.

Printed in the United States of America

Second Printing: July 1213

Trademarks

All terms mentioned in this book that are known to be trademarks or service marks have been appropriately capitalized. Pearson IT Certification cannot attest to the accuracy of this information. Use of a term in this book should not be regarded as affecting the validity of any trademark or service mark.

Warning and Disclaimer

Every effort has been made to make this book as complete and as accurate as possible, but no warranty or fitness is implied. The information provided is on an "as is" basis. The author and the publisher shall have neither liability nor responsibility to any person or entity with respect to any loss or damages arising from the information contained in this book or from the use of the CD or programs accompanying it.

Bulk Sales

Pearson IT Certification offers excellent discounts on this book when ordered in quantity for bulk purchases or special sales. For more information, please contact

U.S. Corporate and Government Sales
1-800-382-3419
corpsales@pearsontechgroup.com

For sales outside of the U.S., please contact

International Sales
international@pearsoned.com

Associate Publisher
Dave Dusthimer

Acquisitions Editor
Betsy Brown

Senior Development Editor
Christopher Cleveland

Managing Editor
Sandra Schroeder

Senior Project Editor
Tonya Simpson

Copy Editor
Sheri Cain

Technical Editors
Shawn Merdinger
Patrick Ramseier

Publishing Coordinator
Vanessa Evans

Multimedia Developer
Timothy Warner

Interior Designer
Gary Adair

Cover Designer
Alan Clements

Compositor
TnT Design, Inc.

Contents at a Glance

Table of Contents

About the Author

As the founder and president of Superior Solutions, Inc., a Houston-based IT security consulting and auditing firm, **Michael Gregg** has more than 20 years of experience in information security and risk management. He holds two associate's degrees, a bachelor's degree, and a master's degree. Some of the certifications he holds include CISA, CISSP, MCSE, CTT+, A+, N+, Security+, CASP, CCNA, GSEC, CEH, CHFI, CEI, CISA, CISM, CGEIT, and SSCP.

In addition to his experience performing security audits and assessments, Michael has authored or coauthored more than 15 books, including *Certified Ethical Hacker Exam Prep* (Que), *CISSP Exam Cram 2* (Que), and *Security Administrator Street Smarts* (Sybex). He is a site expert for TechTarget.com websites, such as SearchNetworking.com. He also serves on their editorial advisory board. His articles have been published on IT websites, and he has been quoted on Fox News and *The New York Times*. He has created more than 15 security-related courses and training classes for various companies and universities. Although audits and assessments are where he spends the bulk of his time, teaching and contributing to the written body of IT security knowledge are how Michael believes he can give something back to the community that has given him so much.

He is a board member for Habitat For Humanity and, when not working, Michael enjoys traveling and restoring muscle cars.

Dedication

I dedicate this book to those who have been my mentors along the way, because without them, this book would not have been possible.

Acknowledgments

I want like to thank everyone who helped make this project a reality, including Betsy Brown, Chris Cleveland, Shawn Merdinger, Patrick Ramseier, and the entire crew at Pearson.

About the Technical Reviewers

Shawn Merdinger is a security researcher and analyst at the University of Florida Academic Health Center. He has worked with Cisco Systems, 3Com/TippingPoint, and as an independent consultant. His current research focuses on medical device security, and he is the founder of the MedSec group on LinkedIn. Shawn regularly presents original research at security/hacker conferences such as DEFCON, Ph-Neutral, ShmooCon, CONfidence, NoConName, O'Reilly, CSI, IT Underground, CarolinaCon, and SecurityOpus.

Patrick Ramseier is a technical editor and author and manages a team of security and unified access consultants. He has held several management and technical positions in different security companies over the past 18 years and currently works on the Borderless Network Security and Unified Access team for Cisco in the Bay Area, where he leads a senior consulting team covering the entire western United States. Patrick has provided many technical edits/reviews for several major publishing companies, including Pearson Education, McGraw Hill, Wiley, and Sybex. He has a BA in Business Administration and MIS and holds CCNA, CISSP, and CISCP certifications.

We Want to Hear from You!

As the reader of this book, *you* are our most important critic and commentator. We value your opinion and want to know what we're doing right, what we could do better, what areas you'd like to see us publish in, and any other words of wisdom you're willing to pass our way.

We welcome your comments. You can email or write to let us know what you did or didn't like about this book—as well as what we can do to make our books better.

Please note that we cannot help you with technical problems related to the topic of this book.

When you write, please be sure to include this book's title and author as well as your name and email address. We will carefully review your comments and share them with the author and editors who worked on the book.

Email: feedback@pearsonitcertification.com

Mail: Dave Dusthimer
Associate Publisher
Pearson IT Certification
800 East 96th Street
Indianapolis, IN 46240 USA

Reader Services

Visit our website and register this book at www.pearsonitcertification.com/register for convenient access to any updates, downloads, or errata that might be available for this book.

Introduction

Welcome to the *CISSP Practice Questions Exam Cram*! This book provides you with practice questions, complete with answers and explanations, that help you learn, drill, and review for the CISSP certification exam.

Who This Book Is For

If you have studied the CISSP exam's content, and you believe that you are ready to put your knowledge to the test but you're not sure you want to take the actual exam yet, this book is for you! Maybe you have answered other practice questions or unsuccessfully taken the real exam, reviewed, and wanted to do more practice questions before retaking the exam. If so, this book is for you, too!

Be aware that *the CISSP exam is difficult and challenging*; therefore, this book shouldn't be your only vehicle for CISSP study. Because of the breadth and depth of knowledge needed to successfully pass the CISSP exam, be sure to use plenty of study material and use this book as a drill, review, and practice vehicle. It is recommended that you use this book with the *CISSP Exam Cram*, Third Edition, by Michael Gregg.

What You Will Find in This Book

This book is all about practice questions. It is divided into the ten domains that you find on the CISSP exam. Each chapter represents a domain, and each chapter has three elements:

- **Practice Questions:** This section includes numerous questions that help you learn, drill, and review.
- **Quick-Check Answer Key:** After you finish answering the questions, you can quickly grade your exam from this section. Only the correct answers are given here. No explanations are offered yet.
- **Answers and Explanations:** This section gives the correct answers and detailed explanations about the content posed in that question. Use this information to learn why an answer is correct and reinforce the content in your mind for exam day.

Hints for Using This Book

Because this book is a paper practice product, you might want to complete its exams on separate pieces of paper so that you can reuse the exams without having previous answers in your way. Also, a rule of thumb across all practice-question products is to make sure that you score into the high 90-percent range in all topics before attempting the actual exam. The higher you score on practice-question products, the better your chances of passing the real exam. Of course, we can't guarantee that you will receive a passing score on the real exam, but we can offer you plenty of opportunities to practice and assess your knowledge levels before you take the exam.

Pearson IT Certification Practice Test Engine and Questions on the CD

This book's accompanying CD includes the Pearson IT Certification Practice Test engine—software that displays and grades a set of exam-realistic multiple-choice questions. Using the Pearson IT Certification Practice Test engine, you can either study by going through the questions in Study Mode or take a simulated exam that mimics real exam conditions.

The installation process requires two major steps: installing the software and activating the exam. The CD has a recent copy of the Pearson IT Certification Practice Test engine. The practice exam—the database of exam questions—is not on the CD.

NOTE

The cardboard CD case in the back of this book includes the CD and a piece of paper. The paper lists the activation code for the practice exam associated with this book. *Do not lose the activation code.* On the opposite side of the paper from the activation code is a unique, one-time-use coupon code for the purchase of the Premium Edition eBook and Practice Test.

Install the Software from the CD

The Pearson IT Certification Practice Test is a Windows-only desktop application. You can run it on a Mac using a Windows virtual machine, but it was built specifically for the PC platform. The minimum system requirements are as follows:

- Windows XP (SP3), Windows Vista (SP2), or Windows 7
- Microsoft .NET Framework 4.0 client
- Microsoft SQL Server Compact 4.0
- Pentium class 1GHz processor (or equivalent)
- 512 MB RAM
- 650 MB disc space plus 50 MB for each downloaded practice exam

The software-installation process is routine compared with other software-installation processes. If you have already installed the Pearson IT Certification Practice Test software from another Pearson product, there is no need for you to reinstall the software. Simply launch the software on your desktop and proceed to activate the practice exam from this book by using the activation code that's included in the CD sleeve.

The following steps outline the installation process:

1. Insert the CD into your PC.
2. The software that automatically runs is the Pearson software to access and use all CD-based features, including the exam engine and the CD-only appendixes. From the main menu, click the **Install the Exam Engine** option.
3. Respond to Windows prompts, like you would with any typical software-installation process.

The installation process gives you the option to activate your exam with the activation code supplied on the paper in the CD sleeve. This process requires you to establish a Pearson website login. You need this login to activate the exam, so please register when prompted. If you already have a Pearson website login, there is no need to register again; just use your existing login.

Activate and Download the Practice Exam

After the exam engine is installed, you should then activate the exam associated with this book (if you did not do so during the installation process), as follows:

1. Start the Pearson IT Certification Practice Test software from the Windows **Start** menu or from your desktop shortcut icon.
2. To activate and download the exam associated with this book, from the **My Products** or **Tools** tab, select the **Activate** button.

3. At the next screen, enter the activation key from the paper inside the cardboard CD holder. Once entered, click the **Activate** button.
4. The activation process downloads the practice exam. Click **Next**, and then click **Finish**.

After the activation process is complete, the **My Products** tab should list your new exam. If you do not see the exam, make sure you have selected the **My Products** tab on the menu. At this point, the software and practice exam are ready to use. Simply select the exam and click the **Open Exam** button.

To update a particular exam that you have already activated and downloaded, simply select the **Tools** tab and select the **Update Products** button. Updating your exams ensures that you have the latest changes and updates to the exam data.

If you want to check for updates to the Pearson IT Certification Practice Test exam engine software, simply select the **Tools** tab and select the **Update Application** button. This ensures that you are running the latest version of the software engine.

Activating Other Exams

The exam software-installation process, and the registration process, has to happen only once. Then, for each new exam, only a few steps are required. For example, if you buy another new Pearson IT Certification Cert Guide or Cisco Press Official Cert Guide, extract the activation code from the CD sleeve in the back of that book—you don't even need the CD at this point. From there, all you have to do is start the exam engine (if it's not still up and running) and perform Steps 2 through 4 from the previous list.

Need Further Study?

If you have a difficult time correctly answering these questions, you probably need further review. Read the sister product to this book, *CISSP Exam Cram*, Third Edition (by Pearson), for further review.

1

CHAPTER ONE

Physical (Environmental) Security

Don't underestimate the challenge of mastering the material in the Physical Security domain. If you are not a physical security expert and don't work in this field on a regular basis, give yourself plenty of time to review the concepts. This domain encompasses all areas of physical security, from choosing a site to securing it against natural or man-made disasters. As a CISSP, you must protect not only the company's assets but also its employees. The following list includes some key areas from this content that you need to master for the CISSP exam:

- Crime Prevention Through Environmental Design (CPTED)
- Facility design
- Fire safety
- Electrical security
- HVAC
- Perimeter security: fences, gates, lighting
- Physical access control: transponders, badges, swipe cards, biometric devices
- Theft, denial, destruction
- Intrusion detection: CCTV, alarms, guards, dogs

Quick Check

Practice Questions

1. Your lab manager is preparing to buy all the equipment that has been budgeted for next year. While reviewing the specifications for several pieces of equipment, he notices that each device has a Mean Time To Repair (MTTR) rating. He asks you what this means. Which of the following is the best response?

   ❍ **A.** The MTTR is used to determine the expected time before the repair can be completed. Higher numbers are better.

   ❍ **B.** The MTTR is used to determine the expected time before the repair can be completed. Lower numbers are better.

   ❍ **C.** The MTTR is used to determine the expected time between failures. Higher numbers are better.

   ❍ **D.** The MTTR is used to determine the expected time between failures. Lower numbers are better.

Quick Answer: **22**
Detailed Answer: **23**

2. Which of the following would you be least likely to find in a data center?

   ❍ **A.** Dry pipe fire control

   ❍ **B.** Smoke detectors

   ❍ **C.** Drop ceilings

   ❍ **D.** Surge protection

Quick Answer: **22**
Detailed Answer: **23**

3. You are asked to serve as a consultant on the design of a new facility. Which of the following is the best location for the server room?

   ❍ **A.** Near the outside of the building

   ❍ **B.** Near the center of the building

   ❍ **C.** In an area that has plenty of traffic so that equipment can be observed by other employees and guests

   ❍ **D.** In an area that offers easy access

Quick Answer: **22**
Detailed Answer: **23**

4. A closed-circuit TV (CCTV) system has been installed to monitor a bank's ATM. The lighting has been adjusted to prevent dark areas, and the depth of field and degree of focus are appropriate for proper monitoring. However, the guard has asked if it would be possible to provide greater width to the area being monitored to permit a subject to be captured for a longer stretch of time. Which adjustment is needed?

Quick Answer: **22**
Detailed Answer: **23**

Quick Check

- ❍ **A.** Decrease the focal length
- ❍ **B.** Increase the focal length
- ❍ **C.** Decrease the iris
- ❍ **D.** Increase the iris

5. When you're choosing the physical location for a new facility, which of the following should you *not* avoid?

Quick Answer: **22**
Detailed Answer: **23**

- ❍ **A.** Airport flight paths
- ❍ **B.** Chemical refineries
- ❍ **C.** Railway freight lines
- ❍ **D.** Hospitals

6. Which one of the following is *not* one of the three main types of fire-detection systems?

Quick Answer: **22**
Detailed Answer: **23**

- ❍ **A.** Heat sensing
- ❍ **B.** Flame sensing
- ❍ **C.** CO_2 sensing
- ❍ **D.** Smoke sensing

7. Above what concentration is Halon considered toxic when inhaled?

Quick Answer: **22**
Detailed Answer: **23**

- ❍ **A.** 5 percent
- ❍ **B.** 6 percent
- ❍ **C.** 10 percent
- ❍ **D.** 15 percent

8. What height of fence is required to deter determined intruders?

Quick Answer: **22**
Detailed Answer: **24**

- ❍ **A.** 4 feet
- ❍ **B.** 5 feet
- ❍ **C.** 8 feet
- ❍ **D.** 6 feet

9. Superior Solutions, Inc., has acquired a contract for the upgrade of a local manufacturer's fire-suppression system. The client wants to find suitable replacements for its Halon fire-suppression system. Which of the following is *not* a suitable replacement?

Quick Answer: **22**
Detailed Answer: **24**

- ❍ **A.** Argon
- ❍ **B.** Hydrogen bromide
- ❍ **C.** Inergen
- ❍ **D.** FM-200

Quick Check

10. You are asked to review the design of your organization's new data center. The proposed data center will be unmanned and typically will not have anyone working inside. With this in mind, which of the following fire-suppression methods works by removing the oxygen element?

 ❍ **A.** Soda acid
 ❍ **B.** CO_2
 ❍ **C.** Water
 ❍ **D.** NO_2

Quick Answer: **22**
Detailed Answer: **24**

11. You are asked to sit in on a meeting with the design team working on the new security data center. Because this facility will have extremely high security, you are concerned about having the appropriate type of fence in place. There will be limited access to this facility, and Class IV gates will be used. What is the correct specification for this perimeter barrier?

 ❍ **A.** 2-inch mesh, 9 gauge
 ❍ **B.** 3/8-inch mesh, 11 gauge
 ❍ **C.** 1-inch mesh, 9 gauge
 ❍ **D.** 2-inch mesh, 6 gauge

Quick Answer: **22**
Detailed Answer: **24**

12. Which of the following is a major drawback of the decision to use security guards as a form of physical deterrent?

 ❍ **A.** Schedule
 ❍ **B.** Salary and benefits
 ❍ **C.** Liability
 ❍ **D.** Culpability

Quick Answer: **22**
Detailed Answer: **24**

13. You are asked to create the new company policy on emergency response and training. You want to make sure that the policy defines how employees are trained to deal with fire drills. Which of the following is the best way to carry out emergency fire drills?

 ❍ **A.** Fire drills should be timed to correspond with company breaks.
 ❍ **B.** Fire drills should be a scheduled event that all employees are told about.
 ❍ **C.** Fire drills should be a random event that the employees are unaware of before the event.
 ❍ **D.** Fire drills are an unnecessary event that cuts into employee work time, thereby reducing productivity.

Quick Answer: **22**
Detailed Answer: **24**

Quick Check

14. Which of the following replacements for Halon has been recommended by the EPA?

Quick Answer: **22**
Detailed Answer: **24**

- ❍ **A.** Argon
- ❍ **B.** FM-200
- ❍ **C.** Inergen
- ❍ **D.** FM-300

15. You are put in charge of the new semiconductor facility, and your boss is concerned about ESD. To protect sensitive equipment from ESD damage, the humidity should be kept at what level?

Quick Answer: **22**
Detailed Answer: **24**

- ❍ **A.** 10–20 percent
- ❍ **B.** 20–40 percent
- ❍ **C.** 40–60 percent
- ❍ **D.** 60–80 percent

16. You are asked to secure the operations of a South American electronics production plant. Because of rising energy prices, this small country has been plagued with power problems over the past several years. One major problem has been the fluctuation of power to greater-than-normal levels. Which of the following best describes this event?

Quick Answer: **22**
Detailed Answer: **25**

- ❍ **A.** Faults and blackouts
- ❍ **B.** Spikes and surges
- ❍ **C.** Sags and brownouts
- ❍ **D.** Noise and EMI

17. You are placed in charge of a small room full of servers. Which of the following is the best protection against brownouts and temporary power loss?

Quick Answer: **22**
Detailed Answer: **25**

- ❍ **A.** RAID
- ❍ **B.** Surge protectors
- ❍ **C.** UPS
- ❍ **D.** Voltage regulators

18. Your manager wants to know which of the following you, as a CISSP, would rank as the item of highest priority. How should you answer?

Quick Answer: **22**
Detailed Answer: **25**

- ❍ **A.** Duty to the ISC[2] code of ethics
- ❍ **B.** Duty to protect company assets
- ❍ **C.** Duty to company policy
- ❍ **D.** Duty to public safety

Quick Check

19. Which of the following is the specification for Halon that can be used as a gas agent?

Quick Answer: **22**
Detailed Answer: **25**

- ❍ **A.** Halon 2800
- ❍ **B.** Halon 1625
- ❍ **C.** Halon 1311
- ❍ **D.** Halon 1301

20. What class of fire suppression should be used against chemical or grease fires?

Quick Answer: **22**
Detailed Answer: **25**

- ❍ **A.** Class A
- ❍ **B.** Class B
- ❍ **C.** Class C
- ❍ **D.** Class D

21. Which of the following is classified as an ASTM Class II gate?

Quick Answer: **22**
Detailed Answer: **25**

- ❍ **A.** Commercial
- ❍ **B.** Industrial
- ❍ **C.** Residential
- ❍ **D.** Restricted access

22. Which of the following heat-activated fire-detection systems provides the fastest warning time?

Quick Answer: **22**
Detailed Answer: **25**

- ❍ **A.** Fixed temperature
- ❍ **B.** Rate of rise
- ❍ **C.** Photoelectric
- ❍ **D.** Piezoelectric

23. Which of the following physical security practices is the best security solution implementation?

Quick Answer: **22**
Detailed Answer: **25**

- ❍ **A.** Placing a Halon fire extinguisher system in the new cafeteria.
- ❍ **B.** Erecting parking-lot lighting on poles in the center of periodic islands, on which trees have been planted for beautification.
- ❍ **C.** Installing emergency-exit fire doors that fail-close in the event of a power failure and that have push panic bars for emergency release.
- ❍ **D.** Placing outside windows in a data center looking at the parking lot so that employees can see their vehicles.

Quick Check

24. Because of an upturn in business, your company has started running a second shift. Some of the line workers complain to your boss that it is very dark in the parking lot. He advises you to investigate the purchase and installation of new exterior lighting. What level of illumination does NIST recommend for lighting critical areas?

- ❍ **A.** Two feet of candlepower at a height of 8 feet
- ❍ **B.** Two feet of candlepower at a height of 10 feet
- ❍ **C.** Four feet of candlepower at a height of 8 feet
- ❍ **D.** Four feet of candlepower at a height of 6 feet

Quick Answer: **22**
Detailed Answer: **25**

25. Why is Halon no longer being produced or sold?

- ❍ **A.** It has been found to cause cancer in laboratory animals.
- ❍ **B.** The base components in Halon are considered rare. This has resulted in a massive price increase. Other options are now much cheaper.
- ❍ **C.** Its use was banned because it was an ozone-depleting agent.
- ❍ **D.** Its use was banned because it is considered a dual-use technology that can be used to produce weapons.

Quick Answer: **22**
Detailed Answer: **25**

26. Which of the following fits in the category of power degradation?

- ❍ **A.** Blackouts
- ❍ **B.** Spikes
- ❍ **C.** Brownouts
- ❍ **D.** Surge

Quick Answer: **22**
Detailed Answer: **25**

27. What is a critical consideration when discussing physical security?

- ❍ **A.** Guard dogs
- ❍ **B.** Layered access control
- ❍ **C.** Fences
- ❍ **D.** CCTV

Quick Answer: **22**
Detailed Answer: **26**

28. Which of the following statements about CCTV is *not* true?

- ❍ **A.** CCTV is a good example of a deterrent system.
- ❍ **B.** CCTV is a good example of an automated intrusion detection system.
- ❍ **C.** CCTV is effective at deterring security violations.
- ❍ **D.** CCTV is a good example of a detection system.

Quick Answer: **22**
Detailed Answer: **26**

Quick Check

29. Which of the following best describes piggybacking?

- ❍ **A.** The act of stealing someone's access card to gain access later
- ❍ **B.** The act of watching over someone's shoulder to steal a password for later use
- ❍ **C.** The act of following someone through a secured door to gain unauthorized access
- ❍ **D.** The act of spoofing someone's identity to gain unauthorized access

Quick Answer: **22**
Detailed Answer: **26**

30. What class of fire suppression should be used against electrical fires, such as computers or electronic equipment?

- ❍ **A.** Class E
- ❍ **B.** Class D
- ❍ **C.** Class C
- ❍ **D.** Class B

Quick Answer: **22**
Detailed Answer: **26**

31. What is one of the largest drawbacks of using guard dogs as a physical security control?

- ❍ **A.** Care
- ❍ **B.** Liability
- ❍ **C.** Investment
- ❍ **D.** Training

Quick Answer: **22**
Detailed Answer: **26**

32. Controlled humidity is important in preventing ESD. What level of static discharge is the approximate amount required to destroy data on hard drives?

- ❍ **A.** 100 static volts
- ❍ **B.** 500 static volts
- ❍ **C.** 1,000 static volts
- ❍ **D.** 1,500 static volts

Quick Answer: **22**
Detailed Answer: **26**

33. While you are consulting for TrayTec, Inc., an employee approaches you with a question. Which of the following would you say is *not* a reason to put a raised floor in the server room?

- ❍ **A.** For increased airflow
- ❍ **B.** To allow easy access to cables
- ❍ **C.** To prevent damage to equipment in case of a flood or water leak
- ❍ **D.** To isolate equipment from harmful vibrations

Quick Answer: **22**
Detailed Answer: **26**

Quick Check

34. Which of the following water-suppression systems contains compressed air or nitrogen?

Quick Answer: **22**
Detailed Answer: **26**

❍ **A.** Wet pipe

❍ **B.** Dry pipe

❍ **C.** Deluge system

❍ **D.** Preaction system

35. Doors with automatic locks can serve as a good form of physical protection. These doors can be configured to respond to power outages in either a fail-safe or fail-open condition. Which of the following describes fail-safe?

Quick Answer: **22**
Detailed Answer: **26**

❍ **A.** If a loss of power occurs, the door opens automatically.

❍ **B.** If a loss of power occurs, the door remains locked.

❍ **C.** In case of a power outage, the door has a BPS and continues to operate normally.

❍ **D.** In case of a power outage, the door will lock but can be opened with a passkey.

36. What is a special type of identification device that does not require action by users because the user only needs to have it passed close to the ID device?

Quick Answer: **22**
Detailed Answer: **26**

❍ **A.** Biometric systems

❍ **B.** Access control badges

❍ **C.** Proximity badges

❍ **D.** CCTV

37. What type of attack relies on the trusting nature of employees and the art of deception?

Quick Answer: **22**
Detailed Answer: **26**

❍ **A.** Hijacking

❍ **B.** Social engineering

❍ **C.** Spoofing

❍ **D.** Deception

38. Which of the following is *not* a valid fire-suppression system?

Quick Answer: **22**
Detailed Answer: **27**

❍ **A.** Wet pipe

❍ **B.** Dry pipe

❍ **C.** Reaction system

❍ **D.** Deluge system

Quick Check

39. You are hired to consult for TrayTec, a small manufacturing firm. This firm is preparing to construct a data center. What is the recommended temperature for rooms containing computer equipment?

Quick Answer: **22**
Detailed Answer: **27**

- ❍ **A.** 50–65 degrees Fahrenheit
- ❍ **B.** 60–75 degrees Fahrenheit
- ❍ **C.** 65–85 degrees Fahrenheit
- ❍ **D.** 70–85 degrees Fahrenheit

40. What class of fire suppression should be used against common fires, such as paper and computer printouts?

Quick Answer: **22**
Detailed Answer: **27**

- ❍ **A.** Class A
- ❍ **B.** Class B
- ❍ **C.** Class C
- ❍ **D.** Class D

41. Which of the following statements about server rooms is incorrect?

Quick Answer: **22**
Detailed Answer: **27**

- ❍ **A.** Server rooms should have barriers on all six sides.
- ❍ **B.** Server rooms should be kept at cold temperatures.
- ❍ **C.** Server rooms should be accessible to IT staff.
- ❍ **D.** Server rooms should not be shared with IT workers.

42. Which of the following would be considered a gas-discharge fire-extinguishing system?

Quick Answer: **22**
Detailed Answer: **27**

- ❍ **A.** Wet pipe
- ❍ **B.** Dry pipe
- ❍ **C.** Flame-activated sprinkler
- ❍ **D.** Handheld CO_2 fire extinguisher

43. What height of fence is required to deter casual intruders?

Quick Answer: **22**
Detailed Answer: **27**

- ❍ **A.** 8 feet
- ❍ **B.** 6 feet
- ❍ **C.** 4 feet
- ❍ **D.** 12 feet

44. Which of the following is *not* a valid intrusion detection system?

Quick Answer: **22**
Detailed Answer: **27**

- ❍ **A.** Wave pattern
- ❍ **B.** Proximity detection
- ❍ **C.** Geometric system
- ❍ **D.** Acoustical system

Quick Check

45. Which of the following fire-suppression systems works by removing the fuel element?

Quick Answer: **22**
Detailed Answer: **27**

- ❍ **A.** Soda acid
- ❍ **B.** CO_2
- ❍ **C.** Water
- ❍ **D.** Oxygen

46. Which of the following is the best HVAC choice for an organization to use in case of fire and smoke?

Quick Answer: **22**
Detailed Answer: **27**

- ❍ **A.** Positive pressurization
- ❍ **B.** Sealed windows
- ❍ **C.** Negative pressurization
- ❍ **D.** Neutral pressurization

47. Which intrusion detection system can sense changes in vibration and noise level in an area?

Quick Answer: **22**
Detailed Answer: **28**

- ❍ **A.** Wave pattern
- ❍ **B.** Proximity detection
- ❍ **C.** Passive infrared system
- ❍ **D.** Acoustical system

48. Doors with automatic locks can serve as a good form of physical protection. These doors can be configured to respond to power outages in either a fail-safe or fail-open condition. Which of the following describes fail-open?

Quick Answer: **22**
Detailed Answer: **28**

- ❍ **A.** If a loss of power occurs, the door remains unlocked.
- ❍ **B.** If a loss of power occurs, the door opens automatically.
- ❍ **C.** In case of a power outage, the door has a BPS and continues to operate normally.
- ❍ **D.** In case of a power outage, the door will unlock, but it can be secured with a special key.

49. Which intrusion detection system can sense changes in heat waves in an area?

Quick Answer: **22**
Detailed Answer: **28**

- ❍ **A.** Wave pattern
- ❍ **B.** Proximity detection
- ❍ **C.** Passive infrared system
- ❍ **D.** Acoustical system

Quick Check

50. What class of fire suppression should be used against oil or gas fires?

Quick Answer: **22**
Detailed Answer: **28**

- ❍ **A.** Class A
- ❍ **B.** Class B
- ❍ **C.** Class C
- ❍ **D.** Class D

51. Your technician is preparing to buy all the equipment that has been budgeted for next year. While reviewing the specifications for several pieces of equipment, he notices that each device has an MTBF rating. He asks if you can explain what this means. Which of the following is the best response?

Quick Answer: **22**
Detailed Answer: **28**

- ❍ **A.** The MTBF is used to determine the expected average time between failures.
- ❍ **B.** The MTBF is used to determine the expected time before a repair is needed.
- ❍ **C.** The MTBF is just a ratio of MTTR used to evaluate product repair time.
- ❍ **D.** The MTBF is used to determine how many backup devices are needed.

52. Which of the following fits into the category of a power loss?

Quick Answer: **22**
Detailed Answer: **28**

- ❍ **A.** Blackouts
- ❍ **B.** Spikes and surges
- ❍ **C.** Brownouts
- ❍ **D.** Surges

53. What is the absolute first requirement of security?

Quick Answer: **22**
Detailed Answer: **28**

- ❍ **A.** Implementation of CPTED
- ❍ **B.** Mitigation of damage
- ❍ **C.** Protecting assets
- ❍ **D.** Protecting people

54. Permitting your data center to be too warm can cause what problem?

Quick Answer: **22**
Detailed Answer: **28**

- ❍ **A.** The equipment turns off.
- ❍ **B.** The equipment works slower.
- ❍ **C.** The computer parts get corroded.
- ❍ **D.** Static electricity is introduced.

Quick Check

55. Halon extinguishers contained a gas that interrupts the chemical reaction of a fire. They were useful and popular for fighting electrical fires that required a nonconductive and noncorrosive control agent. However, Halon was found to be damaging to our environment and was removed from the list of acceptable agents. What document first limited the use of Halon?

❍ **A.** Clean Air Act

❍ **B.** Halon Emissions Reduction Rule

❍ **C.** Environmental Protection Act of 1990

❍ **D.** Montreal Protocol

Quick Answer: **22**
Detailed Answer: **28**

56. Which of the following lock types would you rate as the most secure when installed properly?

❍ **A.** Wafer lock

❍ **B.** Combination lock

❍ **C.** Pin lock

❍ **D.** Cipher lock

Quick Answer: **22**
Detailed Answer: **28**

57. What is the benefit of a contingency plan?

❍ **A.** Perimeter defense

❍ **B.** Diversity of controls

❍ **C.** Defense in layers

❍ **D.** Facility access controls

Quick Answer: **22**
Detailed Answer: **28**

58. Your company is about to begin the parallel test of its latest application, which will then be deployed in house. The company has set up temporary space in a secure room that backs up to the data center. When the equipment in the new lab is powered up, what power anomaly might the computers experience?

❍ **A.** Surge

❍ **B.** Brownout

❍ **C.** Noise

❍ **D.** Sag

Quick Answer: **22**
Detailed Answer: **29**

59. Which of the following describes best practices for a company's evacuation and emergency response plans?

❍ **A.** Once a year, surprise emergency drills should be held to see whether managers understand corporate policy. Employees' demonstrated knowledge of procedures should be discussed in their yearly performance evaluations.

Quick Answer: **22**
Detailed Answer: **29**

Quick Check

❍ **B.** Employees should be provided with written descriptions of emergency actions as part of their corporate indoctrination and should be required to keep the documents in a ready state at their workstations.

❍ **C.** Periodic refresher training should be provided to all employees. Planned exercises with realistic predetermined scenarios should be executed, where managers account for personnel as part of any evacuations.

❍ **D.** Emergency plans should be posted in all work spaces and lounge areas throughout a corporation. All employees should have a way to submit suggestions for improving the plan.

60. You are asked to examine the placement of lighting to be used for perimeter security. The organization is worried about how lighting can be used to detect individuals who are at the fence line of a high-security facility, attempting to gain access to the facility. There is a road outside the fence line and several guard stations near the facility doors. Which of the following would be the best approach?

Quick Answer: **22**
Detailed Answer: **29**

❍ **A.** Place the lighting on the outside of the fence, away from the facility, evenly spaced on poles 5 feet high.

❍ **B.** Place the lighting on the inside of the fence, toward the facility, evenly spaced on poles 8 feet high.

❍ **C.** Place the lighting evenly spaced above the fence 5 feet high.

❍ **D.** Place the lighting evenly spaced above the fence 8 feet high.

61. You are asked to perform a review of the physical controls of your company's data center. Your review will include access control and various preventive and detective controls. With this in mind, what would you say is the primary purpose of CCTV from a control perspective?

Quick Answer: **22**
Detailed Answer: **29**

❍ **A.** CCTV will allow the review of internal or external activity.

❍ **B.** CCTV can mitigate risk by detecting, assessing, and identifying intruders.

❍ **C.** CCTV is only a detective control.

❍ **D.** CCTV cannot generally be used in public areas.

62. Which type of gate is best suited for a prison or restricted-access area that is monitored directly or remotely?

Quick Answer: **22**
Detailed Answer: **29**

❍ **A.** Class IV

❍ **B.** Class D

❍ **C.** Class A

❍ **D.** Class 1

Quick Check

63. When considering external boundary mechanisms, care should be taken to ensure that only authorized individuals are allowed access. Which of the following is *not* one of the services that a boundary mechanism, specifically a fence, provides?

Quick Answer: **22**
Detailed Answer: **29**

- ❍ **A.** Acts as a buffer and delaying mechanism
- ❍ **B.** Offers increased protection
- ❍ **C.** Helps control access
- ❍ **D.** Prevents intruders

64. Although not all facilities have windows, those that do can have varying types. Which window type is used to prevent shattering and maintain its integrity during a fire?

Quick Answer: **22**
Detailed Answer: **29**

- ❍ **A.** Wired
- ❍ **B.** Security film
- ❍ **C.** Laminated glass
- ❍ **D.** Standard glass

65. One important area of physical security is fire detection, suppression, and response. One physical control that may be used in this area is a _________, which is an application that's used primarily in firefighting systems. Its hinged gate remains open only in the inflowing direction. It also has a spring that keeps the gate shut when there is no forward pressure.

Quick Answer: **22**
Detailed Answer: **29**

- ❍ **A.** Backwater valve
- ❍ **B.** Duckbill valve
- ❍ **C.** Clapper valve
- ❍ **D.** Diaphragm valve

Practice Questions (True or False)

66. Warded locks are more secure than pin-and-tumbler locks.

Quick Answer: **22**
Detailed Answer: **29**

- ❍ True
- ❍ False

67. A cipher lock is programmable.

Quick Answer: **22**
Detailed Answer: **29**

- ❍ True
- ❍ False

Quick Check

68. Bump keys are used to bypass cipher locks.

❍ True

❍ False

Quick Answer: **22**
Detailed Answer: **29**

69. The facility and the data center should *not* share a common HVAC system.

❍ True

❍ False

Quick Answer: **22**
Detailed Answer: **30**

70. Data center doors typically are hinged to the outside.

❍ True

❍ False

Quick Answer: **22**
Detailed Answer: **30**

71. Control types such as lights are a type of physical deterrent.

❍ True

❍ False

Quick Answer: **22**
Detailed Answer: **30**

72. Control types such as an annunciation system are a type of intrusion detection.

❍ True

❍ False

Quick Answer: **22**
Detailed Answer: **30**

73. Wire mesh embedded between two sheets of glass typically is used for a fire break.

❍ True

❍ False

Quick Answer: **22**
Detailed Answer: **30**

74. Bollards are used to control the egress and ingress of people.

❍ True

❍ False

Quick Answer: **22**
Detailed Answer: **30**

75. CPTED is designed to deny access by means of physical and man-made barriers, such as locks and fences.

❍ True

❍ False

Quick Answer: **22**
Detailed Answer: **30**

76. A mantrap is a turnstile and a badge reader.

❍ True

❍ False

Quick Answer: **22**
Detailed Answer: **30**

77. Plenum cable is used for environmental reasons.

❍ True

❍ False

Quick Answer: **22**
Detailed Answer: **30**

Quick Check

78. A magnesium fire is best suppressed with a Class D extinguisher.

Quick Answer: **22**
Detailed Answer: **30**

- ❍ True
- ❍ False

79. Placing your headlights on low beam when approaching a security checkpoint is an example of glare protection.

Quick Answer: **22**
Detailed Answer: **30**

- ❍ True
- ❍ False

80. Areas of fixed lighting should be observed with a CCTV camera that supports an auto iris lens.

Quick Answer: **22**
Detailed Answer: **30**

- ❍ True
- ❍ False

Practice Questions (Mix and Match)

81. Match the following power conditions with the proper solution.

Quick Answer: **22**
Detailed Answer: **30**

A. Blackout: _____

B. Brownout: _____

C. Surge: _____

D. Spike: _____

E. Noise: _____

F. Clean power: _____

1. No solution is needed.

2. Power conditioner.

3. Generator.

4. UPS.

5. Surge protector.

Quick-Check Answer Key

1. B
2. C
3. B
4. A
5. D
6. C
7. C
8. C
9. B
10. B
11. B
12. B
13. C
14. B
15. C
16. B
17. C
18. D
19. D
20. D
21. A
22. B
23. C
24. A
25. C
26. C
27. B
28. B
29. C
30. C
31. B
32. D
33. D
34. B
35. B
36. C
37. B
38. C
39. B
40. A
41. C
42. D
43. C
44. C
45. A
46. A
47. D
48. A
49. C
50. B
51. A
52. A
53. D
54. A
55. C
56. D
57. C
58. D
59. C
60. D
61. B
62. A
63. D
64. A
65. C
66. False
67. True
68. False
69. True
60. False
71. True
72. True
73. True
74. False
75. False
76. False
77. False
78. True
79. False
80. False
81. **A.** 3
B. 4
C. 5
D. 5
E. 2
F. 1

Answers and Explanations

1. **Answer: B.** Mean Time To Repair (MTTR) is a value used to calculate the average time to bring a device back up to operating standards. Lower numbers mean reduced downtime. Answers C and D describe Mean Time Before Failures (MTBF) and do not describe MTTR.

2. **Answer: C.** Drop ceilings (plenum space) should not be used in data centers or areas that are adjacent to server rooms. Although these are convenient for hiding cables, the better location is under the raised floor. Drop ceilings offer the intruder a potential path over the wall and into the data center if the wall does not run all the way to the roof. This gives potential intruders easy access. All the other items are recommended for server rooms. Dry pipe fire control offers the potential for water, but also provides adequate time to turn off or power down electronics. Smoke detectors are a must for all areas. Surge protection can be used to protect expensive equipment.

3. **Answer: B.** The best location for a server room is near the center of the building. This location is more secure from natural disasters and helps protect against intruders. This type of configuration requires the intruder to pass multiple employees and possibly checkpoints before reaching the server room. If employees are properly educated, they will ask what the unauthorized person is doing in the area. The theory of layered security applies to physical security just as much as it does to the other domains!

4. **Answer: A.** The focal length adjusts the breadth of view. A shorter focal length permits a wide-angle view, and a long focal length provides a telephoto view. Therefore, answer B is incorrect. In real life, the organization may opt for a zoom lens that permits the guard to redirect the field of view as necessary. Answers C and D are incorrect because the iris controls the amount of light the camera receives and needs to be larger as the amount of light available decreases.

5. **Answer: D.** Any time you start building from scratch, you should consider the surroundings. Areas that are close to airline flight paths, freight lines, or chemical plants may be subject to explosions or crashes. Answer D is correct because having a hospital nearby can be considered an asset. This allows the company to quickly get help to anyone who gets injured.

6. **Answer: C.** CO_2 sensing is not a valid type of fire detection. The three categories of fire-detection systems are heat sensing, flame sensing, and smoke sensing. According to OSHA standard 1910.164, the employer is responsible for ensuring that the number, spacing, and location of fire detectors are based on design data obtained from field experience, tests, engineering surveys, the manufacturer's recommendations, or a recognized testing laboratory listing.

7. **Answer: C.** If Halon is deployed in concentrations of greater than 10 percent and in temperatures of 900 degrees or more, it degrades into hydrogen fluoride, hydrogen bromide, and bromine. This toxic compound is not something that people should breathe. Halon has also been discovered to be three to ten times more damaging to the ozone layer than CFCs.

8. **Answer: C.** Fences 3 to 4 feet high prevent only the casual intruder. Six-foot-high fences are difficult to climb. Critical assets should be physically protected with a fence that is 8 feet high. A three-strand barbed-wire topping is an effective added security measure. If you are trying to keep out the bad guys, you should point the razor wire topping out. If you are really concerned about who's hanging around the perimeter of your facility, consider installing a perimeter intrusion and detection assessment system (PIDAS). This special fencing system has sensors so that it can detect intruders.

9. **Answer: B.** Argon, Inergen, low-pressure water mists, and FM-200 are some of the acceptable replacements for Halon. Halon has been phased out because it acts as an ozone-depleting substance when released into the atmosphere. Hydrogen bromide is a byproduct of Halon and is considered toxic.

10. **Answer: B.** CO_2 works by removing the oxygen from a fire. Soda acid works by removing the fuel element of a fire. Water works by reducing the temperature of a fire. Answer D, nitrous oxide, does not reduce a fire.

11. **Answer: B.** Fences are one of the first lines of defenses and, as such, should be of the right design to protect the physical facility. A 3/8-inch mesh, 11-gauge wire is the specification for an extremely high-security fence. Answer A specifies a normal fence design. Answer C specifies a very high-security fence design, and answer D specifies a greater-than-normal fence design.

12. **Answer: B.** One major drawback of employing guards as a physical security deterrent is the cost of salaries. All other answers are incorrect. Liability is addressed by the fact that security guards typically are bonded and have had to pass state board licensing requirements. The guards' schedule and benefits are also not the primary drawback. Culpability simply means that the guard is deserving of blame.

13. **Answer: C.** Fire drills should be a random event that the employees are unaware of before the drill. Fire drills should not be scheduled, because that defeats the purpose. Fires or natural disasters are not scheduled events. Finally, productivity is not the driving force; rather, it should be employee safety. Employees should have a designated area to go to that is outside the facility in a safe zone. Supervisors or others should be in charge of the safe zones, where there can be an employee count to ensure that everyone is present and accounted for. After the drill, there should be a single point of reentry, and employees should have their IDs checked before returning to work.

14. **Answer: B.** The EPA considers FM-200 the replacement of choice for Halon systems. FM-200 has been adopted by the majority of the world's fire protection companies and has been installed in tens of thousands of systems across the globe. It is similar to Halon but does not affect the ozone layer. Argon and Inergen will work, but they are not as effective. FM-300 does not exist.

15. **Answer: C**. In home environments, electrostatic discharge (ESD) may be an annoyance. In the workplace, its results can be much more severe. ESD can damage or destroy sensitive electronic components, attract contaminants, and cause products to stick together. American National Standards Institute (ANSI) specifications recommend a 40–60 percent humidity range for the prevention of ESD. Humidity above 60 percent is uncomfortable for people, and below 40 percent increases the risk of static generation. Individuals in charge of the environment should consider equipping their areas with active humidity-monitoring equipment to ensure that values stay within the required range.

16. **Answer: B.** A power excess can quickly damage sensitive electronic equipment. The best way to guard against this type of problem is through the use of surge protectors. Brownouts occur when power companies experience an increasingly high demand for power, and blackouts are associated with power loss. EMI is unwanted electrical signals that produce undesirable effects and otherwise disrupt the control system circuits. Electrical noise can cause interference.

17. **Answer: C.** An uninterruptible power supply (UPS) can be used to provide power to critical equipment during short power outages. Surge protectors and voltage regulators help condition the power to ensure that it is clean and smooth. RAID is used for disk drive fault tolerance.

18. **Answer: D.** Although the other items on the list are important, the protection of human life makes duty to public safety the number-one priority of the CISSP.

19. **Answer: D.** Halon can be found in two types: Halon 1211 is used in portable extinguishers, and Halon 1301 is a gas agent used in fixed flooding systems.

20. **Answer: D.** Class D fire suppression should be used against grease or chemical fires. The other answers are incorrect because Class A corresponds to common combustibles, Class B is for burnable fuels, and Class C is for electrical fires.

21. **Answer: A.** A Class II gate is designed for commercial use. Answers B, C, and D are incorrect, because residential gates are Class I, industrial gates are Class III, and restricted access are Class IV.

22. **Answer: B.** The two valid types of heat-activated fire detection systems are fixed temperature and rate of rise. Rate of rise offers the best response time. However, remember that these systems result in more false-positive alarms.

23. **Answer: C.** When possible, you want emergency doors to fail open in the case of a power failure. However, when fail-open is not appropriate, it is critical that the doors have a push panic bar that permits people to exit in the event of an emergency. Not only are Halon fire systems no longer available for deployment, but they would be inappropriate for a cafeteria. On the customer side of a cafeteria, water should be deployed as the suppression agent. On the kitchen side of a cafeteria, wet chemicals are used. Trees should not be planted under the poles that provide safety lighting because their foliage will block the light. Data centers should be located in the center of an organization's building, where outside windows are unavailable and inappropriate.

24. **Answer: A.** Although lighting adds to the security of a facility, it is best when applied with other types of deterrents. The National Institute of Standards and Technology (NIST) states that the standard for perimeter protection using lighting is an illumination of 2 feet of candlepower at a height of 8 feet.

25. **Answer: C.** Halon has been found to destroy the ozone layer. Because of this, it was banned, and an international agreement was signed in 1994. As long as exposure is low, Halon is considered harmless to humans; however, in greater amounts, Halon can cause difficulty breathing, chest pains, and skin irritation.

26. **Answer: C.** A power degradation, such as a brownout, occurs when power companies experience an increasingly high demand for power. Spikes are associated with power excesses. Blackouts are associated with power loss, and surges are associated with excessive power spikes. Sags are another low-voltage condition.

27. **Answer: B.** Access control is the key to physical security, and it works best when deployed in layers. Each layer acts as a physical barrier. At a minimum, a system should have three physical barriers: entrance to the building, entrance to the computer center, and entrance to the computer room itself. These barriers can include guards, biometric access control, locked doors, CCTV, and alarm systems.

28. **Answer: B.** Although closed-circuit TV (CCTV) systems are good deterrent and detection systems, they are not automatic. CCTV requires individuals to watch the captured video, detect the malicious activity, and respond accordingly.

29. **Answer: C.** Piggybacking is the act of following someone through a secured door without being identified to obtain unauthorized access. The act of watching over someone's shoulder as he enters a password is called shoulder surfing. To spoof someone's identity is to pretend to be that person.

30. **Answer: C.** Class C fire suppression should be used against electrical fires. CO_2 and Halon are recommended suppression methods. Class A corresponds to common combustibles, Class B is for burnable fuels, and Class D is for chemical and grease fires.

31. **Answer: B.** Perhaps you've heard the phrase "junkyard dog." In that type of setting, dogs are highly effective, because no one should be in the facility during off hours. However, dogs lack the skill to differentiate between authorized and unauthorized personnel, so they can be a legal liability that results in criminal charges or a civil lawsuit.

32. **Answer: D.** In low-humidity environments, it's not impossible to create static charges in excess of 20,000 volts. It takes only about 1,500 static volts to damage a hard drive or cause destruction of data. Sensitive electronic components can be damaged by less than 100 static volts.

33. **Answer: D.** Using a raised floor provides many benefits, including increased airflow, easy access to cables, prevention of flooding damage to computers, and easier reconfiguration. Vibration is not a critical concern.

34. **Answer: B.** Dry pipe systems contain compressed air instead of water. The pipes are hooked up to a storage tank or water main. The system uses a valve that is sensitive to pressure. When the system is activated, the sprinkler heads open and force the compressed air to rush forward. This results in a drop in pipe pressure, which signals the pressure-sensitive valve connecting to the water supply.

35. **Answer: B.** If a door is considered fail-safe, it remains locked during a power outage. If this type of door is being used, people's safety must take precedence. This means that the door should be equipped with a panic bar or other mechanism that allows individuals to safely exit the building during a power outage or emergency. All other answers are incorrect, because they do not adequately describe the operation of fail-safe locks.

36. **Answer: C.** Proximity identification can be used to activate doors or locks or to identify employees. These systems only require users to pass in proximity to the sensor or sensing system. All other answers are incorrect because they do not describe a proximity system.

37. **Answer: B.** Social engineering is a type of attack in which intruders attempt to gain physical access to your facility by exploiting people's generally trusting nature. A social engineering attack may come from someone posing as a vendor or as someone coming to the facility to repair a problem. Regardless of how the person appears,

social engineering can be hard to detect. Social engineering can also be used to gain logical access by means of tricking a user to giving out some type of sensitive information. Hijacking is a computer-based attack in which someone hijacks a legitimate session. Spoofing is a computer-based attack in which someone's IP or MAC address is stolen. Spoofing can also entail spoofed emails and falsified network-level attacks, such as spoofed SYN floods. Deception is part of social engineering but, by itself, does not adequately describe the attack. Many attacks, such as password theft, make use of social and technical techniques to gain success.

38. **Answer: C.** The four primary fire-suppression systems are wet pipe, dry pipe, deluge system, and preaction system.

39. **Answer: B.** The recommended temperature for rooms containing computer equipment is 60–75 degrees Fahrenheit (15–23 degrees Celsius). Temperatures of 80–85 degrees Fahrenheit are not considered catastrophic; however, higher temperatures can result in lowering the life expectancy of equipment.

40. **Answer: A.** Class A fire suppression should be used to fight common fires. The extinguishing method of choice is water or soda acid. Class B is for burnable fuels and oils, Class C is for electrical fires, and Class D is for chemical fires.

41. **Answer: C.** Server rooms are typically inaccessible to IT staff, because their activities should be done remotely. Even if your employees are fully authorized, they should not share space with the server room where critical equipment is located. Noise and cold temperatures are not conducive to the working environment. Access should be controlled for even authorized IT workers, except when they have specific reasons to access equipment.

42. **Answer: D.** A handheld CO_2 fire extinguisher is considered a gas-discharge fire-extinguishing system. Wet-pipe systems are filled with water. Dry-pipe systems contain compressed air until fire suppression systems are triggered, and then the pipe is filled with water. Flame-activated sprinklers trigger when a predefined temperature is reached.

43. **Answer: C.** Fences 3–4 feet high prevent only casual intruders. Six-foot-high fences become difficult to climb. Critical assets should be physically protected with a fence that is 8 feet high with a three-strand topping of razor wire or razor wire in coils.

44. **Answer: C.** Some of the technologies that can be used to detect intruders are wave pattern, which bounces various frequency waves around a room while verifying that the pattern is undisturbed; proximity detection, which works by detecting changes in the magnetic field; and acoustical systems, which are sensitive to changes in sound and vibration.

45. **Answer: A.** Soda acid works by removing the fuel element of a fire. CO_2 works by removing the oxygen from a fire. Water works by reducing the temperature of a fire. Oxygen would not reduce a fire, but would actually cause it to grow larger.

46. **Answer: A.** Positive pressurization is a heating, ventilation, and air-conditioning (HVAC) design in which positive pressure is maintained in the system, so as a door or window is opened, air is forced out. This protects employees in case of a fire by forcing smoke outside, away from the employees. This positive pressurization also helps keep contaminants out of the building when doors are opened. The air rushes out rather than in, carrying pollen and other substances.

47. **Answer: D.** Acoustical systems are sensitive to changes, sound, and vibration. Proximity detection works by detecting changes to the magnetic field. Passive infrared systems look for the rise of heat waves. Wave pattern bounces various frequency waves around a room while verifying that the pattern is undisturbed.

48. **Answer: A.** If a door is considered fail-open, it remains unlocked during a power outage. All other answers are incorrect, because they do not adequately describe the operation of fail-open systems.

49. **Answer: C.** Passive infrared systems look for the rise of heat waves. Acoustical systems are sensitive to changes in sound and vibration. Proximity detection works by detecting changes in the magnetic field. Wave pattern bounces various frequency waves around a room while verifying that the pattern is undisturbed.

50. **Answer: B.** Class B fire suppression should be used against any type of burnable fuel. The recommended suppressants include CO_2, soda acid, and Halon. The other answers are incorrect because Class A corresponds to common combustibles, Class C is for electrical fires, and Class D is for chemical and grease fires.

51. **Answer: A.** Mean Time Between Failures (MTBF) is the average amount of time between device breakdowns. Higher numbers mean that the devices last longer.

52. **Answer: A.** A power outage, which can be called a blackout, is when power is lost for an extended time. The largest blackout ever to occur in the U.S. happened on August 14, 2003. It affected nearly 60 million people. A brownout occurs when power companies experience an increasingly high demand for power. Spikes are associated with power excesses.

53. **Answer: D.** The absolute first requirement of a CISSP is protecting people. Answers A, B, and C are important, but a CISSP's first goal is always people's safety and welfare.

54. **Answer: A.** Too hot of an environment can cause the equipment to overheat and turn off. Too cold a temperature can cause the performance speed to drop. Corrosion is introduced when there is too much moisture in the air, and static electricity is introduced when the humidity is too low.

55. **Answer: C.** The Montreal Protocol of 1987 was an international agreement to phase out all substances that damaged the ozone layer as soon as possible. Therefore, the Montreal Protocol initiated the effort to reduce the use of Halon, and it led to the ban of Halon. The UK's Environmental Protection Act of 1990 declared that it was illegal to "treat, keep or dispose of controlled waste in a manner likely to cause pollution to the environment." The Halon Emission Reduction Rule banned the manufacturing of Halon and specified methods for proper disposal. The Clean Air Act of 1990, incorporated in U.S. Code, provides legislation to curb the use of materials that are harmful to the environment.

56. **Answer: D.** Of these locks, a cipher lock is considered the most secure. A wafer lock is the least secure; it is the type found on filing cabinets. Pin locks or tumbler locks can be defeated with bump keys, and combination locks can be defeated with a cut aluminum can that is wrapped around the locking bolt. Electronic combination locks are more secure, but without further qualification, "combination locks" refers to the style used on lockers.

57. **Answer: C.** A contingency plan protects you when a primary control fails; it represents the concept of multiple layers in your defense. Perimeter defense identifies your first

line of defense and is a primary control, not a contingency plan. Diversity of controls refers to having a mixture of a type of control (primary or contingency) so that understanding one instance of a control doesn't guarantee knowledge of the next instance. Facility access controls are your physical perimeter's defense.

58. Answer: D. Devices that draw a large amount of current can cause an "in-rush current" that causes a sag in surrounding equipment. A surge is a prolonged period of increased voltage, a brownout is a prolonged period of decreased voltage, and noise is interference—a disruption often caused by RFI or EMI.

59. Answer: C. People need to be focused on the emergency they are practicing a response to in order for that response to become an automatic function in case of a real emergency. The practice should be carried out to completion, including the requirement that managers account for the proper evacuation of all personnel by accounting for those personnel after the rehearsed evacuation. It is also important to look out for any piggybackers going into the facility after the exercise.

60. Answer: D. Answers A, B, and C are incorrect because lighting should be placed over the fence so that trespassers can be easily spotted and their field of view is reduced during an attack. Lighting should not illuminate security guard posts, roads, or security elements. Guards should clearly be able to see the attacking individuals.

61. Answer: B. Answers A, C, and D are incorrect because CCTV is used in public areas and can be used as more than just a detective control, depending on its configuration. CCTV can be used as a preventive, detective, or even compensating control. While CCTV should have some type of recording system for review, what is important to consider is where and how the CCTV system will be used.

62. Answer: A. Answers B, C, and D are incorrect. Gates are broken into four basic groups, which include Class, I, II, III, and IV. Class IV gates are designed for high-security environments that also require monitoring.

63. Answer: D. Answers A, B, and C are incorrect. Although fences can act as buffering and delaying mechanisms, offer increased protection, and can help control access, a fence can be cut, climbed, or bypassed.

64. Answer: A. Answer A is correct, because wired glass is designed to maintain its integrity and not shatter easily. Answers B, C, and D do not match that description.

65. Answer: C. Answers A, B, and D are incorrect. Answer C is correct because a clapper valve uses a hinged gate and only remains open in the inflowing direction. It also has a spring that keeps the gate shut when there is no forward pressure.

66. Answer: False. The two basic types of locks are warded and pin-and-tumbler. Pin-and-tumbler is considered higher security.

67. Answer: True. A cipher lock is typically found in the configuration of a keypad. These locks are programmable and do not use keys.

68. Answer: False. A bump key is a special key that has been cut to a number nine position and has a small amount of extra material shaved from the front and the shank of the key. When slight pressure is applied and the key is bumped or tapped, the pins are driven upward, giving the attacker access. Bump keys are easy to make and easy to obtain on the Internet.

69. **Answer: True.** The organization and the data center should have separate HVAC systems that are not interconnected. The HVAC used in the data center should be dedicated, controlled, and monitored.

70. **Answer: False.** Data center doors should be hinged to the inside to harden the facility and make removing the doors more difficult.

71. **Answer: True.** Lights are a good example of a physical deterrent. Well-lighted areas make an attacker worry that he will be seen or detected.

72. **Answer: True.** The purpose of annunciation is to give the guard or other individuals an early warning of a problem or security breach to allow action to be taken before a situation degrades or further damage occurs.

73. **Answer: True.** Wire mesh secures the glass and prevents it from losing its integrity. As such, a solid barrier is maintained, and a fire break is provided.

74. **Answer: False.** Bollards can be concrete or steel. They are used to block vehicular traffic, particularly at entrances and lobbies, or to protect areas from being rammed by speeding cars, trucks, or vans.

75. **Answer: False.** Crime Prevention Through Environmental Design (CPTED) is designed to deter criminal behavior. An example is placing the parking lot near an area in which employees sit so that they can see and monitor their cars. Lighting the area at night is another example.

76. **Answer: False.** A mantrap is a set of two doors and a small room that is designed to hold someone until he or she is fully cleared for access to prevent piggybacking.

77. **Answer: False.** Plenum-grade cable is used because it is designed to release less toxic gas in case of a fire so that employees' health and welfare are maintained.

78. **Answer: True.** A magnesium fire is considered a Class D fire and would be fought by applying a special dry powder only.

79. **Answer: False.** Glare protection requires a properly designed guardhouse with lights facing away from the guards and toward potential attackers. Approaching vehicles turn off their headlights so that the guards at a security checkpoint can clearly see them and their occupants.

80. **Answer: False.** A CCTV camera that monitors an area of fixed lighting should have a fixed iris lens. An auto iris lens is not needed, because the lighting is maintained at a constant level.

81. **Answer:**

   A. Blackout: **3.** Generator

   B. Brownout: **4.** (UPS) Uninterruptible Power Supply

   C. Surge: **5.** Surge protector

   D. Spike: **5.** Surge protector

   E. Noise: **2.** Power conditioner

   F. Clean power: **1.** No solution is needed

   Being able to match the potential problem with the proper solution helps prepare you for the exam.

CHAPTER TWO

2 Access Control

The Access Control domain tests your knowledge of the large collection of mechanisms available to control authentication, authorization, and accounting. You must not only understand these systems, but also know the advantages and risks of each type as they relate to centralized and decentralized systems. Authentication is but one part of the process; authorization is also a key area of this domain. Individuals should be authorized for only what is required for them to complete required tasks. Finally, there is accounting (or accountability). When things go wrong, there must be a way to establish a chain of responsibility. The following list gives you some key areas from the Access Control domain you need to be aware of for the CISSP exam:

- Authentication methods (types 1, 2, and 3)
- Authorization: DAC, RBAC, MAC
- Accounting: Logging, monitoring, auditing
- Central, decentralized, and hybrid management
- Single sign-on: Kerberos, RADIUS, Diameter, TACACS
- Vulnerabilities: emanations, impersonation, rouge infrastructure, social engineering

Quick Check

Practice Questions

1. Which of the following is not one of the three types of access controls?

   - ❍ **A.** Administrative
   - ❍ **B.** Personnel
   - ❍ **C.** Technical
   - ❍ **D.** Physical

Quick Answer: **52**
Detailed Answer: **53**

2. Your company has just opened a call center in India to handle nighttime operations, and you are asked to review the site's security controls. Specifically, you are asked which of the following is the strongest form of authentication. What will your answer be?

   - ❍ **A.** Something you know
   - ❍ **B.** Something you are
   - ❍ **C.** Passwords
   - ❍ **D.** Tokens

Quick Answer: **52**
Detailed Answer: **53**

3. Your organization has become worried about recent attempts to gain unauthorized access to the R&D facility. Therefore, you are asked to implement a system that will require individuals to present a password and enter a PIN at the security gate before gaining access. What is this type of system called?

   - ❍ **A.** Authorization
   - ❍ **B.** Two-factor authentication
   - ❍ **C.** Authentication
   - ❍ **D.** Three-factor authentication

Quick Answer: **52**
Detailed Answer: **53**

4. Which of the following is not one of the three primary types of authentication?

   - ❍ **A.** Something you remember
   - ❍ **B.** Something you know
   - ❍ **C.** Something you are
   - ❍ **D.** Something you have

Quick Answer: **52**
Detailed Answer: **53**

5. While working as a contractor for Widget, Inc., you are asked what the weakest form of authentication is. What will you say?

   - ❍ **A.** Passwords
   - ❍ **B.** Retina scans
   - ❍ **C.** Facial recognition
   - ❍ **D.** Tokens

Quick Answer: **52**
Detailed Answer: **53**

Quick Check

6. You're preparing a presentation for the senior management of your company. They have asked you to rank the general order of accuracy of the most popular biometric systems, with 1 being the lowest and 5 being the highest. What will you tell them?

Quick Answer: **52**
Detailed Answer: **53**

- ❍ **A.** (1) fingerprint, (2) palm scan, (3) hand geometry, (4) retina scan, (5) iris scan
- ❍ **B.** (1) fingerprint, (2) palm scan, (3) iris scan, (4) retina scan, (5) hand geometry
- ❍ **C.** (1) palm scan, (2) hand geometry, (3) iris scan, (4) retina scan, (5) fingerprint
- ❍ **D.** (1) hand geometry, (2) palm scan, (3) fingerprint, (4) retina scan, (5) iris scan

7. Which of the following items is the least important to consider when designing an access control system?

Quick Answer: **52**
Detailed Answer: **54**

- ❍ **A.** Risk
- ❍ **B.** Threat
- ❍ **C.** Vulnerability
- ❍ **D.** Annual loss expectancy

8. Today, you are meeting with a coworker who is proposing that the number of logins and passwords be reduced. Another coworker has suggested that you investigate single sign-on technologies and make a recommendation at the next scheduled meeting. Which of the following is a type of single sign-on system?

Quick Answer: **52**
Detailed Answer: **54**

- ❍ **A.** Kerberos
- ❍ **B.** RBAC
- ❍ **C.** DAC
- ❍ **D.** RADIUS

9. Which style of authentication is not susceptible to a dictionary attack?

Quick Answer: **52**
Detailed Answer: **54**

- ❍ **A.** CHAP
- ❍ **B.** LEAP
- ❍ **C.** WPA-PSK
- ❍ **D.** PAP

10. Your organization has decided to use a biometric system to authenticate users. If the FAR is high, what happens?

Quick Answer: **52**
Detailed Answer: **54**

- ❍ **A.** Legitimate users are denied access to the organization's resources.

Quick Check

❍ **B.** Illegitimate users are granted access to the organization's resources.

❍ **C.** Legitimate users are granted access to the organization's resources.

❍ **D.** Illegitimate users are denied access to the organization's resources.

11. Which of the following types of copper cabling is the most secure against eavesdropping and unauthorized access?

Quick Answer: **52**
Detailed Answer: **54**

❍ **A.** Single-mode fiber

❍ **B.** Multimode fiber

❍ **C.** Category 6 cabling

❍ **D.** 802.11g wireless

12. Which of the following is not one of the primary categories access control models?

Quick Answer: **52**
Detailed Answer: **54**

❍ **A.** Discretionary

❍ **B.** Mandatory

❍ **C.** Role-based

❍ **D.** Delegated

13. Auditing is considered what method of access control?

Quick Answer: **52**
Detailed Answer: **55**

❍ **A.** Preventive

❍ **B.** Technical

❍ **C.** Administrative

❍ **D.** Physical

14. What method of access control system would a bank teller most likely fall under?

Quick Answer: **52**
Detailed Answer: **55**

❍ **A.** Discretionary

❍ **B.** Mandatory

❍ **C.** Role-based

❍ **D.** Rule-based

15. Which of the following is the easiest and most common form of offline password hash attack used to pick off insecure passwords?

Quick Answer: **52**
Detailed Answer: **55**

❍ **A.** Hybrid

❍ **B.** Dictionary

❍ **C.** Brute-force

❍ **D.** Man-in-the-middle

Quick Check

16. Your company is building a research facility in Bangalore and is concerned about technologies that can be used to pick up stray radiation from monitors and other devices. Specifically, your boss wants copper shielding installed. Which technology does your boss want to know more about?

Quick Answer: **52**
Detailed Answer: **55**

❍ **A.** Radon
❍ **B.** Waveguard
❍ **C.** Tempest
❍ **D.** Van Allen

17. Which of the following is not an example of a single sign-on service?

Quick Answer: **52**
Detailed Answer: **55**

❍ **A.** RADIUS
❍ **B.** Kerberos
❍ **C.** SESAME
❍ **D.** KryptoKnight

18. Christine, a newly certified CISSP, has offered to help her brother-in-law, Gary, at his small construction business. The business currently has 18 computers configured as a peer-to-peer network. All users are responsible for their own security and can set file and folder privileges as they see fit. Which access control model best describes the configuration at this organization?

Quick Answer: **52**
Detailed Answer: **55**

❍ **A.** Discretionary
❍ **B.** Mandatory
❍ **C.** Role-based
❍ **D.** Nondiscretionary

19. Which of the following best describes challenge/response authentication?

Quick Answer: **52**
Detailed Answer: **55**

❍ **A.** It is an authentication protocol in which a salt value is presented to the user, who then returns an MD5 hash based on this salt value.
❍ **B.** It is an authentication protocol in which a system of tickets is used to validate the user's rights to access resources and services.
❍ **C.** It is an authentication protocol in which the username and password are passed to the server using CHAP.
❍ **D.** It is an authentication protocol in which a randomly generated string of values is presented to the user, who then returns a calculated number based on those random values.

Quick Check

20. Your company has installed biometric access control systems. Your director has mentioned that he thinks the systems will have a high FRR. What does this mean?

❍ **A.** Quite a few valid users will be denied access.

❍ **B.** Employees will accept the system.

❍ **C.** Almost all unauthorized users will be denied.

❍ **D.** The system has a high return rate and will quickly pay for itself.

Quick Answer: **52**
Detailed Answer: **55**

21. Which of the following is the most time-intensive type of offline password attack to attempt?

❍ **A.** Hybrid

❍ **B.** Plain text

❍ **C.** Brute-force

❍ **D.** Man-in-the-middle

Quick Answer: **52**
Detailed Answer: **56**

22. You are approached by a junior security officer who wants to know what CVE stands for. What do you tell him?

❍ **A.** Critical Vulnerability and Exploits

❍ **B.** Common Vulnerabilities and Exposures

❍ **C.** Chosen Vulnerabilities and Exploits

❍ **D.** Common Vulnerabilities and Exploits

Quick Answer: **52**
Detailed Answer: **56**

23. Which of the following protocols is recommended to be turned off because it transmits usernames and passwords in clear text?

❍ **A.** SSH

❍ **B.** HTTPS

❍ **C.** Telnet

❍ **D.** TFTP

Quick Answer: **52**
Detailed Answer: **56**

24. Which biometric authentication system is most closely associated with law enforcement?

❍ **A.** Fingerprint recognition

❍ **B.** Iris recognition

❍ **C.** Facial recognition

❍ **D.** Retina pattern recognition

Quick Answer: **52**
Detailed Answer: **56**

Quick Check

25. What type of access control system doesn't give users much freedom to determine who can access their files and is known for its structure and use of security labels?

Quick Answer: 52
Detailed Answer: 56

- ❍ **A.** Discretionary
- ❍ **B.** Mandatory
- ❍ **C.** Role-based
- ❍ **D.** Nondiscretionary

26. As the newly appointed security officer for your corporation, you suggest replacing the password-based authentication system with RSA tokens. Elsa, your CTO, denies your request, citing budgetary constraints. As a temporary solution, Elsa asks that you find ways to increase password security. Which of the following will accomplish this goal?

Quick Answer: 52
Detailed Answer: 56

- ❍ **A.** Disabling password-protected screensavers
- ❍ **B.** Enabling account lockout controls
- ❍ **C.** Enforcing a password policy that requires noncomplex passwords
- ❍ **D.** Enabling users to use the same password on more than one system

27. Which of the following is a major issue with signature-based IDSs?

Quick Answer: 52
Detailed Answer: 56

- ❍ **A.** Signature-based IDSs cannot detect zero-day attacks.
- ❍ **B.** Signature-based IDSs can detect only attacks in which activity deviates from normal behavior.
- ❍ **C.** Signature-based IDSs are available only as host-based systems.
- ❍ **D.** Signature-based IDSs are cost-prohibitive.

28. Administrative controls form an important part of security, and although most of us don't like paperwork, that is a large part of this security control. Which of the following is a high-level document that describes a management plan for how security should be practiced throughout the organization?

Quick Answer: 52
Detailed Answer: 56

- ❍ **A.** Guidelines
- ❍ **B.** Policies
- ❍ **C.** Procedures
- ❍ **D.** Standards

Quick Check

29. A hacker submits a malicious URL request for a help page from an unpatched Apache server that supports an Oracle9i Application Server. This causes a denial of service. Which of the following would have best protected the corporation from this attack?

Quick Answer: 52
Detailed Answer: 57

❍ **A.** HIDS
❍ **B.** NIPS
❍ **C.** HIPS
❍ **D.** NIDS

30. One of your coworkers has joined a CISSP study group and is discussing today's list of topics. One of the topics is this: What is an example of a passive attack?

Quick Answer: 52
Detailed Answer: 57

❍ **A.** Dumpster diving
❍ **B.** Sniffing
❍ **C.** Installing SubSeven
❍ **D.** Social engineering

31. What is one of the major reasons why separation of duties should be practiced?

Quick Answer: 52
Detailed Answer: 57

❍ **A.** Reduced cross-training
❍ **B.** Legal
❍ **C.** Union policies and procedures
❍ **D.** To force collusion

32. There are two basic types of access control policies. Which of the following describes the best approach for a CISSP?

Quick Answer: 52
Detailed Answer: 57

❍ **A.** Begin with deny all.
❍ **B.** Allow some based on needs analysis.
❍ **C.** Begin with allow all.
❍ **D.** Deny some based on needs analysis.

33. Your manager asks you to set up a fake network to identify contractors who may be poking around the network without authorization. What is this type of system called?

Quick Answer: 52
Detailed Answer: 57

❍ **A.** Trap-and-trace
❍ **B.** Honeypot
❍ **C.** Snare
❍ **D.** Prison

Quick Check

34. Various operating systems such as Windows use what to control access rights and permissions to resources and objects?

Quick Answer: **52**
Detailed Answer: **57**

❍ **A.** RBAC

❍ **B.** MITM

❍ **C.** ABS

❍ **D.** ACL

35. While hanging around the watercooler, you hear that your company, Big Tex Bank and Trust, is introducing a new policy. The company will require periodic job rotation and will force all employees to use their vacation time. From a security standpoint, why is this important?

Quick Answer: **52**
Detailed Answer: **57**

❍ **A.** Job rotation is important because it reduces employee burnout.

❍ **B.** Job rotation is important because employees need to be cross-trained in case of man-made or natural disasters.

❍ **C.** Job rotation ensures that no one can easily commit fraud or other types of deception without risking exposure.

❍ **D.** Forcing employees to use their vacation time ensures time away from work, which results in healthy, more productive employees.

36. Your manager persists in asking you to set up a fake network to identify contractors who may be poking around the network without authorization. What is the largest legal issue with these devices?

Quick Answer: **52**
Detailed Answer: **57**

❍ **A.** Enticement

❍ **B.** Federal Statute 1029

❍ **C.** Entrapment

❍ **D.** Liability

37. Your brother-in-law, Mario, is studying for the CISSP exam. He text-messages you with what he believes is an important question: What is a major disadvantage of access control lists? How do you answer him?

Quick Answer: **52**
Detailed Answer: **57**

❍ **A.** Overhead of the auditing function

❍ **B.** Burden of centralized control

❍ **C.** Independence from resource owners

❍ **D.** Lack of centralized control

Quick Check

38. Which of the following was one of the first access control models based on confidentiality?

- ❍ **A.** Clark-Wilson
- ❍ **B.** Biba
- ❍ **C.** Bell-LaPadula
- ❍ **D.** State machine

Quick Answer: **52**
Detailed Answer: **57**

39. What does TACACS+ use as its communication protocol?

- ❍ **A.** TCP
- ❍ **B.** UDP
- ❍ **C.** ICMP
- ❍ **D.** TCP and UDP

Quick Answer: **52**
Detailed Answer: **58**

40. Which of the following attributes does not apply to MAC?

- ❍ **A.** Multilevel
- ❍ **B.** Label-based
- ❍ **C.** Universally applied
- ❍ **D.** Discretionary

Quick Answer: **52**
Detailed Answer: **58**

41. Which of the following is not part of physical access control?

- ❍ **A.** CCTV
- ❍ **B.** Mantraps
- ❍ **C.** Data classification and labeling
- ❍ **D.** Biometrics

Quick Answer: **52**
Detailed Answer: **58**

42. During a weekly staff meeting, your boss reveals that some employees have been allowing other employees to use their passwords. He is determined to put a stop to this and wants you to install biometric access control systems. He has asked about some basic attributes, such as type 1 errors, type II errors, and the CER. What's so important about the CER? How do you respond?

- ❍ **A.** Speed typically is determined by calculating the CER.
- ❍ **B.** The CER has to do with the customer acceptance rate, because some systems are more user-friendly than others.
- ❍ **C.** Accuracy typically is determined by calculating the CER.
- ❍ **D.** The CER has to do with the cost per employee, because some biometric access control systems are very good, but also very expensive.

Quick Answer: **52**
Detailed Answer: **58**

Quick Check

43. Kerberos has some features that make it a good choice for access control and authentication. One of these items is a ticket. What is a ticket used for?

Quick Answer: **52**
Detailed Answer: **58**

- ❍ **A.** A ticket is a block of data that allows users to prove their identity to an authentication server.
- ❍ **B.** A ticket is a block of data that allows users to prove their identity to a service.
- ❍ **C.** A ticket is a block of data that allows users to prove their identity to a ticket-granting server.
- ❍ **D.** A ticket is a block of data that allows users to prove their identity to the Kerberos server.

44. What is the best definition of identification?

Quick Answer: **52**
Detailed Answer: **58**

- ❍ **A.** The act of verifying your identity
- ❍ **B.** The act of claiming a specific identity
- ❍ **C.** The act of finding or testing the truth
- ❍ **D.** The act of inspecting or reviewing a user's actions

45. What term means that a user cannot deny a specific action because there is positive proof that he or she performed it?

Quick Answer: **52**
Detailed Answer: **58**

- ❍ **A.** Accountability
- ❍ **B.** Auditing
- ❍ **C.** Nonrepudiation
- ❍ **D.** Validation

46. What type of cryptography does SESAME use to distribute keys?

Quick Answer: **52**
Detailed Answer: **58**

- ❍ **A.** Public key
- ❍ **B.** Secret key
- ❍ **C.** SHA hashing algorithm
- ❍ **D.** None; it uses clear text.

47. Which of the following is a category of security controls that job rotation fits into?

Quick Answer: **52**
Detailed Answer: **58**

- ❍ **A.** Recovery
- ❍ **B.** Corrective
- ❍ **C.** Detective
- ❍ **D.** Compensation

Quick Check

48. What does RADIUS use for its transport protocol?

Quick Answer: **52**
Detailed Answer: **59**

- ❍ **A.** UDP
- ❍ **B.** TCP
- ❍ **C.** TCP and UDP
- ❍ **D.** ICMP

49. Your coworkers are having a heated discussion about access control models and their differences. To help them move on to more productive endeavors, you offer to answer their question. Specifically, they want to know what the driving force was behind the development of the Biba model. What do you tell them?

Quick Answer: **52**
Detailed Answer: **59**

- ❍ **A.** The Biba model addressed the fact that the Bell-LaPadula model would allow a user with a higher security level rating to write to a subject's information with a higher security level.
- ❍ **B.** The Biba model addressed the fact that the Bell-LaPadula model would allow a user with a lower security level rating to write to a subject's information with a higher security level.
- ❍ **C.** The Biba model addressed the fact that the Clark-Wilson model would allow a user with a lower security level rating to write to a subject's information with a lower security level.
- ❍ **D.** The Biba model addressed the fact that the Clark-Wilson model would allow a user with a higher security level rating to write to a subject's information with a lower security level.

50. Which of the following access control models addresses integrity?

Quick Answer: **52**
Detailed Answer: **59**

- ❍ **A.** Brewer Nash
- ❍ **B.** Biba
- ❍ **C.** Bell-LaPadula
- ❍ **D.** PERT

51. What does strong authentication require?

Quick Answer: **52**
Detailed Answer: **59**

- ❍ **A.** Public/private keys
- ❍ **B.** Using two different methods of identification
- ❍ **C.** Using a method of identification from at least two of type I, II, or III
- ❍ **D.** Authenticating inside an encrypted tunnel

Quick Check

52. You have a homogeneous environment with multiple application servers. Your users are having difficulty remembering all their passwords as they complete their daily activities. What would be the best solution?

- ❍ **A.** Lower the passwords' complexity requirements
- ❍ **B.** Implement harsher penalties
- ❍ **C.** Add assisted user reset capabilities
- ❍ **D.** Use single sign-on

Quick Answer: **52**
Detailed Answer: **59**

53. How do you lower type 1 errors on biometric devices?

- ❍ **A.** By increasing type 2 errors
- ❍ **B.** By decreasing type 2 errors
- ❍ **C.** By increasing precision
- ❍ **D.** By decreasing CER

Quick Answer: **52**
Detailed Answer: **59**

54. When you log into your remote server from home, your server sends you a nonce that you enter into a token device that you were issued when you were hired. Your token device responds with a value you enter at the prompt. What have you entered?

- ❍ **A.** A single sign-on using synchronous authentication
- ❍ **B.** A one-time password using synchronous authentication
- ❍ **C.** A single sign-on using asynchronous authentication
- ❍ **D.** A one-time password using asynchronous authentication

Quick Answer: **52**
Detailed Answer: **59**

55. Which of the following describes a distinction between Kerberos and SESAME?

- ❍ **A.** Kerberos supplies SSO; SESAME does not.
- ❍ **B.** Kerberos uses symmetric encryption; SESAME uses asymmetric encryption.
- ❍ **C.** Kerberos can be used for nonrepudiation; SESAME cannot.
- ❍ **D.** SESAME can be accessed using GSS-API; Kerberos cannot.

Quick Answer: **52**
Detailed Answer: **59**

56. What type of physical control is a mantrap?

- ❍ **A.** Deterrent
- ❍ **B.** Corrective
- ❍ **C.** Preventive
- ❍ **D.** Detective

Quick Answer: **52**
Detailed Answer: **59**

Quick Check

57. What is the best way to store passwords?

- ❍ **A.** In a one-way encrypted file
- ❍ **B.** Using symmetric encryption
- ❍ **C.** Using asymmetric encryption
- ❍ **D.** By means of a digital signature

Quick Answer: **52**
Detailed Answer: **60**

58. The act of professing to be a specific user is

- ❍ **A.** Validation
- ❍ **B.** Authorization
- ❍ **C.** Authentication
- ❍ **D.** Identification

Quick Answer: **52**
Detailed Answer: **60**

59. Which of the following best describes a Zephyr chart?

- ❍ **A.** A means of establishing the accuracy of a biometric system
- ❍ **B.** A means of comparing different biometric systems
- ❍ **C.** A means of comparing type II and type III authentication systems
- ❍ **D.** A chart used to examine the accuracy of IDSs and IPSs

Quick Answer: **52**
Detailed Answer: **60**

60. What is authentication?

- ❍ **A.** Supplying a username
- ❍ **B.** Using criteria to determine what a user can do
- ❍ **C.** Verifying identification
- ❍ **D.** Reviewing audit logs

Quick Answer: **52**
Detailed Answer: **60**

61. Being asked what your maiden name is, what city you were born in, and what your pet's name is is an example of what?

- ❍ **A.** Single sign-on (SSO)
- ❍ **B.** Self-service password reset
- ❍ **C.** Centralized authentication
- ❍ **D.** Assisted passwords

Quick Answer: **52**
Detailed Answer: **60**

62. Which of the following best describes a federated identity?

- ❍ **A.** Simply another term for SSO.
- ❍ **B.** It is restricted to use within a specific domain or area of the network.
- ❍ **C.** Type I authentication (something you know).
- ❍ **D.** It is portable and can be used across business boundaries.

Quick Answer: **52**
Detailed Answer: **60**

Quick Check

63. Which of the following is the most accurate biometric system?

- ❍ **A.** A CER of 1
- ❍ **B.** A CER of 2
- ❍ **C.** A CER of 3
- ❍ **D.** None of the above, because CER is not a numeric rating

Quick Answer: **52**
Detailed Answer: **60**

64. Which type of control that includes fences, password protection, and CCTV is designed to stop an event from occurring?

- ❍ **A.** Detective control
- ❍ **B.** Preventive control
- ❍ **C.** Corrective control
- ❍ **D.** Deterrent control

Quick Answer: **52**
Detailed Answer: **60**

65. Nondiscretionary access control includes which of the following?

- ❍ **A.** Role- and task-based
- ❍ **B.** Rule-based and mandatory
- ❍ **C.** Labeled and mandatory
- ❍ **D.** None of the above, because there are no subcategories

Quick Answer: **52**
Detailed Answer: **60**

66. What is a trust?

- ❍ **A.** A one-way-only bridge established between two domains
- ❍ **B.** A two-way-only bridge established between two domains
- ❍ **C.** A security bridge that is established after a valid authentication
- ❍ **D.** A security bridge that is established between two domains

Quick Answer: **52**
Detailed Answer: **60**

67. What form of authorization is closely associated with labels?

- ❍ **A.** Rule-based access control
- ❍ **B.** Discretionary access control
- ❍ **C.** Mandatory access control
- ❍ **D.** Role-based access control

Quick Answer: **52**
Detailed Answer: **60**

68. How can a swipe card, smart card, or USB dongle be described?

- ❍ **A.** An active token
- ❍ **B.** A static token
- ❍ **C.** Type I authentication
- ❍ **D.** Type III authentication

Quick Answer: **52**
Detailed Answer: **60**

Quick Check

69. The Equal Error Rate is equivalent to what?

- ❍ **A.** The point at which false acceptance and false rejection meet
- ❍ **B.** The crossover error rate minus 10%
- ❍ **C.** The point at which false acceptance is at its highest and false rejection is at its lowest
- ❍ **D.** The point at which false acceptance is at its lowest and false rejection is at its highest

Quick Answer: **52**
Detailed Answer: **60**

70. Which of the following is the most expensive means of verifying a user's identity?

- ❍ **A.** Single sign-on
- ❍ **B.** Tokens
- ❍ **C.** Biometrics
- ❍ **D.** Passwords

Quick Answer: **52**
Detailed Answer: **60**

71. Which biometric system examines the colored portion of the eye that surrounds the pupil?

- ❍ **A.** Iris
- ❍ **B.** Retina
- ❍ **C.** Fovea
- ❍ **D.** Optic disk

Quick Answer: **52**
Detailed Answer: **61**

72. Which of the following best describes a rainbow table?

- ❍ **A.** An attack against a biometric system
- ❍ **B.** An attack against a fingerprint scanner
- ❍ **C.** A table used for digital signatures
- ❍ **D.** A table of precomputed password hashes

Quick Answer: **52**
Detailed Answer: **61**

73. The ticket-granting service is a component of what?

- ❍ **A.** TACACS
- ❍ **B.** Kerberos
- ❍ **C.** RADIUS
- ❍ **D.** SESAME

Quick Answer: **52**
Detailed Answer: **61**

74. The Privilege Attribute Certificate (PAC) is a component of what?

- ❍ **A.** TACACS
- ❍ **B.** Kerberos
- ❍ **C.** RADIUS
- ❍ **D.** SESAME

Quick Answer: **52**
Detailed Answer: **61**

Quick Check

75. What nontechnical attack attempts to lure the victim into giving up financial data, credit card numbers, or other types of account information?

Quick Answer: **52**
Detailed Answer: **61**

- ❍ **A.** Pretexting
- ❍ **B.** Social engineering
- ❍ **C.** Dumpster diving
- ❍ **D.** Phishing

76. You are asked to work on a project where users need to share credentials across multiple domains without forcing them to log in more than once. What technologies might meet this business need?

Quick Answer: **52**
Detailed Answer: **61**

- ❍ **A.** Cookies
- ❍ **B.** Unique X.509 certificates
- ❍ **C.** Web access management
- ❍ **D.** Separate usernames and passwords

77. Your company was initially considering three security models to use to design its new operating system (OS). These models included Biba, Bell-LaPadula, and Clark Wilson. If the company decided to base its OS on the Biba model, which of the following properties is correct?

Quick Answer: **52**
Detailed Answer: **61**

- ❍ **A.** A user cannot write down to a lower level.
- ❍ **B.** The model makes use of transformational procedures and constrained data items.
- ❍ **C.** The user cannot write up to a higher level.
- ❍ **D.** If a user has access to one side of the wall, he does not have access to data on the other side of the wall.

78. Which of the following refers to the process of creation, maintenance, and deletion of user objects?

Quick Answer: **52**
Detailed Answer: **61**

- ❍ **A.** Identification
- ❍ **B.** Verification
- ❍ **C.** Authentication
- ❍ **D.** Provisioning

79. Object reuse can be an important issue when considering which of the following?

Quick Answer: **52**
Detailed Answer: **61**

- ❍ **A.** RAM scraping attacks
- ❍ **B.** Authentication method
- ❍ **C.** Type of biometric system used
- ❍ **D.** Strength of a password

Quick Check

80. Which form of access control has a many-to-many relationship and makes use of mapping between a user and a subset of goals?

Quick Answer: **52**
Detailed Answer: **61**

❍ **A.** MAC
❍ **B.** DAC
❍ **C.** Rule-based access control
❍ **D.** Core RBAC

81. Which of the following is the best example of capabilities tables?

Quick Answer: **52**
Detailed Answer: **61**

❍ **A.** Memory cards
❍ **B.** Kerberos
❍ **C.** Constrained user interface
❍ **D.** Router ACL

82. Which of the following provides an upgrade path from RADIUS?

Quick Answer: **52**
Detailed Answer: **61**

❍ **A.** Diameter
❍ **B.** TACACS
❍ **C.** Kerberos
❍ **D.** NetSP

83. Investigations are a good example of which of the following?

Quick Answer: **52**
Detailed Answer: **61**

❍ **A.** Detective control
❍ **B.** Preventive control
❍ **C.** Deterrent control
❍ **D.** Proactive control

84. Although an authorized sniffer has been connected to a network switch, the user can only see traffic directed to the device and some broadcast traffic. What might be the problem?

Quick Answer: **52**
Detailed Answer: **61**

❍ **A.** An IDS is blocking the traffic.
❍ **B.** The switch port must be spanned.
❍ **C.** The switch detected the sniffer.
❍ **D.** The sniffer is misconfigured.

85. Which type of attack makes use of a time-memory tradeoff?

Quick Answer: **52**
Detailed Answer: **62**

❍ **A.** Rule-based
❍ **B.** Dictionary
❍ **C.** Rainbow table
❍ **D.** Brute-force

Quick Check

Practice Questions (True or False)

86. War dialing is an attack that targets a wireless network.

❍ True

❍ False

Quick Answer: **52**
Detailed Answer: **62**

87. Encryption is an example of a technical control.

❍ True

❍ False

Quick Answer: **52**
Detailed Answer: **62**

88. Access controls should default to full access.

❍ True

❍ False

Quick Answer: **52**
Detailed Answer: **62**

89. TACACS is an example of centralized access technology.

❍ True

❍ False

Quick Answer: **52**
Detailed Answer: **62**

90. Kerberos addresses availability.

❍ True

❍ False

Quick Answer: **52**
Detailed Answer: **62**

91. An example of an IDS engine is signature-based.

❍ True

❍ False

Quick Answer: **52**
Detailed Answer: **62**

92. Stateful matching is a type of signature-based IDS.

❍ True

❍ False

Quick Answer: **52**
Detailed Answer: **62**

93. SATAN is an example of a vulnerability scanner.

❍ True

❍ False

Quick Answer: **52**
Detailed Answer: **62**

94. Software faults can be uncovered with watchdog timers.

❍ True

❍ False

Quick Answer: **52**
Detailed Answer: **62**

95. PAP is considered a secure protocol.

❍ True

❍ False

Quick Answer: **52**
Detailed Answer: **62**

96. Diameter is not an AAA protocol.

❍ True

❍ False

Quick Answer: **52**
Detailed Answer: **62**

Quick Check

97. Attribute value pairs are used with SESAME.

❍ True

❍ False

Quick Answer: **52**
Detailed Answer: **62**

98. A token, ticket, or key can be a capability.

❍ True

❍ False

Quick Answer: **52**
Detailed Answer: **63**

99. MAC allows the owner to determine who has access.

❍ True

❍ False

Quick Answer: **52**
Detailed Answer: **63**

100. Static separation of duties is one way to restrict the combination of duties.

❍ True

❍ False

Quick Answer: **52**
Detailed Answer: **63**

101. Superzapping is a term that relates to data destruction.

❍ True

❍ False

Quick Answer: **52**
Detailed Answer: **63**

102. Retina scanning matches the person's blood vessels on the back of the eye and is very accurate.

❍ True

❍ False

Quick Answer: **52**
Detailed Answer: **63**

103. TACACS+ supports two-factor authentication.

❍ True

❍ False

Quick Answer: **52**
Detailed Answer: **63**

104. Centralized authentication allows a subject to be authenticated by a system only once and then access resource after resource repeatedly.

❍ True

❍ False

Quick Answer: **52**
Detailed Answer: **63**

105. Tokens are an example of type II authentication.

❍ True

❍ False

Quick Answer: **52**
Detailed Answer: **63**

106. Keyboard dynamics is an example of type III authentication.

❍ True

❍ False

Quick Answer: **52**
Detailed Answer: **63**

107. Scrubbing is the act of clearing a hard drive for destruction or resale.

❍ True

❍ False

Quick Answer: **52**
Detailed Answer: **63**

Quick Check

108. Keystroke monitoring is a form of biometrics.

❍ True

❍ False

Quick Answer: **52**
Detailed Answer: **63**

109. A federated identity is an identity management system (IdM) that is considered portable.

❍ True

❍ False

Quick Answer: **52**
Detailed Answer: **63**

110. Type I authentication systems typically have a clipping level set to 3.

❍ True

❍ False

Quick Answer: **52**
Detailed Answer: **64**

Practice Questions (Mix and Match)

111. Match each attack with its definition.

Quick Answer: **52**
Detailed Answer: **64**

A. Smurf: _____

B. LAND: _____

C. TRINOO: _____

D. SYN Attack: _____

E. Chargen: _____

F. Ping of death: _____

1. Uses two systems to bounce a continuous stream of traffic between ports 7 and 19.

2. A SYN packet that is to and from the same address and port.

3. A series of SYN packets are sent that fill the receiving buffer.

4. Uses a ping packet to broadcast addresses spoofed from the victim.

5. An early type of DDOS attack.

6. Sends ICMP packets that are at or exceed maximum size.

Quick-Check Answer Key

1. B
2. B
3. C
4. A
5. A
6. A
7. D
8. A
9. D
10. B
11. C
12. D
13. C
14. C
15. B
16. C
17. A
18. A
19. D
20. A
21. C
22. B
23. C
24. A
25. B
26. B
27. A
28. B
29. B
30. B
31. D
32. A
33. B
34. D
35. C
36. C
37. D
38. C
39. A
40. D
41. C
42. C
43. B
44. B
45. C
46. A
47. C
48. A
49. B
50. B
51. C
52. D
53. A
54. D
55. B
56. C
57. A
58. D
59. B
60. C
61. B
62. D
63. A
64. B
65. A
66. D
67. C
68. B
69. A
70. C
71. A
72. D
73. B
74. D
75. D
76. C
77. C
78. D
79. A
80. D
81. B
82. A
83. A
84. B
85. C
86. False
87. True
88. False
89. True
90. False
91. True
92. True
93. True
94. True
95. False
96. False
97. False
98. True
99. False
100. True
101. False
102. True
103. True
104. False
105. True
106. True
107. False
108. False
109. True
110. True
111. **A.** 4
B. 2
C. 5
D. 3
E. 1
F. 6

Answers and Explanations

1. **Answer: B.** The three types of controls are as follows:
    - *Administrative*: These controls are composed of the policies and procedures the organization has put in place to prevent problems and to ensure that the technical and physical controls are known, understood, and implemented.
    - *Technical*: These controls are used to control access and monitor potential violations. They may be either hardware- or software-based.
    - *Physical*: These control systems are used to protect the welfare and safety of the employees and the organization. Physical controls include such items as smoke alarms, security guards, cameras, and mantraps.
2. **Answer: B.** Authentication can take one of three forms: something you know, something you have, or something you are. Something you are, such as biometrics, is by far the strongest form of authentication. Systems such as retina and iris scans have high levels of accuracy. The accuracy of a biometric device can be assessed by means of the crossover error rate. Remember that, on the exam, questions are sometimes vague, and you will be asked to pick the best available answer.
3. **Answer: C.** The question states that a password and PIN are required. Both passwords and PINs are examples of something you know. Authentication is something you know, something you have, or something you are. Therefore, this is an example of authentication. Answer B is incorrect because two-factor authentication requires two of the three primary categories of authentication to be used. Two-factor authentication is considered more secure than single-factor authentication. Three-factor authentication requires all three categories. Authorization is what you allow the user to do or accomplish.
4. **Answer: A.** Authentication can be based on one or more of the following three factors:
    - *Something you know*: This could be a password, passphrase, or secret number.
    - *Something you have*: This could be a token, bank debit card, or smart card.
    - *Something you are*: This could be a retina scan, fingerprint, DNA sample, or facial recognition.
5. **Answer: A.** Passwords, which belong to the "something you know" category, are the weakest form of authentication. Although there are many more stringent forms of authentication, passwords remain the most widely used. Passwords are insecure because people choose weak ones, don't change them, and have a tendency to write them down or allow others to gain knowledge of them. If more than one person is using the same password, there is no way to properly execute the audit function, and at this point, loss of security occurs. Passwords are also susceptible to cracking and brute-force attacks.
6. **Answer: A.** The general order of accuracy of biometric systems is fingerprint, palm scan, hand geometry, retina scan, and iris scan. However, the accuracy of an individual system is not the only item a security professional needs to consider before implementing a biometric system. Security professionals must examine usability, employee acceptance, and the crossover error rate of the proposed system.

The employee acceptance rate examines the employees' willingness to use the system. For example, technology innovations with RFID tags have made it possible to inject an extremely small tag into an employee's arm. This RFID tag could be used for identification, for authorization, and to monitor employee movement throughout the organization's facility. However, most employees would be hesitant to allow the employer to embed such a device in their arm. Currently issued passports have RFID tags, which has created an issue with identity theft (RFID sniffers).

The crossover error rate examines the capability of the proposed systems to accurately identify the individual. If the system has a high false reject rate, employees will soon grow weary of the system and look for ways to bypass it. Therefore, each of these items is important to consider.

7. **Answer: D.** Before implementing any type of access control system, the security professional needs to consider potential vulnerabilities, because these give rise to threats. Threats must also be considered, because they lead to risks. Risk is the potential that the vulnerability may be exploited. Answer D is incorrect because it relates to the formula used for risk analysis.

8. **Answer: A.** Kerberos is a single sign-on system for distributed systems. It is unlike authentication systems such as NTLM that perform only one-way authentication. It provides mutual authentication for both parties involved in the communication process. Kerberos operates under the assumption that there is no trusted party; therefore, both client and server must be authenticated. After mutual authentication occurs, Kerberos makes use of a ticket stored on the client machine to access network resources. Answers B and C are incorrect because they describe access control models. Answer D describes centralized authentication.

9. **Answer: D.** Only PAP is not susceptible to a dictionary attack; no attack is needed because the password is transmitted in clear text. Answers A, B, and C are incorrect because CHAP, LEAP, and WPA-PSK are all susceptible to dictionary attacks. The only security when forced to use one of these mechanisms is to choose passwords that will not be in any contrived dictionary—although precomputed hashes are now being used for that purpose.

10. **Answer: B.** FAR (False Acceptance Rate) is the percentage of illegitimate users who are granted access to the organization's resources. Keeping this number low is important to keeping unauthorized individuals out of the company's resources.

11. **Answer: C.** The only choice for copper cabling would be Category 6. Answers A and B are incorrect because single-mode and multimode fiber are not examples of copper cabling. However, fiber is considered a more secure transmission medium than copper cabling because it does not emit any EMI. All types of copper cabling emit a certain amount of EMI. Unauthorized personnel can clamp probes to these cables and decode the transmitted messages. Answer D is incorrect because wireless also is not an example of copper cabling.

12. **Answer: D.** There are three types of access control models. Discretionary access control places the data owners in charge of access control. Mandatory access control uses labels to determine who has access to data. Role-based access control is based on the user's role in the organization. Answer D is incorrect because there is no category called delegated access control.

13. **Answer: C.** Auditing is considered an administrative control. The three types of controls are discussed in answer 1.

14. **Answer: C.** Bank tellers would most likely fall under a role-based access control system. These systems work well for organizations in which employee roles are identical.

15. **Answer: B.** Dictionary attacks are an easy way to pick off insecure passwords. Passwords based on dictionary words allow attackers to simply perform password guessing or to use more advanced automated methods employing software programs. LCP, Cain and Able, and John the Ripper are commonly used password-cracking programs that can launch dictionary attacks. Answer A is incorrect because a hybrid attack must try a combination of words and special characters. Answer C is incorrect because a brute-force attack must try all combinations of characters, numbers, and special characters. Answer D is incorrect because a man-in-the-middle attack is one in which the attacker stands between the victim and the service and attempts to steal or sniff passwords or information.

16. **Answer: C.** Tempest is the standard for electromagnetic shielding of computer equipment. Answer B is a distracter, answer A is the name of a radioactive gas, and answer D is the name of the individual who discovered the radiation belts that surround the Earth.

17. **Answer: A.** Single sign-on is an authentication process that requires a user to enter only one username and password. The user can then access multiple systems without being burdened by additional logins. Single sign-on is implemented by using ticket-based systems such as Kerberos, SESAME, and KryptoKnight. RADIUS is a centralized remote authentication service that can be used for dial-in user service or wireless clients.

18. **Answer: A.** Answer A is correct because a discretionary access system places the data owners in charge of access control. Answers B, C, and D are incorrect because mandatory access control uses labels to determine who has access to data, and role-based access control is based on organizational roles. This is also known as nondiscretionary and is based on the user's role in the organization.

19. **Answer: D.** Challenge/response authentication is a secure authentication scheme that works in the following way: First, a randomly generated string of values is presented to the user, who then returns a calculated number based on those random values. Second, the server performs the same process locally and compares the result to the saved value. Finally, if these values match, the user is granted access; otherwise, access is denied. Answer A is a distracter. Answer B is an example of Kerberos. Answer C is an example of Challenge Handshake Authentication Protocol (CHAP).

20. **Answer: A.** FRR (False Rejection Rate) measures the number of authorized users who were incorrectly denied access. If a system has a high FRR, many valid users will be denied access. Answer B is incorrect because valid users who are denied access may attempt to bypass or subvert the authentication system because they believe it does not work correctly. Answer C is incorrect because the FRR is separate from the False Acceptance Rate (FAR). The FAR is used to measure statistics of unauthorized users. Answer D is incorrect because FRR has nothing to do with the rate of return.

21. **Answer: C.** Password attacks are the easiest way to attempt to bypass access control systems. Password attacks can range from simple password guessing to more advanced automated methods in which software programs are used. Whereas dictionary attacks may be the fastest, brute-force is considered the most time-intensive. If the user has chosen a complex password, this may be the attacker's only choice. Brute-force uses a combination of all numbers and letters, making substitutions as it progresses. It continues until all possible combinations have been attempted. If the password is very long or complex, this may take a considerable amount of time. A plain-text password would require no cracking at all.

22. **Answer: B.** CVE stands for Common Vulnerabilities and Exposures. CVE was a database developed to standardize the naming system of security vulnerabilities where information could be easily exchanged between different vendors and software platforms. You can find more information about the CVE database at http://cve.mitre.org.

23. **Answer: C.** Telnet transmits username and password information in clear text and thus can be used by attackers to gain unauthorized access. Answers A and B are incorrect because SSH and HTTPS are secure protocols. Although some versions of SSH are more secure than others, it is always better to go with some form of encryption. Answer D is incorrect because even though TFTP transmits in clear text, no username and password information is exchanged, because TFTP does not require authentication.

24. **Answer: A.** Fingerprints are most closely associated with law enforcement. Close behind this is facial recognition. Facial recognition has made great strides since 9/11. Common methods include the Markov model, eigenface, and fisherface. Iris and retina recognition typically are not associated with law enforcement.

25. **Answer: B.** Under the mandatory access control model, the system administrator establishes file, folder, and account rights. It is a very restrictive model in which users cannot share resources dynamically.

26. **Answer: B.** Password-based authentication systems can be made more secure if complex passwords are used, account lockouts are put in place, and tools such as Passprop are implemented. Passprop places remote lockout restrictions on the administrator account. Passprop is Microsoft-specific, and the test will not quiz you on that level of detail. Just understand that tools are available on both Windows and *NIX platforms to accomplish this task. Many routers, switches, and network gear also support varying degrees of lockout (usually tied to RADIUS). Disabling password-protected screensavers would decrease security, as would allowing users to reuse passwords.

27. **Answer: A.** Signature-based IDSs can detect only attack signatures that have been previously stored in their databases. These systems rely on the vendor for updates. Until then they are vulnerable to new zero-day or polymorphic attacks. Answer B is incorrect because it describes a statistical-based IDS. Answer C is incorrect because signature-based IDSs are available as both host and network configurations. Answer D is incorrect because the costs of signature-based IDS and statistical anomaly-based IDS are comparable.

28. **Answer: B.** Policies provide a high-level overview of how security should be practiced throughout the organization. Answers A, C, and D all describe the details of how these policies are to be implemented. What is most important about these particular concepts is that security policy must flow from the top of the organization.

29. **Answer: B.** A Network Intrusion Prevention System (NIPS) provides protective/reactive responses to a network. This malicious attack was submitted via port 80 HTTP service and is identified by network monitoring. Answer A is incorrect because a Host Intrusion Detection System (HIDS) focuses on services that cannot be seen from the network. Answer C is incorrect because a Host Intrusion Prevention System (HIPS) is focused on the system but can respond. Answer D is incorrect because a Network Intrusion Detection System (NIDS) identifies suspicious activity in a log file but cannot take action.

30. **Answer: B.** Sniffing is an example of a passive attack. Attackers performing the sniff simply wait and capture data when they find the information they are looking for. This might be usernames, passwords, credit card numbers, or proprietary information. All other answers are incorrect because installing programs, dumpster diving, and social engineering (which uses the art of deception) are all active attacks.

31. **Answer: D.** Forcing collusion is one of the primary reasons why separation of duties should be practiced. Simply stated, collusion requires two or more employees to work together to bypass security. This means that one person working alone cannot pull off an attack. The practice of separation of duties vastly reduces this risk.

32. **Answer: A.** The best access control policy is "deny all." This strategy starts by denying all access and privileges to all employees. Then, only as required by the job needs should access and privilege be granted. Some organizations start with "allow all." This should not be done, because it presents a huge security risk.

33. **Answer: B.** Honeypots, which also have been expanded into honeynets, are network decoys or entire networks that are closely monitored systems. These devices allow security personnel to monitor when the systems are being attacked or probed. They can also provide advance warning of a pending attack and act as a jail until you have decided how to respond to the intruder.

34. **Answer: D.** ACLs, as seen in the context of the CISSP exam, are used to set discretionary access controls. The three basic types are read, write, and execute. RBAC refers to role-based access controls, MITM is an acronym for man-in-the-middle, and ABS is simply a distracter.

35. **Answer: C.** Although job rotation does provide backup for key personnel and may help in all the other ways listed, its primary purpose is to prevent fraud or financial deception.

36. **Answer: C.** Some of the issues surrounding honeypots include entrapment and enticement. Although liability could be an issue if the honeypot is compromised and then used to attack an outside organization, entrapment is illegal and unethical, and ISC2-certified professionals are bound by a code of ethics. Statute 1029 is related to hacking and is not the primary concern of honeypots. Answer D is incorrect because although liability is an issue, it is not the primary concern in the context of this question.

37. **Answer: D.** The major disadvantages of ACLs are the lack of centralized control and the fact that many OSs default to full access. This method of access control is burdened by the difficulty of implementing a robust audit function. Therefore, answers A, B, and C are incorrect.

38. **Answer: C.** Bell-LaPadula, which was developed in the early 1970s, uses confidentiality as its basis of design. Answers A and B are integrity models and answer D is a state model that examines the state a system can enter.

39. **Answer: A.** TACACS+ uses TCP port 49 for communication. The strength of TACACS+ is that it supports authentication, authorization, and accounting. Each is implemented as a separate function, which allows the organization to determine which services it wants to deploy. This makes it possible to use TACACS+ for authorization and accounting, while choosing a technology such as RADIUS for authentication.

40. **Answer: D.** MAC (Mandatory Access Control) typically is built in and is a component of most OSs. MAC's attributes include the following: it's nondiscretionary because it is hard-coded and cannot easily be modified, it is capable of multilevel control, it is label-based because it can be used to control access to objects in a database, and it is universally applied because changes affect all objects.

41. **Answer: C.** CCTV, mantraps, biometrics, and badges are just some of the items that are part of physical access control. Data classification and labeling are preventive access control mechanisms.

42. **Answer: C.** The CER (Crossover Error Rate) is used to determine the device's accuracy. A lower CER means that the device is more accurate. The CER is determined by mapping the point at which the FAR (False Acceptance Rate) and the FRR (False Rejection Rate) meet. The CER does not determine speed, customer acceptance, or cost per employee.

43. **Answer: B.** Kerberos is a network authentication protocol that provides single sign-on service for client/server networks. A ticket is a block of data that allows users to prove their identity to a service. The ticket is valid only for a limited amount of time. Allowing tickets to expire helps raise the barrier for possible attackers, because the ticket becomes invalid after a fixed period. Answer A is incorrect because an authentication server provides each client with a ticket-granting ticket. Answer C is incorrect because clients use a ticket-granting server to grant session tickets and reduce the workload of the authentication server.

44. **Answer: B.** Identification is defined as the act of claiming a specific identity. Authentication is the act of verifying your identity, validation is the act of finding or testing the truth, and auditing is the act of inspecting or reviewing a user's actions.

45. **Answer: C.** Nonrepudiation is closely tied to accountability. It is defined as a means to ensure that users cannot deny their actions. Therefore, nonrepudiation is what makes users accountable. Digital signatures and timestamps are two popular methods used to prove nonrepudiation. Answer A is incorrect because accountability is more closely related to activities, intrusions, events, and system conditions. Answer B is incorrect because auditing is the act of review. Answer D is incorrect because validation is more closely associated with certification and accreditation.

46. **Answer: A.** SESAME uses public key cryptography to distribute secret keys. It also uses the MD5 algorithm to provide a one-way hashing function. It does not distribute keys in clear text, use SHA, or use secret key encryption.

47. **Answer: C.** There are six categories of security controls: preventive, detective, corrective, deterrent, recovery, and compensation. Job rotation would help in the detective category because it could be used to uncover violations. It would not help in recovery, corrective, or compensation.

48. **Answer: A.** RADIUS (Remote Authentication Dial-in User Service) uses UDP ports 1812 and 1813. RADIUS performs authentication, authorization, and accounting for remote users. RADIUS can also use UDP 1645 for authentication and UDP 1646 for accounting. Answers B, C, and D are wrong because RADIUS does not use TCP or ICMP as a transport protocol.

49. **Answer: B.** The Biba model was developed in 1977 largely to address the fact that the Bell-LaPadula model allowed a user with a lower security level rating to write to a subject's information with a higher security level. Therefore, its goal was to build in integrity by making sure that individuals could not write to a more secure (higher-level) object.

50. **Answer: B.** Biba is based on the concept of integrity. The Bell-LaPadula access control model is based on confidentiality. Brewer Nash was designed to protect equal competition. The Program Evaluation Review Technique (PERT) model is a program management technique.

51. **Answer: C.** Each answer is a good authentication method, but C is the best description of two-factor authentication. Answer A describes asymmetric encryption. Answer B does not specify what types or categories are being used. Answer D could be the description of IPSec or another tunneling protocol.

52. **Answer: D.** Single sign-on (SSO) can be difficult in a heterogeneous environment, where not all manufacturers may support the same authentication method. But it is a great solution in a homogeneous environment, where all vendors support the same mechanism. But the password must be complex, or you've given a malicious hacker a single point where he can breach your network.

53. **Answer: A.** Type 1 errors result from rejection of authenticated persons. You lower this count by relaxing the precision of the equipment (decreasing precision), which increases type 2 errors (accepting unauthenticated persons). You stop your tuning when type 1 errors equal type 2 errors (the crossover error rate [CER]). Under no circumstances do you want to let in more unauthenticated persons, because then you risk rejecting authorized persons.

54. **Answer: D.** Your token uses the nonce to create a one-time password. This is called asynchronous authentication. Answers A, B, and C are incorrect because synchronous token authentication takes place when the token has a timing device that is in sync with a timing mechanism on the server.

55. **Answer: B.** Because SESAME uses asymmetric authentication, it can be used for non-repudiation, whereas Kerberos cannot. Both Kerberos and SESAME support single sign-on (SSO), and both can be accessed by applications that use GSS-API function calls.

56. **Answer: C.** A mantrap is a preventive control, because it prevents the entry of unauthorized individuals. Deterrent controls slow down unauthorized behavior, corrective controls remove inappropriate actions, and detective controls discover that unauthorized behavior occurred. The CISSP exam expects you to understand the difference between various types of controls.

57. **Answer: A.** A salted, one-way encrypted file is the best way to store passwords. Cryptographic solutions to accomplish this include MD5, SHA, and HAVAL. Answer B, C, and D are incorrect because symmetric, asymmetric, and digital signatures are not the preferred way of storing passwords.

58. **Answer: D.** The act of professing to be a specific user is identification. It is not validation, authorization, or authentication.

59. **Answer: B.** A Zephyr chart can be used to compare and measure different types of biometric systems. For example, consider a situation in which you are asked to compare a fingerprint scanner to a palm scanner. Answer A is incorrect because the Crossover Error Rate (CER) is better suited for that task. Answer C also refers to the CER. Answer D is incorrect because a Zephyr chart is not used for intrusion detection.

60. **Answer: C.** Authentication can best be described as the act of verifying identity.

61. **Answer: B.** The best answer is a self-service password reset. Many websites allow users to reset their passwords by supplying some basic information. This is not an example of single sign-on, centralized authentication, or assisted passwords.

62. **Answer: D.** A federated identity is portable and can be used across business boundaries. Federated identity is not SSO or one that is restricted for use within a single domain. Federated identity also is not restricted to type I authentication.

63. **Answer: A.** The lower the crossover error rate (CER), the more accurate the biometric system. Therefore, a system with a CER of 1 would be the most accurate.

64. **Answer: B.** Preventive systems are designed to stop an unwanted event from occurring. Detective controls are designed to discover an event. Corrective controls are designed to provide a countermeasure to the unwanted event, and deterrent controls are used for discouragement.

65. **Answer: A.** Nondiscretionary access control includes role- and task-based mechanisms. Mandatory access controls are an example of label-based security and are not considered nondiscretionary.

66. **Answer: D.** A trust can be defined as a security bridge that is established between two domains. The trust can be one-way, two-way, or transitive and is not restricted to any mode.

67. **Answer: C.** Labels are associated with Mandatory Access Control (MAC). MAC is not permissive; it is considered prohibitive. MAC is more secure and less flexible than DAC; if access is not specifically granted, it is forbidden. Answers A, B, and D are not associated with labels.

68. **Answer: B.** A static token can be a swipe card, smart card, or USB token. These tokens are not active and are not considered type I (something you know) or type III (something you are) authentication.

69. **Answer: A.** The Equal Error Rate (EER) is simply another name for the Crossover Error Rate (CER). It is not the CER minus 10%, or where the FAR is lowest or highest.

70. **Answer: C.** Biometric systems are the most expensive means of performing authentication. They cost more than tokens, single sign-on, or passwords.

71. **Answer: A.** The optic disk and the fovea are parts of the eye, but an iris scan looks at the colored portion of the eye. A retina scan looks at the blood vessels at the back of the eye.

72. **Answer: D.** A rainbow table is a type of precomputed hash. It utilizes the time memory trade-off principle. It is not an attack against a biometric or fingerprint system and has nothing to do with digital certificates.

73. **Answer: B.** The ticket-granting service is a component of Kerberos.

74. **Answer: D.** SESAME uses a PAC in much the same way that Kerberos uses a key distribution center. RADIUS and TACACS do not use PACs.

75. **Answer: D.** Phishing is a nontechnical attack that attempts to trick the victim into giving up account or password information. Pretexting is the act of using established personal information to gain access to accounts, cell phone records, or other information. Social engineering is a more general term used to describe this entire category of attacks. Dumpster diving is accomplished by means of digging through the trash.

76. **Answer: C.** Web-access management allows web users to share user credentials across multiple domains without having to log into each site. Cookies will not work because they are domain-specific, and a unique certificate for each domain would not address the problems.

77. **Answer: C.** Under the Biba model, users cannot write up. Answer A describes the Bell-LaPadula model. Answer B describes the Clark Wilson Model. Answer D described the Brewer Nash model.

78. **Answer: D.** Provisioning is the management of user access. Answers A. B, and C are incorrect because they do not define the term.

79. **Answer: A.** Object reuse refers to the allocation or reallocation of system resources (storage objects) to a subject. RAM-scraping attacks, such as the cold boot attack, demonstrates that object reuse can be a real problem. The authentication method, biometric system, or strength of the password do not apply.

80. **Answer: D.** Core RBAC makes use of a many-to-many relationship and is useful in organizations that have well-defined roles. Answer A describes MAC, which makes use of labels. Answer B describes DAXC, which is a nondiscretionary model. Answer C describes rule-based access control, which makes use of ACLs.

81. **Answer: B.** A good example of a capability table is Kerberos. When a ticket is issued, it is bound to the user and specifies what resources a user can access. Answers A, C, and D do not meet that specification.

82. **Answer: A.** Diameter is the only option that provides an upgrade path from RADIUS.

83. **Answer: A.** Investigations are a good example of a detective control.

84. **Answer: B.** Switched networks are segmented, and as such require a port to be spanned. Answer A is incorrect because an IDS does not block traffic. An IPS would, but that type of control is not discussed in this question. Answer C is incorrect because MAC filtering would have most likely disabled the port. Answer D is incorrect because no traffic would have been captured.

85. **Answer: C.** A rainbow table uses a table of precomputed hashes. Answers A, B, and D are incorrect.

86. **Answer: False.** War dialing is the act of using a phone dialer program to dial a series of numbers in search of an open modem. Some people now use VoIP for war dialing, such as the I-War tool, WarVOX and IAX protocol (Asterisk).

87. **Answer: True.** Encryption is an example of a technical control. Something like policies is an example of an administrative control, whereas a fence is a physical control.

88. **Answer: False.** Access control should default to no access. You should also restrict the user to allow access to only what is needed and nothing more. As a default, no access should be provided unless a business justification can be shown as to why access should be provided.

89. **Answer: True.** TACACS, RADIUS, and Diameter are all examples of centralized access controls. For example, RADIUS is widely used by ISPs to authenticate dialup users. This central point of authentication provides an easy mechanism if users do not pay their monthly fees.

90. **Answer: False.** Although Kerberos provides single sign-on capability, it does not provide availability. Kerberos is a network authentication protocol created at the Massachusetts Institute of Technology that uses secret-key cryptography. Kerberos has three parts: a client, a server, and a trusted third party (KDC) to mediate between them. Clients obtain tickets from the Kerberos Key Distribution Center (KDC), and they present these tickets to servers when connections are established.

91. **Answer: True.** IDS engines typically include signature and anomaly. Valid types of IDSs include host and network. Knowing the difference in these terms is an important distinction for the exam.

92. **Answer: True.** Signature-based IDSs can be pattern-matching or stateful. Pattern matching looks to map the results to a known signature. Stateful compares patterns to the user's activities.

93. **Answer: True.** SATAN was actually the first vulnerability assessment tool ever created. The cocreator was fired for releasing the program. The creator released a second tool named repent to rename the program SANTA. Although the CISSP exam is not platform-specific, you may be asked about well-known tools and open-source technologies, such as SATAN or Tripwire.

94. **Answer: True.** Watchdog timers can prevent timing problems, infinite loops, deadlocks, and other software issues.

95. **Answer: False.** Password Authentication Protocol (PAP) is not a secure protocol, because passwords are passed in clear text.

96. **Answer: False.** Diameter got its name as a takeoff on RADIUS. Diameter is considered a centralized AAA protocol. Diameter was designed for all forms of remote connectivity, not just dialup.

97. **Answer: False.** Attribute pairs are used with RADIUS. RADIUS is a UDP-based client/server protocol defined in RFCs 2058 and 2059. RADIUS provides three services: authentication, authorization, and accounting. RADIUS facilitates centralized user administration and keeps all user profiles in one location that all remote services share. SESAME is a single sign-on mechanism created in Europe.

98. Answer: True. A capability can be a token, ticket, or key. Capabilities define specific use. For example, a movie ticket lets the holder watch the show. As another example, before access is granted to read a file, the capability is verified.

99. Answer: False. MAC is mandatory access control and, as such, the user has little freedom. Therefore, in a MAC-based system, access is determined by the system rather than the user. The MAC model typically is used by organizations that handle highly sensitive data, such as the DoD, NSA, CIA, and FBI.

100. Answer: True. Static separation of duties is one way to restrict the combination of duties. This means of control is commonly found in RBAC environments. For example, the individual who initiates the payment cannot also authorize the payment.

101. Answer: False. Superzapping is a generic term, derived from an IBM mainframe tool, that describes a program that can bypass normal security restrictions. The term is not associated with data destruction.

102. Answer: True. Retina scanning matches blood vessels on the back of the eye and is very accurate. Iris scanning looks at the colored portion of the eye.

103. Answer: True. Terminal Access Controller Access Control System (TACACS) is available in three variations: TACACS, XTACACS (Extended TACACS), and TACACS+, which features two-factor authentication. TACACS also allows the division of the authentication, authorization, and accounting function, which gives the administrator more control over its deployment.

104. Answer: False. This is actually a description of single sign-on (SSO).

105. Answer: True. Tokens are an example of type II authentication. Tokens, which are something you have, can be synchronous dynamic password tokens or asynchronous password devices. These devices use a challenge-response scheme and are form-factored as smart cards, USB plugs, key fobs, or keypad-based units. These devices generate authentication credentials that often are used as one-time passwords. Another great feature of token-based devices is that they can be used for two-factor authentication.

106. Answer: True. Keyboard dynamics is an example of type III authentication. Keyboard dynamics analyzes the speed and pattern of typing. Different biometric systems such as keyboard dynamics have varying levels of accuracy. The accuracy of a biometric device is measured by the percentage of type 1 and type 2 errors it produces.

107. Answer: False. Scrubbing is an activity undertaken by a user to erase evidence of illegal or unauthorized acts.

108. Answer: False. Keystroke monitoring can be used to watch employees' activities. Keystroke monitors can be either hardware or software devices. One important issue with their use is acceptable use policies (AUPs). Users must understand that their activities can be monitored and that privacy is not implied.

109. Answer: True. A federated identity is an IdM that is considered portable. For example, consider someone who travels by both plane and rental car. If both the airline and the rental car company use a federated identity management system, the traveler's authentication can be used between the two organizations.

110. **Answer: True.** Type I authentication systems typically have a clipping level set to 3. This limits logon attempts to three tries or successive attempts.

111. The answers are as follows:

   A. **Smurf: 4.** Uses a ping packet to broadcast addresses spoofed from the victim. The victim is flooded with ping replies.

   B. **LAND: 2.** Sends a spoofed SYN packet that is addressed with the target's address and port as the source and destination.

   C. **TRINOO: 5.** An early type of DDoS attack.

   D. **SYN attack: 3.** Sends a rapid series of spoofed SYN packets that are designed fill up the receiver queue.

   E. **Chargen: 1.** Loops traffic between echo and chargen on ports 7 and 19.

   F. **Ping of death: 6.** Sends ICMP ping packets that are at or exceed maximum size.

   Being able to identify common DoS and DDoS attacks will help you be prepared for the exam.

CHAPTER THREE

Cryptography

The Cryptography domain examines ways to prevent the disclosure of critical information and to ensure integrity. The word *cryptography* is based on Greek words that loosely translate into "hidden writing." Cryptography is based on old-world science that strived to find ways to provide secrecy. Today it is used for privacy, integrity, nonrepudiation, and authentication.

If you are not actively involved in this field, the concepts may truly appear to be hidden—but there is no need to worry. With a little reading and some study, anyone can master these concepts. Like other CISSP domains, this one is also a mile wide and an inch deep! The following list gives you some key areas to focus on:

- History of cryptography
- Symmetric algorithms
- Asymmetric algorithms
- Hashing
- Cryptosystems such as SSL, S/MIME, PGP, IPsec
- Public Key Infrastructure
- Cryptanalysis

Quick Check

Practice Questions

1. Which of the following ciphers is/are symmetric?

   Quick Answer: **86**
   Detailed Answer: **87**

   - ❍ **A.** DES
   - ❍ **B.** DES and Skytale
   - ❍ **C.** DES, Skytale, and Caesar's cipher
   - ❍ **D.** DES, Skytale, Caesar's cipher, and RSA

2. An employee is leaving your company. You debrief the individual and escort him to the door. After reviewing the materials in his office, you realize he left with the VPN router that had been configured for him to use when he worked from home. This router had a certificate issued to that employee, and it is not deemed worth the effort to retrieve it. What action should be taken in regards to the certificate?

   Quick Answer: **86**
   Detailed Answer: **87**

   - ❍ **A.** Suspend it.
   - ❍ **B.** Destroy it.
   - ❍ **C.** Revoke it.
   - ❍ **D.** Transfer it.

3. Which algorithm provides for key distribution but does not provide encryption or nonrepudiation?

   Quick Answer: **86**
   Detailed Answer: **87**

   - ❍ **A.** Diffie-Hellman
   - ❍ **B.** ElGamal
   - ❍ **C.** RSA
   - ❍ **D.** Elliptic Curve Cryptosystem (ECC)

4. A coworker reports that she has lost her public key ring. What does this mean?

   Quick Answer: **86**
   Detailed Answer: **87**

   - ❍ **A.** This is a security violation. You need to revoke her digital certificate.
   - ❍ **B.** She can regenerate it.
   - ❍ **C.** She will be unable to decrypt her stored files.
   - ❍ **D.** The PKI is gone.

5. What is the risk to an organization when a cryptosystem fails to use the full keyspace available?

   Quick Answer: **86**
   Detailed Answer: **87**

   - ❍ **A.** Keys are too short.
   - ❍ **B.** Keys cause a collision.
   - ❍ **C.** Keys are clustered.
   - ❍ **D.** Keys repeat.

Quick Check

6. Which DES modes of operation encrypt blocks of 1 to 8 bits?

Quick Answer: **86**
Detailed Answer: **87**

- ❍ **A.** CTR, OFB, CFB
- ❍ **B.** OFB, CFB, EFB
- ❍ **C.** CBC, OFB, EFB
- ❍ **D.** OFB, CTR, CBC

7. Which type of cipher causes confusion?

Quick Answer: **86**
Detailed Answer: **87**

- ❍ **A.** Transposition
- ❍ **B.** Substitution
- ❍ **C.** Concealment
- ❍ **D.** Running key

8. When an attacker is questioned about his attack vector, he confesses that he analyzed the messages based on the lengths of the encrypted messages. What type of cipher was the attacker most likely attacking?

Quick Answer: **86**
Detailed Answer: **87**

- ❍ **A.** Block
- ❍ **B.** Symmetric
- ❍ **C.** Stream
- ❍ **D.** Asymmetric

9. Which type of encryption uses only one shared key to encrypt and decrypt?

Quick Answer: **86**
Detailed Answer: **88**

- ❍ **A.** Public key
- ❍ **B.** Asymmetric
- ❍ **C.** Symmetric
- ❍ **D.** TCB key

10. Which type of cipher operates in real time on a single character or single bits of data?

Quick Answer: **86**
Detailed Answer: **88**

- ❍ **A.** Block
- ❍ **B.** Rolling
- ❍ **C.** Stream
- ❍ **D.** Continuous

11. Your CISSP exam study group has asked you to prepare a list of the various DES modes of operation. Which of the following is most similar to output feedback mode?

Quick Answer: **86**
Detailed Answer: **88**

- ❍ **A.** Cipher Block Chaining (CBC)
- ❍ **B.** Electronic Code Book (ECB)
- ❍ **C.** Cipher Feedback mode (CFB)
- ❍ **D.** Counter mode (CTR)

Quick Check

12. Because of the excellent material you provided your study group on DES encryption, you are assigned a new task for next week's meeting. You are asked to discuss the weakest mode of DES. Which of the following will you discuss?

Quick Answer: **86**
Detailed Answer: **88**

- ❍ **A.** CBC
- ❍ **B.** ECB
- ❍ **C.** CFB
- ❍ **D.** RID

13. Bob, a member of your CISSP study group, asks you to explain the functionality of Triple DES. How do you respond?

Quick Answer: **86**
Detailed Answer: **88**

- ❍ **A.** Triple DES works by always using three separate 128-bit encryption keys that produce an effective key strength of 384 bits.
- ❍ **B.** Triple DES works by first using two separate 56-bit encryption keys and then using a meet-in-the-middle function.
- ❍ **C.** Triple DES works by using either two or three separate 56-bit encryption keys that can encrypt/encrypt/encrypt or encrypt/decrypt/encrypt.
- ❍ **D.** Triple DES works by first using either two or three keys that must always encrypt/encrypt/encrypt to work correctly.

14. Which of the following is *not* a component of PKI?

Quick Answer: **86**
Detailed Answer: **88**

- ❍ **A.** Rejection authority
- ❍ **B.** Certificate authority
- ❍ **C.** Repository
- ❍ **D.** Archive

15. Your manager asks you to use a hashing algorithm to verify the integrity of a software program he received from the R&D branch in Hyderabad, India. Which of the following would you recommend?

Quick Answer: **86**
Detailed Answer: **88**

- ❍ **A.** IDEA
- ❍ **B.** MD5
- ❍ **C.** AES
- ❍ **D.** DES

16. Black Hat Bob has decided to attempt a chosen plaintext attack. Which of the following accurately describes this attack?

Quick Answer: **86**
Detailed Answer: **88**

Quick Check

❍ **A.** Black Hat Bob chooses the ciphertext to be decrypted. Then, based on the results, he chooses another sample to be decrypted and compares the results.

❍ **B.** Black Hat Bob chooses the plaintext to be encrypted and obtains the corresponding ciphertext.

❍ **C.** Black Hat Bob attempts to exploit the probability that two messages will use the same hashing algorithm and produce the same ciphertext.

❍ **D.** Black Hat Bob intercepts messages between two parties and attempts to modify the ciphertext.

17. Alice, a member of the web development group, is preparing to load a demo version of the company's new software onto the updated website. She wants to know which of the following message authentication algorithms can be used to validate the demo software as authentic. Which of the following would you *not* recommend?

Quick Answer: **86**
Detailed Answer: **88**

❍ **A.** HAVAL

❍ **B.** SHA

❍ **C.** PEM

❍ **D.** MD5

18. CISSPs need to understand how digital signatures are generated and verified; therefore, place the following four items in the proper order:

Quick Answer: **86**
Detailed Answer: **88**

1. Encrypt the digest with your private key.

2. Compare the message digest to one you created.

3. Generate a message digest.

4. Decrypt the signature with the sender's public key.

❍ **A.** 4, 2, 1, 3

❍ **B.** 1, 4, 3, 2

❍ **C.** 3, 1, 4, 2

❍ **D.** 3, 4, 2, 1

19. Which of the following is *not* a good choice to secure email?

Quick Answer: **86**
Detailed Answer: **88**

❍ **A.** S/MIME

❍ **B.** SSH

❍ **C.** PEM

❍ **D.** PGP

Quick Check

20. Which type of cipher works on a single segment of data, such as 64 bits, at a time to produce a corresponding segment of encrypted data?

- ❍ **A.** Block
- ❍ **B.** Segmented
- ❍ **C.** Stream
- ❍ **D.** Continuous

Quick Answer: **86**
Detailed Answer: **89**

21. Jan asks you to explain asymmetric encryption. You respond by saying, "With asymmetric encryption, some keys are freely shared among communicating parties, and others are kept secret." Which keys are shared, and which are secret?

- ❍ **A.** Public, private
- ❍ **B.** Secret, private
- ❍ **C.** Public, public
- ❍ **D.** Domain, controlled

Quick Answer: **86**
Detailed Answer: **89**

22. Which of the following provides communicating parties with the assurance that they are communicating with people or entities who truly are who they claim to be?

- ❍ **A.** Hashing
- ❍ **B.** Biometric signatures
- ❍ **C.** Symmetric encryption
- ❍ **D.** Digital certificates

Quick Answer: **86**
Detailed Answer: **89**

23. Which of the following would you define as a neutral organization that notarizes digital certificates?

- ❍ **A.** Certificate authority
- ❍ **B.** Public key authority
- ❍ **C.** Public key infrastructure
- ❍ **D.** Authorization zone

Quick Answer: **86**
Detailed Answer: **89**

24. Which method of encryption was reported to have been used by al Qaeda before 9/11 and functions by hiding information inside a picture or graphic?

- ❍ **A.** Port redirection
- ❍ **B.** Stealthography
- ❍ **C.** Steganography
- ❍ **D.** Tunneling

Quick Answer: **86**
Detailed Answer: **89**

Quick Check

25. Your manager wants to implement PKI and wants to make sure that the system is fully standardized. Therefore, your digital certificates should comply with which standard?

Quick Answer: **86**
Detailed Answer: **89**

- ❍ **A.** X.501
- ❍ **B.** X.509
- ❍ **C.** IEEE 802.3
- ❍ **D.** IEEE 802.11

26. Your manager asks you to explain the ways in which certificates can be revoked. What do you tell her?

Quick Answer: **86**
Detailed Answer: **89**

- ❍ **A.** Online certificate status protocol and certificate revocation lists
- ❍ **B.** Certificate revocation lists and certificate denial lists
- ❍ **C.** Online certificate status update and certificate denial lists
- ❍ **D.** Certificate denial lists and online certificate status update

27. What is the maximum key length for the Blowfish algorithm?

Quick Answer: **86**
Detailed Answer: **89**

- ❍ **A.** 56 bits
- ❍ **B.** 128 bits
- ❍ **C.** 256 bits
- ❍ **D.** 448 bits

28. Which of the following is one of the algorithms that might be used in PGP for encryption?

Quick Answer: **86**
Detailed Answer: **89**

- ❍ **A.** Tiger
- ❍ **B.** DES
- ❍ **C.** SHA
- ❍ **D.** IDEA

29. Your CISSP study group asks you to research the various hashing algorithms. They want you to report back and let them know which one was designed to be used in high-speed computations. What will you say?

Quick Answer: **86**
Detailed Answer: **90**

- ❍ **A.** HMAC
- ❍ **B.** MD4
- ❍ **C.** SHA
- ❍ **D.** MD5

Quick Check

30. Your nephew, Richard, has been putting in lots of time trying to learn about security. He comes to you with a question: What is the science of taking plaintext and converting it to ciphertext with the goal of providing confidentiality, integrity, authenticity, and nonrepudiation? What will your answer be?

- ❍ **A.** Cryptosystems
- ❍ **B.** Cryptanalysis
- ❍ **C.** Cryptology
- ❍ **D.** Cryptography

Quick Answer: **86**
Detailed Answer: **90**

31. Which asymmetric algorithm uses a 160-bit key that offers the equivalent protection of a 1024-bit RSA key?

- ❍ **A.** ElGamal
- ❍ **B.** Elliptic Curve Cryptosystem
- ❍ **C.** Triple DES
- ❍ **D.** Blowfish

Quick Answer: **86**
Detailed Answer: **90**

32. Which standard was proposed by MasterCard and Visa as a method of more secure credit card transactions?

- ❍ **A.** One-time pad
- ❍ **B.** S/MIME
- ❍ **C.** SET
- ❍ **D.** HAVAL

Quick Answer: **86**
Detailed Answer: **90**

33. Ralph, the branch manager, asks you to give an informal talk to his security team about wireless networking dos and don'ts. Which of the following standards will you say is used to provide confidentiality in wireless networks?

- ❍ **A.** SET
- ❍ **B.** WEP
- ❍ **C.** PAP
- ❍ **D.** IEEE 802.3

Quick Answer: **86**
Detailed Answer: **90**

34. Someone in the Loss Prevention department asks if you can recommend a hashing algorithm that is stronger than MD5. What will you recommend?

- ❍ **A.** RSA
- ❍ **B.** SHA-1
- ❍ **C.** IDEA
- ❍ **D.** MARS

Quick Answer: **86**
Detailed Answer: **90**

Quick Check

35. Which encryption system did the Japanese use during World War II?

Quick Answer: **86**
Detailed Answer: **90**

- ❍ **A.** Enigma
- ❍ **B.** Scytale
- ❍ **C.** Runic stones
- ❍ **D.** Purple Machine

36. Which of the following is *not* contained in a digital certificate?

Quick Answer: **86**
Detailed Answer: **90**

- ❍ **A.** Serial number
- ❍ **B.** Subject's name
- ❍ **C.** Subject's private key
- ❍ **D.** X.509 version

37. Your recent speech on wireless network vulnerabilities and attacks has generated several emails. The one question you keep receiving is this: What type of encryption is WEP built on? What is the correct answer?

Quick Answer: **86**
Detailed Answer: **91**

- ❍ **A.** MD5
- ❍ **B.** RC4
- ❍ **C.** Triple DES
- ❍ **D.** DES

38. Your organization is considering using IPsec for its mobile users. Which mode of IPsec encrypts only the payload?

Quick Answer: **86**
Detailed Answer: **91**

- ❍ **A.** Transport mode
- ❍ **B.** Transfer mode
- ❍ **C.** Tunnel mode
- ❍ **D.** Channel mode

39. Michael believes that Black Hat Bob altered an encrypted message he received from a client. Which of the following should Michael check to verify his assumptions?

Quick Answer: **86**
Detailed Answer: **91**

- ❍ **A.** The message header
- ❍ **B.** The digital signature
- ❍ **C.** Time and date stamps
- ❍ **D.** The sender's public key

40. Which of the following can emulate a stream cipher?

Quick Answer: **86**
Detailed Answer: **91**

- ❍ **A.** DES ECB
- ❍ **B.** RC4
- ❍ **C.** IDEA
- ❍ **D.** Blowfish

Quick Check

41. Secure Electronic Transaction (SET) is a proven method to perform financial transactions on the Internet. Before a SET session is established, what underlying protocol typically is used to provide a secure session between the consumer and the merchant?

Quick Answer: **86**
Detailed Answer: **91**

- ❍ **A.** PGP
- ❍ **B.** SSL
- ❍ **C.** DES
- ❍ **D.** SSH

42. Your organization is looking for an IP layer VPN solution. You believe that IPsec is the best option. In which of the following modes would you configure IPsec to obtain the greatest amount of security?

Quick Answer: **86**
Detailed Answer: **91**

- ❍ **A.** Tunnel mode
- ❍ **B.** Channel mode
- ❍ **C.** Transport mode
- ❍ **D.** Transfer mode

43. Which of the following statements is *not* true of one-time pads?

Quick Answer: **86**
Detailed Answer: **91**

- ❍ **A.** The pads must not be reused.
- ❍ **B.** The key must be generated randomly.
- ❍ **C.** The key must be at least as long as the message to be encrypted.
- ❍ **D.** The pads, much like a public key, do not need to be protected from physical disclosure.

44. Which of the following key size version of DES is *not* considered secure?

Quick Answer: **86**
Detailed Answer: **91**

- ❍ **A.** 56-bit DES
- ❍ **B.** 64-bit DES
- ❍ **C.** 128-bit DES
- ❍ **D.** 256-bit DES

45. Which of the following encryption machines did the Germans use?

Quick Answer: **86**
Detailed Answer: **92**

- ❍ **A.** Enigma
- ❍ **B.** Scytale
- ❍ **C.** Runic stones
- ❍ **D.** Purple Machine

Quick Check

46. Kara is studying for her CISSP exam and comes to you for help. She needs some information about Boolean logic and the XOR function. Her question is this: If she has a plaintext input of 0 and a key bit of 1, what will the output be? How do you answer?

Quick Answer: **86**
Detailed Answer: **92**

- ❍ **A.** 0
- ❍ **B.** 1
- ❍ **C.** 10
- ❍ **D.** 01

47. Bob and Alice want to use symmetric encryption to exchange information. How many keys are required?

Quick Answer: **86**
Detailed Answer: **92**

- ❍ **A.** One
- ❍ **B.** Two
- ❍ **C.** Three
- ❍ **D.** Four

48. Jeff wants to make sure that the cryptographic mechanisms he chooses provide integrity and authentication. Which of the following must he use?

Quick Answer: **86**
Detailed Answer: **92**

- ❍ **A.** Steganography
- ❍ **B.** Hashing
- ❍ **C.** Digital signatures
- ❍ **D.** Kerberos

49. Which of the following is considered unbreakable as long as key requirements are met?

Quick Answer: **86**
Detailed Answer: **92**

- ❍ **A.** DES
- ❍ **B.** Vernam cipher
- ❍ **C.** ECB DES
- ❍ **D.** Double DES

50. Which of the following is *not* an example of symmetric encryption?

Quick Answer: **86**
Detailed Answer: **92**

- ❍ **A.** Merkle-Hellman
- ❍ **B.** IDEA
- ❍ **C.** RC5
- ❍ **D.** Twofish

Quick Check

51. Using cryptography could be considered a two-step process. What is the information to be concealed called, and what is the operation to conceal it?

- ❍ **A.** Plaintext, encryption
- ❍ **B.** Ciphertext, algorithm
- ❍ **C.** Message, cryptogram
- ❍ **D.** Encryption, plaintext

Quick Answer: **86**
Detailed Answer: **92**

52. When working with ciphers, you have several ways to handle the encryption process. Which of the following best describes these two main methods?

- ❍ **A.** Timed and blocked
- ❍ **B.** Rolling and parsed
- ❍ **C.** Analog and digital
- ❍ **D.** Stream and block

Quick Answer: **86**
Detailed Answer: **92**

53. Alice has been reading about hackers stealing credit-card numbers and other personal information. She wants to learn more about how this is accomplished. What is it called when hackers try to decipher ciphertext without the cryptographic key?

- ❍ **A.** Cracking
- ❍ **B.** Cryptography
- ❍ **C.** Cryptology
- ❍ **D.** Cryptanalysis

Quick Answer: **86**
Detailed Answer: **92**

54. Which block cipher standard was developed as a replacement for DES?

- ❍ **A.** IDEA
- ❍ **B.** ElGamal
- ❍ **C.** Diffie-Hellman
- ❍ **D.** AES

Quick Answer: **86**
Detailed Answer: **92**

55. Which encryption mechanism did the ancient Spartans use?

- ❍ **A.** Enigma
- ❍ **B.** Scytale
- ❍ **C.** Runic stones
- ❍ **D.** Purple Machine

Quick Answer: **86**
Detailed Answer: **93**

Quick Check

56. Which of the following is *not* a weakness of symmetric encryption?

- ❍ **A.** Problematic key distribution
- ❍ **B.** Scalability
- ❍ **C.** Limited security
- ❍ **D.** Slower than asymmetric encryption

Quick Answer: **86**
Detailed Answer: **93**

57. Which type of encryption uses two keys that use a trap door function?

- ❍ **A.** MD5
- ❍ **B.** Asymmetric
- ❍ **C.** Secret key
- ❍ **D.** Symmetric

Quick Answer: **86**
Detailed Answer: **93**

58. Which mode of DES works as described here? It encrypts the preceding block of ciphertext with the DES algorithm. This block is then XORed with the next block of plaintext to produce the next block of ciphertext.

- ❍ **A.** CFB
- ❍ **B.** OFB
- ❍ **C.** 3DES (EEE3)
- ❍ **D.** ECB

Quick Answer: **86**
Detailed Answer: **93**

59. Which algorithm is similar to MD4 and is used for integrity?

- ❍ **A.** RIPEMD
- ❍ **B.** LUC
- ❍ **C.** RSA
- ❍ **D.** ECC

Quick Answer: **86**
Detailed Answer: **93**

60. You are hired as a reviewer for an upcoming movie. After signing a release stating that you will not make copies of or redistribute the movie, you notice that the contract states that the files have been watermarked. Which term best describes the category of cryptographic solution that has been applied?

- ❍ **A.** Symmetric encryption
- ❍ **B.** Asymmetric encryption
- ❍ **C.** Steganography
- ❍ **D.** Integrity verification

Quick Answer: **86**
Detailed Answer: **93**

Quick Check

61. Which of the following best describes LUC?

❍ **A.** A symmetric algorithm that uses discrete logarithms and Lucas functions

❍ **B.** A symmetric algorithm that uses large prime numbers and Lucas functions

❍ **C.** A hashing algorithm that uses XOR logic and Lucas functions

❍ **D.** An asymmetric algorithm that uses discrete logarithms and Lucas functions

Quick Answer: **86**
Detailed Answer: **93**

62. Which algorithm was designed for 64-bit systems and is used in Merkle hash trees?

❍ **A.** SHA

❍ **B.** MD5

❍ **C.** Tiger

❍ **D.** CAST

Quick Answer: **86**
Detailed Answer: **93**

63. Observe the following chart, and determine which answer best describes its purpose:

Quick Answer: **86**
Detailed Answer: **94**

A	B	C	D	E	F	G	H	I	J	K	L	M	N	O	P	Q	R	S	T	U	V	W	X	Y	Z
A	B	C	D	E	F	G	H	I	J	K	L	M	N	O	P	Q	R	S	T	U	V	W	X	Y	Z
B	C	D	E	F	G	H	I	J	K	L	M	N	O	P	Q	R	S	T	U	V	W	X	Y	Z	A
C	D	E	F	G	H	I	J	K	L	M	N	O	P	Q	R	S	T	U	V	W	X	Y	Z	A	B
D	E	F	G	H	I	J	K	L	M	N	O	P	Q	R	S	T	U	V	W	X	Y	Z	A	B	C
E	F	G	H	I	J	K	L	M	N	O	P	Q	R	S	T	U	V	W	X	Y	Z	A	B	C	D
F	G	H	I	J	K	L	M	N	O	P	Q	R	S	T	U	V	W	X	Y	Z	A	B	C	D	E
G	H	I	J	K	L	M	N	O	P	Q	R	S	T	U	V	W	X	Y	Z	A	B	C	D	E	F
H	I	J	K	L	M	N	O	P	Q	R	S	T	U	V	W	X	Y	Z	A	B	C	D	E	F	G
I	J	K	L	M	N	O	P	Q	R	S	T	U	V	W	X	Y	Z	A	B	C	D	E	F	G	H
J	K	L	M	N	O	P	Q	R	S	T	U	V	W	X	Y	Z	A	B	C	D	E	F	G	H	I
K	L	M	N	O	P	Q	R	S	T	U	V	W	X	Y	Z	A	B	C	D	E	F	G	H	I	J
L	M	N	O	P	Q	R	S	T	U	V	W	X	Y	Z	A	B	C	D	E	F	G	H	I	J	K
M	N	O	P	Q	R	S	T	U	V	W	X	Y	Z	A	B	C	D	E	F	G	H	I	J	K	L
N	O	P	Q	R	S	T	U	V	W	X	Y	Z	A	B	C	D	E	F	G	H	I	J	K	L	M
O	P	Q	R	S	T	U	V	W	X	Y	Z	A	B	C	D	E	F	G	H	I	J	K	L	M	N
P	Q	R	S	T	U	V	W	X	Y	Z	A	B	C	D	E	F	G	H	I	J	K	L	M	N	O
Q	R	S	T	U	V	W	X	Y	Z	A	B	C	D	E	F	G	H	I	J	K	L	M	N	O	P
R	S	T	U	V	W	X	Y	Z	A	B	C	D	E	F	G	H	I	J	K	L	M	N	O	P	Q
S	T	U	V	W	X	Y	Z	A	B	C	D	E	F	G	H	I	J	K	L	M	N	O	P	Q	R
T	U	V	W	X	Y	Z	A	B	C	D	E	F	G	H	I	J	K	L	M	N	O	P	Q	R	S
U	V	W	X	Y	Z	A	B	C	D	E	F	G	H	I	J	K	L	M	N	O	P	Q	R	S	T
V	W	X	Y	Z	A	B	C	D	E	F	G	H	I	J	K	L	M	N	O	P	Q	R	S	T	U
W	X	Y	Z	A	B	C	D	E	F	G	H	I	J	K	L	M	N	O	P	Q	R	S	T	U	V
X	Y	Z	A	B	C	D	E	F	G	H	I	J	K	L	M	N	O	P	Q	R	S	T	U	V	W
Y	Z	A	B	C	D	E	F	G	H	I	J	K	L	M	N	O	P	Q	R	S	T	U	V	W	X
Z	A	B	C	D	E	F	G	H	I	J	K	L	M	N	O	P	Q	R	S	T	U	V	W	X	Y

Quick Check

- ❍ **A.** The chart is an example of a Vernam cipher.
- ❍ **B.** The chart is an example of a one-time pad.
- ❍ **C.** The chart is an example of the atbash cipher.
- ❍ **D.** The chart is an example of the Vigenere cipher.

64. What does the following formula define?

number of keys = [n * (n – 1)]/2

Quick Answer: **86**
Detailed Answer: **94**

- ❍ **A.** The number of keys needed in a symmetric encryption network
- ❍ **B.** The number of keys needed to distribute hashed messages in a network
- ❍ **C.** The number of keys required to prevent collisions
- ❍ **D.** The number of keys needed in an asymmetric encryption network

65. In an asymmetric system, how many keys are required for 10 users to fully communicate?

Quick Answer: **86**
Detailed Answer: **94**

- ❍ **A.** 10
- ❍ **B.** 20
- ❍ **C.** 100
- ❍ **D.** 110

66. In a symmetric system, how many keys are required for 10 users to fully communicate?

Quick Answer: **86**
Detailed Answer: **94**

- ❍ **A.** 10
- ❍ **B.** 20
- ❍ **C.** 45
- ❍ **D.** 100

67. Which cryptographic system can be used for integrity, authenticity, and nonrepudiation?

Quick Answer: **86**
Detailed Answer: **94**

- ❍ **A.** Asymmetric encryption
- ❍ **B.** Symmetric encryption
- ❍ **C.** Hashing
- ❍ **D.** None of the above

Quick Check

68. Which algorithm was scheduled for use to give law enforcement authorities the ability to obtain legal authorization to encrypt data?

Quick Answer: **86**
Detailed Answer: **94**

- ❍ **A.** DES
- ❍ **B.** Skipjack
- ❍ **C.** Blowfish
- ❍ **D.** Twofish

69. You are reviewing some documentation that mentions the Clipper Chip. To what is this document referring?

Quick Answer: **86**
Detailed Answer: **94**

- ❍ **A.** Government access to keys
- ❍ **B.** Hardware encryption
- ❍ **C.** Hard drive encryption
- ❍ **D.** PGP encryption keys

70. You are given an encrypted file. You know what a portion of the file says, but not the entire document. Which of the following attacks should you attempt to recover the encrypted data?

Quick Answer: **86**
Detailed Answer: **94**

- ❍ **A.** Ciphertext only
- ❍ **B.** Chosen plaintext
- ❍ **C.** Chosen ciphertext
- ❍ **D.** Known plaintext

71. Black Hat Bob is monitoring an encrypted channel and notices that the volume of traffic has increased between two parties. Bob makes assumptions about what types of activities the two parties have planned. What most accurately describes the type of attack that has taken place?

Quick Answer: **86**
Detailed Answer: **94**

- ❍ **A.** Session hijacking
- ❍ **B.** Sniffing attack
- ❍ **C.** Data mining
- ❍ **D.** Inference attack

72. To prevent an attacker from seeing the original source and the final destination of two parties communicating via encryption, which of the following techniques should be used?

Quick Answer: **86**
Detailed Answer: **95**

- ❍ **A.** IPsec tunnel
- ❍ **B.** IPsec transport
- ❍ **C.** Secure Shell (SSH)
- ❍ **D.** Source routing

Quick Check

73. What is the effective length of the DES encryption key?

Quick Answer: **86**
Detailed Answer: **95**

- ❍ **A.** 48 bits
- ❍ **B.** 56 bits
- ❍ **C.** 64 bits
- ❍ **D.** 8 bits

74. Which of the following is an authenticating and encrypting protocol that is used with IPsec to provide source authentication, confidentiality, and message integrity?

Quick Answer: **86**
Detailed Answer: **95**

- ❍ **A.** Encapsulating Security Payload (ESP)
- ❍ **B.** IPsec Internet Key Exchange (IKE)
- ❍ **C.** Security Association (SA)
- ❍ **D.** Authentication Header (AH)

75. Which of the following best describes collisions?

Quick Answer: **86**
Detailed Answer: **95**

- ❍ **A.** When two cleartext inputs fed into an asymmetric algorithm produce the same encrypted output
- ❍ **B.** When two different messages produce the same hash value.
- ❍ **C.** When two cleartext inputs fed into a symmetric algorithm produce the same encrypted output
- ❍ **D.** When a steganographic program produces two images that look the same, except that one has text hidden in it.

76. You are asked to help a coworker who produces digital art for the company website. You want to make sure that the digital photos and art she produces are recognizable as hers even if they are stolen and placed on another website. What is the best solution?

Quick Answer: **86**
Detailed Answer: **95**

- ❍ **A.** Copyright the art
- ❍ **B.** Use steganography
- ❍ **C.** Use a digital watermark
- ❍ **D.** Use a digital certificate

77. Programs such as Tripwire, MD5sum, and Windows System File Protection (WFP) all rely on what?

Quick Answer: **86**
Detailed Answer: **95**

- ❍ **A.** Digital certificates
- ❍ **B.** Hashing
- ❍ **C.** Digital signatures
- ❍ **D.** Steganography

Quick Check

78. How many characters long is the output of an MD5sum?

Quick Answer: **86**
Detailed Answer: **95**

- ❍ **A.** 128 characters
- ❍ **B.** 64 characters
- ❍ **C.** 32 characters
- ❍ **D.** 16 characters

79. What binary coding is most commonly used for e-mail purposes?

Quick Answer: **86**
Detailed Answer: **95**

- ❍ **A.** UUencode
- ❍ **B.** SMTP
- ❍ **C.** XOR
- ❍ **D.** Base64

80. Which of the following is a good example of zero proof knowledge?

Quick Answer: **86**
Detailed Answer: **95**

- ❍ **A.** Symmetric encryption
- ❍ **B.** Hashing
- ❍ **C.** Caesar's cipher
- ❍ **D.** Digital signatures

81. When using HMACs, what process can be used for symmetric key exchange?

Quick Answer: **86**
Detailed Answer: **96**

- ❍ **A.** The key is included in the function.
- ❍ **B.** Diffie–Hellman.
- ❍ **C.** AES.
- ❍ **D.** DSA.

82. Which of the following has been adopted by the International Organization for Standardization (ISO) and the International Electrotechnical Commission (IEC) as part of the joint ISO/IEC 10118-3 international-standard hashing algorithms?

Quick Answer: **86**
Detailed Answer: **96**

- ❍ **A.** Whirlpool
- ❍ **B.** Tiger
- ❍ **C.** CAST
- ❍ **D.** Elliptic curve

83. What is another name for a collision?

Quick Answer: **86**
Detailed Answer: **96**

- ❍ **A.** Meet-in-the-middle attack
- ❍ **B.** Birthday attack
- ❍ **C.** Brute-force attack
- ❍ **D.** Key clustering

Quick Check

84. Which of the following is *not* a symmetric algorithm?

Quick Answer: **86**
Detailed Answer: **96**

- ❍ **A.** Serpent
- ❍ **B.** SAFER
- ❍ **C.** CAST
- ❍ **D.** Lucas

85. Which of the following attributes best describes symmetric encryption?

Quick Answer: **86**
Detailed Answer: **96**

- ❍ **A.** Used for key distribution.
- ❍ **B.** The algorithms are less complex.
- ❍ **C.** Used for digital signatures.
- ❍ **D.** Used for nonrepudiation.

Practice Questions (True or False)

86. DES ECB is susceptible to frequency analysis.

Quick Answer: **86**
Detailed Answer: **96**

- ❍ True
- ❍ False

87. DES OFB can be implemented to emulate a stream cipher.

Quick Answer: **86**
Detailed Answer: **96**

- ❍ True
- ❍ False

88. Double DES is more secure than DES.

Quick Answer: **86**
Detailed Answer: **96**

- ❍ True
- ❍ False

89. Nonrepudiation can be provided by digital signatures.

Quick Answer: **86**
Detailed Answer: **96**

- ❍ True
- ❍ False

90. Digital signatures require the sender to use the private key.

Quick Answer: **86**
Detailed Answer: **96**

- ❍ True
- ❍ False

91. DES uses 32 rounds for encryption.

Quick Answer: **86**
Detailed Answer: **96**

- ❍ True
- ❍ False

92. Side channel attacks require cleartext and ciphertext.

Quick Answer: **86**
Detailed Answer: **96**

- ❍ True
- ❍ False

Quick Check

93. Message Security Protocol (MSP) is considered an x.400 protocol.
❍ True
❍ False

Quick Answer: **86**
Detailed Answer: **97**

94. AES and RSA can be used for privacy-enhanced mail (PEM).
❍ True
❍ False

Quick Answer: **86**
Detailed Answer: **97**

95. PPTP is found at the session layer.
❍ True
❍ False

Quick Answer: **86**
Detailed Answer: **97**

96. The major weakness of public key cryptography is its slow speed of operation.
❍ True
❍ False

Quick Answer: **86**
Detailed Answer: **97**

97. Symmetric encryption is best used for small blocks of data, digital signatures, digital envelopes, and digital certificates.
❍ True
❍ False

Quick Answer: **86**
Detailed Answer: **97**

98. A running key cipher is also known as a book cipher.
❍ True
❍ False

Quick Answer: **86**
Detailed Answer: **97**

99. Caesar's cipher is also known as a ROT3 cipher.
❍ True
❍ False

Quick Answer: **86**
Detailed Answer: **97**

100. A cipher is a cryptographic system of symbols that represent words or phrases that may be secret but not always confidential.
❍ True
❍ False

Quick Answer: **86**
Detailed Answer: **97**

101. Collisions are a well-known weakness in cryptography in which plaintext messages can generate identical ciphertext messages using different keys and the same algorithm.
❍ True
❍ False

Quick Answer: **86**
Detailed Answer: **97**

102. Rijndael was chosen to replace DES and be the new U.S. standard for encrypting sensitive but unclassified data.
❍ True
❍ False

Quick Answer: **86**
Detailed Answer: **97**

103. Keystroke loggers such as Magic Lantern can be used to bypass cryptographic systems and capture keystrokes of a targeted computer.
❍ True
❍ False

Quick Answer: **86**
Detailed Answer: **97**

Quick Check

104. X.509 is the standard for digital signatures because it specifies information and attributes required to identify a person or computer system.
- ❍ True
- ❍ False

Quick Answer: **86**
Detailed Answer: **97**

105. A Rijndael 128-bit key goes through 14 rounds.
- ❍ True
- ❍ False

Quick Answer: **86**
Detailed Answer: **97**

106. Anyone who can verify a message authentication code can also create one.
- ❍ True
- ❍ False

Quick Answer: **86**
Detailed Answer: **97**

107. Wireless Transport Layer Security (WTLS) protocol is used by wireless application protocol.
- ❍ True
- ❍ False

Quick Answer: **86**
Detailed Answer: **97**

108. The hashing algorithm in the Digital Signature Standard (DSS) generates a message digest of 128 bits.
- ❍ True
- ❍ False

Quick Answer: **86**
Detailed Answer: **98**

109. The NIST Advanced Encryption Standard uses Blowfish.
- ❍ True
- ❍ False

Quick Answer: **86**
Detailed Answer: **98**

Practice Questions (Mix and Match)

110. Match each cryptographic term with its definition.

A. SHA2: _____

B. Diffie-Hellman: _____

C. Digital signature: _____

D. 3DES: _____

E. Steganography: _____

F. Public key infrastructure: _____

1. Nonrepudiation

2. Integrity

3. Symmetric encryption

4. Hidden, not encrypted

5. Facilitates trust

6. Key exchange

Quick Answer: **86**
Detailed Answer: **98**

Quick-Check Answer Key

1. C
2. C
3. A
4. B
5. D
6. A
7. B
8. C
9. C
10. C
11. D
12. B
13. C
14. A
15. B
16. B
17. C
18. C
19. B
20. A
21. A
22. D
23. A
24. C
25. B
26. A
27. D
28. D
29. B
30. D
31. B
32. C
33. B
34. B
35. D
36. C
37. B
38. A
39. B
40. B
41. B
42. A
43. D
44. A
45. A
46. B
47. A
48. C
49. B
50. A
51. A
52. D
53. D
54. D
55. B
56. D
57. B
58. A
59. A
60. C
61. D
62. C
63. D
64. A
65. D
66. C
67. A
68. B
69. A
70. D
71. D
72. A
73. B
74. A
75. B
76. C
77. B
78. C
79. A
80. D
81. B
82. A
83. B
84. D
85. B
86. True
87. True
88. False
89. True
90. True
91. False
92. False
93. True
94. True
95. False
96. True
97. False
98. True
99. True
100. False
101. False
102. True
103. True
104. True
105. False
106. True
107. True
108. False
109. False
110. **A.** 2
    B. 6
    C. 1
    D. 3
    E. 4
    F. 5

Answers and Explanations

1. **Answer: C.** Symmetric refers to the fact that the "key" used to encrypt a message is also used to decrypt. This is the case with DES, Skytale, and Caesar's cipher (although with DES and Caesar's cipher the actual mechanism—or cipher—performed when encrypting is opposite the process for decrypting). RSA is an asymmetric process involving two keys—one to encrypt and one to decrypt.

2. **Answer: C.** A certificate is revoked if lost or stolen. Certificates are suspended when it is expected that the cognizant authority will resume use in the future. PKI does define a mechanism (PKCS #12) for transferring private and public certificates. However, because this is an issue from your corporation, it is unlikely that you would want to transfer it to another individual. You cannot destroy the certificate after it is out of your control. However, you can prevent the public from recognizing the certificate as legitimate by revoking it. The certificate authority (CA) adds the certificate to the Certificate Revocation List (CRL).

3. **Answer: A.** Diffie-Hellman enables key distribution over an insecure channel but does not provide encryption or digital signatures. ElGamal, RSA, and ECC provide key distribution, encryption, and nonrepudiation.

4. **Answer: B.** A key ring refers to all the keys a person has collected in support of PGP, a peer-to-peer public key cryptography. The user should be able to recollect the public keys she requires. Digital certificates are revoked when someone has lost (or had stolen) a private key. Files are encrypted with session-type keys, which are then encrypted with the user's public key. These encrypted session keys are stored as part of the Encrypting File System (EFS) mechanism on an NTFS drive.

5. **Answer: D.** The keyspace represents the entire range of values from which keys can be derived. Uniqueness is maximized by ensuring use of the entire keyspace; otherwise, patterns and repetitions surface. The size of the key, collisions, and clusters are all characteristics that are associated with the cipher itself, not with the keyspace. Collisions occur when two files form the same hash result. Clustering results when different keys yield the same result.

6. **Answer: A.** Counter mode (CTR), output feedback mode (OFB), and cipher feedback (CFB) all are ciphers that can handle small or streaming input. They are distinguished by how data is chained forward for successive blocks of encryption. Electronic code book (ECB) is the only one that does not involve chaining, and it always yields the same result for a given input. It is satisfactory for small, nonrepeating transmissions. Both OFB and CBC use 64-bit blocks with chaining.

7. **Answer: B.** Transposition causes diffusion, and substitution causes confusion. When encoding with block ciphers, S-boxes are used. These S-boxes perform a certain number of transpositions and substitutions, because today's complex ciphers require both methods. A concealment cipher uses an agreed-on pattern to embed or hide the message. A running key cipher uses patterns found in the environment.

8. **Answer: C.** Stream ciphers do not alter the lengths of the encrypted message. Block ciphers pad the message to conform to the needed block size. Symmetric ciphers can be block or stream. Asymmetric ciphers are not used for bulk encryption but are used to create tunnels, encrypt session keys, perform authentication, and create digital signatures.

9. **Answer: C.** Symmetric encryption uses a single key to encrypt and decrypt. This was the default standard before the 1970s. Public key refers to asymmetric encryption, and TCB is not a valid form of encryption.

10. **Answer: C.** Stream ciphers typically are implemented in hardware and operate in real time on a continuous stream of bits or characters of data. Answer A is incorrect because a block cipher processes blocks of data, Answers B and D are distracters.

11. **Answer: D.** CBC, ECB, and CFB are all modes of DES but are not the most similar to output feedback mode (OFB). Counter mode uses a counter and XORs each block, whereas OFB uses a randomly generated initialization vector (IV).

12. **Answer: B.** ECB (Electronic Code Book) is the weakest implementation of DES because identical blocks of plaintext always produce the same ciphertext. Any type of encryption system that produces a pattern is subject to attack. CBC (Cipher Block Chaining) and CFB (Cipher Feedback Mode) are considered more secure. RID is a distracter.

13. **Answer: C.** Triple DES can use either two or three keys, depending on the mode that is used. For example, two-key DES uses the first key to encrypt, the second key to decrypt (which further scrambles the data), and the first key to reencrypt.

14. **Answer: A.** PKI (Public Key Infrastructure) has four key components: certificate authority, registration authority, repository, and archive. There is no such component as the rejection authority.

15. **Answer: B.** MD5 is a one-way hashing algorithm that is often used to check file integrity. The creator of a file or message can use MD5 to create an MD5 checksum. Then, when the message or program is received, a new MD5 checksum can be created. If the two checksums match, the data is unchanged. Programs such as Tripwire automate this process. You can check out Tripwire at www.tripwire.org. The other answers are incorrect because they are not hashing algorithms. IDEA is asymmetric, AES is asymmetric, and DES is a symmetric algorithm.

16. **Answer: B.** The attacker chooses the plaintext to be encrypted and then obtains the corresponding ciphertext. Answer A describes an adaptive chosen ciphertext attack. Answer C describes a birthday attack. Answer D describes a man-in-the-middle attack.

17. **Answer: C.** SHA, MD5, and HAVAL are three hashing algorithms that can be used for file integrity and authentication. Each produces a message digest that cannot be reversed. Message digests are produced using one-way hashing functions. They are not intended to be used to reproduce the data. The purpose of a digest is to verify the integrity of data and messages. PEM is the correct answer because it is not a hashing algorithm.

18. **Answer: C.** Digital signatures are generated and verified as follows: First, you generate a message digest, and then you encrypt the digest with your private key. Next, you verify the digital signature by decrypting the signature with the sender's public key. Finally, you compare the message digest to one you originally generated. If they match, the message is authentic.

19. **Answer: B.** Secure email solutions are important because email is one of the most widely used Internet applications and is cleartext by default. S/MIME, PEM, and PGP are all good options to protect the confidentiality of email. Secure Shell (SSH) is the incorrect answer because it cannot be used to protect email. SSH is a program designed for secure computer-to-computer communication. SSH allows remote users to execute

commands and move files, and it serves as a replacement for insecure communication protocols. SSH is a replacement for Berkley programs such as rlogin and rcp.

20. **Answer: A.** Block ciphers work on a single block of data at a time to produce a corresponding block of encrypted data. Block ciphers pad the message to conform to the needed block size. Block ciphers are widely used; they are implemented in software, and most work with 64-bit blocks. Answers B and D are distracters. Answer C is incorrect because stream ciphers do not alter the lengths of the encrypted message.

21. **Answer: A.** Asymmetric encryption or public key cryptography is unlike symmetric encryption in that it uses two unique keys. One key is used to encrypt the data, and another is used to decrypt it. One of the great things about asymmetric encryption is that it overcomes one of the main barriers of symmetric encryption, key distribution. Asymmetric encryption works by freely sharing public keys among communicating parties, whereas private keys are kept secret and are not released to other parties.

22. **Answer: D.** A digital signature is a way to prove the authenticity of a person or entity you are communicating with. Answers A, B, and C are incorrect because hashing is used for integrity, biometric signatures is a distracter, and symmetric encryption provides confidentiality.

23. **Answer: A.** A certificate authority is a neutral organization that offers notarization for digital certificates. One analogy for a CA is the Department of Motor Vehicles (DMV). This is the state entity that is responsible for issuing driver's licenses. A driver's license is a standard for physical identification. Whenever you cash a check, go to a nightclub, or catch a plane, your driver's license is the one document accepted at all these locations to prove your identity. Certificate authorities are like the DMV because they vouch for your identity in the digital world.

24. **Answer: C.** Steganographic programs take a piece of information and hide it within another. Steganography can use pictures, graphics, or sound files. For example, I could take a picture of Sara Lee and embed a text file that contains my mother's secret German chocolate cake recipe and then send it to a friend.

25. **Answer: B.** Digital certificates conform to the X.509 international standard for interoperability. Answer A is the ITU-T standard for directory models, answer C refers to IEEE Ethernet standards, and answer D refers to IEEE wireless standards.

26. **Answer: A.** There are two ways to verify the authenticity of certificates and to verify that they have not been revoked. The first method involves certificate revocation lists. These are maintained by various certificate authorities. The user must download and cross-reference the list to verify that the certificate has been revoked. The second method is via the online certificate status protocol. This is a more automated method by which to handle this process, because it offers a real-time response to the user's question about a certificate's validity. All the other answers do not represent real services.

27. **Answer: D.** The maximum key length for the Blowfish algorithm is 448 bits. Blowfish is a block cipher that processes 64 bits of data at a time. Make sure to take the time to review the various encryption types, block sizes, and key lengths, because you can expect to find these items on the exam.

28. **Answer: D.** IDEA (International Data Encryption Algorithm) is a symmetric encryption used in PGP software. This 64-bit block cipher uses a 128-bit key. Although it has

been patented by a Swiss company, it is freely available for noncommercial use. It is considered a secure encryption standard, and there have been no known attacks against it. DES, SHA, and Tiger typically are not used in PGP.

29. **Answer: B.** All the MD algorithms were developed by Ron Rivest. These have progressed through the years as technology has advanced. MD4 was designed to be used in high-speed computations.

30. **Answer: D.** Cryptography is the science (some claim it is an art) of taking plaintext and converting it into ciphertext with the goal of providing confidentiality, integrity, authenticity, and nonrepudiation. These are the four main potential goals of cryptography. Cryptanalysis is the science of cracking ciphertext with a cryptographic key. Cryptology is the science that encompasses both cryptography and cryptanalysis.

31. **Answer: B.** Elliptic Curve Cryptosystem provides much of the same functionality as RSA, except that it is much more efficient. Elliptic Curve Cryptosystem uses a 160-bit key that offers the equivalent protection of a 1024-bit RSA key. It is widely used in wireless devices and other handheld electronic units that have limited power and processing capability. The term cryptosystem is short for "cryptographic system." A cryptographic system is any computer system that involves cryptography.

32. **Answer: C.** SET (Secure Electronic Transaction) is an industry-standard protocol proposed by MasterCard and Visa that provides a secure end-to-end payment process. The three main parties in the SET transaction are the cardholder, the merchant, and the bank card network. SET provides both confidentiality and integrity. S/MIME is used for secure email, one-time pads are highly secure encryption systems, and HAVAL is a hashing algorithm.

33. **Answer: B.** WEP (Wired Equivalent Privacy) was created to give users a subjectively equivalent amount of confidentiality as that of a wired area network. More-secure forms of protection are now available, such as WPA (Wi-Fi Protected Access) and 802.11i (WPA2). Secure Electronic Transaction (SET) is used for credit card transactions, IEEE 802.3 is the standard for Ethernet, and Password Authentication Protocol (PAP) is a distracter.

34. **Answer: B.** SHA (Secure Hash Algorithm) was developed by NIST. Unlike MD5, SHA produces a 160-bit or greater output, depending on the version. This fixed-length output is known as a message digest or fingerprint. This fingerprint is used to guarantee that you have an original, unaltered file, because you can compare your hashed value to the original. This ensures file integrity. All other answers are incorrect because they are not hashing algorithms.

35. **Answer: D.** During the 1930s and 1940s, the Japanese used the Red Machine and Purple Machine to transmit encrypted messages. The machine made use of a rotation cipher with multialphabets. As with most encryption mechanisms, it did not withstand the test of time. Runic stones were used by the Vikings, Scytale was used by the Egyptians, and Enigma was used by the Germans.

36. **Answer: C.** Digital certificates are at the heart of the PKI system. The digital certificate serves two roles. It ensures the integrity of the public key, and it ensures that the key remains unchanged and remains in a valid form. Second, it validates that the public key is tied to the stated owner and that all associated information is true and correct.

The subject's private key is not contained in an X.509 certificate. The certificate does contain serial number, version of X.509, signature identifier, issuer's name, validity period, subject's name, and subject's public key.

37. **Answer: B.** WEP (Wired Equivalent Privacy) uses RC4, a symmetric stream cipher. Although RC4 is significantly weaker than RC5, it was used because it was simple and fast and didn't violate any of the encryption export laws that were in place at the time. WEP was designed to provide the same privacy than a user would have on a wired network. WEP is based on the RC4 symmetric encryption standard and uses either 64-bit or 128-bit keys. However, the keys are not really this many bits, because a 24-bit initialization vector (IV) is used to provide randomness. So the "real key" is actually 40 or 104 bits long. The other answers are incorrect because they are not used in WEP. DES and Triple DES are symmetric ciphers, and MD5 is a hashing algorithm.

38. **Answer: A.** IPsec (IP Security) is a set of protocols that support secure exchange of packets at the internetworking layer. IPsec was developed by the IETF and is available in either transport mode, in which only the payload is encrypted, or tunnel mode, in which the payload and the header are encrypted.

39. **Answer: B.** Digital signatures provide message integrity. When a recipient receives a message, he or she can perform a hashing function to verify its integrity. This value is then compared to the sender's hash value that was transported along with the original message. The message header gives only the IP address and related transport information. Time and date stamps can be forged and cannot prove integrity, nor does the sender's public key.

40. **Answer: B.** RC4 can emulate a stream cipher. All other answers are incorrect because they are implemented as block ciphers.

41. **Answer: B**. SSL (Secure Socket Layer) is a transport layer application-independent protocol originally developed by Netscape. It is used in conjunction with Secure Electronic Transaction. It is an industry-standard protocol that MasterCard and Visa developed to provide a secure end-to-end online payment process.

42. **Answer: A.** Tunnel mode is the most secure because it encrypts both the header and the payload. IPsec is available in either transport mode or tunnel mode. Answers B and D are distracters, and answer C is incorrect because this mode of IPsec encrypts only the payload.

43. **Answer: D.** One-time pads are also known as Vernam ciphers. They can be a highly secure means of data encryption if the following conditions are met: The pads must not be reused, the key must be generated randomly, the key must be at least as long as the message to be encrypted, and the key must be protected against physical disclosure.

44. **Answer: A.** DES uses an actual key size of 56 bits for encryption and decryption. An additional 8 bits are used for parity checking. The original 56-bit version of DES was released as a national standard in 1977, but it is not sufficiently long to provide security. 128-bit DES is now considered the minimum. In 1998, a group of distributed crackers broke the 56-bit version of DES. This shocked and dismayed many individuals, because it was assumed that 56-bit DES would be secure for much longer.

45. **Answer: A.** During World War II, the Germans used Enigma to transmit encrypted messages. Although it was considered complex, it was eventually cracked. Enigma was actually a substitution cipher machine that could be used in the field. During WWII it was broken by a group of individuals located at Station X, which was an estate in Bletchley, England. Runic stones were used by the Vikings, Scytale was used by the Egyptians, and the Purple Machine was used by the Japanese.

46. **Answer: B.** XORing is used to create a more random ciphertext. The XOR (exclusive OR) function is a Boolean logic operation that states that if 2 bits are the same, the output is 0, and if 2 bits are different, the output is 1.

47. **Answer: A.** Symmetric encryption uses a shared secret key; therefore, only one key is required. The single shared secret key is used for encryption and decryption. These dual-use keys can be used to lock and unlock data. Symmetric encryption is the oldest form of encryption. Systems such as Scytale and Caesar's cipher are examples of symmetric encryption. Symmetric encryption provides confidentiality. It keeps people who do not have the key from knowing the true contents of the message.

48. **Answer: C.** Digital signatures are based on public key cryptography and are used to verify the authenticity and integrity of a message. Encryption provides confidentiality, and hashing provides integrity.

49. **Answer: B.** One-time pads, or Vernam ciphers, are considered unbreakable as long as certain key requirements are met, such as secure distribution of the key, no key reuse, and a key length that is as long as the actual message. The inherent problems with one-time pads are the same as with symmetric encryption: distribution and key management.

50. **Answer: A.** Merkle-Hellman is an example of an asymmetric encryption algorithm. IDEA, RC5, and Twofish are all examples of symmetric encryption. Remember that symmetric encryption uses a shared secret key; therefore, only one key is required. The single shared secret key is used for encryption and decryption. These dual-use keys can be used to lock and unlock data.

51. **Answer: A.** In cryptography, the information to be concealed is called plaintext, and the operation to conceal it is called encryption. Encryption is the transformation of data into a form that makes it unreadable by anyone without the proper encryption key.

52. **Answer: D.** When plaintext is converted into ciphertext, there are basically two ways in which the transformation can be accomplished—block and stream ciphers. Block ciphers function by dividing the message into blocks for processing. Stream ciphers function by dividing the message into bits for processing. Data is encrypted by means of a key. A key is simply a secret sequence of bits used to encode/decode data.

53. **Answer: D.** The science of cracking ciphertext without a cryptographic key is known as cryptanalysis. Cracking is a general term for criminal hacking. Cryptography is the science of taking plaintext and converting it into ciphertext with the goal of providing confidentiality, integrity, and nonrepudiation. Cryptology is the science of secure communications.

54. **Answer: D.** AES (Advanced Encryption Standard) is a type of block cipher that was developed to replace DES. ElGamal is a public key algorithm, IDEA is a block cipher but is not the scheduled replacement for DES, and Diffie-Hellman is a public key asymmetric algorithm.

55. **Answer: B.** Scytale was an encryption mechanism in which the message to be encoded was written lengthwise on a rod that had been wrapped with leather. Afterward, the leather was unwrapped and carried to the front line by a carrier. The awaiting general would then wrap the leather around a similar-sized rod and decode the message. If anyone captured the carrier, the message in its unwrapped form appeared to be nothing more than random characters. Enigma was used by the Germans, runic stones were used by the Vikings, and the Purple Machine was used by the Japanese.

56. **Answer: D.** Symmetric encryption offers some benefits over asymmetric encryption. Symmetric encryption is much faster than asymmetric encryption. Weaknesses of symmetric encryption include the following: secure key distribution is problematic, it's not very scalable because a large number of keys are required to communicate with a large number of people, and security is limited because symmetric encryption provides only confidentiality.

57. **Answer: B.** Asymmetric cryptography is made possible by the use of one-way functions. A one-way function (trap door) is a math operation that is easy to compute in one direction yet next to impossible to compute in the other. This difficulty is achieved by using large prime numbers or logarithmic functions. MD5 is a type of hashing algorithm, and secret key describes symmetric encryption.

58. **Answer: A.** DES (Data Encryption Standard) is a form of symmetric encryption. CFB mode encrypts the preceding block of ciphertext with the DES algorithm and then XORs this block with the next block of plaintext to produce the next block of ciphertext. The XOR operation in this mode is what conceals the plaintext. Answer B is incorrect because OFB works somewhat differently. OFB uses plaintext to feed back into a stream of ciphertext. Transmission errors do not propagate throughout the encryption process. Answer C is incorrect because 3DES (EEE3) uses three different keys and goes through three encryption processes. Answer D is incorrect because ECB is not chained, nor does it emulate a stream cipher. ECB is the native encryption mode of DES. Although it produces the highest throughput, it is also the easiest form of DES to break. If used with large amounts of data, it can be easily attacked, because the same plaintext encrypted with the same key always produces the same ciphertext.

59. **Answer: A.** RIPEMD is similar to MD4 and was designed in Europe. Lucas functions, RSA, and Elliptic Curve Cryptosystem are all asymmetric standards, not hashing algorithms.

60. **Answer: C.** Watermarking is a legal form of steganography. The goal of steganography is to hide information by embedding it in other messages. Computer graphics and digital pictures such as bitmaps are commonly used. Steganography works by altering the least significant bit of each byte of information. Symmetric encryption, asymmetric encryption, and integrity verification are not used for watermarking.

61. **Answer: D.** LUC is an asymmetric algorithm that uses discrete logarithms and Lucas functions. LUC is not a symmetric or hashing algorithm.

62. **Answer: C.** Tiger is a hashing algorithm that was designed to work efficiently on 64-bit systems and to be used in items such as the Merkle hash tree. Although SHA and MD5 are both hashing algorithms, they are not designed for 64-bit systems. CAST is a symmetric encryption standard.

63. **Answer: D.** The chart is an example of the Vigenere cipher. The Vigenere cipher is actually a polyalphabetic substitution cipher. It was considered an improvement over Caesar's cipher. Answers A and B are names for the same thing. Atbash was similar to Caesar's cipher. It used a single alphabet that worked from opposite ends. For example, if you wanted a cleartext A, you would encrypt the value Z.

64. **Answer: A.** One of the major problems of symmetric encryption is key management. As the number of users grows, so does the number of keys. The number of keys can go quite large rather quickly. For 100 users, you would need 4,950 keys!

65. **Answer: D.** Each user would have his private key, plus his public key, plus each of the nine other public keys. The total keys required would be 110.

66. **Answer: C.** The network would require a total of 45 keys. The formula is number of keys = $[n * (n-1)]/2$

67. **Answer: A.** Asymmetric encryption or public key cryptography is unlike symmetric encryption because it can be used for integrity, authenticity, and nonrepudiation. Symmetric encryption and hashing cannot accomplish this.

68. **Answer: B.** Skipjack was the proposed standard for use with law enforcement authorities as the algorithm to use to obtain legal authorization for encrypted data. The purpose of the government maintaining this information is stated as being that legal authorities could decrypt communications between the affected parties when approved by a warrant or approval of the court. DES, Blowfish, and Twofish were never designated for this purpose.

69. **Answer: A.** The Clipper Chip was a government-devised method for commercial encryption. It was designed to make use of the skipjack algorithm. Skipjack faces opposition, because the government would maintain a portion of the information required to reconstruct a Skipjack key. The purpose of the government's maintaining this information is stated as being that legal authorities could decrypt communications between the affected parties when approved by a warrant or approval of the court.

70. **Answer: D.** Known-plaintext attacks are effective when you have the known cleartext and encrypted text. Although this may seem unlikely, consider the example given in the question, or the fact that many messages may start with the same type of beginning or may close with a common ending. Here is an example:

```
*****************************************************************
This email may contain confidential material.
If you were not an intended recipient, please notify the sender
and delete all copies.
We may monitor email to and from our network.
*****************************************************************
```

Knowing that each message has this same ending can aid the attacker in decrypting the encrypted text.

71. **Answer: D.** The question defines an inference attack. Although the data is encrypted, the attacker can still observe the volume of data being transmitted. Answer A is incorrect because a session hijack requires the attacker to hijack a user's session. Answer B is incorrect because sniffing is a general term and does not best define the attack described. Answer C is incorrect because a database is not mentioned.

72. **Answer: A.** The answer here is to use IPsec. Internet Protocol Security (IPsec) is an end-to-end security technology that allows two devices to communicate securely. Transport mode encrypts the data that is sent between peers. Tunnel mode is the correct choice because it encapsulates the entire packet and adds a new IPv4 header. Tunnel mode is designed to be used by VPNs. SSH and source routing do not meet the stated requirements.

73. **Answer: B.** DES is a symmetric encryption standard that is based on a 64-bit block. DES processes 64 bits of plaintext at a time to output 64-bit blocks of ciphertext. The effective length of the DES encryption key is 56 bits. Even though the block size of DES is 64 bits, 8 bits are used for parity.

74. **Answer: A.** ESP is an authenticating and encrypting protocol that provides source authentication, confidentiality, and message integrity. The authentication header (AH) provides integrity and uses a hashing algorithm and symmetric key to calculate a message authentication code. The security association (SA) performs the information exchange to set up the secure session. The Diffie-Hellman algorithm is used to generate this shared key. Internet Key Exchange (IKE) is the default standard for exchanging symmetric keys. IKE is considered a hybrid protocol because it combines the functions of two other protocols, Internet Security Association and Key Management Protocol (ISAKMP) and the OAKLEY protocol.

75. **Answer: B.** Collisions occur when two message digests produce the same hash value. This is undesirable, because it could mask the fact that someone may have changed the contents of a file or message. Common hashing algorithms include MD5, SHA, and HAVAL. Message digests are not based on symmetric, asymmetric, or steganographic functions.

76. **Answer: C.** Digital watermarks are specifically used to mark materials for copyright and fingerprinting. See www.digitalwatermarkingalliance.org/ for more information. Copyrights and digital certificates do not meet this need.

77. **Answer: B.** Programs such as Tripwire, MD5sum, and WFP all rely on hashing programs, such as SHA and the MD series of algorithms. Digital signatures, digital certificates, and steganography cannot meet this requirement.

78. **Answer: C.** The output of an MD5sum is 32 characters long. For example, 4145bc316b0bf78c2194b4d635f3bd27 is the hash for a text file that contains the words "hello world."

79. **Answer: A.** UUencode was developed to aid in the transport of binary images via email. Answer B is incorrect because Simple Mail Transport Protocol (SMTP) is not an encoding method; it is used to send standard email. Answer C is incorrect because XOR is not commonly used to encode email, although it is used for weak password management. Answer D is incorrect because Base64 is used not for email but primarily for weak password management.

80. **Answer: D.** Zero proof knowledge is achieved when you give someone just the information they need to know without having to give up too much information. As an example, encrypting a hash with a private key and allowing someone to verify the hash with a public key proves the message was sent by the sender without having to provide the private key. Answers A, B, and C do not provide this.

81. **Answer: B.** When HMACs are used, the sender and receiver are using the same symmetric key; however, the key must be sent securely through some other process. Common techniques include Diffie-Hellman and RSA key exchange. Answer A is incorrect because the key is not included in the function. Answer C is incorrect because AES is a symmetric algorithm and will not work. Answer D is incorrect because the digital algorithm is not used for that process.

82. **Answer: A.** Whirlpool is a hashing algorithm that is part of the ISO 10118 standard. Although Tiger is a hashing algorithm, it is not part of the above standard. CAST is a symmetric algorithm and Elliptic curve is an asymmetric algorithm.

83. **Answer: B.** Another name for a collision is a birthday attack, because it deals with probabilities. Answers A, C, and D are incorrect. Answer A describes an attack against double DES. Answer C describes a general cryptographic attack that attempts all possible values. Answer D describes a vulnerability where two different keys result in the same output.

84. **Answer: D.** Lucas is an example of an asymmetric algorithm. All other answers are symmetric.

85. **Answer: B.** Symmetric algorithms are less complex. They are not used for key distribution, digital signatures, or nonrepudiation.

86. **Answer: True.** ECB is the native encryption mode of DES. Although it produces the highest throughput, it is also the easiest form of DES to break. If used with large amounts of data, it can be easily attacked because the same plaintext encrypted with the same key always produces the same ciphertext.

87. **Answer: True.** OFB can emulate a stream cipher. Unlike CFB, transmission errors do not propagate throughout the encryption process, because OFB uses plaintext to feed back into a stream of ciphertext.

88. **Answer: False.** Double DES is not commercially viable and is susceptible to a meet-in-the-middle attack.

89. **Answer: True.** A digital signature is much like a written signature because the signature validates the integrity of the document and the sender. Five basic steps are used in the digital signature process: 1. Mike produces a message digest by passing a message through a hashing algorithm. 2. The message digest is encrypted using Mike's private key. 3. The message is forwarded to the recipient, David. 4. David creates a message digest from the message with the same hashing algorithm that Mike used. 5. David decrypts Mike's signature digest by using Mike's public key. David compares the two message digests—the one originally created by Mike and the other one he created. If the two values match, David can be confident that the message is unaltered.

90. **Answer: True.** The sender creates the message digest and then applies his or her private key.

91. **Answer: False.** DES uses 16 rounds in the encryption process. Because DES has been cracked, it has not been used by the U.S. government since 1998.

92. **Answer: False.** Side channel attacks target the encryption device itself. Items of interest include how big the device is, how much power it uses, and how long it takes to encrypt or decrypt data.

93. **Answer: True.** The role of MSP is to provide a framework for secure message transmission. MSP is not widely used. Both PGP and S/MIME have greater market share.

94. **Answer: True.** PEM is another secure email protocol that is not widely used. PEM can use both AES and RSA. PEM is addressed in RFCs 1421 and 1424.

95. **Answer: False.** Point-to-Point Tunneling Protocol (PPTP) is used in virtual private networks and can be found at the data link layer.

96. **Answer: True.** This is why many systems incorporate both symmetric and asymmetric systems into a hybrid encryption system. Such a design allows the asymmetric system to be used for key exchange and allows the symmetric system to be used to encrypt and decrypt the data.

97. **Answer: False.** Asymmetric encryption is best used for small blocks of data, digital signatures, digital envelopes, and digital certificates. Symmetric encryption is used for privacy and bulk encryption.

98. **Answer: True.** Such a system uses a book or length of text as a key. Such systems have even been used with games and other electronic access control. For example, to get bonus material for this book, go to our website, www.hackthestack.com, and enter the text on page 5, second paragraph, first word.

99. **Answer: True.** A ROT3 cipher is one that rotates by 3. This is just how Caesar's cipher works. For example, using Caesar's cipher to encrypt the word *cat* results in *fdw*.

100. **Answer: False.** A code is a cryptographic system of symbols that represent words or phrases that may be secret but not always confidential. Codes are not as secure as ciphers and can be broken.

101. **Answer: False.** Clustering is a well-known weakness in cryptography in which plaintext messages can generate identical ciphertext messages using different keys and the same algorithm. You may have seen this in mechanical locks and keys in which one key actually works in another lock/key set.

102. **Answer: True.** Rijndael has variable block and key lengths of 128, 192, or 256 bits.

103. **Answer: True.** Keystroke loggers can be hardware or software devices that act as shims and sit between the keyboard and computer. They can be used to capture all the user's keystrokes.

104. **Answer: True.** When viewing a web page that begins with https, you can click the lock icon displayed in the corner of the web browser to display the contents of the X.509 certificate.

105. **Answer: False.** The Rijndael cipher varies its rounds based on its key size. For example, a 256-bit key performs 14 rounds, a 192-bit key performs 12 rounds, and a 128-bit key performs 10 rounds.

106. **Answer: True.** Message authentication codes (MACs) can be used to verify integrity. MACs are generated and verified using the same shared key. At the receiving end or the point of verification, a MAC that is identical would indicate that the message was not modified en route. To provide stronger protection, hashing MACs (HMACs) can be used.

107. **Answer: True.** WTLS provides three classes of security. Class 3 is the most secure, because the client and server are both authenticated.

108. Answer: False. The hashing algorithm in the Digital Signature Standard (DSS) generates a message digest of 160 bits. DSS is used to provide authenticity and nonrepudiation of electronic documents. It was developed and approved by the National Security Agency (NSA).

109. Answer: False. The NIST Advanced Encryption Standard uses Rijndael. Rijndael beat out several other competitors, including Blowfish. Rijndael can be implemented in one of three key sizes, including 128, 192, and 256 bits. It is considered a fast, simple, robust encryption mechanism.

110. The answers are as follows:

A. SHA2: **2.** Integrity

B. Diffie-Hellman: **6.** Key exchange

C. Digital signature: **1.** Nonrepudiation

D. 3DES: **3.** Symmetric encryption

E. Steganography: **4.** Hidden, not encrypted

F. Public key infrastructure: **5.** Facilities trust

SHA2 is a message digest algorithm that ranges from SHA 224 to SHA 512 and that is used to verify integrity. Diffie-Hellman was one of the first asymmetric algorithms created and is used for key exchange. Digital signatures work much like a notary in the real world in that they provide nonrepudiation. 3DES is a symmetric algorithm. Steganography is used to hide information or data. One common method is to use digital images. The public key infrastructure (PKI) provides trust. I may want to do business with a party I have never met, and I can do so through the Internet via PKI because it provides third-party trust.

CHAPTER FOUR

Security Architecture and Design

The focus of the Security Architecture and Design domain is system architecture. This domain is of critical importance because in many ways the design of a computer system determines its amount of security. Therefore, security professionals should know and understand the underlying technology of computer systems and the various system security guidelines, certifications, and security and assurance ratings that infosec security professionals use. The following list gives you some key areas to focus on:

- Layering, data hiding, and abstraction
- Processors
- Memory: segmentation/rings, types of memory
- Operating systems
- Models
- Assurance: TCSEC, ITSEC, CC
- Architecture problems: covert channels, denial of service, TOC/TOU attacks

Quick Check

Practice Questions

1. TCSEC provides levels of security that are classified in a hierarchical manner. Each level has a corresponding set of security requirements that must be met. Which of the following does Level A correspond to?

   ❍ **A.** Mandatory protection
   ❍ **B.** Required protection
   ❍ **C.** Verified protection
   ❍ **D.** Validated protection

Quick Answer: **122**
Detailed Answer: **123**

2. TCSEC offers numbered divisions of security that can occur in each category. With this in mind, which of the following represents the highest level of security?

   ❍ **A.** B2
   ❍ **B.** D2
   ❍ **C.** B1
   ❍ **D.** D1

Quick Answer: **122**
Detailed Answer: **123**

3. Jim has been asked to assist with a security evaluation. He has heard other members of the teams speak of TCB. What does TCB stand for?

   ❍ **A.** Taking care of business
   ❍ **B.** Total computer base
   ❍ **C.** Trusted computer base
   ❍ **D.** Total communication bandwidth

Quick Answer: **122**
Detailed Answer: **123**

4. Which of the following is *not* one of the valid states in which a CPU can operate?

   ❍ **A.** Processor
   ❍ **B.** Supervisor
   ❍ **C.** Problem
   ❍ **D.** Wait

Quick Answer: **122**
Detailed Answer: **123**

5. Which organization began developing the Common Criteria standard in 1990?

   ❍ **A.** IEEE
   ❍ **B.** ISC2
   ❍ **C.** ISO
   ❍ **D.** NIST

Quick Answer: **122**
Detailed Answer: **123**

Quick Check

6. Which security model uses security labels to grant access to objects through the use of transformation procedures?

 - ❍ **A.** Biba
 - ❍ **B.** Bell-LaPadula
 - ❍ **C.** Trusted Computer System
 - ❍ **D.** Clark-Wilson

Quick Answer: **122**
Detailed Answer: **123**

7. Your CISSP study group is reviewing the Security Architecture and Design domain in preparation for the exam. One of the members has a question. Which of the following is *not* one of the requirements for memory management?

 - ❍ **A.** Processing
 - ❍ **B.** Sharing
 - ❍ **C.** Protection
 - ❍ **D.** Relocation

Quick Answer: **122**
Detailed Answer: **123**

8. Ted has been working with one of the contract programmers and comes to you with a question: What is a thread? What do you tell him?

 - ❍ **A.** A thread is a set of instructions that the computer understands and processes in a virtual machine.
 - ❍ **B.** A thread is a single sequential flow of control within a program.
 - ❍ **C.** A thread is a highly privileged routine that is executed within a computer system.
 - ❍ **D.** A thread is a program in execution that can communicate only with its controlling process.

Quick Answer: **122**
Detailed Answer: **123**

9. During which of the following states does a CPU execute code or process application data?

 - ❍ **A.** Processor
 - ❍ **B.** Supervisor
 - ❍ **C.** Problem
 - ❍ **D.** Wait

Quick Answer: **122**
Detailed Answer: **123**

10. TCSEC provides levels of security that are classified in a hierarchical manner. Each level has a corresponding set of security requirements that must be met. Which of the following does Level B correspond to?

 - ❍ **A.** Mandatory protection
 - ❍ **B.** Required protection
 - ❍ **C.** Verified protection
 - ❍ **D.** Validated protection

Quick Answer: **122**
Detailed Answer: **123**

Quick Check

11. The Clark-Wilson security model defines several procedures that make it a good choice for commercial application. Which procedure scans data items and confirms their reliability?

Quick Answer: **122**
Detailed Answer: **123**

- ❍ **A.** Constrained Data Item (CDI)
- ❍ **B.** Integrity Verification Procedure (IVP)
- ❍ **C.** Transformational Procedure (TP)
- ❍ **D.** Invocation Property (IP)

12. TCSEC's security ratings can be applied to all types of computer systems. Which rating would a Windows 2003 computer be classified as?

Quick Answer: **122**
Detailed Answer: **124**

- ❍ **A.** D2
- ❍ **B.** C2
- ❍ **C.** B2
- ❍ **D.** A2

13. What process is used to transfer portions of an active program between an I/O device and main memory?

Quick Answer: **122**
Detailed Answer: **124**

- ❍ **A.** Paging
- ❍ **B.** Scatter-gather
- ❍ **C.** Multitasking
- ❍ **D.** Multiprocessing

14. What was the first security model developed to address integrity?

Quick Answer: **122**
Detailed Answer: **124**

- ❍ **A.** Bell-LaPadula
- ❍ **B.** Biba
- ❍ **C.** Lattice-based access control
- ❍ **D.** Clark-Wilson

15. Which Bell-LaPadula state machine property dictates that a subject may not read information at a higher sensitivity level?

Quick Answer: **122**
Detailed Answer: **124**

- ❍ **A.** Simple security property
- ❍ **B.** * (star) security property
- ❍ **C.** Mandatory security property
- ❍ **D.** Discretionary security property

16. The Biba model was developed to protect which of the following?

Quick Answer: **122**
Detailed Answer: **124**

- ❍ **A.** Availability
- ❍ **B.** Integrity
- ❍ **C.** Confidentiality
- ❍ **D.** Access control

Quick Check

17. Your boss has questions about ports and protocols that must be allowed through the firewall. He is concerned about egress from inside the firewall to outside, as well as ingress from outside to inside. He also wants to know how attackers may use resources in a way not intended, or a possible attack in which a resource may be modulated to signal unauthorized information. Which of the following best describes this possible method of attack?

- ❍ **A.** Data pipe
- ❍ **B.** Backdoor
- ❍ **C.** Tunneling
- ❍ **D.** Covert channel

Quick Answer: **122**
Detailed Answer: **124**

18. What is it called when a class of objects is assigned permissions?

- ❍ **A.** Attribute
- ❍ **B.** Fault tolerance
- ❍ **C.** Abstraction
- ❍ **D.** Security model

Quick Answer: **122**
Detailed Answer: **124**

19. The Bell-LaPadula model was developed to protect which of the following?

- ❍ **A.** Availability
- ❍ **B.** Integrity
- ❍ **C.** Confidentiality
- ❍ **D.** Access control

Quick Answer: **122**
Detailed Answer: **124**

20. TCSEC (Orange Book) provides levels of security that are classified in a hierarchical manner. Each level has a corresponding set of security requirements that must be met. What does Level C correspond to?

- ❍ **A.** Minimal security
- ❍ **B.** Discretionary protection
- ❍ **C.** Verified protection
- ❍ **D.** Unsecured

Quick Answer: **122**
Detailed Answer: **125**

21. Which assurance standard was developed through collaboration with the U.S., UK, France, Germany, and others to align existing standards and provide for a globally accepted standard?

- ❍ **A.** CTCPEC
- ❍ **B.** Common Criteria
- ❍ **C.** TCSEC
- ❍ **D.** ITSEC

Quick Answer: **122**
Detailed Answer: **125**

Quick Check

22. Dana has been studying computer system design and has a question: What is another name for a PLC?

Quick Answer: **122**
Detailed Answer: **125**

- ❍ **A.** RAM
- ❍ **B.** Small computer typically used in automation
- ❍ **C.** Scalar processor
- ❍ **D.** Superscalar processor

23. Which technology allows data to be moved to and from memory directly, without going through the CPU?

Quick Answer: **122**
Detailed Answer: **125**

- ❍ **A.** Programmed I/O
- ❍ **B.** DMA
- ❍ **C.** Masked processing
- ❍ **D.** Himem

24. In the realm of security architecture, what does the term *open system* mean?

Quick Answer: **122**
Detailed Answer: **125**

- ❍ **A.** Open systems are vendor-dependent. They have proprietary specifications and interface with approved validated products from other suppliers.
- ❍ **B.** Open systems are insecure and are not subject to independent examinations.
- ❍ **C.** Open systems are vendor-independent, have published specifications, and operate with the products of other suppliers.
- ❍ **D.** Open systems use vendor-dependent proprietary hardware and are not subject to publicly published specifications.

25. Which Bell-LaPadula state machine property dictates that the subject is not allowed to write information to a lower level of confidentiality?

Quick Answer: **122**
Detailed Answer: **125**

- ❍ **A.** Simple security property
- ❍ **B.** * (star) security property
- ❍ **C.** Mandatory security property
- ❍ **D.** Discretionary security property

26. Which of the following best describes a conceptual portion of the security kernel that is used as a system access control mechanism? Specifically, it validates users' requests.

Quick Answer: **122**
Detailed Answer: **125**

- ❍ **A.** Segmentation
- ❍ **B.** Reference monitor
- ❍ **C.** Security controller
- ❍ **D.** Protection rings

Quick Check

27. In a discussion of rings of protection, if ring 0 is the innermost ring and ring 4 is the outermost ring, which would be considered the most secure?

❍ **A.** 4
❍ **B.** 2
❍ **C.** 1
❍ **D.** 0

Quick Answer: **122**
Detailed Answer: **125**

28. Which of the following does the security kernel implement?

❍ **A.** Core dump
❍ **B.** Reference monitor
❍ **C.** Process manager
❍ **D.** Security control

Quick Answer: **122**
Detailed Answer: **125**

29. Which information security mode states that "the system may handle multiple classification levels and all users have authorization and the need to know for all information that is processed by that system"?

❍ **A.** Controlled
❍ **B.** Limited Access
❍ **C.** Dedicated
❍ **D.** Compartmented

Quick Answer: **122**
Detailed Answer: **125**

30. Which of the following corresponds to Level D TCSEC security?

❍ **A.** Minimal security
❍ **B.** Discretionary protection
❍ **C.** Verified protection
❍ **D.** Unsecured

Quick Answer: **122**
Detailed Answer: **126**

31. This project's goal has been to find a new standard for specifying and evaluating the security features of computer products and systems that will be accepted in North America, Europe, and the rest of the world. What is this standard called?

❍ **A.** TCSEC
❍ **B.** ITSEC
❍ **C.** CTCPEC
❍ **D.** Common Criteria

Quick Answer: **122**
Detailed Answer: **126**

Quick Check

32. Which of the following is one type of NIACAP accreditation?

❍ **A.** Site accreditation
❍ **B.** Summary accreditation
❍ **C.** Program accreditation
❍ **D.** Process accreditation

Quick Answer: **122**
Detailed Answer: **126**

33. Which Biba property states that a subject cannot read down?

❍ **A.** Discretionary security property
❍ **B.** Simple security property
❍ **C.** * (star) integrity property
❍ **D.** Simple integrity property

Quick Answer: **122**
Detailed Answer: **126**

34. Which type of memory is used in conjunction with the CPU to present a larger address space than actually exists?

❍ **A.** Secondary memory
❍ **B.** Virtual memory
❍ **C.** Sequential memory
❍ **D.** Cache memory

Quick Answer: **122**
Detailed Answer: **126**

35. One of the primary U.S. government and defense certification and accreditation standards is DITSCAP. How many phases does the DITSCAP process have?

❍ **A.** One
❍ **B.** Two
❍ **C.** Four
❍ **D.** Six

Quick Answer: **122**
Detailed Answer: **126**

36. Which Bell-LaPadula state machine property dictates that the subject may not write information to an object at a lower sensitivity level?

❍ **A.** Simple security property
❍ **B.** The * (star) security property
❍ **C.** The mandatory security property
❍ **D.** The discretionary security property

Quick Answer: **122**
Detailed Answer: **126**

37. Which CPU instruction execution type can execute only one instruction at a time?

❍ **A.** RISC
❍ **B.** Superscalar
❍ **C.** CISC
❍ **D.** Scalar

Quick Answer: **122**
Detailed Answer: **126**

Quick Check

38. The failure to check the size of input streams destined for temporary storage specified by program parameters can result in what?

Quick Answer: **122**
Detailed Answer: **126**

- ❍ **A.** Failover
- ❍ **B.** Backdoor
- ❍ **C.** Buffer overflow
- ❍ **D.** Maintenance hook

39. Which information security mode states that "All users have a clearance for the highest level of classified information, but they may not necessarily have the authorization or a need to know for all the data handled by the computer system"?

Quick Answer: **122**
Detailed Answer: **127**

- ❍ **A.** Controlled
- ❍ **B.** Limited Access
- ❍ **C.** Dedicated
- ❍ **D.** Compartmented

40. The Clark-Wilson security model defines several procedures that make it a good choice for commercial application. Which of the following describes data that is to be input and hasn't been validated?

Quick Answer: **122**
Detailed Answer: **127**

- ❍ **A.** Constrained data item
- ❍ **B.** Initial data item
- ❍ **C.** Transformational data item
- ❍ **D.** Unconstrained data item

41. Concerning the concept of the security kernel, which of the following statements is not true?

Quick Answer: **122**
Detailed Answer: **127**

- ❍ **A.** The security kernel implements the reference monitor concept.
- ❍ **B.** The security kernel must allow maintenance hooks.
- ❍ **C.** The security kernel must be verified as correct.
- ❍ **D.** The security kernel must be protected from unauthorized changes.

42. Christine is trying to learn more about discretionary access control. "A Guide to Understanding Discretionary Access Control in Trusted Systems" is also known as what?

Quick Answer: **122**
Detailed Answer: **127**

- ❍ **A.** The Purple Book
- ❍ **B.** The Tan Book
- ❍ **C.** The Neon Orange Book
- ❍ **D.** The Green Book

Quick Check

43. Mark has been placed on a security team and has a question: How is accreditation defined?

Quick Answer: **122**
Detailed Answer: **127**

❍ **A.** It is the technical evaluation of security components and their compliance.

❍ **B.** It is a technical requirement for assessment that must be completed before a contract is awarded.

❍ **C.** It is the formal acceptance of the system's overall security.

❍ **D.** It is an agreed-upon level of security that has the backing of policies and procedures.

44. The Take-Grant model addresses what requirement?

Quick Answer: **122**
Detailed Answer: **127**

❍ **A.** Confidentiality

❍ **B.** Integrity

❍ **C.** Authentication

❍ **D.** Availability

45. Which of the following describes a system element that is required to implement security services that are essential to meet the needs of users and the performance levels required of the system for its security and usability needs?

Quick Answer: **122**
Detailed Answer: **127**

❍ **A.** Security model

❍ **B.** Security architecture

❍ **C.** TCB

❍ **D.** Security kernel

46. A TOC/TOU (Time of Check to Time of Use) attack is best described by which of the following?

Quick Answer: **122**
Detailed Answer: **127**

❍ **A.** A type of session hijack

❍ **B.** An asynchronous attack

❍ **C.** A buffer overflow

❍ **D.** A spoofing attack

47. Your assistant is attempting to learn more about security evaluation criteria. She wants to know how many levels are in ITSEC. What do you tell her?

Quick Answer: **122**
Detailed Answer: **128**

❍ **A.** Two

❍ **B.** Four

❍ **C.** Six

❍ **D.** Seven

Quick Check

48. What is the definition of certification?

Quick Answer: **122**
Detailed Answer: **128**

- ❍ **A.** Certification is the technical evaluation of security components and their compliance.
- ❍ **B.** Certification is a technical requirement for assessment that must be completed before a contract is awarded.
- ❍ **C.** Certification is the formal acceptance of the system's overall security.
- ❍ **D.** Certification is an agreed-upon level of security that has the backing of policies and procedures.

49. Which integrity model best meets the all the primary goals of integrity?

Quick Answer: **122**
Detailed Answer: **128**

- ❍ **A.** Biba
- ❍ **B.** Bell-LaPadula
- ❍ **C.** Clark-Wilson
- ❍ **D.** Lattice-based access control

50. Which model is concerned with who is authorized to give access to files and folders to other users? Specifically, this model is focused on nonadministrators' file-granting privilege results in a discretionary access control system.

Quick Answer: **122**
Detailed Answer: **128**

- ❍ **A.** Clark-Wilson
- ❍ **B.** Bell-LaPadula
- ❍ **C.** Biba
- ❍ **D.** Take-Grant

51. Alicia has sat down to log onto a computer so that she can complete a customer order form. She has not yet typed anything. The cursor is flashing in the field following a prompt asking for her username. Assuming that the computer is running properly, and all is as it appears, what state is the login process in?

Quick Answer: **122**
Detailed Answer: **128**

- ❍ **A.** New state
- ❍ **B.** Running state
- ❍ **C.** Ready state
- ❍ **D.** Blocked state

52. In terms of the TCB, which of the following statements best describes the purpose of a trusted path?

Quick Answer: **122**
Detailed Answer: **128**

- ❍ **A.** The path or shell that a process cannot break out of.
- ❍ **B.** The path or channel between a user and a program for protected communications.

Quick Check

❍ **C.** The path between a user and the kernel for protected communications.

❍ **D.** The path or shell that a user cannot break out of.

53. Which security model prevents a user from directly accessing data stored on the computer?

Quick Answer: **122**
Detailed Answer: **128**

❍ **A.** Biba

❍ **B.** Clark-Wilson

❍ **C.** Bell-LaPadula

❍ **D.** Brewer-Nash

54. A host intrusion detection program has logged a process that continually wakes up to access a file and update the file's timestamp and then goes back to sleep. The process has been waking and sleeping on an erratic but consistent schedule. The alert has documented the event as suspicious covert activity. What minimum certification level specifies a security requirement to ensure that no covert activity will occur?

Quick Answer: **122**
Detailed Answer: **128**

❍ **A.** A1

❍ **B.** B1

❍ **C.** C1

❍ **D.** D1

55. The CPU knows if it should be working in a problem state (user mode) or a kernel state (privileged mode) by checking which component in a computer's architecture?

Quick Answer: **122**
Detailed Answer: **128**

❍ **A.** The program status word (PSW) register

❍ **B.** The arithmetic logic unit (ALU)

❍ **C.** The control unit

❍ **D.** The stack pointer register

56. The operating system maintains the tightest control over access to which of the following?

Quick Answer: **122**
Detailed Answer: **128**

❍ **A.** Application memory

❍ **B.** Relative memory

❍ **C.** Logical memory

❍ **D.** Absolute memory

Quick Check

57. Prolog, LISP, and other artificial-intelligence languages are good examples of what?

Quick Answer: **122**
Detailed Answer: **129**

- ❍ **A.** 3GL languages
- ❍ **B.** 2GL languages
- ❍ **C.** 5GL languages
- ❍ **D.** 4GL languages

58. Which of the following is an example of an interpreted language?

Quick Answer: **122**
Detailed Answer: **129**

- ❍ **A.** Pascal
- ❍ **B.** Java
- ❍ **C.** C+
- ❍ **D.** FORTRAN

59. Computer systems and their design have made drastic strides over the last decade. The increase in the speed of memories and other processor components, along with the ability to get more out of fewer clock cycles, led to what advancement?

Quick Answer: **122**
Detailed Answer: **129**

- ❍ **A.** Complex Instruction Set Computer (CISC)
- ❍ **B.** Reduced Instruction Set Computer (RISC)
- ❍ **C.** Multitasking
- ❍ **D.** Multiprocessors

60. Which of the following best describes a macro?

Quick Answer: **122**
Detailed Answer: **129**

- ❍ **A.** A programming language designed for use in a distribute environment that makes use of a sandbox design
- ❍ **B.** A low-level compiled language that uses simple commands instead of machine language
- ❍ **C.** A very high-level language that uses a declarative style
- ❍ **D.** A group of statements used to perform a specific function

61. What occurs when a system suffers a total TCB or media failure and the system must be restored to a reliable, secure state?

Quick Answer: **122**
Detailed Answer: **129**

- ❍ **A.** System restart
- ❍ **B.** Cold start
- ❍ **C.** Fail-safe
- ❍ **D.** Fail-secure

Quick Check

62. According to CSC-STD-003-85 (Light Yellow Book), which operational mode allows two or more classification levels of information to be processed simultaneously within the same system when some users are not cleared for all levels of information present?

Quick Answer: **122**
Detailed Answer: **129**

- ❍ **A.** Multilevel
- ❍ **B.** Dedicated
- ❍ **C.** Controlled
- ❍ **D.** No access

63. Jack is at a low level of security. Jill, Jack's boss, is at a high level of security. Jack is responsible for preparing a weekly report for Jill and has embedded a hidden macro in it. Jack has told Jill not to worry about any macros, because they are just there for formatting. However, the macro actually writes top-secret information to a shared network folder to which Jack has access. What type of attack has Jack launched?

Quick Answer: **122**
Detailed Answer: **129**

- ❍ **A.** Maintenance hook
- ❍ **B.** Backdoor
- ❍ **C.** Covert channel
- ❍ **D.** TOC/TOU attack

64. Which of the following best describes the rings of protection concept?

Quick Answer: **122**
Detailed Answer: **129**

- ❍ **A.** Ring 0 is located near the center of the design and is the home of the reference monitor. This serves as the heart of every OS.
- ❍ **B.** Rings are organized with the most privileged domain near the outside of the domain; this ring is home to the security kernel.
- ❍ **C.** Rings are organized with the most privileged domain located in the center of the design; this ring is home to the security kernel.
- ❍ **D.** Rings are organized with the most privileged domain near the outside of the domain; this ring is home to the reference monitor.

65. What coordinates activities of the other CPU components during program execution?

Quick Answer: **122**
Detailed Answer: **129**

- ❍ **A.** Arithmetic logic unit
- ❍ **B.** Bus interface unit
- ❍ **C.** Control unit
- ❍ **D.** Memory management unit

Quick Check

66. What is not one of the four primary functions of the operating system?

Quick Answer: **122**
Detailed Answer: **129**

- ❍ **A.** Process management
- ❍ **B.** BIOS management
- ❍ **C.** File management
- ❍ **D.** I/O device management

67. Which of the following best describes a grouping of electronic conductors that interconnect components of the computer? These conductors transmit signals, addresses, and data between the components.

Quick Answer: **122**
Detailed Answer: **130**

- ❍ **A.** Hardware
- ❍ **B.** Firmware
- ❍ **C.** Bus
- ❍ **D.** Registers

68. A coworker asks you what E^2PROMs are and how they work. What do you tell her?

Quick Answer: **122**
Detailed Answer: **130**

- ❍ **A.** An E^2PROM is the same as an EPROM in that both require a UV light to erase.
- ❍ **B.** An E^2PROM is another name for an EEPROM, and both are one-time programmable.
- ❍ **C.** An E^2PROM is the same as an EEPROM in that both require a UV light to erase.
- ❍ **D.** An E^2PROM is another name for an EEPROM and is programmed and erased electrically.

69. You have noticed that your new computer has a page.sys file. When you open many files and applications simultaneously, you notice that the system begins to slow down. With that in mind, how is the page.sys file being used?

Quick Answer: **122**
Detailed Answer: **130**

- ❍ **A.** Page.sys is used as virtual memory so that actual RAM is extended by means of using space on the system's hard drive.
- ❍ **B.** Page.sys is used as a cache. Reducing its size increases the system's speed.
- ❍ **C.** Page.sys is used as a cache. Increasing its size reduces the system's speed.
- ❍ **D.** Page.sys is used to hold programs that have been loaded from firmware.

Quick Check

70. What performs calculations of a numeric nature and comparative logic functions?

Quick Answer: **122**
Detailed Answer: **130**

- ❍ **A.** Arithmetic logic unit
- ❍ **B.** Bus interface unit
- ❍ **C.** Control unit
- ❍ **D.** Memory management unit

71. A local user has gained root access by exploiting a vulnerability that leverages the difference between when a value is written by an application and when the application uses the value for processing. Which term best describes this issue?

Quick Answer: **122**
Detailed Answer: **130**

- ❍ **A.** TOC/TOU
- ❍ **B.** Backdoor
- ❍ **C.** Maintenance hook
- ❍ **D.** Covert channel

72. While attending a security conference, you overhear several individuals discussing Van Eck phreaking. What does this type of attack do?

Quick Answer: **122**
Detailed Answer: **130**

- ❍ **A.** It is similar to a blue box attack in that analog phone systems are targeted.
- ❍ **B.** It is similar to a blue box attack in that digital phone systems are targeted.
- ❍ **C.** This coding attack allows the attacker to gain access to a higher level of information than he or she should have access to.
- ❍ **D.** This attack allows the attacker to intercept information dispersed by radio waves.

73. Which statement(s) is/are incorrect?

Quick Answer: **122**
Detailed Answer: **130**

I. Fault-tolerant systems must be able to detect and correct or circumvent a fault.

II. Fail-safe systems pause program execution to prevent the system from compromise.

III. Fail-soft systems terminate noncritical processing and allow the system to continue functioning in a degraded mode.

IV. Failover systems detect failures and automatically transfer processing to a backup component or system.

- ❍ **A.** I and III
- ❍ **B.** II and III
- ❍ **C.** II
- ❍ **D.** IV

Quick Check

74. What is the name of the TCSEC B1 specification?

Quick Answer: 122
Detailed Answer: 130

- ❍ A. Labeled security protection
- ❍ B. Structured protection
- ❍ C. Security domains
- ❍ D. Verified design

75. What supervises data transfers over the bus system between the CPU and I/O devices?

Quick Answer: 122
Detailed Answer: 130

- ❍ A. Arithmetic logic unit
- ❍ B. Bus interface unit
- ❍ C. Control unit
- ❍ D. Memory management unit

76. What is the name of the TCSEC B3 specification?

Quick Answer: 122
Detailed Answer: 131

- ❍ A. Labeled security protection
- ❍ B. Structured protection
- ❍ C. Security domains
- ❍ D. Verified design

77. Which of the following is a requirement for the TCSEC B3 specification?

Quick Answer: 122
Detailed Answer: 131

- ❍ A. Trusted path requirements
- ❍ B. Protection from covert channels
- ❍ C. First level to require sensitivity labels
- ❍ D. Configuration management procedures must be enforced

78. Which of the following is a requirement for the TCSEC B1 specification?

Quick Answer: 122
Detailed Answer: 131

- ❍ A. Trusted path requirements
- ❍ B. Protection from covert channels
- ❍ C. First level to require sensitivity labels
- ❍ D. Configuration management procedures must be enforced

79. Which Orange Book level is considered discretionary and does not distinguish between individual users?

Quick Answer: 122
Detailed Answer: 131

- ❍ A. C2
- ❍ B. C1
- ❍ C. B1
- ❍ D. B2

Quick Check

80. What handles addressing and cataloging of data stored in memory and translates logical addressing into physical addressing?

Quick Answer: **122**
Detailed Answer: **131**

- ❍ **A.** Arithmetic logic unit
- ❍ **B.** Bus interface unit
- ❍ **C.** Control unit
- ❍ **D.** Memory management unit

81. Common Criteria defines which of the following?

Quick Answer: **122**
Detailed Answer: **131**

- ❍ **A.** A target of review
- ❍ **B.** Ten functionality classes and seven evaluation levels
- ❍ **C.** Rainbow series requirements
- ❍ **D.** Seven assurance levels

82. Which EAL level could be described as "methodically designed, tested, and reviewed"?

Quick Answer: **122**
Detailed Answer: **131**

- ❍ **A.** EAL 2
- ❍ **B.** EAL 4
- ❍ **C.** EAL 6
- ❍ **D.** EAL 7

83. Which EAL level could be described as "structurally tested"?

Quick Answer: **122**
Detailed Answer: **131**

- ❍ **A.** EAL 2
- ❍ **B.** EAL 4
- ❍ **C.** EAL 6
- ❍ **D.** EAL 7

84. A local user uses a program that sends information inside ICMP ping packets to an attacker outside the organization. Because ping is allowed by the organization, the traffic has not yet been detected. Which of the following best describes the type of attack the insider has launched?

Quick Answer: **122**
Detailed Answer: **131**

- ❍ **A.** TOC/TOU
- ❍ **B.** Backdoor
- ❍ **C.** Maintenance hook
- ❍ **D.** Covert channel

85. Which of the following best describes the code or computer programs that are stored in ROM?

Quick Answer: **122**
Detailed Answer: **132**

- ❍ **A.** Hardware
- ❍ **B.** Firmware
- ❍ **C.** Bus
- ❍ **D.** Registers

Quick Check

86. You are the security administrator for an investment company. At the beginning of each month, you have an employee review all logs and look for discrepancies or problems. This month, your employee reported e-mail system error log reports. Large numbers of unsuccessful login attempts have occurred after several port scans. What type of attack may be occurring?

Quick Answer: **122**
Detailed Answer: **132**

- ❍ **A.** Software exploitation attack
- ❍ **B.** Backdoor attack
- ❍ **C.** Trojan
- ❍ **D.** TOC/TOU attack

87. Which European standard addresses confidentiality, integrity, and availability?

Quick Answer: **122**
Detailed Answer: **132**

- ❍ **A.** Information Technology Security Evaluation Criteria (ITSEC)
- ❍ **B.** Trusted Computer System Evaluation Criteria (TCSEC)
- ❍ **C.** Common Criteria (CC)
- ❍ **D.** ISO 17799

88. Which service normally is granted by a senior executive or Designated Approving Authority and is used to verify that the system is approved for operation?

Quick Answer: **122**
Detailed Answer: **132**

- ❍ **A.** Evaluation
- ❍ **B.** Accreditation
- ❍ **C.** Certification
- ❍ **D.** Approval

89. Which model is not confidentiality-driven and can be described as a state machine model based on a classification lattice with mandatory access controls?

Quick Answer: **122**
Detailed Answer: **132**

- ❍ **A.** Bell-LaPadula
- ❍ **B.** Sutherland
- ❍ **C.** Brewer-Nash
- ❍ **D.** Biba

90. Of all the security models, which one is most commonly mentioned as being designed for and used in the commercial environment?

Quick Answer: **122**
Detailed Answer: **132**

- ❍ **A.** Bell-LaPadula
- ❍ **B.** Lipner
- ❍ **C.** Brewer-Nash
- ❍ **D.** Clark-Wilson

Quick Check

91. Which model is primarily concerned with conflicts of interest?

Quick Answer: **122**
Detailed Answer: **132**

- ❍ **A.** Bell-LaPadula
- ❍ **B.** Sutherland
- ❍ **C.** Brewer-Nash
- ❍ **D.** Biba

92. Which of the following is/are not a valid information security model?

Quick Answer: **122**
Detailed Answer: **132**

I. Reference monitor

II. Bell-LaPadula

III. Goguen-Meseguer

IV. Bobert and Kain

- ❍ **A.** I
- ❍ **B.** I, II, and III
- ❍ **C.** III
- ❍ **D.** III and IV

93. Which of the following is a commercial integrity model that addresses all the goals of integrity?

Quick Answer: **122**
Detailed Answer: **133**

- ❍ **A.** Bell-LaPadula
- ❍ **B.** Lipner
- ❍ **C.** Brewer-Nash
- ❍ **D.** Clark-Wilson

94. Bob wants to set the permissions shown in Table 4-1.

Quick Answer: **122**
Detailed Answer: **133**

TABLE 4-1 Permissions

Subject	Object	Access
Bob	File A	Read
Christine	Printer	No access
Melvin	Network share	Read/write

Which of the following statements is most accurate?

- ❍ **A.** The table dictates how rights can be passed from one subject to another or from a subject to an object.
- ❍ **B.** In the table, each row is a capability list.
- ❍ **C.** The table is an example of the Simple Integrity Axiom.
- ❍ **D.** The table defines how information flow can be between subjects and objects at the same classification level and different classification levels.

Quick Check

95. Which of the following defines process isolation?

Quick Answer: 122
Detailed Answer: 133

- ❍ **A.** The use of controls to separate memory spaces for each process's instructions and data
- ❍ **B.** The use of hardware controls to separate memory spaces for each process's instructions and data
- ❍ **C.** One level of security is not visible to processes running at different security levels.
- ❍ **D.** Objects don't necessarily need to know the details of how something works.

96. Which of the following best matches the ITSEC rating of "networks with high confidentiality and integrity requirements"?

Quick Answer: 122
Detailed Answer: 133

- ❍ **A.** F6
- ❍ **B.** F8
- ❍ **C.** F10
- ❍ **D.** F9

97. Which of the following best matches the ITSEC rating of "high confidentiality requirements during data communications"?

Quick Answer: 122
Detailed Answer: 133

- ❍ **A.** F6
- ❍ **B.** F8
- ❍ **C.** F10
- ❍ **D.** F9

98. Programming languages are considered generational. As such, what type of programming language is considered a 3GL?

Quick Answer: 122
Detailed Answer: 133

- ❍ **A.** Prolog
- ❍ **B.** Assembly
- ❍ **C.** FORTRAN
- ❍ **D.** SQL

99. Which of following is the best example of using a storage mechanism that searches from the beginning rather than directly accessing the location?

Quick Answer: 122
Detailed Answer: 133

- ❍ **A.** Optical drives
- ❍ **B.** Tape backup
- ❍ **C.** Hard drive
- ❍ **D.** Floppy disk

Quick Check

100. Programming languages are considered generational. As such, what type of programming language is considered a 4GL?

- ❍ **A.** Prolog
- ❍ **B.** Assembly
- ❍ **C.** FORTRAN
- ❍ **D.** SQL

Quick Answer: **122**
Detailed Answer: **133**

101. Which cloud-based service would handle support functions during the SDLC process?

- ❍ **A.** MaaS
- ❍ **B.** IaaS
- ❍ **C.** SaaS
- ❍ **D.** PaaS

Quick Answer: **122**
Detailed Answer: **133**

102. Which of the following cloud-based solutions enables the user to buy or rent infrastructure?

- ❍ **A.** MaaS
- ❍ **B.** IaaS
- ❍ **C.** SaaS
- ❍ **D.** PaaS

Quick Answer: **122**
Detailed Answer: **133**

103. Which cloud-based solution is designed to watch over networks, applications, servers, and applications?

- ❍ **A.** MaaS
- ❍ **B.** IaaS
- ❍ **C.** SaaS
- ❍ **D.** PaaS

Quick Answer: **122**
Detailed Answer: **133**

104. Which type of memory is faster than DRAM and has a type of look-ahead feature?

- ❍ **A.** EDO DRAM
- ❍ **B.** BEDO DRAM
- ❍ **C.** DDR SDRAM
- ❍ **D.** SDRAM

Quick Answer: **122**
Detailed Answer: **134**

Quick Check

105. Which of the following refers to when an attacker is able to run malware or code on a virtual machine that allows an operating system running within it to break out and interact directly with the hypervisor?

Quick Answer: **122**
Detailed Answer: **134**

- ❍ **A.** VLANhopping
- ❍ **B.** VLANscaping
- ❍ **C.** VMhopping
- ❍ **D.** VMEscaping

Practice Questions (True or False)

106. The security kernel must control all access, must be protected from modification or change, and must be verified and tested to be correct.

Quick Answer: **122**
Detailed Answer: **134**

- ❍ True
- ❍ False

107. The Bell-LaPadula model supports the Simple Security Property (ss Property), which states that a subject at one level of confidentiality is not allowed to write information at a higher level of confidentiality.

Quick Answer: **122**
Detailed Answer: **134**

- ❍ True
- ❍ False

Practice Questions (Mix and Match)

108. Match each TCSEC security level with its definition.

Quick Answer: **122**
Detailed Answer: **134**

A. A1: _____

B. B1: _____

C. B2: _____

D. C1: _____

E. D: _____

1. Considered minimal protection
2. The highest supported level. Systems rated as such must meet formal methods and proof of integrity of TCB.
3. The first level to use labeled security protection
4. The highest MAC level of security shown here.
5. These systems don't need to distinguish between individual users and types of access.

Quick Check Answer Key

1. C
2. A
3. C
4. A
5. C
6. D
7. A
8. B
9. C
10. A
11. B
12. B
13. A
14. B
15. A
16. B
17. D
18. C
19. C
20. B
21. B
22. B
23. B
24. C
25. B
26. B
27. D
28. B
29. C
30. A
31. D
32. A
33. D
34. B
35. C
36. B
37. D
38. C
39. D
40. D
41. B
42. C
43. C
44. A
45. B
46. B
47. D
48. A
49. C
50. D
51. D
52. C
53. B
54. A
55. A
56. D
57. C
58. B
59. B
60. D
61. B
62. A
63. C
64. C
65. C
66. B
67. C
68. D
69. A
70. A
71. A
72. D
73. C
74. A
75. B
76. C
77. B
78. C
79. B
80. D
81. D
82. B
83. A
84. D
85. B
86. A
87. A
88. B
89. D
90. D
91. C
92. A
93. D
94. B
95. A
96. C
97. D
98. C
99. B
100. D
101. D
102. B
103. A
104. A
105. D
106. True
107. False
108. **A.** 2
B. 3
C. 4
D. 5
E. 1

Answers and Explanations

1. **Answer: C.** The TCSEC (Trusted Computer System Evaluation Criteria), also known as the Orange Book, was originally developed for the military to classify its computer systems. It is now widely used throughout the computer industry. It ranks security in categories ranging from A to D. A is verified protection, B is mandatory protection, C is discretionary protection, and D is minimal security.

2. **Answer: A.** Lower letters of the alphabet represent higher levels of security. Higher numbers indicate a greater level of trust. Therefore, B2 offers the highest level of trust of the four possible answers.

3. **Answer: C.** The TCB (trusted computer base) includes all the hardware, software, and firmware within a system that is used for its protection. TCB standards dictate that all hardware, software, and firmware have been tested and validated to ensure that they are implementing the system security policy and it do not violate it.

4. **Answer: A.** Processor is not a valid state. The four valid states in which a CPU can operate are Ready, Supervisor, Problem, and Wait.

5. **Answer: C.** The International Organization for Standardization began working on a new standard of criteria in 1990. This standard has come to be known as Common Criteria.

6. **Answer: D.** Clark-Wilson uses security labels to grant access to objects through the use of transformation procedures. This helps ensure that data is protected from changes by anyone who is unauthorized.

7. **Answer: A.** The five requirements for memory management are relocation, protection, sharing, physical organization, and logical organization.

8. **Answer: B.** A thread is a single sequential flow of control within a program. It takes advantage of the resources allocated for that program and the program's environment.

9. **Answer: C.** Although it may sound as if it is the result of an error, the problem state is used when the CPU is executing an application or its data. The four valid states in which a CPU can operate are Ready, Supervisor, Problem, and Wait. Problem is a non-privileged state, whereas Supervisor is a privileged state.

10. **Answer: A.** The TCSEC (Trusted Computer System Evaluation Criteria), also known as the Orange Book, was originally developed for the military to classify its computer systems. It ranks security in categories ranging from A to D. A is verified protection, B is mandatory protection, C is discretionary protection, and D is minimal security.

11. **Answer: B.** The Clark-Wilson model was created in 1987. It differed from other models because it was developed with the intention of being used for commercial activities and meets all the goals of integrity. This model dictates that the separation of duties must be enforced, that subjects must access data through an application, and that auditing is required. The IVP scans data items and confirms their integrity. Although CDI and TP are valid Clark-Wilson procedures, they do not match the description. IP is not a valid answer because it is associated with the Biba model and deals with integrity.

12. **Answer: B.** An example of a C2 certified system is a Windows 2000 computer. A C2 system requires that users must identify themselves individually to gain access to objects. Although the exam might not ask product-specific questions, it's important that a CISSP candidate understand how various systems are rated within the TCSEC ratings.

13. **Answer: A.** Paging is the process that makes it seem that a computer can hold much more information in memory than is possible. It accomplishes this by transferring data between an I/O device, such as a hard drive, and memory (RAM). Answer B is incorrect because scatter/gather is used to transfer data to noncontiguous areas of memory. Answer C is incorrect because multiprocessing occurs when a single CPU performs multiple tasks. Answer D is incorrect because multiprocessing is performed by a system containing two or more processors.

14. **Answer: B.** Biba was the first security model developed to address integrity in computer systems. Bell-LaPadula is a confidentiality model. Lattice-based access control models were originally designed to address confidentiality of information and can be considered a broad category of access control. Clark-Wilson is a commercial integrity model that was developed after Biba.

15. **Answer: A.** The simple security property of the Bell-LaPadula model, also known as no read up, dictates that a subject at a specific classification level cannot read data with a higher classification level. Bell-LaPadula was actually the first formal model developed to protect confidentiality. It uses mandatory access control to enforce the DoD multilevel security policy. The star property deals with writing. The mandatory security model deals with B-level (mandatory protection) systems as defined by TCSEC. The discretionary security model deals with C-level (discretionary protection) systems as defined by TCSEC.

16. **Answer: B.** The Biba model was developed to protect the integrity of data. Biba addresses only integrity, not availability or confidentiality. It also assumes that internal threats are being protected by good coding practices and therefore focuses on external threats. Therefore, all other answers are incorrect.

17. **Answer: D.** A covert channel is any method used to pass information that is not for legitimate communication. For example, an organization may allow ICMP ping traffic. If an attacker can redirect other traffic onto this communication path, he or she would be able to use this channel as an illicit communication path. All other answers are incorrect because a data pipe is a port redirection tool, a backdoor is a maintenance hook or hole left in a legitimate program, and tunneling is the act of sending one data stream inside another. Protocols such as PPTP and L2TP are considered tunneling protocols.

18. **Answer: C.** Abstraction allows the simplification of security by allowing the assignment of security controls to a group of objects rather than singularly. It works by placing similar elements into groups, classes, or roles that collectively can be assigned security controls, restrictions, or permissions. An attribute is the characteristic of an object. Fault tolerance is the act of providing backup or redundant systems. Security models include Biba, Clark-Wilson, and Bell-LaPadula.

19. **Answer: C.** The Bell-LaPadula model was developed to protect confidentiality of data. To achieve this goal, it uses data classifications such as confidential, secret, and top-secret.

20. **Answer: B.** The TCSEC (Trusted Computer System Evaluation Criteria), also known as the Orange Book, was originally developed for the U.S. military to classify its computer systems. It is now widely used throughout the computer industry. It ranks security in categories ranging from A to D. A is verified protection, B is mandatory protection, C is discretionary protection, and D is minimal security.

21. **Answer: B.** The Common Criteria was developed through collaboration with the U.S., UK, France, Germany, and others to align existing standards and provide for a globally accepted standard. CTCPEC was developed by Canada. TCSEC is a U.S. government-based standard. ITSEC was developed by the European Union.

22. **Answer: B.** A PLC (programmable logic controller) is a small computer commonly used in automation or assembly lines. PLCs generally are used in process control scenarios, especially in harsh or unpleasant environments where more traditional general-purpose computers would not work well. RAM is random-access memory. A scalar processor can perform one instruction at a time, whereas a superscalar processor can perform several concurrent operations at a time.

23. **Answer: B.** DMA (Direct Memory Access) allows data to be moved directly from and to memory without going through the CPU. DMA replaces programmed I/O, which requires a considerable amount of overhead because it requires the attention of the system CPU. Masked processing and Himem are distracters.

24. **Answer: C.** Open systems are vendor-independent systems that have published specifications and that operate with products from other suppliers. They are subject to review and evaluation by third parties, which helps truly validate the system's robustness.

25. **Answer: B.** The * (star) property dictates that the subject is not allowed to write information to a lower level of confidentiality. Bell-LaPadula was actually the first formal model developed to protect confidentiality. It uses mandatory access control to enforce the DoD multilevel security policy. The mandatory security model deals with B-level systems as defined by TCSEC.

26. **Answer: B.** The reference monitor is the part of the security kernel that is used as a system access control mechanism. User requests must be validated by the reference monitor before operations can be completed. Segmentation can occur via hardware or software and deals with separation. Security controller is a distracter. Protection rings is an example of a hierarchical protection design used by computer architecture.

27. **Answer: D.** Rings of protection are one form of security mechanism. As the ring number increases, the security level decreases. The innermost ring is the most secure and protects the operating system security kernel. Correctly designing rings of protection can improve security by preventing programs at a lower level of access from misusing resources at a higher level of access.

28. **Answer: B.** The reference monitor is the primary component that enforces access control on data and devices and is implemented by the security kernel. The security kernel must also control all access, must be protected from modification or change, and must be verified and tested to be correct. All other answers are distracters.

29. **Answer: C.** Information security modes allow systems to operate at different security levels, depending on the information's classification level and the users' clearance. A

dedicated mode system may handle a single classification level, and all users have authorization and the need to know for all information that is processed by that system.

30. **Answer: A.** The TCSEC (Trusted Computer System Evaluation Criteria), also known as the Orange Book, was originally developed for the U.S. military to classify its computer systems. It is now widely used throughout the computer industry. It ranks security in categories ranging from A to D. A is verified protection, B is mandatory protection, C is discretionary protection, and D is minimal security.

31. **Answer: D.** The Common Criteria defines a protection profile that has been developed as a joint project involving the security organizations of many countries, including the U.S., Canada, Britain, France, and Germany. You can learn more about the Common Criteria at www.commoncriteriaportal.org/.

32. **Answer: A.** The NIACAP (National Information Assurance Certification and Accreditation Process) process accreditation is composed of three valid types: site, type, and system. Although country-specific laws are being removed from the CISSP exam, understanding the various accreditations helps security professionals build good security architectures.

33. **Answer: D.** The simple integrity property states that a subject cannot read an object of a lower integrity level. The Biba integrity model is similar to Bell-LaPadula and was developed in 1977.

34. **Answer: B.** Virtual memory is used in conjunction with the CPU to present a larger address space than actually exists. Systems such as Windows make use of this concept via the page.sys file, whereas *NIX systems often use swap space. Secondary memory is all the system's RAM. Sequential memory is memory that must be read in sequential order, such as a backup tape. Cache memory is the RAM inside the CPU that is used for fast lookups.

35. **Answer: C.** The DITSCAP (Defense Information Technology Security Certification and Accreditation Process) is composed of four phases. These phases outline a standard process that is used to certify and accredit IT systems that need to maintain a required security posture. DITSCAP is being phased out in favor of Defense Information Assurance Certification and Accreditation Process (DIACAP).

36. **Answer: B.** The * (star) security property of the Bell-LaPadula model, also known as no write down, dictates that the subject may not write information to an object at a lower sensitivity level. The simple security property deals with reading, not writing. The mandatory security model deals with B-level systems as defined by TCSEC. Discretionary security deals with C-level systems.

37. **Answer: D.** Scalar can execute only one instruction at a time. Reduced Instruction Set Computer (RISC) offers a reduced instruction set. Complex Instruction Set Computer (CISC) can execute several low-level instructions in a single instruction. Superscalar offers a parallel instruction set for increased performance.

38. **Answer: C.** The failure to check the size of input streams destined for temporary storage (buffer) specified by program parameters can result in a buffer overflow. When too much data goes into the buffer, any excess is written into the area of memory immediately following the reserved area. This area may be another temporary storage area, a pointer to the next instruction, or another program's output area. Regardless of

what is there, it is overwritten and destroyed. Many times the result is that an attacker can use this to gain control of a system. Failover systems are used for backup. Backdoors are used for unauthenticated access. Maintenance hooks can be used during testing but should be removed before release.

39. **Answer: D.** Information security modes allow systems to operate at different security levels, depending on the information's classification level and the users' clearance. With a compartmented system, all users have clearance for the highest level of classified information, but they may not necessarily have the authorization or a need to know for all the data handled by the computer system.

40. **Answer: D.** The Clark-Wilson model differs from previous models because it was developed to be used for commercial activities. This model dictates that the separation of duties must be enforced, subjects must access data through an application, and that auditing is required. An Unconstrained Data Item is considered any data that is to be input and that hasn't been validated. The only other valid answer is Constrained Data Item, and it describes any data item whose integrity is protected by the Clark-Wilson security model.

41. **Answer: B.** The security kernel implements the reference monitor concept. It must be verified as correct, and it must be protected from unauthorized changes. The security kernel should not allow maintenance hooks, because they can be used as a method to bypass system security.

42. **Answer: C.** The Neon Orange Book was published in 1987. Its formal name is NCSC-TG-003, "A Guide to Understanding Discretionary Access Control in Trusted Systems." The Purple Book is "Guidelines for Formal Verification System." The Tan Book is "A Guide to Understanding Audit in Trusted Systems." The Green Book, "DoD 5220.22-M," provides DoD password management guidelines.

43. **Answer: C.** Accreditation is the formal acceptance of the system's overall security. Normally, it is provided by a senior executive or another designated approving authority. Certification is the process of validating that the systems that are being implemented are configured and operating as expected.

44. **Answer: A.** The Take-Grant system model addresses confidentiality. It uses rights for this process that are divided into four basic operations: create, revoke, grant, and take.

45. **Answer: B.** The security architecture is the culmination of system elements required to implement security services that are essential to meet the needs of users and the performance levels required of the system for its security and usability needs. Security models are used to describe models such as Biba and Bell-LaPadula. The Trusted Computer Base (TCB) is all software, hardware, and controls used to protect the system's security. The security kernel is found at ring 0 and implements the reference monitor concept.

46. **Answer: B.** An asynchronous attack exploits the timing difference between when a security control is applied and when the authorized service is used. Check out http://en.wikipedia.org/wiki/Time_of_check_to_time_of_use or www.slideshare.net/amiable_indian/security-architecture for more information. A session hijack is used to bypass normal identification and authentication. Attackers can use buffer overflows to gain control of a system. Spoofing is a person or process pretending to be another person or process.

47. **Answer: D.** ITSEC (European Information Technology Security Evaluation Criteria) has seven assurance classes, from E0 to E6. ITSEC is different from TCSEC because it was developed to look at more than just confidentiality. It separates the required functionality from the level of assurance that the system is evaluated for.

48. **Answer: A.** Certification is the technical evaluation of security components and their compliance. The certification process is a technical evaluation of the system that can be carried out by independent security teams or by the existing staff. Its goal is to uncover any vulnerabilities or weaknesses in the implementation. Answer C describes accreditation, and answers B and D are distracters.

49. **Answer: C.** Clark-Wilson best meets all the primary goals of integrity. It prevents unauthorized users from making unauthorized changes, blocks unauthorized users from modifying data, and maintains internal and external reliability. Biba addresses only one goal of integrity. Bell-LaPadula is a confidentiality model. Lattice-based models describe a wide category of models, including Biba and Bell-LaPadula.

50. **Answer: D.** The Take-Grant model is concerned with who is authorized to give access to files and folders to other users and the results of these actions. Its purpose is to better understand object transference. Bell-LaPadula addresses confidentiality. Clark-Wilson and Biba are integrity models.

51. **Answer: D.** A process is in a blocked state when it is waiting for user input. It is in a ready state when it is waiting to send instructions to the CPU. It is in a running state while the CPU is executing those instructions. The process is in a new state before it has been loaded into memory.

52. **Answer: C.** The trusted path is a protected communications channel between a user and the kernel or between a process and the kernel. The trusted shell is another trusted computing base term that refers to space that users cannot break out of and that other processes cannot break into. Answers A, B, and D do not adequately describe the trusted path.

53. **Answer: B.** The Clark-Wilson model requires an access triple that consists of the operator, a program, and the data. A user cannot directly change data. Data can be changed by a qualified application after the user has authenticated to it. Biba is concerned with maintaining integrity. Bell-LaPadula is concerned with maintaining confidentiality. The Brewer-Nash model ensures that no conflict of interest occurs when information is accessed.

54. **Answer: A.** The lowest division and class that accounts for covert channels is B2, which is not one of the possible answers. So B2, B3, and A1 (B2 or higher) all satisfy the stipulated requirement.

55. **Answer: A.** The PSW holds the application's operating state. The ALU performs calculations, the control unit synchronizes operations, and the stack pointer register holds the address of the next instruction to be executed.

56. **Answer: D.** The operating system prohibits direct access to absolute memory. Applications each operate within their own memory spaces and make use of calls to relative memory (back a few, forward a few using offsets) or logical memory (using indexes or variable names).

57. **Answer: C.** Prolog, LISP, and other artificial-intelligence languages are good examples of 5GL languages. A 2GL language would include assembly. A 3GL would be C+, and an example of a 4GL would be SQL.

58. **Answer: B.** Interpreted languages include those such as Java and BASIC. Answers A, C, and D are examples of compiled languages.

59. **Answer: B.** RISC was the result of an increase in the speed of memories and the ability to get more work from fewer clock cycles. Answer A is incorrect because CISC is designed to perform many operations per instruction. Multitasking systems can alternate among tasks. Multiprocessor systems have two or more processors.

60. **Answer: D.** A macro is a group of statements used to perform a specific function. Answer A is incorrect because it more closely describes Java. Answer B is incorrect because it describes assembly language. Answer C is incorrect because it describes a 5GL language such as Prolog.

61. **Answer: B.** A cold start must be performed when a system suffers a total TCB or media failure and the system must be restored to a reliable, secure state. A system restart typically occurs when an application or process cannot be terminated or the system enters an unstable state. Both fail-safe and fail-secure are designed to stop program execution and protect the system from being compromised.

62. **Answer: A.** A multilevel security control system allows two or more classification levels of information to be processed simultaneously within the same system when some users are not cleared for all levels of information present. Answer B is incorrect because a dedicated system requires all users to have clearance and a need to know for all information processed by the system. Answer C is incorrect because a controlled system places a limited amount of trust in the hardware base. Answer D is incorrect because no access is not a valid type of system.

63. **Answer: C.** Jack is attempting to launch a covert channel attack. He is using Jill's level of access to write data to a lower level of security. Answer A is incorrect because a maintenance hook is an attack in which the attacker uses code that should have been removed before the program was released to the public. Answer B is incorrect because backdoor is a term that describes a program or application that gives an attacker unauthorized access to a system. Answer D is incorrect because a TOC/TOU attack is a type of trying attack that acts as a race condition.

64. **Answer: C.** Although answer A is correct in that Ring 0 is located toward the center of the design, this is not the best explanation. Answer C is most accurate. Rings are organized with the most-privileged domain located in the center and the least-privileged domain in the outermost ring. Ring 0 is where the security kernel is located.

65. **Answer: C.** The control unit coordinates activities of the other CPU components during program execution. The arithmetic logic unit performs calculations of a numeric nature and comparative logic functions. The bus interface unit supervises data transfers over the bus system between the CPU and I/O devices. The memory management unit handles addressing and cataloging of data stored in memory and translates logical addressing into physical addressing.

66. **Answer: B.** An operating system's four functions are process management, I/O device management, file management, and memory management. The BIOS is an independent function that does not fall under the control of the OS.

67. **Answer: C.** A bus is a grouping of electronic conductors that interconnect components of the computer. These conductors transmit signals, addresses, and data between these components. A bus can be used for data, addresses, or control. Hardware is just the physical devices. Firmware is the code or computer programs that are stored in ROM. Registers are buffers used to hold data, addresses, and instructions in temporary storage.

68. **Answer: D.** An E^2PROM is another name for an EEPROM and is programmed and erased electrically. EPROMs are not the same as an EEPROM and are erased via an ultraviolet light.

69. **Answer: A.** Virtual memory is used to make the CPU believe that more memory is present than is actually available. It accomplishes this by means of presenting both physical memory and available hard drive space.

70. **Answer: A.** The arithmetic logic unit performs calculations of a numeric nature and comparative logic functions. The bus interface unit supervises data transfers over the bus system between the CPU and I/O devices. The control unit coordinates activities of the other CPU components during program execution. The memory management unit handles addressing and cataloging of data stored in memory and translates logical addressing into physical addressing.

71. **Answer: A.** The question describes a race condition that is also known as a time of check to time of use (TOC/TOU) attack. The TOC/TOU attack targets changes in a system between the checking of a condition and the use of the results of that check. A backdoor is a condition used in programming to describe a program that can be used to bypass authentication. A maintenance hook allows the programmer to examine operations of a program while in production. The maintenance hooks should be stripped from the code when it's moved to production and before release. A covert channel is an unknown communication that takes place over an allowed communication path.

72. **Answer: D.** Van Eck phreaking is a form of eavesdropping. It was developed on the theory that the contents of a CRT display could be sniffed and decoded by intercepting the monitor's electromagnetic emissions. TEMPEST is one technology that was created to prevent Van Eck phreaking. Van Eck phreaking does not have to do with analog or digital phone systems and is not a coding attack.

73. **Answer: C.** A fail-safe systems does not pause program execution to protect the system from compromise. Fault-tolerant systems can detect and correct or circumvent a fault. Fail-soft systems can terminate noncritical processing and allow the system to continue functioning in a degraded mode. Failover systems detect failures and provide a means of redundancy.

74. **Answer: A.** The name for the TCSEC B1 specification is labeled. B2 is structured, B3 is security domains, and verified design is used for A1.

75. **Answer: B.** The bus interface unit supervises data transfers over the bus system between the CPU and I/O devices. The arithmetic logic unit performs calculations of a numeric nature and comparative logic functions. The control unit coordinates activities of the other CPU components during program execution. The memory management unit handles addressing and cataloging of data stored in memory and translates logical addressing into physical addressing.

76. **Answer: C.** The name for TCSEC B3 is security domains. B2 is structured, B1 is labeled security, and verified design is used for A1.

77. **Answer: B.** Although the Orange Book is now considered somewhat dated, you should know about it for the exam. B3 systems must have protections against covert channels. B2 systems must possess trusted path requirements. B1 systems are the first level to require sensitivity labels. Configuration management requirements are part of Orange Book A1 classification.

78. **Answer: C.** B1 systems are the first level to require sensitivity labels. B2 systems must possess trusted path requirements. B3 systems must have protections against covert channels. Configuration management requirements are part of Orange Book A1 classification.

79. **Answer: B.** C1 systems offer only minimum controls. A C1 system does not distinguish between users or the types of access possible. C2 systems require separation of user accounts. B1 requires sensitivity labels, and B2 adds trusted path requirements.

80. **Answer: D.** The memory management unit handles addressing and cataloging of data stored in memory and translates logical addressing into physical addressing. The arithmetic logic unit performs calculations of a numeric nature and comparative logic functions. The bus interface unit supervises data transfers over the bus system between the CPU and I/O devices. The control unit coordinates activities of the other CPU components during program execution.

81. **Answer: D.** Common Criteria (CC) defines seven assurance levels. CC was designed as a way to improve assurance efforts between Europe and North America. Common Criteria lists seven levels, with EAL 1 being the most basic (and therefore the cheapest to implement and evaluate) and EAL 7 being the most stringent. Answer A is incorrect because CC does not use a target of review. Answer B is incorrect because 10 functionality classes and seven evaluation levels are also defined by ITSEC. Answer C is incorrect because rainbow series requirements apply to Trusted Computer System Evaluation Criteria (TCSEC).

82. **Answer: B.** The Common Criteria defines seven assurance levels (EALs). EAL 4 is methodically designed, tested, and reviewed. EAL 2 is structurally tested. EAL 6 is semiformally verified, designed, and tested. EAL 7 is formally verified, designed, and tested.

83. **Answer: A.** EAL 2 is structurally tested. EAL 4 is methodically designed, tested, and reviewed. EAL 6 is semiformally verified, designed, and tested. EAL 7 is formally verified, designed, and tested.

84. **Answer: D.** A covert channel is an unknown communication that takes place over an allowed communication path. The question describes a covert channel known as Loki. A TOC/TOU attack targets changes in a system between the checking of a condition and the use of the results of that check. A backdoor is a condition used in programming to describe a program that can be used to bypass authentication. A maintenance hook allows the programmer to examine operations of a program while in production. The maintenance hooks should be stripped from the code when it's moved to production and before release.

85. **Answer: B.** Firmware is the code or computer programs that are stored in ROM. Hardware is just the physical devices. A bus is a grouping of electronic conductors that interconnect components of the computer. These conductors transmit signals, addresses, and data between these components. A bus can be used for data, addresses, or control. Registers are buffers used to hold data, addresses, and instructions in temporary storage.

86. **Answer: A.** A software exploitation attack attempts to exploit weaknesses in software. Attackers first attempt to enumerate a service to determine any weakness. This is accomplished via a port scan. E-mail servers use TCP port 25 for e-mail connections using SMTP and TCP port 110 for POP3. A list of ports can be found at www.iana.org/assignments/port-numbers. A backdoor is a condition used in programming to describe a program that can be used to bypass authentication. Trojans attempt to trick the user into installing a program he thinks he wants while another, malicious program is embedded inside. A time of check to time of use (TOC/TOU) attack targets changes in a system between the checking of a condition and the use of the results of that check.

87. **Answer: A.** ITSEC was developed in the late 1980s to address the needs of the European Union. TCSEC was developed for the U.S. government. Common Criteria was developed to harmonize standards between the U.S., Europe, and others. ISO 17799 was developed for information security and auditing.

88. **Answer: B.** Although certification can be thought of as the technical review of a system, accreditation is the approval of such a system by a senior executive or Designated Approving Authority. Accreditation is used to verify that the system is approved for operation.

89. **Answer: D.** Biba is a state machine model that is integrity-based. Biba is designed on a classification lattice with mandatory access controls. Bell-LaPadula is also based on the state machine concept but is based on confidentiality. The Sutherland model is based on the problem of inference. Brewer-Nash addresses conflicts of interest.

90. **Answer: D.** Clark-Wilson is the model most frequently mentioned in relation to commercial use. The Clark-Wilson model dictates that the separation of duties must be enforced, that subjects must access data through an application, and that auditing is required. Answer A is incorrect because Bell-LaPadula was actually the first formal model developed to protect confidentiality. Bell-LaPadula uses mandatory access control to enforce the DoD multilevel security policy. Answer B is incorrect because Lipner was never used as a commercial model but was the first to separate objects so that data and programs were viewed separately. Brewer-Nash addresses conflicts of interest.

91. **Answer: C.** Brewer-Nash addresses conflicts of interest. It is similar to the Bell-LaPadula model and is also called the Chinese Wall model. Biba is a state machine model that is integrity based. Bell-LaPadula is also based on the state machine concept but is based on confidentiality. The Sutherland model is based on the problem of inference. Biba is designed on a classification lattice with mandatory access controls.

92. **Answer: A.** The reference monitor is an abstract machine that is used to implement security. Bell-LaPadula, Goguen-Meseguer, and Bobert and Kain are all valid information security models.

93. **Answer: D.** Clark-Wilson is the model most frequently mentioned in relation to commercial use. It addresses all goals of integrity. The Clark-Wilson model dictates that the separation of duties must be enforced, that subjects must access data through an application, and that auditing is required. Answer A is incorrect because Bell-LaPadula was actually the first formal model developed to protect confidentiality. Bell-LaPadula uses mandatory access control to enforce the DoD multilevel security policy. Answer B is incorrect because Lipner was never used as a commercial model. It was the first to separate object so that data and programs were viewed separately. Brewer-Nash addresses conflicts of interest.

94. **Answer: B.** Answer B defines an access control list. Each row is a capability list. Answer A defines an attribute of the Take-Grant model, which specifies how rights can be passed from one subject to another or from a subject to an object. Answer C is incorrect because the Simple Integrity Axiom is a component of the Biba model. Answer D is incorrect because it defines the information flow model.

95. **Answer: A.** Process isolation is the use of controls to separate memory spaces for each process's instructions and data. Process isolation is not implemented in hardware that would be performed by hardware segmentation. Data hiding is the process of making sure that information at one level of security is not visible at different security levels. Abstraction is the concept that objects are limited in knowing how something works.

96. **Answer: C.** F10 matches networks with high confidentiality and integrity requirements. F8 systems match high integrity during data communications. F9 matches networks with high confidentiality requirements during data communications. F6 is equal to high integrity.

97. **Answer: D.** F9 matches networks with high confidentiality requirements during data communications. F10 matches networks with high confidentiality and integrity requirements. F8 systems match high integrity during data communications. F6 is equal to high integrity.

98. **Answer: C.** Languages have been grouped into five generations, from 1GL to 5GL. FORTRAN is considered a 3GL. Prolog is considered a 5GL, assembly is a 2GL, and SQL is a 4GL.

99. **Answer: B.** Sequential memory searches from the beginning rather than directly accessing the location. The most commonly used sequential device is for tape drives and backup. Many companies still use a tape backup system. Optical drives, hard drives, and floppy drives do not search sequentially to access data.

100. **Answer: D.** Languages have been grouped into five generations, from 1GL to 5GL. SQL is a 4GL. FORTRAN is considered a 3GL. Prolog is considered a 5GL. Assembly is a 2GL.

101. **Answer: D.** PaaS provides a platform for your use. Services provided by this model can help during all phases of system development life cycle (SDLC) and can use application program interfaces (API), website portals, or gateway software.

102. **Answer: B.** IaaS describes a cloud solution where you are buying infrastructure. You purchase virtual power to execute your software as needed.

103. **Answer: A.** MaaS offers a cloud-based solution to monitoring solutions. This includes monitoring for networks, servers, applications, and remote-systems management.

104. Answer: A. EDO DRAM is faster than DRAM and has a type of look-ahead feature. It is different than the types in answers B, C, and D in that it can capture the next block of data while the previous block is being sent to the CPU.

105. Answer: D. VMEscaping is a form of attack that occurs when an attacker is able to run malware or code on a virtual machine that allows an operating system running within it to break out and interact directly with the hypervisor. Answers A, B, and C do not describe this attack.

106. Answer: True. The security kernel must control all access, be protected from modification or change, must be verified, and must be tested to be correct.

107. Answer: False. The Bell-LaPadula model supports the Simple Security Property (ss Property). This property states that a subject at one level of confidentiality is not allowed to read information at a higher level of confidentiality. Bell-LaPadula was actually the first formal model developed to protect confidentiality. It uses mandatory access control to enforce the DoD multilevel security policy.

108. The answers are as follows:

- **A.** A1: **2**
- **B.** B1: **3**
- **C.** B2: **4**
- **D.** C1: **5**
- **E.** D: **1**

A1 is the highest supported rating. Systems rated as such must meet formal methods and proof of integrity of the trusted computer base (TCB). It must be tested, installed, and delivered under secure conditions. Examples of A1 systems include Gemini Trusted Network Processor and the Honeywell SCOMP. B1 is the first level to use labeled security protection. B1 systems require sensitivity labels for all subjects and storage objects. Examples of B1-rated systems are the Cray Research Trusted Unicos 8.0 and the Digital SEVMS. B2 is the highest rating of MAC level security listed here. TCSEC ranks security levels as B3, B2, and B1 (most secure to least secure). C-level or DAC systems are ranked as C1 and C2. C1 systems don't need to distinguish between individual users and types of access. D-level systems either have failed TCSEC or were not tested. DOS is an example of a D-rated system.

CHAPTER FIVE

Telecommunications and Network Security

The Telecommunications and Network Security domain is one of the larger CISSP domains. Individuals actively involved in the networking end of the business may consider this one of the easier domains. However, it's advisable not to be lulled into complacency, because this domain encompasses a large body of knowledge. It's possible that many test questions may come from this domain. The following list gives you some key areas from telecommunications and network security that you need to be aware of for the CISSP exam:

- ▶ OSI model
- ▶ TCP/IP model
- ▶ Protocols such as TCP, UDP, ICMP, and IP
- ▶ Ethernet and local-area networking protocols
- ▶ Hardware: routers, gateways, switches, and hubs
- ▶ Firewalls and their deployments
- ▶ Wireless systems WLANs/cell phones/satellite
- ▶ WAN technologies: T1s/T3s/Frame Relay/PPP/ISDN/DSL/cable
- ▶ Voice: PBX/cell phones/VoIP
- ▶ IPsec
- ▶ Network vulnerabilities

Quick Check

Practice Questions

1. Which of the following is considered a connection-oriented protocol?

   Quick Answer: **158**
   Detailed Answer: **159**

   ❍ **A.** UDP
   ❍ **B.** TCP
   ❍ **C.** ICMP
   ❍ **D.** ARP

2. Which connectionless protocol is used for its low overhead and speed?

   Quick Answer: **158**
   Detailed Answer: **159**

   ❍ **A.** UDP
   ❍ **B.** TCP
   ❍ **C.** ICMP
   ❍ **D.** ARP

3. Information security is not built on which of the following?

   Quick Answer: **158**
   Detailed Answer: **159**

   ❍ **A.** Confidentiality
   ❍ **B.** Availability
   ❍ **C.** Accessibility
   ❍ **D.** Integrity

4. Which data communications solution transmits timing information to the receiver by using a "preamble" of alternating 1s and 0s?

   Quick Answer: **158**
   Detailed Answer: **159**

   ❍ **A.** Modem communication
   ❍ **B.** Ethernet communication
   ❍ **C.** Instant messaging
   ❍ **D.** Serial communication

5. LAN data transmissions can take on several different forms. Which of the following can be both a source and a destination address?

   Quick Answer: **158**
   Detailed Answer: **159**

   ❍ **A.** Unicast
   ❍ **B.** Multicast
   ❍ **C.** Broadcast
   ❍ **D.** Anycast

Quick Check

6. Data transmission technologies vary. Which one does Ethernet use?

   ❍ **A.** CSMA/CA
   ❍ **B.** CSMA/CS
   ❍ **C.** CSNA/CD
   ❍ **D.** CSMA/CD

Quick Answer: **158**
Detailed Answer: **159**

7. Which of the following best describes ISDN BRI?

   ❍ **A.** Twenty-four D channels
   ❍ **B.** One D channel and 23 B channels
   ❍ **C.** Two B channels and one D channel
   ❍ **D.** Two D channels and one B channel

Quick Answer: **158**
Detailed Answer: **159**

8. Because some of your organization's employees use fax machines to send and receive confidential information, you have become concerned about their level of security. Which of the following is the most effective security measure to protect against unauthorized disclosure?

   ❍ **A.** Activity logs
   ❍ **B.** Exception reports
   ❍ **C.** Confidential cover pages
   ❍ **D.** Removing fax machines from insecure areas

Quick Answer: **158**
Detailed Answer: **159**

9. Protocols are used to set up rules of operation. One well-known protocol is the OSI model. Between what layers of the OSI model does ARP operate?

   ❍ **A.** Presentation and session
   ❍ **B.** Network and data link
   ❍ **C.** Data link and physical
   ❍ **D.** Physical and session

Quick Answer: **158**
Detailed Answer: **160**

10. TCP and UDP reside at which layer of the OSI model?

   ❍ **A.** Session
   ❍ **B.** Transport
   ❍ **C.** Data link
   ❍ **D.** Presentation

Quick Answer: **158**
Detailed Answer: **160**

Quick Check

11. Which of the following describes the OSI model?

Quick Answer: **158**
Detailed Answer: **160**

- ❍ **A.** RFC 1700
- ❍ **B.** IEEE 802.3
- ❍ **C.** ISO 7498
- ❍ **D.** NIST 812D

12. What is the purpose of ARP?

Quick Answer: **158**
Detailed Answer: **160**

- ❍ **A.** To resolve known MAC addresses to unknown IP addresses
- ❍ **B.** To resolve domain names to unknown IP addresses
- ❍ **C.** To resolve NetBIOS names to IP addresses
- ❍ **D.** To resolve known IP addresses to unknown physical addresses

13. Do ARP requests leave the broadcast domain?

Quick Answer: **158**
Detailed Answer: **160**

- ❍ **A.** Only when traffic is bound for another network.
- ❍ **B.** ARP requests never leave the broadcast domain.
- ❍ **C.** It depends on the router's configuration.
- ❍ **D.** Only when using routable IP addresses.

14. Which device operates at the network interface layer of the TCP/IP model?

Quick Answer: **158**
Detailed Answer: **160**

- ❍ **A.** Router
- ❍ **B.** Firewall
- ❍ **C.** PBX
- ❍ **D.** Switch

15. Which device operates at the internetworking layer of the TCP/IP model?

Quick Answer: **158**
Detailed Answer: **160**

- ❍ **A.** Router
- ❍ **B.** Firewall
- ❍ **C.** PBX
- ❍ **D.** Switch

16. An IP protocol field of 0x06 indicates that IP is carrying what as its payload?

Quick Answer: **158**
Detailed Answer: **160**

- ❍ **A.** TCP
- ❍ **B.** ICMP
- ❍ **C.** UDP
- ❍ **D.** IGRP

Quick Check

17. From a security standpoint, what is the most common complaint about email?

Quick Answer: **158**
Detailed Answer: **160**

❍ **A.** Spam

❍ **B.** Clear-text passwords

❍ **C.** Incompatible mail programs

❍ **D.** Weak authentication

18. Which of the following presents the largest security risk?

Quick Answer: **158**
Detailed Answer: **161**

❍ **A.** RAS

❍ **B.** Cable or DSL Internet access

❍ **C.** Dialup Internet access

❍ **D.** Shotgun modems

19. What is a secure private connection through a public network or the Internet called?

Quick Answer: **158**
Detailed Answer: **161**

❍ **A.** Tunneling protocol

❍ **B.** IPsec

❍ **C.** PSTN

❍ **D.** VPN

20. Which of the following is the least secure communications protocol?

Quick Answer: **158**
Detailed Answer: **161**

❍ **A.** CHAP

❍ **B.** IPsec

❍ **C.** PAP

❍ **D.** EAP

21. RAID is a powerful technology because it provides fault tolerance. The following describes which level of RAID? The data is striped over all drives while parity is held on one drive. If a drive failure occurs, the defective drive can be rebuilt by accessing the parity drive.

Quick Answer: **158**
Detailed Answer: **161**

❍ **A.** Level 0

❍ **B.** Level 1

❍ **C.** Level 2

❍ **D.** Level 3

Quick Check

22. TCP is a widely used protocol. Which of the following attributes makes TCP reliable?

❍ **A.** Connection establishment

❍ **B.** Low overhead

❍ **C.** Connectionless establishment

❍ **D.** Null sessions

Quick Answer: **158**
Detailed Answer: **161**

23. RAID is a powerful technology because it provides fault tolerance. The following describes which level of RAID? This version of RAID is used for performance gains because data is striped over several drives, but no one drive is used for redundancy or parity.

❍ **A.** Level 0

❍ **B.** Level 1

❍ **C.** Level 2

❍ **D.** Level 3

Quick Answer: **158**
Detailed Answer: **161**

24. Which protocol resides at the transport layer of the OSI model?

❍ **A.** ARP

❍ **B.** ICMP

❍ **C.** UDP

❍ **D.** IP

Quick Answer: **158**
Detailed Answer: **161**

25. What protocol resolves FQDN to IP addresses?

❍ **A.** ARP

❍ **B.** DNS

❍ **C.** FTP

❍ **D.** RARP

Quick Answer: **158**
Detailed Answer: **161**

26. Which routing protocol makes a routing decision based on hop count?

❍ **A.** RIP

❍ **B.** IGRP

❍ **C.** OSPF

❍ **D.** IPX

Quick Answer: **158**
Detailed Answer: **162**

27. Intrusion detection is a critical component of security. Which of the following phases of security does intrusion detection fit into?

❍ **A.** Response

❍ **B.** Prevention

❍ **C.** Detection

❍ **D.** Bastion

Quick Answer: **158**
Detailed Answer: **162**

Quick Check

28. Your firm has just hired a newly certified CISSP named Sam as an intern. He wants to learn more about detection-based security systems. He asks you to explain intrusion detection. Which of the following is one of the two types of intrusion detection engines?

Quick Answer: **158**
Detailed Answer: **162**

- ❍ **A.** Host
- ❍ **B.** Signature
- ❍ **C.** Network
- ❍ **D.** Hybrid

29. At which layer of the OSI model does IPsec operate?

Quick Answer: **158**
Detailed Answer: **162**

- ❍ **A.** Transport
- ❍ **B.** Network
- ❍ **C.** Data link
- ❍ **D.** Session

30. While preparing for your CISSP exam, you have been reading more about IPsec. This has worked in your favor, because your boss has asked you to explain IPsec at the next staff meeting. How will you explain the operation of IPsec transport mode?

Quick Answer: **158**
Detailed Answer: **162**

- ❍ **A.** Transport mode works by encrypting the data and then encapsulating the entire packet. This provides two layers of security.
- ❍ **B.** Transport mode works by tunneling the entire packet inside an encrypted tunnel.
- ❍ **C.** Transport mode only provides nonrepudiation. That is, all data and the header are sent in clear text. A cryptographic checksum is used to verify that the data remains unchanged.
- ❍ **D.** Transport mode works by encrypting the data. The header and associated information are sent in their natural, unencrypted form.

31. The e-commerce branch of your parent company's organization has become increasingly worried about attacks against the network that is hosting its web servers. The department head has asked you to explain what a smurf attack is and how it might affect the web server. How will you respond?

Quick Answer: **158**
Detailed Answer: **162**

- ❍ **A.** A smurf attack uses ICMP packets of a rather large size. These packets overwhelm the receiving device, causing a denial of service for legitimate devices attempting legitimate connections.

Quick Check

❍ **B.** Smurf targets the TCP session setup. As such, a large number of spoofed SYN packets are launched against the target device. As the queue of illegitimate connections grows, the system slows down, finally reaching the point where no users can obtain access.

❍ **C.** A smurf attack uses ICMP packets with forged source and target addresses. The packets are addressed to the local broadcast address. The attack eventually chokes the web server.

❍ **D.** Smurf attacks work by changing the length and fragmentation field of the IP header. This causes a system to slow down or hang.

32. IPsec can be used to ensure integrity, confidentiality, and authenticity. Which of the following does IPsec provide principally through the use of the encapsulated security payload?

Quick Answer: **158**
Detailed Answer: **162**

❍ **A.** Integrity

❍ **B.** Confidentiality

❍ **C.** Authenticity

❍ **D.** Nonrepudiation

33. Your assistant is starting to learn about routing and IP addressing. She comes to you with a question. She wants to know how many host addresses are possible with a 16-bit host field. What do you tell her?

Quick Answer: **158**
Detailed Answer: **162**

❍ **A.** 256

❍ **B.** 65,534

❍ **C.** 65,536

❍ **D.** 254

34. Which of the following is an example of a Class D network address?

Quick Answer: **158**
Detailed Answer: **162**

❍ **A.** 10.10.10.1

❍ **B.** 224.0.0.1

❍ **C.** 172.16.3.4

❍ **D.** 192.168.4.1

35. Securing networked computers is a critical task. Many organizations choose to place some services such as web or email in an area of the network that is neither fully internal nor fully external to the organization. These services are placed behind an Internet-facing router, but in front of a firewall or another device that protects the internal network. What is the area in which these services are deployed called?

Quick Answer: **158**
Detailed Answer: **163**

Quick Check

- ❍ **A.** Dual-homed gateway
- ❍ **B.** Intranet
- ❍ **C.** Demilitarized zone (DMZ)
- ❍ **D.** Extranet

36. You are the security administrator for a large medical device company. You are asked to determine whether NAT should be used at your organization for Internet connectivity. Which of the following is *not* one of the three types of NAT?

Quick Answer: **158**
Detailed Answer: **163**

- ❍ **A.** PAT
- ❍ **B.** Dynamic NAT
- ❍ **C.** DAT
- ❍ **D.** Static NAT

37. Which of the following is considered an OSI application layer security protocol?

Quick Answer: **158**
Detailed Answer: **163**

- ❍ **A.** RIP
- ❍ **B.** SSL
- ❍ **C.** SKIP
- ❍ **D.** S/MIME

38. Your new intern, Christine, has been asking about private addressing. She wants to know which of the following blocks of IP addresses is reserved for this purpose. What do you tell her?

Quick Answer: **158**
Detailed Answer: **163**

- ❍ **A.** 10.0.0.0/8
- ❍ **B.** 12.0.0.0/8
- ❍ **C.** 127.0.0.1/8
- ❍ **D.** 169.254.0.0/12

39. Some of your coworkers are studying for the CISSP exam. Because you're considered an expert, they ask you the following question: Which of the following would be considered a disadvantage of using a router as a firewall? What do you tell them?

Quick Answer: **158**
Detailed Answer: **163**

- ❍ **A.** Routers are more expensive than firewalls.
- ❍ **B.** Routers are more difficult to configure than firewalls.
- ❍ **C.** Routers are stateless by design.
- ❍ **D.** Routers can function as firewalls only if the user has purchased the ACL plug-ins.

Quick Check

40. VPNs have become very popular as a way to connect users to corporate networks by means of the Internet. Which of the following is *not* a VPN protocol?

Quick Answer: **158**
Detailed Answer: **163**

- ❍ **A.** SLIP
- ❍ **B.** PPTP
- ❍ **C.** L2TP
- ❍ **D.** L2F

41. Which VPN protocol was developed by Cisco and operates at Layer 2 of the OSI model?

Quick Answer: **158**
Detailed Answer: **164**

- ❍ **A.** TACACS
- ❍ **B.** PPTP
- ❍ **C.** IPsec
- ❍ **D.** L2F

42. Your manager, Ed, has decided that passwords are too easily broken to be used to authenticate remote users. Ed wants you to implement some type of RAS authentication that uses some type of token card. Which system meets this critical requirement?

Quick Answer: **158**
Detailed Answer: **164**

- ❍ **A.** PAP
- ❍ **B.** EAP
- ❍ **C.** CHAP
- ❍ **D.** PPP

43. The product design group of the corporation you work for has requested the installation of 802.11g wireless access points secured with WEP. The request cites ease of network access and enhanced mobile computing as the reasons why they need this technology. You are the senior IT security officer; what should your response be?

Quick Answer: **158**
Detailed Answer: **164**

- ❍ **A.** Wireless offers good security, so you should approve the request.
- ❍ **B.** If the wireless systems implement WEP, you will have no problem approving the request, because WEP is highly secure.
- ❍ **C.** Because many cordless phones are used in the design area, wireless would be a poor choice, because interference would be high.
- ❍ **D.** Wireless is not a good choice because the design area maintains critical information, and 802.11g has some known vulnerabilities when WEP is used.

Quick Check

44. Maxwell has more than 100 workstations at his site. He is looking for a method of centralized management. Which of the following is his best choice?

- ❍ **A.** APIPA
- ❍ **B.** RARP
- ❍ **C.** DHCP
- ❍ **D.** Host tables

Quick Answer: **158**
Detailed Answer: **164**

45. Your company is performing a study to determine the most unsecured protocols that are currently being used. Which of the following is considered a secure protocol?

- ❍ **A.** SSH
- ❍ **B.** FTP
- ❍ **C.** SNMP
- ❍ **D.** Telnet

Quick Answer: **158**
Detailed Answer: **164**

46. What is the most commonly used AAA solution?

- ❍ **A.** SLIP
- ❍ **B.** TACACS
- ❍ **C.** PPP
- ❍ **D.** RADIUS

Quick Answer: **158**
Detailed Answer: **164**

47. You are asked to configure the border routers to block ICMP messages and prevent the return of any error messages to external networks. Which of the following will accomplish this task?

- ❍ **A.** Drop
- ❍ **B.** Filter
- ❍ **C.** Reject
- ❍ **D.** Bounce

Quick Answer: **158**
Detailed Answer: **164**

48. What is the maximum distance of a single run of Category 5 cable?

- ❍ **A.** 100 feet
- ❍ **B.** 200 feet
- ❍ **C.** 235 feet
- ❍ **D.** 328 feet

Quick Answer: **158**
Detailed Answer: **164**

Quick Check

49. Which type of malicious software is a self-replicating program?

Quick Answer: **158**
Detailed Answer: **164**

- ❍ **A.** Virus
- ❍ **B.** Trojan
- ❍ **C.** Worm
- ❍ **D.** Trapdoor

50. Your organization is considering switching to single-mode fiber-optic cable. What is the maximum distance this cable can be extended?

Quick Answer: **158**
Detailed Answer: **165**

- ❍ **A.** 2,000 meters
- ❍ **B.** 200 feet
- ❍ **C.** 2 miles
- ❍ **D.** 200 miles

51. Which field of the IP header does traceroute manipulate?

Quick Answer: **158**
Detailed Answer: **165**

- ❍ **A.** Fragmentation
- ❍ **B.** TTL
- ❍ **C.** IPID
- ❍ **D.** Offset

52. The protection of employees' health and welfare is of critical importance to an organization's security officer. Therefore, it is critical that the proper type of networking cable be chosen for each task. What type of network cabling should be used in drop ceilings or areas that might be exposed to fire?

Quick Answer: **158**
Detailed Answer: **165**

- ❍ **A.** Plenum grade
- ❍ **B.** A1 fire-rated cable
- ❍ **C.** Polyvinyl chloride-coated cable
- ❍ **D.** Nonpressurized conduit-rated cable

53. Which of the following is an example of baseband technology?

Quick Answer: **158**
Detailed Answer: **165**

- ❍ **A.** DSL
- ❍ **B.** Cable modem
- ❍ **C.** Cable television
- ❍ **D.** Ethernet

54. Which of the following is not an option in IPv4?

Quick Answer: **158**
Detailed Answer: **165**

- ❍ **A.** Unicast
- ❍ **B.** Multicast
- ❍ **C.** Anycast
- ❍ **D.** Broadcast

Quick Check

55. Which type of technology uses a ring topology?

Quick Answer: **158**
Detailed Answer: **165**

- ❍ **A.** Ethernet
- ❍ **B.** Token Ring
- ❍ **C.** ISDN
- ❍ **D.** PPP

56. Your lead technician has been reviewing the marketing materials of several network switch manufacturers. She wants to know what the spec sheet means when it says, "The switch is a 'cut-through' design."

Quick Answer: **158**
Detailed Answer: **165**

- ❍ **A.** This terminology applies only to the board design of the switch.
- ❍ **B.** It means that the switch can support port spanning.
- ❍ **C.** It means that the switch can prioritize traffic for QoS, thereby increasing switching speed.
- ❍ **D.** It means that the switch is designed to examine only a portion of the frame, thereby increasing throughput.

57. Which type of network is set up similar to the Internet but is private to an organization?

Quick Answer: **158**
Detailed Answer: **165**

- ❍ **A.** Extranet
- ❍ **B.** VLAN
- ❍ **C.** Intranet
- ❍ **D.** VPN

58. What is the total multiplexed rate of a T1 carrier?

Quick Answer: **158**
Detailed Answer: **165**

- ❍ **A.** 1 Mbps
- ❍ **B.** 1.54 Mbps
- ❍ **C.** 10 Mbps
- ❍ **D.** 44.736 Mbps

59. Sam, one of your help-desk technicians, wants to learn more about long-haul data transmission technologies. You kindly take a few minutes to explain wide-area networks (WANs). WANs can be either circuit-switched or packet-switched. Which of the following is an example of circuit switching?

Quick Answer: **158**
Detailed Answer: **165**

- ❍ **A.** Frame Relay
- ❍ **B.** DDS
- ❍ **C.** X.25
- ❍ **D.** ATM

Quick Check

60. Regina is preparing to perform a penetration test. Which of the following is the most important item for Regina to complete?

Quick Answer: **158**
Detailed Answer: **165**

- ❍ **A.** Assigning team members to specific tasks
- ❍ **B.** Signing a written agreement stating the details of the assessment
- ❍ **C.** Performing a thorough preassessment that includes passive information gathering
- ❍ **D.** Gathering all network maps and associated information about the network's configuration

61. What is the total multiplexed rate of a T3 carrier?

Quick Answer: **158**
Detailed Answer: **165**

- ❍ **A.** 1 Mbps
- ❍ **B.** 1.54 Mbps
- ❍ **C.** 10 Mbps
- ❍ **D.** 44.736 Mbps

62. Layer 2 switches can be either cut-through or store-and-forward. Which of the following statements is true about cut-through switches?

Quick Answer: **158**
Detailed Answer: **166**

- ❍ **A.** Cut-through switches introduce more latency into the network.
- ❍ **B.** Cut-through switches must validate the frame's CRC before making a switching decision.
- ❍ **C.** Although cut-through switches are faster, they may propagate more errors.
- ❍ **D.** Although cut-through switches are faster, they are cost-prohibitive and expensive to manufacture.

63. A portion of the MAC address can be used to identify the manufacturer of the NIC used. How many bytes is this portion of the address, and what is the total length of a MAC address?

Quick Answer: **158**
Detailed Answer: **166**

- ❍ **A.** A MAC address is 4 bytes long, and the first 2 bytes identify the manufacturer of the NIC.
- ❍ **B.** A MAC address is 4 bytes long, and the first byte identifies the manufacturer of the NIC.
- ❍ **C.** A MAC address is 6 bytes long, and the first 2 bytes identify the manufacturer of the NIC.
- ❍ **D.** A MAC address is 6 bytes long, and the first 3 bytes identify the manufacturer of the NIC.

Quick Check

64. What process do criminal hackers use to identify remote-access modems?

Quick Answer: **158**
Detailed Answer: **166**

- ❍ **A.** War driving
- ❍ **B.** War dialing
- ❍ **C.** War chalking
- ❍ **D.** Modem scanning

65. Several coworkers are discussing the operation of network equipment. To help them finish this discussion and get back to more productive endeavors, you have agreed to answer their question: Does an Ethernet switch perform logical segmentation? What is your answer?

Quick Answer: **158**
Detailed Answer: **166**

- ❍ **A.** Ethernet switches perform logical segmentation.
- ❍ **B.** Ethernet switches do not perform logical segmentation.
- ❍ **C.** The answer depends on whether the switch supports port spanning.
- ❍ **D.** Ethernet switches do not perform logical segmentation if connected to a hub.

66. What three items are known as the three A's of security?

Quick Answer: **158**
Detailed Answer: **166**

- ❍ **A.** Accountability, allocation, and authorization
- ❍ **B.** Accountability, authentication, and allocation
- ❍ **C.** Accountability, activation, and authorization
- ❍ **D.** Access control, authentication, and auditing

67. Backing up network data and software is an important part of maintaining an organization's resources. Without backup, disasters or failures could cause catastrophic loss. Which of the following is *not* a valid type of backup?

Quick Answer: **158**
Detailed Answer: **166**

- ❍ **A.** Full
- ❍ **B.** Differential
- ❍ **C.** Sequential
- ❍ **D.** Incremental

68. James does not want to pretend to be a valid user; he wants to become that user. With that in mind, why would James want to alter the relationship between the IP address and MAC address in one of your ARP table entries?

Quick Answer: **158**
Detailed Answer: **166**

- ❍ **A.** Spoofing
- ❍ **B.** Hijacking
- ❍ **C.** ICMP redirect
- ❍ **D.** Backscatter

Quick Check

69. Attackers who want to overcome the segmentation of a switch are forced to use one of two types of attacks. Which of the following is one of these attacks?

Quick Answer: **158**
Detailed Answer: **166**

❍ **A.** Bouncing
❍ **B.** Flooding
❍ **C.** DNS poisoning
❍ **D.** IP forwarding

70. What type of IDS matches the following description? This IDS uses small programs or pieces of code that reside on various host systems throughout the network. These programs monitor the OS continuously and can set off triggers or send alarms if they detect activity that is deemed inappropriate.

Quick Answer: **158**
Detailed Answer: **167**

❍ **A.** Network-based
❍ **B.** Signature-based
❍ **C.** Host-based
❍ **D.** Behavior-based

71. Which protocol offers the least confidentiality?

Quick Answer: **158**
Detailed Answer: **167**

❍ **A.** PPTP
❍ **B.** L2TP
❍ **C.** TKIP
❍ **D.** WEP

72. A research and development team working in a laboratory for an antimalware manufacturer will be testing the performance of new behavioral analysis network software. In support of the acceptance testing of their latest adaptive module, they have created a zero-day virus. As an additional safety net to their testing, they will modify the default TTL value for the TCP/IP stack of the attacking machine to ensure that the virus cannot travel beyond the current subnet. What should they set the TTL to?

Quick Answer: **158**
Detailed Answer: **167**

❍ **A.** Null
❍ **B.** 0
❍ **C.** 1
❍ **D.** 2

73. RIP is a legacy distance-vector protocol that has largely been replaced by OSPF and IGRP. What is one of the deficiencies of RIP?

Quick Answer: **158**
Detailed Answer: **167**

❍ **A.** The protocol has a limit of 15 hops and weak authentication.
❍ **B.** The protocol has a limit of 16 hops and weak authentication.

Quick Check

❍ **C.** The protocol has a limit of 254 hops and weak authentication.

❍ **D.** The protocol has a limit of 255 hops and weak authentication.

74. To prevent packets from being captured and redirected to another geographic location where they might be replayed, an organization has added content to the packet header, identifying the acceptable area where the packet will be considered valid. What attack is the organization trying to prevent?

Quick Answer: **158**
Detailed Answer: **167**

❍ **A.** Black hole attack

❍ **B.** Tunneled attack

❍ **C.** Wormhole attack

❍ **D.** Out-of-band attack

75. Your manager asks you to immediately set up a honeypot on the intranet. He hopes to catch an employee who is suspected of using the network for activities that are prohibited by the company's acceptable-use policy. You tell your manager that you can set up a honeypot, but not in the way he wants, because this would constitute entrapment. You also explain that the honeypot:

Quick Answer: **158**
Detailed Answer: **167**

❍ **A.** Must quickly be authorized by policy so that it represents enticement.

❍ **B.** Must be set up on a screened subnet.

❍ **C.** Must be installed on a screened host.

❍ **D.** Must be installed on all employees' computers directly and equally.

76. What is the most reliable and secure form of IPsec that can be deployed?

Quick Answer: **158**
Detailed Answer: **167**

❍ **A.** Authenticating headers (AH)

❍ **B.** Encapsulating Security Payload (ESP)

❍ **C.** Iterated tunneling

❍ **D.** Transport adjacency

77. Which of the following shows the sequence of layers as Layers 1, 4, 7, 2, and 5?

Quick Answer: **158**
Detailed Answer: **167**

❍ **A.** Physical, transport, application, data link, and presentation

❍ **B.** Physical, transport, application, data link, and session

❍ **C.** Physical, session, application, data link, and transport

❍ **D.** Physical, transport, application, transport, and session

Quick Check

78. Which protocols work at the application, transport, data link, and session layers, respectively?

Quick Answer: **158**
Detailed Answer: **167**

- ❍ **A.** File Transfer Protocol, User Datagram Protocol, NetBIOS, and Structured Query Language
- ❍ **B.** Telnet, Transmission Control Protocol, High-Speed Serial Interface (HSSI), and MPEG
- ❍ **C.** Simple Network Management Protocol, Stream Control Transmission Protocol, Serial Line Internet Protocol, and Structured Query Language
- ❍ **D.** Internet Group Management Protocol, User Datagram Protocol, Point-to-Point Protocol, and Structured Query Language

79. Secure Socket Layer (SSL) resides between which layers of the OSI model?

Quick Answer: **158**
Detailed Answer: **167**

- ❍ **A.** Between application and presentation
- ❍ **B.** Between presentation and network
- ❍ **C.** Between data link and transport
- ❍ **D.** Between transport and session

80. Which of the following is a Class D IPv4 address?

Quick Answer: **158**
Detailed Answer: **168**

- ❍ **A.** 225.0.0.0
- ❍ **B.** 241.0.0.0
- ❍ **C.** 223.0.0.0
- ❍ **D.** 192.168.0.0

81. Which of the following best describes communication between modems?

Quick Answer: **158**
Detailed Answer: **168**

- ❍ **A.** Synchronization takes place before communication begins.
- ❍ **B.** It does not frame the data in start and stop bits.
- ❍ **C.** It transfers data as a stream of bits.
- ❍ **D.** The transmitted data can travel at any time, can be any length, and uses stop and start delimiters.

82. Which of the following is designed to work with wireless devices when only limited resources and applications are available and two-way client/server authentication is needed?

Quick Answer: **158**
Detailed Answer: **168**

- ❍ **A.** WEP with RC4
- ❍ **B.** Class 1 Wireless Application Protocol
- ❍ **C.** Class 3 Wireless Application Protocol
- ❍ **D.** WPA2 with AES

Quick Check

83. You are asked to work on a smart phone application project that will initially be rolled out in the Far East. Your company wants the application to work with Compact HTML (cHTML). Which protocol should you recommend after reviewing these requirements?

Quick Answer: 158
Detailed Answer: 168

- ❍ **A.** 802.15
- ❍ **B.** Wireless Application Protocol (WAP)
- ❍ **C.** 802.16
- ❍ **D.** i-Mode

84. You company's sales force is going mobile because the corporate office has decided that the best way to increase sales is to get the salespeople out of the office. Each member will be responsible for using the company's RAS connection to report sales each night. With this in mind, which protocol is the most widely used for this type of data link connectivity?

Quick Answer: 158
Detailed Answer: 168

- ❍ **A.** IMAP
- ❍ **B.** IPsec
- ❍ **C.** PPTP
- ❍ **D.** PPP

85. Which protocol is the most commonly used replacement for SLIP?

Quick Answer: 158
Detailed Answer: 168

- ❍ **A.** IMAP
- ❍ **B.** IPsec
- ❍ **C.** PPTP
- ❍ **D.** PPP

86. Which of the following is true of SLIP?

Quick Answer: 158
Detailed Answer: 168

- ❍ **A.** It can relay IP packets over a dialup line.
- ❍ **B.** It provides authentication.
- ❍ **C.** It supports multiple protocols.
- ❍ **D.** It supports link monitoring.

87. You are asked to prepare a proposal for upgrading the organization's email servers. Although SPAM and junk mail have become a big concern, you are asked to upgrade to the most current Internet mail application while maintaining support for port 25 transmissions. Which protocol is most appropriate?

Quick Answer: 158
Detailed Answer: 168

- ❍ **A.** POP3
- ❍ **B.** POP2
- ❍ **C.** SMTP
- ❍ **D.** IMAP

Quick Check

88. What is the target data rate for a 2g cell phone?

- ❍ **A.** 14.4 Kbps
- ❍ **B.** 28.8 Kbps
- ❍ **C.** 2 Mbps
- ❍ **D.** 10 Mbps

Quick Answer: **158**
Detailed Answer: **168**

89. What is the target data rate for a 3g cell phone?

- ❍ **A.** 14.4 Kbps
- ❍ **B.** 28.8 Kbps
- ❍ **C.** 2 Mbps
- ❍ **D.** 10 Mbps

Quick Answer: **158**
Detailed Answer: **168**

90. You are asked to implement a telecommunication solution for two buildings that are within line of site. You do not own the land in between, and easement costs are high. What technology should you suggest?

- ❍ **A.** Twisted pair
- ❍ **B.** Microwave
- ❍ **C.** Infrared
- ❍ **D.** Coaxial

Quick Answer: **158**
Detailed Answer: **169**

91. You have configured a wireless device to pass WTLS traffic to a gateway before it is forwarded to a web server. You are concerned about any shortcomings in security after traffic leaves the gateway. How should this concern be addressed?

- ❍ **A.** There is no way to address this problem.
- ❍ **B.** The Wireless Application Protocol (WAP) gateway should implement SSL.
- ❍ **C.** WAP should be configured for mutual authentication.
- ❍ **D.** The WAP gateway should implement i-Mode.

Quick Answer: **158**
Detailed Answer: **169**

92. As your organization has grown, so has the need for switching at OSI Layer 3. You believe that by switching at this layer and by using a Tag Information Base, you can increase the speed of delivery of packets on your network. Based on this information, which of the following is incorrect?

- ❍ **A.** Tagging is also known as Multiprotocol Label Switching (MPLS).
- ❍ **B.** Tagging allows better use of QoS.
- ❍ **C.** Tagging makes use of the IP header and the tag.
- ❍ **D.** Tagging guarantees minimum data delivery rates.

Quick Answer: **158**
Detailed Answer: **169**

Quick Check

93. What is an older form of scripting that was used extensively in early web systems?

Quick Answer: **158**
Detailed Answer: **169**

- ❍ **A.** ActiveX
- ❍ **B.** WAP
- ❍ **C.** CGI
- ❍ **D.** ODBC

94. What standard was finalized in 2002 and defines the development and deployment of broadband wireless metropolitan-area networks?

Quick Answer: **158**
Detailed Answer: **169**

- ❍ **A.** 802.11
- ❍ **B.** 802.16
- ❍ **C.** 802.3
- ❍ **D.** 802.5

95. What routing protocol enables routers on different autonomous systems to share routing information?

Quick Answer: **158**
Detailed Answer: **169**

- ❍ **A.** RIP
- ❍ **B.** OSPF
- ❍ **C.** BGP
- ❍ **D.** IGMP

96. When discussing routing, which of the following best describes a black hole attack?

Quick Answer: **158**
Detailed Answer: **169**

- ❍ **A.** Using OSPF to perform partial updates
- ❍ **B.** Using RIP to perform full updates
- ❍ **C.** Transmitting bogus routing updates to redirect traffic for a man-in-the-middle attack
- ❍ **D.** Transmitting traffic to a nonexistent router or network

97. In terms of Ethernet, what is a backoff algorithm?

Quick Answer: **158**
Detailed Answer: **169**

- ❍ **A.** A random collision timer
- ❍ **B.** A transmission method
- ❍ **C.** A latency prevention mechanism
- ❍ **D.** A CSMA/CA technology

98. What do wireless LAN technologies use?

Quick Answer: **158**
Detailed Answer: **169**

- ❍ **A.** Polling
- ❍ **B.** Token passing
- ❍ **C.** CSMA/CA
- ❍ **D.** CSMA/CD

Quick Check

99. The Boot Protocol uses the same ports as what?

Quick Answer: **158**
Detailed Answer: **169**

- ❍ **A.** SNMP
- ❍ **B.** DHCP
- ❍ **C.** DNS
- ❍ **D.** ARP

100. Which of the following statements about a bridge is incorrect?

Quick Answer: **158**
Detailed Answer: **170**

- ❍ **A.** It filters traffic based on IP address.
- ❍ **B.** It forwards broadcast traffic.
- ❍ **C.** It does not alter header information.
- ❍ **D.** It forwards traffic to all ports if the targeted address is unknown.

101. Which of the following items is different in 3G cellular than older 1G and 2G implementations?

Quick Answer: **158**
Detailed Answer: **170**

- ❍ **A.** Supports packet switching
- ❍ **B.** Interfaces with IrDa
- ❍ **C.** First to support caller ID
- ❍ **D.** First to support voicemail

102. IPv6 will no longer make use of ARP. Which of the following will be used in its place?

Quick Answer: **158**
Detailed Answer: **170**

- ❍ **A.** Directed physical addressing
- ❍ **B.** Nonlogical addressing
- ❍ **C.** ARPv6
- ❍ **D.** Network Discovery Protocol

103. What is *not* one of the potential types of VoIP servers?

Quick Answer: **158**
Detailed Answer: **170**

- ❍ **A.** Proxy server
- ❍ **B.** Redirect server
- ❍ **C.** Signaling server
- ❍ **D.** Registrar

104. Transaction signatures (TSIG) are used to secure which of the following?

Quick Answer: **158**
Detailed Answer: **170**

- ❍ **A.** DNS
- ❍ **B.** IPv6
- ❍ **C.** VoIP
- ❍ **D.** HDLC

105. SOCKS can best be described as what?

Quick Answer: **158**
Detailed Answer: **170**

- ❍ **A.** Application-level proxy
- ❍ **B.** Circuit-level proxy
- ❍ **C.** Stateful firewall
- ❍ **D.** Stateless firewall

Quick Check

Practice Questions (True or False)

106. RARP is useful for thin clients.

Quick Answer: **158**
Detailed Answer: **170**

- ❍ True
- ❍ False

107. Plenum-grade cables have a polyvinyl chloride (PVC) jacket covering.

Quick Answer: **158**
Detailed Answer: **170**

- ❍ True
- ❍ False

108. L2TP is a hybrid of PPTP and L2F.

Quick Answer: **158**
Detailed Answer: **170**

- ❍ True
- ❍ False

109. Routers can implement ACLs and stateful inspection.

Quick Answer: **158**
Detailed Answer: **170**

- ❍ True
- ❍ False

110. A proxy server is also known as a circuit-level firewall.

Quick Answer: **158**
Detailed Answer: **170**

- ❍ True
- ❍ False

Practice Questions (Mix and Match)

111. Match each attack with its definition.

Quick Answer: **158**
Detailed Answer: **170**

A. Sniffing: _____

B. War dialing: _____

C. Man-in-the-middle attack: _____

D. DNS spoofing: _____

E. ARP poisoning: _____

F. Salami attack: _____

1. Financial attack

2. Passive attack

3. Considered a WAN attack

4. Phreaking

5. Corrupts MAC and IP addresses

6. Bypasses identification and authentication

Quick Check Answer Key

1. B
2. A
3. C
4. B
5. A
6. D
7. C
8. D
9. B
10. B
11. C
12. D
13. B
14. D
15. A
16. A
17. B
18. B
19. D
20. C
21. D
22. A
23. A
24. C
25. B
26. A
27. C
28. B
29. B
30. D
31. C
32. B
33. B
34. B
35. C
36. C
37. D
38. A
39. C
40. A
41. D
42. B
43. D
44. C
45. A
46. D
47. A
48. D
49. C
50. D
51. B
52. A
53. D
54. C
55. B
56. D
57. C
58. B
59. B
60. B
61. D
62. C
63. D
64. B
65. B
66. D
67. C
68. B
69. B
70. C
71. B
72. C
73. A
74. C
75. B
76. D
77. B
78. C
79. D
80. A
81. D
82. C
83. D
84. D
85. D
86. A
87. D
88. A
89. C
90. B
91. B
92. C
93. C
94. B
95. C
96. D
97. A
98. C
99. B
100. A
101. A
102. D
103. C
104. A
105. B
106. True
107. False
108. True
109. False
110. True
111. **A.** 2
    B. 4
    C. 6
    D. 3
    E. 5
    F. 1

Answers and Explanations

1. **Answer: B.** TCP (Transmission Control Protocol) is considered a connection-oriented protocol because it provides for startup, shutdown, flow control, and acknowledgments. It is covered in detail in RFC 793. UDP (User Datagram Protocol) is connectionless. ICMP (Internet Control Message Protocol) is used for logical errors and diagnostics. ARP (Address Resolution Protocol) is used to resolve known IP addresses to unknown MAC addresses.

2. **Answer: A.** UDP (User Datagram Protocol) is a connectionless protocol that is built for speed. It has low overhead. It often sends data in small blocks, such as 512 bytes, and its header is 8 bytes long. The fields in the header include source port, target port, message length, and checksum. TCP (Transmission Control Protocol) is considered a connection-oriented protocol because it provides for startup, shutdown, flow control, and acknowledgments. It is covered in detail in RFC 793. ICMP (Internet Control Message Protocol) is used for logical errors and diagnostics. ARP (Address Resolution Protocol) is used to resolve known IP addresses to unknown MAC addresses.

3. **Answer: C.** All security is based on the goals of confidentiality, integrity, and availability. Confidentiality refers to limiting information access and disclosure to the set of authorized users. Availability relates to the availability and accessibility of information resources. Integrity refers to the validity of information resources. Accessibility is not provided by the CIA triad.

4. **Answer: B.** Ethernet transmits timing information to the receiver using a "preamble" of alternating 1s and 0s. Its unit of transmission is known as a frame. A frame has three sections: control information, a data field, and a frame check sequence. Although asynchronous is widely used, it suffers from high overhead. All other answers are incorrect because these systems do not use a preamble of 1s and 0s.

5. **Answer: A.** All data transmissions must originate from a single source. As such, only a unicast can be both a source and a destination address.

6. **Answer: D.** CSMA/CD (Carrier Sense Multiple Access Collision Detection) is Ethernet's mode of operation. A device that wants to send a frame must monitor the transmission line. When the line is available, a frame is sent. Afterward, the transmitting device must monitor the line to verify that no collision has taken place. If a collision is detected, the device must resend the frame. Answer A describes collision avoidance. Answers B and C are distracters.

7. **Answer: C.** ISDN is a communication protocol that operates similar to POTS, except that all-digital signaling is used. ISDN uses separate frequencies called channels on a special digital connection. The B channels are used for voice, data, video, and fax services. The D channel is used for signaling by the service provider and user equipment. The D channel operates at a low 16 Kbps, and the B channels operate at a speed up to 64 Kbps.

8. **Answer: D.** Although fax usage is declining, it is still in use and as such offers a service that may be vulnerable to attack. To improve the security of fax transmissions, these machines can be moved from insecure areas to locations where access can be controlled. Activity logs and exception reports are useful in detecting misuse or possible attack. Other useful items for the protection of fax machines and their transmissions include fax encryptors and link encryption. Fax over IP and VoIP are also becoming security issues.

9. **Answer: B.** Not all protocols fit perfectly into the OSI (Open System Interconnect) model, because many were designed for the TCP/IP model. ARP is one example of this, because some books show it at the data link layer and others show it at the network layer. One good way to conceptualize ARP is to remember that it actually operates between the data link and network layers. ARP resolves known IP addresses to unknown MAC addresses. Reverse ARP (RARP) resolves known MAC addresses to unknown IP addresses.

10. **Answer: B.** The layers of the OSI model include physical, data link, network, transport, session, presentation, and application. The OSI model was developed to give the different equipment vendors a common set of rules they could use to communicate with each other. TCP and UDP reside at the transport layer of the OSI model. The transport layer is responsible for host-to-host communication.

11. **Answer: C.** The OSI model was developed in 1984 by the International Organization for Standardization (ISO). The model is based on a specific hierarchy, in which each layer builds on the output of each adjacent layer. It was originally designed as a network communication standard. ISO 7498 describes the OSI model. It defines the responsibilities of each layer.

12. **Answer: D.** ARP (Address Resolution Protocol) is a helper protocol that performs address resolution on a LAN. ARP resolves known IP addresses to unknown physical addresses. The results are stored in the ARP cache. Attackers can manipulate ARP because it is a trusting protocol. Bogus ARP responses are accepted as valid, which can allow attackers to redirect traffic on a switched network. This attack is the basis of a man-in-the-middle attack.

13. **Answer: B.** ARP requests are sent to the broadcast address 0xFFFFFFFFFFFF. Therefore, these remain within the local broadcast domain and do not pass through routers. Physical addresses (MAC) are at Layer 2, and logical addresses (IP) are at Layer 3. Routers are designed to look at logical traffic.

14. **Answer: D.** The network interface layer of the TCP/IP model is equivalent to Layers 1 and 2 of the OSI model. Switches reside at this layer because they are involved in the processing of frames on the LAN. The four layers of the TCP/IP model are (from bottom to top) network interface, internetworking, transport, and application.

15. **Answer: A.** The internetworking layer is home to the IP protocol. Routers are responsible for routing IP and, as such, are the primary piece of equipment found at this layer. The TCP/IP protocol suite is the most widely used networking protocol in the world.

16. **Answer: A.** The protocol field carries the ID number of the next-higher-layer protocol. These values allow IP to demultiplex the data packet as it progresses up the stack. Common protocol numbers include 0x01 (ICMP), 0x06 (TCP), 0x11 (UDP), and 0x58 (IGRP). FTP resides at the application layer and is addressed by TCP port 21. FTP also uses TCP port 20 for data transfer.

17. **Answer: B.** Clear-text usernames and passwords are a major problem of email. Anyone who has access to the network can potentially sniff this information, thereby breaching confidentiality. Although spam is a nuisance, it is not a security risk. Spam is the most widely despised and unwanted aspect of email. Spam is technically known as unsolicited commercial email (UCE).

18. **Answer: B.** Dialup is slower and usually is connected for a short period of time. It also has different IP addresses when connections take place. Unlike dialup modems, cable modems and DSL are always connected to the Internet. This makes these computers prime targets for hackers. These individuals look for poorly protected always-on connections to use for DDoS, illegal wares, and other malicious activities. Dialup modems and dialup services represent a much lower security risk.

19. **Answer: D.** A VPN (virtual private network) is a secure private connection. It allows remote users to use the public Internet for a secure connection. VPNs are possible because of tunneling protocols. These use encapsulation and encryption for security.

20. **Answer: C.** PAP (Password Authentication Protocol) is the least secure type of authentication. PAP is used by remote users for authentication. It is insecure because it sends credentials in clear text. Anyone using a network sniffer could capture these credentials and use them to gain access to unauthorized resources. Other well-known authentication protocols include CHAP (Challenge Handshake Authentication Protocol) and EAP (Extensible Authentication Protocol). IPsec is a VPN protocol.

21. **Answer: D.** There are several RAID levels. RAID 3 provides fault tolerance by spreading data over two or more drives at the byte level. The parity information is sent to a dedicated disk. RAID is commonly used on servers or in situations in which data integrity and/or availability are important.

22. **Answer: A.** TCP is the choice for reliability, whereas UDP is used for speed. The TCP header contains all the items needed for reliable network communication. Some of the features that ensure the reliability of TCP sessions include connection establishment, flow control, adaptive timeouts, and sequence numbers. TCP is covered in detail in RFCs 793 and 2581 and others.

23. **Answer: A.** RAID (redundant array of independent disks) is used to provide fault tolerance or performance gains. It functions by spreading data over two or more drives. The most common levels of RAID are as follows:

    RAID 0: Multiple drive striping

    RAID 1: Disk mirroring

    RAID 3: Single parity drive

    RAID 5: Distributed parity information

24. **Answer: C.** Two distinct protocols operate at the transport layer. These protocols, TCP and UDP, behave quite differently. TCP is a connection-oriented protocol that provides reliable connection-oriented features to applications, whereas UDP is simplistic and connectionless by design. ARP resides lower in the stack because it resolves known IP addresses to unknown MAC addresses. IP resides at the network layer of the OSI model, as does ICMP.

25. **Answer: B.** DNS (domain name service) resolves fully qualified domain names (FQDNs) to IP addresses. DNS maintains a hierarchy of servers. In other words, if the initial server you query does not know the domain name you are looking for, the service queries the next DNS server in the chain. It functions as a helper protocol and is a key component in the functionality and operation of the Internet. DNS receives a name (such as www.hackthestack.com) and converts it into a corresponding IP address (63.240.93.157).

26. **Answer: A.** Routing protocols determine the optimum path by either hop count or link state. RIP versions 1 and 2 base their routing decision on hops. This underlying process is known as the Bellman Ford algorithm. These distance vector algorithms are well-suited for small, simple networks.

27. **Answer: C.** Security is not a product but a process. As such, security can be divided into three distinct phases: prevention, detection, and response. Without detection-based systems, security breaches cannot be discovered.

28. **Answer: B.** The two primary types of intrusion detection engines are signature and anomaly. Signature-based intrusion detection systems work much like virus scanners in that they have databases of known attacks. Although these systems work well, they are vulnerable to new exploits or those not yet added to the systems' database. Anomaly-based intrusion detection systems look for a deviation from normal behavior. For example, these systems would quickly send an alert if someone who worked the day shift attempted multiple logins at 3 a.m.

29. **Answer: B.** IPsec operates at the network layer of the OSI model. IPsec can be used to ensure integrity, confidentiality, and authenticity. Its two modes of operation are tunnel and transport. IPsec users are free to perform security assessments to determine which mode of operation is optimum for their organization.

30. **Answer: D.** IPsec (Internet Protocol Security) is on open standard developed by the Internet Engineering Task Force. Since its inception, it has been and continues to be one of the most popular choices of VPN protocols. It can operate in one of two modes: transport mode or tunnel mode. Transport mode encrypts only the data. Tunnel mode encrypts the entire packet.

31. **Answer: C.** A smurf attack uses ICMP packets with forged source and target addresses. The packets are addressed to the local broadcast address, and the source address is pointed toward the device to be attacked. The result is that all devices on the broadcast network respond to this spoofed ICMP ping packet. This floods the target device, thereby preventing legitimate traffic. Answer A describes a ping of death. Answer B describes a SYN attack. Answer D describes a Fraggle attack.

32. **Answer: B.** IPsec uses two protocols: authentication header and encapsulated security payload. The authentication header provides nonrepudiation, integrity, and authentication. The encapsulated security payload provides confidentiality because it shields the payload from unauthorized access. The configuration of IPsec requires the establishment of a security association. This association is a one-way connection, which means that at least two security associations are required for an IPsec session to commence.

33. **Answer: B.** With 16 bits reserved for the host field, there is a total of 65,534 host addresses, two of which cannot be assigned to host devices. These two addresses are reserved addresses. All host bits off, address 0, is the network address. All host bits on, 65,536, is the broadcast address for the network.

34. **Answer: B.** Classful addressing, as specified in RFC 791, designates four primary classes of IP addresses:

    Class A: 1 to 127

    Class B: 128 to 191

    Class C: 192 to 223

    Class D: 224 to 239

224.0.0.1 is a Class D address and therefore is reserved for multicast purposes. Multicast addressing is used as a mechanism to contact groups of devices without the overhead of sending individual packets to each device.

35. **Answer: C.** This is commonly called a DMZ (demilitarized zone). DMZs offer several advantages to security professionals. They allow an organization to distance critical internal services from the Internet and web services. They enable the organization to design a network that has a layered defense. This design allows some filtering of traffic before Internet users can reach web-based services. Traffic attempting to proceed deeper into the network must pass this inspection. Intranets are internal to an organization, and extranets are external; typically they may be shared with a business partner.

36. **Answer: C.** DAT is not a form of NAT. NAT (network address translation) allows organizations connected to the Internet to use private addresses. These same private addresses can be used by many different organizations because they are nonroutable and are hidden to the direct Internet. These are the three primary types of NAT:

    PAT: Port address translation permits only outbound sessions and allows one public address to be used by many internal, private addresses.

    Dynamic NAT: This method of translation allows an external address to be mapped directly to an internal address. This method is useful when an organization has a pool of external IP addresses that must be shared among many internal devices.

    Static NAT: This method of NAT allows one internal address to be permanently mapped to a specific external address.

37. **Answer: D.** S/MIME (Secure Multipurpose Internet Mail Extensions) is an application layer security protocol used to send emails securely. RIP is a routing protocol and is not used for security services. SSL (Secure Socket Layer) and SKIP (Simple Key Management for Internet Protocol) are examples of transport layer protocols.

38. **Answer: A.** Private addressing is defined in RFC 1918. The addresses allow the creation of pockets of IP addresses that are independent of each other and are not connected to the Internet. Private IP addressing is composed of three blocks of nonroutable IP addresses to be used by organizations: 10.0.0.0/8, 172.16.0.0/12, and 192.168.0.0/16. Answer C is incorrect because it is the address used for loopback testing. Answer D is incorrect because it is the address used for Automatic Private IP Addressing (APIPA).

39. **Answer: C.** A router is considered a stateless firewall because it treats each packet individually. A router has no way of maintaining a record of which packets respond to which connection. Therefore, if a packet meets the condition of the rule set in the ACL, it is passed as valid network traffic. Although these devices are easy to deploy, they offer only limited protection. It is best to use a router as a screening device in conjunction with another chokepoint or firewall. This principle is known as defense-in-depth. Answer A is incorrect because routers are already in place, so there is no additional cost. Answer B is incorrect because routers are not difficult to configure. Answer D is incorrect because ACLs are not plug-ins, but simply a script that must be configured in a specific order to be effective.

40. **Answer: A.** Serial Line Internet Protocol (SLIP) is a very old protocol that was used to connect systems by means of a modem. SLIP offers no secure services. Protocols used for VPNs include PPTP (Point-to-Point Tunneling Protocol), L2TP (Layer 2 Tunneling Protocol), and L2F (Layer 2 Forwarding Protocol). When properly configured, these protocols allow users to establish a secure tunnel through the Internet.

41. **Answer: D.** Although answers B and C are VPN protocols, they do not fit the description. L2F was developed by Cisco and operates at Layer 2 of the OSI model. Answer A is incorrect because TACACS is a control protocol.

42. **Answer: B.** Extensible Authentication Protocol (EAP) is the method of choice because it can work with more than just passwords as authentication. EAP can use token cards, MD5 challenge, and digital certificates as possible authentication mechanisms. Although Password Authentication Protocol (PAP) is used for RAS, it sends passwords in clear text. Challenge Handshake Authentication Protocol (CHAP) uses an MD5 challenge. Answer D describes a method of sending IP packets over phone lines.

43. **Answer: D.** Although wireless is very popular, you must be careful when installing a wireless system. Some cordless phones do operate on the same frequencies, but this should not be the driving consideration in this decision. WEP has been shown to be vulnerable. Originally the Wired Equivalent Privacy (WEP) protocol was developed to address this issue. It was designed to provide the same privacy that a user would have on a wired network. WEP is based on the RC4 symmetric encryption standard and uses either 64-bit or 128-bit keys. However, the keys are not really this many bits, because a 24-bit initialization vector (IV) is used to provide randomness. So the "real" key is actually 40 or 104 bits long. WEP has been surpassed by WPA and WPA2. Other controls, such as PEAP and LEAP (and the v2 versions of both), are also used to protect wireless communication. Encryption is now provided by AES.

44. **Answer: C.** DHCP (Dynamic Host Configuration Protocol) is an effective method of centralized management. IP addresses can be managed from one location. This can ease administration and make changes easier. DHCP has four steps: discover, offer, request, and acknowledgment. APIPA is an automatic address scheme that is used when no address server can be found. RARP resolves MAC addresses to IP addresses. Host tables do not provide IP addressing services.

45. **Answer: A.** FTP (File Transfer Protocol), SNMP (Simple Network Management Protocol), and Telnet are all considered insecure because they transmit information in clear text. SSH (Secure Shell) encrypts data before transmitting it over the network. SNMP versions 1 and 2 are cleartext. SNMPv3 supports encryption. SSHv1 is considered vulnerable.

46. **Answer: D.** The RADIUS protocol is an IETF standard and the most widely deployed AAA solution. RADIUS has been implemented by most of the major operating system manufacturers. RADIUS can be managed centrally. Although the name denotes dialup, it is used with many more modern solutions, such as 802.1x.

47. **Answer: A.** The two primary ways in which routers can deal with ICMP messages are reject and drop. Reject allows failed traffic to create an ICMP error message and return it to the sending device. Drop silently discards any traffic that is not allowed into the network or that creates an ICMP error message.

48. **Answer: D.** Category 5 can support cable distances of up to 328 feet (100 meters). These cables are spliced to RJ-45 connectors on each end and contain four pairs of wire within each run.

49. **Answer: C.** A worm is a piece of self-replicating code. Worms use parts of the OS that are automatic and invisible to the user. At no time does the worm need assistance from the end user. The first known worm was released into the wild by Robert Morris in 1988. Hence, it was called the Morris worm.

50. **Answer: D.** Single-mode fiber-optic cable can be extended up to 200 miles before regeneration is required. These tiny fibers of glass have a core of about 8 microns and depend on laser light for digital signaling. Answer A describes the maximum distance of multimode fiber.

51. **Answer: B.** Traceroute increments the TTL (time-to-live) by 1 for each hop discovered along the way to the destination device. This causes the packet to expire and return IP address information about that particular device. TCP traceroute tools also are available. Answers A, C, and D are incorrect because they are not manipulated by the traceroute process.

52. **Answer: A.** Plenum-grade cabling is required to meet fire codes and protect the organization's employees. Nonplenum-grade cables, such as those coated with PVC (polyvinyl chloride), can give off noxious gas when burned or exposed to high heat. Proper consideration should be given when choosing a network cable type and location. Loose cables present a potential trip hazard. There is no such standard as A1 fire-rated.

53. **Answer: D.** Ethernet is an example of baseband technology. Baseband technologies use the full spectrum for a single transmission. DSL, cable modems, and cable television divide the available spectrum into separate channels, thereby allowing different types of data to all be transmitted at the same time.

54. **Answer: C.** IPv4 uses unicast, multicast, and broadcast. Although anycast is not an option, it is available to IPv6. With this new type of address, the network delivers the packet that has this address to anyone in an anycast group.

55. **Answer: B.** A Token Ring network uses a ring topology in which all computers are connected by a unidirectional transmission loop. Answer A is incorrect because Ethernet is an example of a star or bus topology. Answers C and D are not the proper technologies.

56. **Answer: D.** Switches typically come in two designs: cut-through and store-and-forward. Cut-through switches examine only a portion of the frame that contains the destination MAC address, thereby increasing throughput. The term does not apply to the board design or provide QoS. Port spanning is the ability to mirror traffic from one port to the next.

57. **Answer: C.** Many organizations use intranets to provide internal communications between employees and resources. Extranets give external business partners and clients access to specific company resources.

58. **Answer: B.** T1 lines are composed of 24 DS0 (64KB) channels. This gives a total multiplexed rate of 24 * 64KB = 1.54Mbps. T1s are considered a circuit-switched technology.

59. **Answer: B.** DDS (Digital Data Service) is an example of a circuit-switched technology. DDS was developed in the 1970s and was one of the first digital services used by telephone companies. It has a maximum data rate of 56 KB. Frame Relay, X.25, and ATM are all examples of packet-switched technologies.

60. **Answer: B.** Although all the possible answers are important, it's critical that a legal agreement be reviewed and signed before the assessment begins.

61. **Answer: D.** T-carrier service is used for leased lines. A leased line is locked in between two locations. It is very secure. Users pay a fixed monthly fee for this service regardless of usage. The most common T-carriers are T1 and T3. T3 lines are composed of

672 DS0 (64 KB) channels. This gives a total multiplexed rate of 672 * 64 KB = 44.736 Mbps. T3s are deployed as dedicated lines that can carry voice and data. They typically are sold to organizations as a point-to-point service.

62. **Answer: C.** Cut-through switches are faster because they read only the beginning of the Ethernet frame. Store-and-forward switches read the entire frame before processing the data. Therefore, the decision of which to use comes down to a choice of speed versus reliability.

63. **Answer: D.** MAC addresses are 6 bytes long (48 bits). The first 3 bytes identify the manufacturer of the NIC card. These 3 bytes are called the OUI (Organizational Unique Identifier). The IEEE is responsible for assigning these codes. A complete listing can be found at http://standards.ieee.org/regauth/oui/oui.txt. There are some problems with the first 3 identifying bytes due to poor engineering practices, spoofing, and counterfeiting.

64. **Answer: B.** War dialing is the process of calling large numbers of phone numbers in search of a modem. Although rather dated, this method is still used to attempt to find out-of-band access points into a network. A good example of war dialing can be seen in the 1983 movie *WarGames.* Programs used to war dial include ToneLoc. Answers A and C refer to hacking technologies associated with wireless networks. War dialing is gaining resurgence because of the ability to use VoIP (which is cheaper and more anonymous).

65. **Answer: B.** Switches operate at Layer 2 of the OSI model. Switches, in the classic Layer 2 perspective, provide physical segmentation because they separate collision domains. Port spanning is used to allow one port to see another port's traffic.

66. **Answer: D.** Access control, authentication, and auditing are the three pillars of security that are used to support CIA (confidentiality, integrity, and availability). Access control is concerned with the methods that give users access to network equipment and resources. Authentication is the act of validating that the person attempting to use network equipment or resources is who he says he is. Auditing is the act of monitoring users, events, errors, and access for compliance and accountability. When used in conjunction with the principle of least privilege, these items can be used to effectively control and monitor company resources. The three A's of security are discussed in detail in RFC 3127.

67. **Answer: C.** Full, incremental, and differential are the three basic types of backups. This is a critical operation, because it is only a matter of time before hard drives fail or other disasters happen. Policies should be developed to determine what type of backup procedure is right for your organization. Full backups take the longest to perform, whereas incremental backups take the least amount of time.

68. **Answer: B.** Hijacking is the process of poisoning someone's ARP table with bogus ARP responses. Because ARP is a trusting protocol, no verification is used to ensure that received ARP replies match a previous ARP request. This allows the attacker to issue bogus ARP responses that can be used to poison the ARP table. This poisoned ARP table allows the attacker to redirect communication and attempt a man-in-the-middle attack. Hunt, Cain and Abel, and ETTERCAP are several of the tools commonly used for this type of attack.

69. **Answer: B.** Flooding is the process of sending large amounts of traffic onto the network. The goal is to flood the switch's CAM (Content Addressable Memory) with so many MAC addresses that it overflows and begins to operate like a hub. The other method by which

an attacker can overcome the functionality of a switch is with ARP poisoning. ARP poisoning is the process of sending faked ARP response packets in an attempt to change entries in the victim's ARP table, thereby redirecting traffic to the attacker.

70. **Answer: C.** Host-based IDSs monitor the OS continuously and can set off triggers or send alarms if they detect inappropriate activity. Some IDSs can even change firewall or router rule sets to prohibit certain types of traffic or block suspicious IP addresses.

71. **Answer: B.** The confidentiality of these protocols in increasing order is L2TP (no encryption is provided), WEP (weak encryption, shared key authentication), PPTP (PPP with MPPE, MS-CHAP, or EAP-TLS authentication), and TKIP (encryption with dynamic keying, and all EAP authentications are supported).

72. **Answer: C.** The TTL is an 8-bit value that is decremented at each router. Each router decrements the TTL by at least 1, and when the value reaches 0, the router discards the packet and returns an ICMP message to the sender.

73. **Answer: A.** The protocol used the value 16 to denote an unreachable network. RIPv1 had no authentication. RIPv2 allowed for cleartext or MD5 hashed passwords. Although TTL can count up to 254, remember that RIP was an internal routing protocol.

74. **Answer: C.** Wormhole attacks result from an attacker tunneling valid data to an accomplice who can replay the data out of context. A black hole is the destination when data is sent to a nonexistent receiver. Tunneling is the method used to move the data between the attackers. The out-of-band attack was a DoS attack against Windows 95 and Windows for Workgroups (WFW) machines.

75. **Answer: B.** Honeypots are installed in the DMZ, or a screened subnet. (The original design was to install on the Internet directly, and temporarily, to study attack styles.) The honeypot would not be installed on the firewall itself (screened host). Policies and logging that employees are subjected to must be established as normal business procedures before any malicious behavior is noted. You would not install honeypots on all employee computers.

76. **Answer: D.** AH provides for higher integrity. ESP provides for confidentiality. Transport adjacency combines AH and ESP. Iterated tunneling means that messages using IPsec can be placed inside other tunnels using IPsec, but it does not state what level of security IPsec is being deployed with.

77. **Answer: B.** The Open System Interconnect (OSI) model was developed in 1984 by the International Organization for Standardization (ISO). The model is based on a specific hierarchy, in which each layer builds on the output of each adjacent layer. The correct layers of the OSI model are physical, data link, network, transport, session, presentation, and application.

78. **Answer: C.** The proper order for the application, transport, data link, and session layers is Simple Network Management Protocol, Stream Control Transmission Protocol, Serial Line Internet Protocol, and Structured Query Language. It is a good idea to know what protocols can be found at specific layers of the OSI model before attempting the CISSP exam.

79. **Answer: D.** SSL is actually composed of two protocols and works closely around the transport and session layers. This makes some potential questions tricky, because the exam may not ask you *at* what layer the protocol works but *between* what layers the

protocol works. This is because the OSI model tries to draw clear definitions around some protocols that actually straddle several layers.

80. **Answer: A.** Class D addresses run from 224.0.0.0 to 239.255.255.255. 241.0.0.0 is a Class E address. 223.0.0.0 and 192.168.0.0 are Class C addresses.

81. **Answer: D.** Modems are asynchronous devices. They transmit data that can travel at any time, can be any length, and use stop and start delimiters. Answers A, B, and C all describe synchronous communication.

82. **Answer: C.** Wireless Application Protocol (WAP) was designed to meet the needs of a variety of wireless devices. Some of these devices may have a full TCP/IP stack, and others may be small, mobile, low-powered devices. As such, WAP has three classes of service. Class 1 is anonymous authentication, Class 2 is server authentication, and Class 3 is two-way client/server authentication. Both WEP with RC4 and WPA2 with AES would not meet these requirements because they were simply designed for wireless security.

83. **Answer: D.** i-Mode is designed for cell phones and has achieved success in Japan. i-Mode uses a custom version of HTML known as compact HTML (cHTML). WAP uses Wireless Markup Language. Both WEP with RC4 and WPA2 with AES would not meet these requirements because they are simply designed for wireless security.

84. **Answer: D.** Point-to-Point Protocol (PPP) is widely used for dialup connections and is a replacement for Serial Line Internet Protocol (SLIP). Internet Message Access Protocol (IMAP) is used for email, so it would not work given the requirements. IPsec is used to secure Internet traffic, not to allow for connectivity over modems. Point-to-Point Tunneling Protocol (PPTP) is designed for VPNs.

85. **Answer: D.** Serial Line Internet Protocol (SLIP) is an older dialup technology. Because of its shortcomings, it was replaced with Point-to-Point Protocol (PPP). Internet Message Access Protocol (IMAP) is used for email, so it would not work given the requirements. IPsec is used to secure Internet traffic, not to allow for connectivity over modems. Point-to-Point Tunneling Protocol (PPTP) is designed for VPNs.

86. **Answer: A.** Serial Line Internet Protocol (SLIP) offers very little, but it can relay packets over a dialup line. SLIP cannot provide authentication, does not support multiple protocols, and does not support link monitoring.

87. **Answer: D.** Internet Message Access Protocol (IMAP) is one of the most prevalent standards for Internet mail. IMAP allows mail to be forwarded and stored in information areas called stores. IMAP also allows for faster email access. POP2 and POP3 are versions of Post Office Protocol. POP is cleartext and not as capable as IMAP. Simple Mail Transfer Protocol (SMTP) is used for outgoing mail.

88. **Answer: A.** Cell phones have progressed through what are known as generations. 1G cell phones have a target data rate of 2 Kbps, 2G cell phones have a target data rate of 14.4 Kbps, 3G cell phones have a target data rate of 2 Mbps, and 4G cell phones have a target data rate of 100 Mbps to 1 Gbps.

89. **Answer: C.** Cell phones have progressed through what are known as generations. 1G cell phones have a target data rate of 2 Kbps, 2G cell phones have a target data rate of 14.4 Kbps, 3G cell phones have a target data rate of 2 Mbps, and 4G cell phones have a target data rate of at least 100 Mbps.

90. **Answer: B.** Microwave would be the best choice because it offers high bandwidth and can easily be installed as line of site between the two facilities. Twisted pair and coaxial are not optimum solutions because the land between the sites belongs to a third party. Infrared is designed for very short distances.

91. **Answer: B.** One big concern is how data is protected after it leaves the Wireless Application Protocol (WAP) gateway. The industry-standard solution is to use Secure Socket Layer (SSL). Answer A is incorrect because SSL protects the data much more than common clear text. Even if WAP is configured for mutual authentication, that only protects the data between the WAP gateway and the client. WAP and i-Mode are competing technologies, so answer D is incorrect.

92. **Answer: C.** Tagging, which is also known as Multiprotocol Label Switching (MPLS), allows better use of QoS. Tagging also guarantees minimum data delivery rates. Tagging does not make use of the IP header and the tag. That would defeat the purpose that the tag is used to pass the information from one device to the next. Only when the information is at the last hop is the header examined. This speeds up delivery.

93. **Answer: C.** CGI scripts were an early web technology used to capture data from a user using simple forms. CGI is not widely used in new systems and has been replaced with technologies such as Java and ActiveX. Wireless Application Protocol (WAP) was designed to meet the needs of a variety of wireless devices. Some of these devices may have a full TCP/IP stack, and others may be small, mobile, low-powered devices. WAP is not used for scripting. Open Database Connectivity (ODBC) is also not used for scripting; it is a database technology.

94. **Answer: B.** 802.16 is the IEEE standard that defines the development and deployment of broadband wireless metropolitan-area networks. 802.3 is for Ethernet, 802.11 is for wireless LAN communication, and 802.5 is the standard for Token Ring.

95. **Answer: C.** Border Gateway Protocol (BGP) is an exterior routing protocol that enables routers on different autonomous systems to share routing information. BGP is widely used on the Internet. RIP and OSPF are interior routing protocols. IGMP is a router management protocol used to communicate group information.

96. **Answer: D.** Some routing protocols, such as RIP, have no means of authentication. This allows an attacker to use ICMP or bogus routing updates to redirect traffic to a nonexistent router or network, which results in a denial of service. Using RIP or OSPF for partial or full updates would be considered their normal behavior and not a black hole attack. A man-in-the-middle attack is done for interception, not DoS.

97. **Answer: A.** Ethernet maintains a method to reduce the effect of collisions. Should a collision occur, both systems are subject to a random back-off timer that causes each system to wait a random amount of time before retransmitting. It is not a transmission method or a latency prevention mechanism, and it is not used in CSMA/CA.

98. **Answer: C.** Wireless systems use CSMA/CA. This allows each wireless device to signal that it will transmit before the event occurs. Wireless devices do not use polling, token passing, or CSMA/CD.

99. **Answer: B.** BootP uses the same ports as DHCP, UDP ports 67 and 68. SNMP uses UDP ports 161 and 162. DNS uses TCP/UDP port 53. ARP does not use a port because it is a lower-layer protocol.

100. Answer: A. Bridges are dated device, so you probably will not hear too much about them outside the test environment. Bridges forward broadcast traffic, do not alter header information, and forward traffic to all ports if the targeted address is unknown. Bridges are Layer 2 devices and do not filter based on IP addresses.

101. Answer: A. One of the big differences between 3G and older technologies is that 3G was the first to support packet switching. Support for circuit switching, IrDa, and caller ID was present in older technologies.

102. Answer: D. While ARP goes away in IPv6, it is replaced by Network Discovery Protocol. Answers A, B, and D are incorrect because they do not properly describe the replacement for ARP.

103. Answer: C. VoIP servers can use several types of servers, which include proxy servers, registrar servers, and redirect servers. A signaling server is not a valid category.

104. Answer: A. TSIGs are used by DNS to implement secure DNS services. Because DNS lookups are generally a UDP-based network service, it has several major inherent security vulnerabilities, and TSIGs are useful for securing communications between DNS servers and helping prevent DNS spoofing. Answers B, C, and D are not associated with TSIGs.

105. Answer: B. SOCKS can best be described as a circuit-level proxy. Because it does not provide detailed protocol-specific control, it cannot be categorized as an application proxy, stateful firewall, or stateless firewall.

106. Answer: True. Reverse Address Resolution Protocol (RARP) is used to resolve known physical addresses to unknown IP address and therefore would be helpful for a thin client.

107. Answer: False. PVC is toxic during fires and should not be used in areas where people are located.

108. Answer: True. This was an agreed-upon standard by Microsoft and Cisco.

109. Answer: False. Routers can implement ACLs, but they perform stateless inspection.

110. Answer: True. Proxy servers can be configured as circuit-level firewalls. As such, they cause a break in the connection between the client and the server.

111. The answers are as follows:

- **A.** Sniffing: **2.** Passive attack
- **B.** War dialing: **4.** Phreaking
- **C.** Man-in-the-middle attack: **6.** Bypasses identification and authentication
- **D.** DNS spoofing: **3.** Considered a WAN attack
- **E.** ARP poisoning: **5.** Corrupts MAC and IP addresses
- **F.** Salami attack: **1.** Financial attack

Sniffing is a passive attack. War dialing is used to find unsecure modems and is considered a phreaking attack. Man-in-the-middle attacks bypass identification and authentication. DNS spoofing is considered a WAN attack. ARP poisoning corrupts MAC and IP addresses. A salami attack is a financial attack.

CHAPTER SIX

Business Continuity and Disaster Recovery Planning

The Business Continuity Planning and Disaster Recovery Planning domain addresses the issues businesses face whenever a natural or man-made act threatens the continuation of business. Whereas other domains are concerned with preventing and mitigating risk, this domain works under the assumption that these items have or will have happened. Therefore, it is focused on the tasks needed to keep critical business services operational and on how to recover quickly while protecting the safety of the employees. This is an important domain, so expect to see questions on the exam about all areas of business continuity and disaster recovery. As an example, you need to understand that there is no demonstrated recovery unless the plan has been tested.

The following list gives you some key areas of knowledge from the Business Continuity domain that you should know for the CISSP exam:

- Policy
- Roles and teams
- BIA
- Data backups, vaulting, journaling, shadowing
- Alternate sites
- Emergency response
- Required notifications
- Tests

Quick Check

Practice Questions

1. Place the following four elements of the Business Continuity Plan in the proper order.

Quick Answer: **195**
Detailed Answer: **196**

- ❍ **A.** Scope and plan initiation, plan approval and implementation, business impact assessment, business continuity plan development
- ❍ **B.** Scope and plan initiation, business impact assessment, business continuity plan development, plan approval and implementation
- ❍ **C.** Business impact assessment, scope and plan initiation, business continuity plan development, plan approval and implementation
- ❍ **D.** Plan approval and implementation, business impact assessment, scope and plan initiation, business continuity plan development

2. Risk assessment is a critical component of the BCP process. As such, which risk-assessment method is scenario-driven and does not assign numeric values to specific assets?

Quick Answer: **195**
Detailed Answer: **196**

- ❍ **A.** Qualitative Risk Assessment
- ❍ **B.** Statistical Weighted Risk Assessment
- ❍ **C.** Quantitative Risk Assessment
- ❍ **D.** Asset-Based Risk Assessment

3. Which of the following best describes the concept and purpose of BCP?

Quick Answer: **195**
Detailed Answer: **196**

- ❍ **A.** BCPs are used to reduce outage times.
- ❍ **B.** BCPs and procedures are put in place for the response to an emergency.
- ❍ **C.** BCPs guarantee the reliability of standby systems.
- ❍ **D.** BCPs are created to prevent interruptions to normal business activity.

4. What are the three goals of a business impact analysis?

Quick Answer: **195**
Detailed Answer: **196**

- ❍ **A.** Downtime estimation, resource requirements, defining the continuity strategy
- ❍ **B.** Defining the continuity strategy, criticality prioritization, resource requirements
- ❍ **C.** Criticality prioritization, downtime estimation, documenting the continuity strategy
- ❍ **D.** Criticality prioritization, downtime estimation, resource requirements

Quick Check

5. Which of the following is the number-one priority for all Business Continuity Plans (BCPs) and Disaster Recovery Plans (DRPs)?

- ❍ **A.** The reduction of potential critical outages
- ❍ **B.** The minimization of potential outages
- ❍ **C.** The elimination of potential outages
- ❍ **D.** The protection and welfare of employees

Quick Answer: **195**
Detailed Answer: **196**

6. During which step of the BIA do implementers ensure that all critical business processes are identified and ranked?

- ❍ **A.** Criticality prioritization
- ❍ **B.** Defining the continuity strategy
- ❍ **C.** Resource requirements
- ❍ **D.** Downtime estimation

Quick Answer: **195**
Detailed Answer: **196**

7. During the BCP process, which group directs the planning, implementation, and development of the test procedures?

- ❍ **A.** Senior business unit management
- ❍ **B.** BCP committee
- ❍ **C.** Executive management staff
- ❍ **D.** Functional business units

Quick Answer: **195**
Detailed Answer: **196**

8. Concerns arose many years ago regarding the integrity of the international business dealings of U.S. corporations. Bribery, for instance, was not unheard of. Which 1977 law imposes civil and criminal penalties on organizations that fail to act responsibly?

- ❍ **A.** U.S. Computer Act
- ❍ **B.** Gramm-Leach-Bliley Act
- ❍ **C.** FCPA
- ❍ **D.** HIPAA

Quick Answer: **195**
Detailed Answer: **196**

9. During a BIA, a vulnerability assessment is usually performed. What is its purpose?

- ❍ **A.** To determine the financial cost of preventing an identified vulnerability
- ❍ **B.** To comply with due diligence requirements
- ❍ **C.** To determine the impact of the loss of a critical business function
- ❍ **D.** To determine the nonmonetary cost to the organization of the loss of a critical business function

Quick Answer: **195**
Detailed Answer: **197**

Quick Check

10. Which of the following elements of the BCP process includes the completion of a vulnerability assessment?

Quick Answer: 195
Detailed Answer: 197

❍ A. Plan approval and implementation
❍ B. Business impact assessment
❍ C. Scope and plan initiation
❍ D. Business continuity plan development

11. Which phase of the BIA has the objective of making sure that the most time-sensitive processes receive the most resources to help prevent or reduce a potential outage?

Quick Answer: 195
Detailed Answer: 197

❍ A. Criticality prioritization
❍ B. Documenting the continuity strategy
❍ C. Resource requirements
❍ D. Downtime estimation

12. What is the practice of routing traffic through different cable facilities?

Quick Answer: 195
Detailed Answer: 197

❍ A. Alternate routing
❍ B. Long-haul diversity
❍ C. Diverse routing
❍ D. Last-mile protection

13. Which of the following is an example of risk transference?

Quick Answer: 195
Detailed Answer: 197

❍ A. Spare equipment
❍ B. Insurance
❍ C. Offsite storage
❍ D. Fire suppression

14. During the BCP process, which group identifies and prioritizes time-critical systems that are of great importance to an organization?

Quick Answer: 195
Detailed Answer: 197

❍ A. Senior management
❍ B. BCP committee
❍ C. Functional business units
❍ D. Executive management staff

15. Which phase of the BCP process involves getting senior management sign-off?

Quick Answer: 195
Detailed Answer: 197

❍ A. Plan approval and implementation
❍ B. Business impact assessment
❍ C. Scope and plan initiation
❍ D. Business continuity plan development

Quick Check

16. Houston-based Sea Breeze Industries has determined that there is a possibility that it may be hit by a hurricane once every 10 years. The losses from such an event are calculated to be $1 million. What is the SLE for this event?

Quick Answer: **195**
Detailed Answer: **197**

❍ **A.** $1 million

❍ **B.** $10 million

❍ **C.** $100,000

❍ **D.** $10,000

17. Houston-based Sea Breeze Industries has expanded the scope of your work. The organization has determined that there is a possibility that it may be hit by a hurricane once every 10 years. The losses from such an event are calculated to be $1 million. Based on this information, Sea Breeze Industries wants you to calculate the ALE. What result do you get?

Quick Answer: **195**
Detailed Answer: **197**

❍ **A.** $10,000

❍ **B.** $100,000

❍ **C.** $1 million

❍ **D.** $10 million

18. Your contact at Sea Breeze Industries comes to you with the following question: When calculating the ALE just described, what do the results denote? What should your answer be?

Quick Answer: **195**
Detailed Answer: **197**

❍ **A.** All occurrences of hurricane risk affecting Sea Breeze Industries in the next 10 years divided by the SLE

❍ **B.** All occurrences of the hurricane risk affecting Sea Breeze Industries during the next 10 years

❍ **C.** All occurrences of the hurricane risk affecting Sea Breeze Industries in any given year

❍ **D.** All occurrences of the hurricane risk affecting Sea Breeze Industries during the lifetime of the business

19. Your contact at Sea Breeze Industries is now worried that your calculations for the hurricane service outage are inaccurate. She is concerned that the calculations you developed do not take into consideration the loss of prestige and goodwill that this possible outage would cause. What is the best way to factor in her considerations?

Quick Answer: **195**
Detailed Answer: **197**

❍ **A.** Perform a quantitative assessment.

❍ **B.** Reassure your contact that this is not an issue to be concerned about.

❍ **C.** Reassure your contact that this issue will be handled during the DRP.

❍ **D.** Perform a qualitative assessment.

Quick Check

20. Which phase of the BCP process includes project parameter definition?

Quick Answer: **195**
Detailed Answer: **198**

- ❍ **A.** Plan approval and implementation
- ❍ **B.** Business impact assessment
- ❍ **C.** Scope and plan initiation
- ❍ **D.** Business continuity plan development

21. Which phase of the BIA has the following goal? Determine what is the longest period of time a critical process can remain interrupted before the company can never recover.

Quick Answer: **195**
Detailed Answer: **198**

- ❍ **A.** Outage assessment
- ❍ **B.** Documenting the continuity strategy
- ❍ **C.** Resource requirements
- ❍ **D.** Downtime estimation

22. Greg, your eccentric brother-in-law, has cashed out his 401(k) plan. He claims to have come up with a great business idea. He has purchased several large tractor-trailer rigs that have been retrofitted with backup power, computers, networking equipment, satellite Internet connectivity, work area, and HVAC. He has hired a sales team to sign contracts with local companies because he claims to offer a full backup alternative that's functional during almost any kind of organizational disaster. What is the best description for his new business venture?

Quick Answer: **195**
Detailed Answer: **198**

- ❍ **A.** Cold site
- ❍ **B.** Warm site
- ❍ **C.** Rolling hot site
- ❍ **D.** Mobile backup site

23. Backups ensure that information stored on a workstation or server can be restored if a disaster or failure occurs. Which type of backup makes a complete archive of every file?

Quick Answer: **195**
Detailed Answer: **198**

- ❍ **A.** Complete backup
- ❍ **B.** Differential backup
- ❍ **C.** Incremental backup
- ❍ **D.** Full backup

24. Which of the following is *not* essential when planning a backup strategy?

Quick Answer: **195**
Detailed Answer: **198**

- ❍ **A.** Selecting a media supplier
- ❍ **B.** Managing the backup media

Quick Check

❍ **C.** Tracking the location of all backup media

❍ **D.** Providing mechanisms to duplicate sets of backed-up data so that while a copy remains onsite, another copy can be taken offsite for disaster protection

25. Which phase of the BCP process describes plan implementation, plan testing, and ongoing plan maintenance?

Quick Answer: **195**
Detailed Answer: **198**

❍ **A.** Plan approval and implementation

❍ **B.** Business impact assessment

❍ **C.** Scope and plan initiation

❍ **D.** Business continuity plan development

26. Your organization performed a full backup on Monday. On Tuesday and Wednesday, incremental backups were performed. Then, on Thursday morning, a hardware failure destroyed all data on the server. Which of the following represents the proper restore method?

Quick Answer: **195**
Detailed Answer: **198**

❍ **A.** Monday's full backup

❍ **B.** Monday's full backup and Wednesday's incremental backup

❍ **C.** Monday's full backup and Tuesday's and Wednesday's incremental backups

❍ **D.** Wednesday's incremental backup

27. What type of backup scheme requires the following? Full backups are done once a week, and daily backups are differential or incremental. The daily tapes are reused after a week, and the weekly tapes are not reused until the following month. The last tape of the month is known as the monthly backup and is retained for a year before being reused.

Quick Answer: **195**
Detailed Answer: **198**

❍ **A.** Bimodal rotation

❍ **B.** Yearly rotation

❍ **C.** GFS rotation

❍ **D.** Monthly rotation

28. Which of the following is *not* a feature of a hot site?

Quick Answer: **195**
Detailed Answer: **199**

❍ **A.** Hot sites contain preexisting Internet and network connectivity.

❍ **B.** Equipment and software must be compatible with the data being backed up.

❍ **C.** Hot sites can be ready to use in a few hours to at most several days.

❍ **D.** A company may have exclusive rights to the facility at which the hot site is located.

Quick Check

29. Which of the following is *not* one of the primary reasons data is backed up?

Quick Answer: **195**
Detailed Answer: **199**

- ❍ **A.** Disaster recovery
- ❍ **B.** Legal requirements
- ❍ **C.** Hardware failure protection
- ❍ **D.** Continuous availability

30. Which of the following best describes the concept and purpose of DRP?

Quick Answer: **195**
Detailed Answer: **199**

- ❍ **A.** DRPs help reduce the risk of financial loss during a potential outage.
- ❍ **B.** DRPs and procedures are put in place for the response to an emergency.
- ❍ **C.** DRPs are created to prevent interruptions to normal business activity.
- ❍ **D.** DRPs are developed to estimate total allowable downtime.

31. An old friend sends you an email with the following question: What is the most resource-intensive and costly DRP testing method? How will you answer?

Quick Answer: **195**
Detailed Answer: **199**

- ❍ **A.** Checklist
- ❍ **B.** Structured walk-through
- ❍ **C.** Simulation
- ❍ **D.** Full interruption

32. What is the best backup option for an organization that is geographically dispersed and does not want to make arrangements with outside vendors?

Quick Answer: **195**
Detailed Answer: **199**

- ❍ **A.** Failsafe site
- ❍ **B.** Hot site
- ❍ **C.** Warm site
- ❍ **D.** Multiple data centers

33. What is the minimum frequency at which disaster recovery drills should be performed?

Quick Answer: **195**
Detailed Answer: **199**

- ❍ **A.** Daily
- ❍ **B.** Weekly
- ❍ **C.** Yearly
- ❍ **D.** Bi-monthly

Quick Check

34. You just received an instant message from a coworker who wants to know what the term is for the longest time an organization can survive without a critical function. What will your answer be?

Quick Answer: 195
Detailed Answer: 199

- A. Mean time between failures
- B. Maximum tolerable downtime
- C. Maximum outage time
- D. Mean time to repair

35. Which of the following is the best example of a natural disaster?

Quick Answer: 195
Detailed Answer: 199

- A. Sabotage
- B. DoS
- C. Fire
- D. Strikes

36. Which of the following backup types ensures that data will be restored in the shortest available time?

Quick Answer: 195
Detailed Answer: 199

- A. Tape backup
- B. Differential backup
- C. Incremental backup
- D. Full backup

37. Which of the following is the best reason to conduct disaster recovery drills and exercises?

Quick Answer: 195
Detailed Answer: 199

- A. To enforce policy and ensure that all employees understand the need to participate
- B. To ensure that the entire organization is confident about and competent with the disaster recovery plan
- C. To make the same type of decisions you would when responding to a real disaster
- D. To force the staff to assume the workload of the backup site to help them prepare for the stress

38. Which of the following best describes the differences between DRP and BCP?

Quick Answer: 195
Detailed Answer: 200

- A. DRP is the process of identifying critical data systems and business functions, analyzing the risks of disruption to the data systems, and developing methods to measure how the loss of these services would affect the organization. The BCP is used to plan for business continuity in the event of a natural or man-made disaster.

Quick Check

❍ **B.** BCP is the process of identifying critical data systems and business functions, analyzing the risks of disruption to the data systems, and developing methods to measure how the loss of these services would affect the organization. The DRP is used to plan for business continuity in the event of a natural or man-made disaster.

❍ **C.** DRP is an all-encompassing term that includes both DRP and BCP. As a subcomponent, the goal of a BCP is to facilitate and expedite the resumption of business after a disruption of critical or impacting data systems and operations has occurred.

❍ **D.** The BCP is reactive in that critical data systems and business functions are analyzed to measure how the loss of these services would affect the organization. The DRP is proactive because it is used in response to any type of disaster that threatens the organization's viability.

39. Which type of backup method takes the most time to restore?

Quick Answer: **195**
Detailed Answer: **200**

❍ **A.** Complete backup
❍ **B.** Differential backup
❍ **C.** Incremental backup
❍ **D.** Partial backup

40. Your manager has concerns about the viability of one of the organization's major custom software providers. Which of the following should you suggest to ensure that your organization has continued access to mission-critical software should the provider go bankrupt?

Quick Answer: **195**
Detailed Answer: **200**

❍ **A.** Ask the provider to agree to periodic financial audits
❍ **B.** Ask for a viability contract
❍ **C.** Ask for a software escrow agreement
❍ **D.** Invest in a hot site facility

41. A full backup was made on Monday, and differential backups were made each day during that week. Friday night at midnight, lightning struck the server and destroyed the hard drive. Which of the following is the proper restore method?

Quick Answer: **195**
Detailed Answer: **200**

❍ **A.** Friday's differential backup
❍ **B.** Monday's full backup and Tuesday's, Wednesday's, Thursday's, and Friday's differential backups
❍ **C.** Monday's full backup and Friday's differential backup
❍ **D.** Monday's full backup

Quick Check

42. Kelly has been assigned to develop a DR testing plan. He would like a test in which representatives from each department come together to discuss the plan and then walk through various scenarios to make sure that all the important items were covered. Which of the following plan types meets these criteria?

Quick Answer: **195**
Detailed Answer: **200**

- ❍ **A.** Checklist
- ❍ **B.** Simulation
- ❍ **C.** Structured walk-through
- ❍ **D.** Parallel

43. As director of IT, you have spent some time drafting a new security policy for all your employees. The policy addresses password change policies on the servers under your control, tape backup, configuration management, and other items concerning the security and functionality of the equipment you are in charge of. Now that the policy is finished, what should be your next step?

Quick Answer: **195**
Detailed Answer: **200**

- ❍ **A.** Release the policy
- ❍ **B.** Submit the policy to other department heads for their comments
- ❍ **C.** Allow your employees to review the policy
- ❍ **D.** Obtain approval from your management to proceed

44. Don believes he has come up with a plan that will save his company money while providing operations backup. He has brokered a deal with a company 10 miles away that has agreed to provide office space, computing services, and resources in exchange for the same in case of emergency. What is the name of this type of situation?

Quick Answer: **195**
Detailed Answer: **200**

- ❍ **A.** Mutual aid agreement
- ❍ **B.** Hot site
- ❍ **C.** Redundant site
- ❍ **D.** Parallel site

45. BCP practices require consideration from both a long-term and short-term perspective. Which of the following would *not* be considered a long-term BCP goal?

Quick Answer: **195**
Detailed Answer: **200**

- ❍ **A.** Fiscal management
- ❍ **B.** Contractual obligations
- ❍ **C.** Priorities for restoration
- ❍ **D.** Strategic plans

Quick Check

46. Which type of DR test distributes copies of the plan to each department head for review?

Quick Answer: 195
Detailed Answer: 200

- ❍ **A.** Checklist
- ❍ **B.** Simulation
- ❍ **C.** Structured walk-through
- ❍ **D.** Verification

47. Your company's database contains critical information. Because of this, your president has asked you to ensure that database backup is included in any BCP/DR plan you develop. Which database backup method transfers copies of the database transaction logs to an offsite facility?

Quick Answer: 195
Detailed Answer: 200

- ❍ **A.** Remote duplexing
- ❍ **B.** Electronic vaulting
- ❍ **C.** Remote mirroring
- ❍ **D.** Remote journaling

48. Which of the following is *not* one of the primary goals of the disaster recovery plan?

Quick Answer: 195
Detailed Answer: 201

- ❍ **A.** Minimize the length of the disruption
- ❍ **B.** Build an effective recovery team
- ❍ **C.** Build a criticality assessment
- ❍ **D.** Reduce the complexity of the recovery

49. Which backup type does not clear the archive bit for the files it has copied?

Quick Answer: 195
Detailed Answer: 201

- ❍ **A.** Complete backup
- ❍ **B.** Differential backup
- ❍ **C.** Incremental backup
- ❍ **D.** Archived backup

50. During the BCP process, which group grants final approval and provides ongoing support?

Quick Answer: 195
Detailed Answer: 201

- ❍ **A.** Senior business unit management
- ❍ **B.** BCP committee
- ❍ **C.** Functional business units
- ❍ **D.** Executive management

Quick Check

51. Today is Thursday, and the network server just crashed and needs to be restored. Which backup method results in the fastest recovery?

Quick Answer: **195**
Detailed Answer: **201**

- ❍ **A.** Completing a differential backup every Sunday, followed by a differential backup every day
- ❍ **B.** Completing a differential backup every Sunday, followed by an incremental backup every day
- ❍ **C.** Completing a full backup every Sunday, followed by a differential backup every day
- ❍ **D.** Completing a full backup every Sunday, followed by an incremental backup every day

52. In which facility recovery model is it most important to periodically test the successful recovery of data from backup tapes?

Quick Answer: **195**
Detailed Answer: **201**

- ❍ **A.** Hot
- ❍ **B.** Cold
- ❍ **C.** Warm
- ❍ **D.** Redundant

53. Which configuration facilitates the best retrieval of evidence of a code injection attack during a dead acquisition?

Quick Answer: **195**
Detailed Answer: **201**

- ❍ **A.** A computer with little memory but a huge swap space
- ❍ **B.** A computer with a lot of memory but a small amount of swap space
- ❍ **C.** A computer in which the memory equals the swap space
- ❍ **D.** A virtual machine

54. What is the hardest recovery implementation to enforce?

Quick Answer: **195**
Detailed Answer: **201**

- ❍ **A.** Rolling hot site
- ❍ **B.** Reciprocal site
- ❍ **C.** Cold site
- ❍ **D.** Redundant site

55. A small but talented company has developed proprietary code for you. You are concerned that in the future the employees and maybe even the company may break up and move on. What is the best way for you to protect the value of your purchased product?

Quick Answer: **195**
Detailed Answer: **201**

- ❍ **A.** Demand the source code
- ❍ **B.** Hire the lead developer
- ❍ **C.** Only buy from well-established vendors
- ❍ **D.** Use a software escrow

Quick Check

56. You work for a service organization that provides value-added networks (VANs) to fulfill supply requests of several large firms. What is the best offsite backup method for maximizing recovery of transactions?

Quick Answer: **195**
Detailed Answer: **201**

- ❍ **A.** Electronic vaulting
- ❍ **B.** Tape vaulting
- ❍ **C.** Remote journaling
- ❍ **D.** Tape rotation

57. What is another name for a mirrored striped set?

Quick Answer: **195**
Detailed Answer: **202**

- ❍ **A.** RAID 0
- ❍ **B.** RAID 5
- ❍ **C.** RAID 6
- ❍ **D.** RAID 0+1

58. Which of the following best describes the term DRP?

Quick Answer: **195**
Detailed Answer: **202**

- ❍ **A.** Training employees in critical functions, designing systems to reduce outage times, backing up and restoring from backup to return to normal operations
- ❍ **B.** Showing employees how to respond to incidents, developing emergency procedures, reducing the impact of immediate dangers, restoring critical systems
- ❍ **C.** Long-term planning to keep a business functional after a disaster
- ❍ **D.** Performing a risk analysis, identifying critical systems, determining criticality, researching resource requirements

59. When you're calculating the maximum tolerable downtime (MTD), which of the following best defines how long a company can survive without an important item?

Quick Answer: **195**
Detailed Answer: **202**

- ❍ **A.** Minutes to hours
- ❍ **B.** 24 hours
- ❍ **C.** 72 hours
- ❍ **D.** Seven days

60. With what form of RAID does losing one drive result in total failure?

Quick Answer: **195**
Detailed Answer: **202**

- ❍ **A.** RAID 0
- ❍ **B.** RAID 5
- ❍ **C.** RAID 6
- ❍ **D.** RAID 0+1

Quick Check

61. Which of the following best describes the business impact analysis (BIA)?

Quick Answer: 195
Detailed Answer: 202

- ❍ **A.** Training employees on critical functions, designing systems to reduce outage times, backing up and restoring from backup to return to normal operations
- ❍ **B.** Showing employees how to respond to incidents, developing emergency procedures, reducing the impact of immediate dangers, restoring critical systems
- ❍ **C.** Long-term planning to keep the business functional after a disaster
- ❍ **D.** Performing a risk analysis, identifying critical systems, determining criticality, researching resource requirements

62. When you're calculating the maximum tolerable downtime (MTD), which of the following best defines how long a company can survive without an item of normal importance?

Quick Answer: 195
Detailed Answer: 202

- ❍ **A.** Minutes to hours
- ❍ **B.** 24 hours
- ❍ **C.** 72 hours
- ❍ **D.** Seven days

63. Which of the following best describes "the level of service provided by alternate processes while primary processing is offline"?

Quick Answer: 195
Detailed Answer: 202

- ❍ **A.** Maximum tolerable outage
- ❍ **B.** Service level objective
- ❍ **C.** Core processing
- ❍ **D.** Maximum acceptable outage

64. When you're calculating the maximum tolerable downtime (MTD), which of the following best defines how long a company can survive without an item of critical importance?

Quick Answer: 195
Detailed Answer: 203

- ❍ **A.** Minutes to hours
- ❍ **B.** 24 hours
- ❍ **C.** 72 hours
- ❍ **D.** Seven days

65. What form of RAID is designed to tolerate two simultaneous HDD failures yet requires a much more complex method of encoding?

Quick Answer: 195
Detailed Answer: 203

- ❍ **A.** RAID 0
- ❍ **B.** RAID 5
- ❍ **C.** RAID 6
- ❍ **D.** RAID 0+1

Quick Check

66. Which of the following best describes "the maximum amount of time the organization can provide services at the alternate site"?

Quick Answer: **195**
Detailed Answer: **203**

- ❍ **A.** Maximum tolerable outage
- ❍ **B.** Service level objective
- ❍ **C.** Core processing
- ❍ **D.** Maximum acceptable outage

67. Which of the following describes the greatest advantage of JBOD?

Quick Answer: **195**
Detailed Answer: **203**

- ❍ **A.** In case of drive failure, only the data on the affected drive is lost.
- ❍ **B.** It is superior to disk mirroring.
- ❍ **C.** It offers greater performance gains than RAID.
- ❍ **D.** Compared to RAID, it offers greater fault tolerance.

68. Which process is most critical in terms of revenue generation?

Quick Answer: **195**
Detailed Answer: **203**

- ❍ **A.** Discretionary
- ❍ **B.** Supporting
- ❍ **C.** Core
- ❍ **D.** Critical

69. What tape backup method is known as Tower of Hanoi?

Quick Answer: **195**
Detailed Answer: **203**

- ❍ **A.** This scheme uses one tape for every day of the week and then repeats the next week. One tape can be for Mondays, one for Tuesdays, and so on. You add a set of new tapes each month and then archive the monthly sets.
- ❍ **B.** This scheme includes four tapes for weekly backups, one tape for monthly backups, and four tapes for daily backups.
- ❍ **C.** This scheme involves using five sets of tapes, each set labeled A through E.
- ❍ **D.** This scheme uses only one set of tapes. After a predetermined number of months, you need the newest set of tapes.

70. Which of the following is considered the most common form of fault-tolerant RAID technology?

Quick Answer: **195**
Detailed Answer: **203**

- ❍ **A.** RAID 0
- ❍ **B.** RAID 5
- ❍ **C.** RAID 6
- ❍ **D.** RAID 0+1

Quick Check

71. Which tape backup method is known as grandfather, father, son?

Quick Answer: **195**
Detailed Answer: **204**

- ❍ **A.** This scheme uses one tape for every day of the week and then repeats the next week. One tape can be for Mondays, one for Tuesdays, and so on. You add a set of new tapes each month and then archive the monthly sets.
- ❍ **B.** This scheme includes four tapes for weekly backups, one tape for monthly backups, and four tapes for daily backups.
- ❍ **C.** This scheme involves using five sets of tapes, each set labeled A through E.
- ❍ **D.** This scheme uses only one set of tapes. After a predetermined number of months, you need the newest set of tapes.

72. Which of the following does a business impact analysis not provide?

Quick Answer: **195**
Detailed Answer: **204**

- ❍ **A.** Detailing how training and awareness will be performed and how the plan will be updated
- ❍ **B.** Determining the maximum outage time before the company is permanently crippled
- ❍ **C.** Determining the need for BCP
- ❍ **D.** Selecting recovery strategies to be implemented

73. What is the practice of routing traffic through different cable facilities called?

Quick Answer: **195**
Detailed Answer: **204**

- ❍ **A.** Alternate routing
- ❍ **B.** Long-haul diversity
- ❍ **C.** Diverse routing
- ❍ **D.** Final-mile protection

74. Which of the following should you not do with disaster recovery plans?

Quick Answer: **195**
Detailed Answer: **204**

- ❍ **A.** Perform drills with the plan.
- ❍ **B.** Place the plan on the website so that everyone has access.
- ❍ **C.** Verify that the plan details who is in charge of the disaster recovery process.
- ❍ **D.** Keep a copy of the plans offsite.

Quick Check

75. Which of the following is not one of the reasons to perform a disaster recovery test?

Quick Answer: **195**
Detailed Answer: **204**

- ❍ **A.** All necessary contingency arrangements have been completed.
- ❍ **B.** The outcome of the test is known.
- ❍ **C.** Procedures are in place that will facilitate recovery should a disaster occur.
- ❍ **D.** The design of computer systems, networks, and applications conforms to the requirements set forth in the disaster recovery plan and the company's application design standards.

76. What is the most visible way to demonstrate senior management's support of and commitment to disaster recovery?

Quick Answer: **195**
Detailed Answer: **204**

- ❍ **A.** Personally appoint the team members to perform the business impact analysis.
- ❍ **B.** Ensure that a disaster recovery procedure has been created.
- ❍ **C.** Verify that all regulatory requirements have been met.
- ❍ **D.** Perform disaster recovery tests.

77. You are asked to set up a personnel notification system to be used in case of emergency. Which of the following is the best way for you to notify off-duty employees quickly?

Quick Answer: **195**
Detailed Answer: **204**

- ❍ **A.** Software escrow
- ❍ **B.** Provide a website for employees to check
- ❍ **C.** Require employees to list emergency numbers upon hiring
- ❍ **D.** Phone tree

78. When a company must decide if a backup generator is needed, which of the following is the most critical decision-making factor?

Quick Answer: **195**
Detailed Answer: **205**

- ❍ **A.** The organization's electrical rates
- ❍ **B.** The cost of fuel
- ❍ **C.** The distance to the hot site
- ❍ **D.** The maximum potential outage

Quick Check

79. When you're classifying critical systems, which category can be described as follows? "These functions are important and can be performed by a backup manual process but not for a long period of time."

- ❍ **A.** Vital
- ❍ **B.** Sensitive
- ❍ **C.** Critical
- ❍ **D.** Driven by demand

Quick Answer: **195**
Detailed Answer: **205**

80. Which of the following statements about backup media is most correct?

- ❍ **A.** Backup media should be stored between 50 and 55 degrees.
- ❍ **B.** Backup media should be stored at specialized offsite facilities.
- ❍ **C.** Backup media should be stored at employees' homes.
- ❍ **D.** Backup media should be stored in the data center in a locked cabinet.

Quick Answer: **195**
Detailed Answer: **205**

81. After performing a full backup on Sunday and an incremental on Monday and Tuesday, you suffer an outage. What is needed to restore operations?

- ❍ **A.** Sunday's full backup
- ❍ **B.** Sunday's full backup and Monday's incremental
- ❍ **C.** Sunday's full backup and Tuesday's incremental
- ❍ **D.** Sunday's full backup, Monday's incremental, and Tuesday's incremental

Quick Answer: **195**
Detailed Answer: **205**

82. Which of the following defines how current the data must be?

- ❍ **A.** Service level agreement (SLA)
- ❍ **B.** Recovery point objective (RPO)
- ❍ **C.** Recovery time objective (RTO)
- ❍ **D.** Maximum tolerable downtime (MTD)

Quick Answer: **195**
Detailed Answer: **205**

83. Because of the need to provide almost continuous service, your organization has invested in a hot site. Which of the following was most likely a major consideration in this decision?

- ❍ **A.** Service level agreement (SLA)
- ❍ **B.** Recovery point objective (RPO)
- ❍ **C.** Recovery time objective (RTO)
- ❍ **D.** Maximum tolerable downtime (MTD)

Quick Answer: **195**
Detailed Answer: **205**

Quick Check

84. Which of the following is not the responsibility of the BCP team and could be considered a senior management duty?

Quick Answer: **195**
Detailed Answer: **205**

- ❍ **A.** Participating in the testing
- ❍ **B.** Initiating the project
- ❍ **C.** Performing the BIA
- ❍ **D.** Directing the planning, implementation, and test process

85. After performing a full backup on Sunday and a differential on Monday and Tuesday, you suffer an outage. What is needed to restore operations?

Quick Answer: **195**
Detailed Answer: **206**

- ❍ **A.** Sunday's full backup
- ❍ **B.** Sunday's full backup and Monday's differential
- ❍ **C.** Sunday's full backup and Tuesday's differential
- ❍ **D.** Sunday's full backup, Monday's differential, and Tuesday's differential

86. Which of the following specifies the maximum elapsed time to recover an application at an alternate site?

Quick Answer: **195**
Detailed Answer: **206**

- ❍ **A.** Service level agreement (SLA)
- ❍ **B.** Recovery point objective (RPO)
- ❍ **C.** Recovery time objective (RTO)
- ❍ **D.** Maximum tolerable downtime (MTD)

87. When you're performing the BIA, which of the following would not be considered a quantitative loss criteria?

Quick Answer: **195**
Detailed Answer: **206**

- ❍ **A.** Financial loss from loss of revenue
- ❍ **B.** Additional operational expense due to the disruptive event
- ❍ **C.** The loss of competitive advantage
- ❍ **D.** Financial loss from violation of compliance requirements

88. Your organization has reached an agreement with the bank across the street to exchange services should a disaster occur and the bank's data center become nonfunctional. What should be the primary concern with this proposal?

Quick Answer: **195**
Detailed Answer: **206**

- ❍ **A.** It would be a useful arrangement for only a short time.
- ❍ **B.** A major outage could easily disable both companies.
- ❍ **C.** Are the businesses similar enough in nature for the agreement to work?
- ❍ **D.** Will the service provider be available for the hours and times needed by the primary business?

Quick Check

89. Your organization has reached an agreement with the bank across the street to exchange services should a disaster occur and the bank's data center become nonfunctional. Which of the following is the best description of what this agreement is called?

Quick Answer: **195**
Detailed Answer: **206**

- ❍ **A.** Mutual aid
- ❍ **B.** Reciprocal site
- ❍ **C.** Hot site
- ❍ **D.** Redundant site

90. Which of the following describes parallel processing of transactions to an alternate site?

Quick Answer: **195**
Detailed Answer: **206**

- ❍ **A.** Electronic vaulting
- ❍ **B.** Remote journaling
- ❍ **C.** Database shadowing
- ❍ **D.** Tape backup

91. Your company has started providing outsourced help desk services to a number of clients worldwide. The provider you have chosen is equipped to handle more than a thousand calls a day, with an average call length of 10 minutes. Should the help desk need to move to an alternate facility in the event of some disaster or disruption, management wants to be able to provide at least 80% of the current capacity. What metric would need to be determined in the business impact analysis (BIA)?

Quick Answer: **195**
Detailed Answer: **206**

- ❍ **A.** Recovery time objectives
- ❍ **B.** Service level objectives
- ❍ **C.** Maximum tolerable downtime
- ❍ **D.** Recovery point objectives

92. You are asked to create disaster recovery plans for your IT group. After being briefed by senior management, you are concerned that the paper-based tests that management has suggested are not realistic enough. You believe that more should be done, but you are concerned with risking downtime of production systems. With this in mind, what test type is most appropriate?

Quick Answer: **195**
Detailed Answer: **206**

- ❍ **A.** Structured walk-through
- ❍ **B.** Warm
- ❍ **C.** Simulation
- ❍ **D.** Parallel

Quick Check

93. Which of the following describes parallel processing of transactions to an alternate site?

Quick Answer: **195**
Detailed Answer: **207**

- ❍ **A.** Electronic vaulting
- ❍ **B.** Remote journaling
- ❍ **C.** Database shadowing
- ❍ **D.** Tape backup

94. Recently, Specialized Solutions suffered a fire, requiring the company to relocate. Management was concerned because a member of the recovery team failed to appear at the site when backup operations were required. When he was contacted, the individual claimed he was unclear on his role and did not realize he was named in the plan. What caused this disconnect, and where should the team manager look to verify the names of people who are required to attend?

Quick Answer: **195**
Detailed Answer: **207**

- ❍ **A.** Reconstitution plans
- ❍ **B.** Recovery procedures
- ❍ **C.** Service level agreement
- ❍ **D.** Memorandum of understanding

95. Which of the following describes duplicating database sets to multiple servers?

Quick Answer: **195**
Detailed Answer: **207**

- ❍ **A.** Electronic vaulting
- ❍ **B.** Remote journaling
- ❍ **C.** Database shadowing
- ❍ **D.** Tape backup

96. After a disaster, when returning to the restored primary site

Quick Answer: **195**
Detailed Answer: **207**

- ❍ **A.** Order is not important.
- ❍ **B.** Order is determined by policy.
- ❍ **C.** Order is from most critical to least critical.
- ❍ **D.** Order is from least critical to most critical.

97. Which of the following would have the longest recovery point objective?

Quick Answer: **195**
Detailed Answer: **207**

- ❍ **A.** Tape backup
- ❍ **B.** A redundant array of hard drives (RAID)
- ❍ **C.** Clustering
- ❍ **D.** Journaling

Quick Check

98. Once a plan is complete, who can issue final approval?

- ❍ **A.** DR project manager
- ❍ **B.** DR team
- ❍ **C.** Business managers
- ❍ **D.** Senior management

Quick Answer: **195**
Detailed Answer: **207**

99. Which of the following best describes a cold site?

- ❍ **A.** It's ready within hours
- ❍ **B.** It's ready within a month
- ❍ **C.** It's ready within a few days
- ❍ **D.** It's ready within a few weeks

Quick Answer: **195**
Detailed Answer: **207**

Practice Questions (True or False)

100. A parallel test is the most complete test of a BCP.

- ❍ True
- ❍ False

Quick Answer: **195**
Detailed Answer: **207**

101. A hot site is an example of a subscription service.

- ❍ True
- ❍ False

Quick Answer: **195**
Detailed Answer: **207**

102. The disaster is over as soon as operations have been moved to an alternate site.

- ❍ True
- ❍ False

Quick Answer: **195**
Detailed Answer: **207**

103. The primary disadvantage of a hot site recovery is cost.

- ❍ True
- ❍ False

Quick Answer: **195**
Detailed Answer: **207**

Practice Questions (Mix and Match)

104. Match each term with its definition:

Quick Answer: **195**
Detailed Answer: **208**

A. Checklist: _____

B. Structured walk-through: _____

C. Simulation: _____

D. Parallel: _____

E. Full interruption: _____

1. Can cause its own disaster because of interruption.

2. The most common type of disaster recovery test.

3. The plan is copied to each business unit manager.

4. Relocate to an alternative site, but do not perform offsite processing.

5. Representatives meet to review the plan.

Quick Check Answer Key

1. B
2. A
3. D
4. D
5. D
6. A
7. B
8. C
9. C
10. B
11. C
12. C
13. B
14. A
15. A
16. A
17. B
18. C
19. D
20. C
21. D
22. C
23. D
24. A
25. D
26. C
27. C
28. C
29. D
30. B
31. D
32. D
33. C
34. B
35. C
36. D
37. B
38. B
39. C
40. C
41. C
42. C
43. D
44. A
45. C
46. A
47. D
48. C
49. B
50. D
51. C
52. A
53. A
54. B
55. D
56. A
57. D
58. B
59. C
60. A
61. D
62. D
63. B
64. A
65. C
66. A
67. A
68. C
69. C
70. B
71. B
72. B
73. C
74. B
75. B
76. D
77. D
78. D
79. A
80. B
81. D
82. B
83. C
84. B
85. C
86. C
87. C
88. B
89. A
90. B
91. B
92. C
93. B
94. D
95. C
96. D
97. A
98. D
99. B
100. False
101. True
102. False
103. True
104. **A.** 3
    B. 5
    C. 4
    D. 2
    E. 1

Answers and Explanations

1. **Answer: B.** BCP (Business Continuity Plan) and DR (Disaster Recovery) are two closely related topics. DR looks at what needs to happen after an adverse event, whereas BCP looks at the planning and plan development that should take place up front. The four elements of the BCP are

   Scope and plan initiation

   Business impact assessment

   Business continuity plan development

   Plan approval and implementation

2. **Answer: A.** Qualitative Risk Assessment does not assign numeric values to specific assets. Quantitative Risk Assessment does assign numeric values. Statistical Weighted Risk Assessment and Asset-Based Risk Assessment are distracters.

3. **Answer: D.** BCP is designed to help organizations prevent interruptions to normal business activity. All other answers fail to describe BCP. It is worth remembering that the BCP is developed to prevent interruptions to normal business. If these events cannot be prevented, the goal of the plan is to minimize the outage. The other goal of the plan is to reduce the potential costs of such disruptions on the organization.

4. **Answer: D.** The three goals of a BIA (Business Impact Analysis) are criticality prioritization, downtime estimation, and resource requirements. The purpose of a BIA is to help the organization understand what impact a disruptive event would have on the health and well-being of the business. The BIA should present a clear picture of what is needed to continue operations should a disaster occur. The individuals responsible for the BIA must look at the organizations from many different angles and use information from a variety of inputs. For the BIA to succeed, the team must know what the key business processes are.

5. **Answer: D.** The number-one priority for all BCP and DRPs is always the protection and welfare of employees.

6. **Answer: A.** Performing the BIA is no easy task. It requires not only knowledge of business processes but also a thorough understanding of the organization itself. Criticality prioritization is the portion of the BIA that identifies and prioritizes all critical business processes. It also is used to analyze the impact a disruption would have on services or processes.

7. **Answer: B.** Developing and carrying out a successful business continuity plan takes much work and effort. It is something that should be done in a modular way. Each step builds on the last. It requires that the BCP team members know the business and have worked with other departments and management to determine critical processes. The BCP committee is the group that directs the planning, implementation, and development of the test procedures.

8. **Answer: C.** The FCPA (Foreign Corrupt Practices Act) imposes civil and criminal penalties if publicly held organizations fail to maintain sufficient controls over their information systems and data. The U.S. Computer Act of 1987 targets federal agencies, the Gramm-Leach-Bliley Act deals with financial reform and control, and HIPAA addresses the healthcare industry. Although questions dealing with laws specific to any one country are not common on the CISSP exam, it is still important to have a good understanding of the applicable laws under which your organization does business.

9. **Answer: C.** The goal of the vulnerability assessment is to determine the impact of the loss of a critical business function. This includes the dollar and nondollar costs. For example, it may be winter in Galveston, Texas, and the possibility of a hurricane extremely low. However, this doesn't mean that a vulnerability assessment shouldn't take place to reduce the potential negative impact. Answers A, B, and D do not completely address the reason for a vulnerability assessment.

10. **Answer: B.** The business impact assessment includes the completion of a vulnerability assessment. It is used to help departments within the organization understand the result of a disruptive event.

11. **Answer: C.** The resource requirements phase of the BIA identifies the most time-sensitive processes in order to receive the most resource allocation to help mitigate a potential outage. Criticality prioritization, documenting the continuity strategy, and downtime estimation do not meet those requirements.

12. **Answer: C.** Diverse routing is the practice of routing traffic through different cable facilities. Alternate routing is the ability to use another transmission line if the regular line is busy or unavailable. Long-haul diversity is the practice of having different long-distance communication carriers. Last-mile protection provides a second local loop connection.

13. **Answer: B.** Insurance is an example of risk transference. It is usually easier to mitigate risk than it is to eliminate or transfer it. Keep in mind that insurance is not without its drawbacks, such as high premiums, delayed claim payout, denied claims, and problems with proving financial loss.

14. **Answer: A.** Senior management identifies and prioritizes time-critical systems that are of great importance to an organization. Although management personnel may not always feel they have time to be involved in this process, it's important that they invest the time, because any disruptive event that affects the business's profitability may cause stockholders and board directors to hold them responsible.

15. **Answer: A.** The plan approval and implementation phase is the final step and, as such, must be approved by senior management.

16. **Answer: A.** SLE (single loss expectancy) is the total cost of a single occurrence of the specified event. Therefore, the SLE is $1 million. All other answers are incorrect because no calculations need to be performed to arrive at the correct answer.

17. **Answer: B.** The ALE (annualized loss expectancy) is computed this way: SLE $\times$ annualized rate of occurrence = ALE. This works out to $1 million $\times$ 0.1, which equals an ALE of $100,000.

18. **Answer: C.** The ALE (annualized loss expectancy) covers the loss expectancy from the risk of a hurricane during a single year.

19. **Answer: D.** A complete business impact assessment includes both a quantitative and qualitative analysis. Intangible items such as loss of prestige or customer dissatisfaction therefore would be addressed in the qualitative portion of the assessment. Answer A is incorrect because this issue would not be addressed during a quantitative assessment. Answer B is incorrect because this is a valid concern of your client. Answer C is incorrect because this issue is not handled during the DRP.

20. **Answer: C.** Before the BCP process can begin, management must be onboard. They are ultimately responsible and need to be actively involved in the process. Management sets the budget, determines the team leader, and gets the process started. The BCP team leader determines who will be on the BCP team. After it is established, the team has a host of duties. The scope and plan initiation includes everything needed to define the scope and parameters of the project.

21. **Answer: D.** Downtime estimation, which is sometimes called maximum tolerable downtime, is the phase of the BIA at which the calculations are made to determine what is the longest period of time a critical process can remain interrupted before the company can never recover.

22. **Answer: C.** Rolling hot sites are tractor-trailer rigs or portable buildings that can be quickly brought to a disaster area and used as a network center or data processing facility. Rolling hot sites usually are converted tractor-trailer rigs that have been converted into data processing centers. They contain all the necessary equipment and can be transported to a business location quickly. These can be chained together to provide space for data processing and can provide communication capabilities. They are a good choice for areas where no recovery facilities exist.

23. **Answer: D.** Although backup strategy is a rather straightforward implementation, it can take some planning when you're deciding what to back up, how to back it up, and what type of backup to perform. A full backup makes a complete archive of every file on the system. No category of backup is called a complete backup.

24. **Answer: A.** An organization's backup strategy must be able to achieve the following: manage the backup media, track the location of all backup media, and provide mechanisms to duplicate sets of backed-up data. While a copy remains onsite, another copy can be taken offsite for disaster protection and recovery. The disposal of used backup media falls under general security guidelines that cover the disposal of sensitive information. However, this is a valid concern. Because old media may have sensitive information, they need to be disposed of in a reasonably secure way. The selection of media supplier would not take precedence over the other items.

25. **Answer: D.** The goal of business continuity plan development includes everything related to defining and documenting the continuation strategy. The team meets with senior management to accomplish this. The purpose is to discuss plan implementation, plan testing, and ongoing plan maintenance. This should give everyone present some idea of how the BCP is to be implemented and tested.

26. **Answer: C.** An incremental backup makes a copy of all the files that were changed since the last backup. This means that for the organization to fully restore the lost data, Monday's full backup and Tuesday's and Wednesday's incremental backups must be performed. Incremental backups use substantially less storage media than full backups but require more work and time to restore.

27. **Answer: C.** GFS (grandfather, father, son) rotation is a standard rotation scheme for backup. Although the other answers do not match the rotation description given in the question, valid modes include daily, weekly, and monthly backup media rotation. Bimodal rotation does not exist.

28. **Answer: C.** A hot site may belong exclusively to one organization, contain preexisting Internet and network connectivity, and have equipment and software that are compatible with the data being backed up. However, a hot site typically would be ready to use within a few minutes to a couple of hours at the most.

29. **Answer: D.** Although there are many reasons why data may be backed up, the ultimate decision of what to back up must involve a team of individuals. This includes the data owner, IT security, and management. Only then can those involved in the BIA process make an informed decision about the impact that this data loss would have on the organization. Continuous availability is *not* a primary reason why data is backed up, because some data may be deemed low priority or nonessential to business continuation. If concerns such as continuous availability are important, items such as redundant drives, power supplies, and servers should be investigated.

30. **Answer: B.** DRPs are the procedures used to respond to an emergency. They do not help prevent the incident, but simply help prepare the organization to deal with it.

31. **Answer: D.** A full interruption test is the most intensive method of those listed, because normal systems are powered down and mission-critical operations are moved to the backup recovery systems. A full interruption test mimics a real disaster; all steps are performed to start backup operations. It involves all the individuals who would be involved in a real emergency, including internal and external organizations. Checklists, walk-throughs, and simulations do not provide this level of review or this amount of cost.

32. **Answer: D.** For organizations that are geographically dispersed and do not want to make arrangements with outside vendors, one possible solution is multiple data centers. Multiple data centers allow rapid recovery and a trained staff who are already onsite and familiar with the organization's business practices and procedures. Their disadvantage is cost.

33. **Answer: C.** Disaster recovery drills should be performed at least once a year. Without periodic drills, there is no way an organization can have any confidence that its disaster recovery plan will succeed. Periodic drills ensure that the organization is confident and competent about its disaster recovery plan.

34. **Answer: B.** Maximum tolerable downtime is the longest time that an organization can survive without a critical function. This is a measurement of the longest period a business can be without a function and survive. MTBF and MTTR deal with equipment reliability. Maximum outage time is a distracter.

35. **Answer: C.** A fire is an example of a natural disaster. Disasters can be broadly grouped into several categories, including man-made, technical, and natural. Even though we must all be prepared to deal with disasters, most surveys show that U.S. companies continue to spend less than recommended.

36. **Answer: D.** Full backups result in the shortest available recovery time. Answers A, B, and C do not meet this requirement.

37. **Answer: B.** Tests and drills prepare individuals for the real event and ensure that the entire organization is confident and competent about the plan. No demonstrated recovery exists until the plan has been tested. Without testing the plan, there is no guarantee that it will work. Testing helps move theoretical plans into reality. To build confidence, the BCP team should start with easier parts of the plan and build to more complex items.

38. **Answer: B.** Business continuity planning is an umbrella term that includes both BCP and DRP. The goal of BCP is to identify the systems and processes that are critical to the organization's continued operation. The goal of DRP is to develop methods to ensure that the items identified during the BCP will be operational during a disaster. Examples of these items include hot sites, warm sites, cold sites, redundant network connectivity, and backup systems. The BCP process is proactive because it is a planning process. The DRP is reactive because it is implemented after a disaster occurs.

39. **Answer: C.** Although incremental backups use the fewest resources, they take the longest time to restore.

40. **Answer: C.** Software escrow agreements ensure that your organization has access to the source code of a business's software should the provider go out of business or go into bankruptcy. Audits, viability contracts, and hot sites do not provide this function.

41. **Answer: C.** Although most administrators use a combination of two of the three types of backups, your individual choice should be based on the speed of the backup, the quickness of the restore, and the volume of the backup media used. Differential backups take up more resources than incremental; however, differential backups possess the latest versions of all the files that were modified since the last full backup. This means that a restore requires only the last full backup and the last differential backup.

42. **Answer: C.** A structured walk-through test has individuals from each department meet and discuss the plan. Then the group discusses various scenarios of the plan to make sure that all the important items were covered and that nothing was missed. A checklist DR review is when a document is sent to each manager for review. A simulation reenacts a specific scenario such as a power outage or loss of communication. A parallel DR test verifies the backup facility while the primary site continues to operate.

43. **Answer: D.** Before the policy is put in place, it is advisable to have your management review its content, because all policy should flow from the top of the organization. Policies typically are not passed to subordinates for review. Nor is a review from other department heads required, because the policy targets only your employees. Finally, if you release the policy without your management's buy-in, you most likely have overstepped your boundaries.

44. **Answer: A.** A mutual aid agreement is used by two or more parties to provide assistance if one of the parties experiences a disaster. Although mutual aid agreements are cost-effective, they do not provide the level of redundancy that a hot/warm/cold site would. Furthermore, if a disaster strikes a large area and both parties are affected, the agreement becomes useless.

45. **Answer: C.** Priorities for restoration would fall under the category of DR and would be considered a short-term goal.

46. **Answer: A.** With a checklist, copies of the proposed plan are sent to each department head. This gives all managers time to review the plan, determine whether any changes need to be made, or see whether anything has been left out. Simulation tests require a large amount of time and effort. Walk-through tests require the participants to come together. No category of drill is called verification test.

47. **Answer: D.** Remote journaling transfers copies of the database transaction logs to an offsite facility. No category of database backup is called remote duplexing. Electronic vaulting takes place when database backups are transferred to a remote site in a bulk transfer fashion. Remote mirroring maintains a live database server at the backup site.

48. **Answer: C.** The disaster recovery plan should seek to reduce the complexity of the recovery, minimize the length of the disruption and the damage to business operations, pinpoint weaknesses in the current resumption plan, and build an effective recovery team. A criticality assessment is part of the BCP process.

49. **Answer: B.** A differential backup does not clear the archive bit for the files it has copied. This approach ensures that all the files with the archive bit on will be backed up until a full or incremental backup is performed. This would reset the archive bit.

50. **Answer: D.** Ultimately, executive management is responsible for all phases of the plan. As such, all completed plans must be approved by executive management.

51. **Answer: C.** A full backup is complete and provides for recovery at the time it is taken; it also resets the archive bit on all files. Incremental backups save only changed files and reset the archive bit. Differential backups save all changed files but do not reset the archive bit. Differential backups are slower to create but faster to restore. Every sequential differential includes files from the previous differential. Incremental backups are faster to create but are slower to recover because they must be restored in sequential order.

52. **Answer: A.** Cold and warm sites seldom have all the hardware to permit the restore process from your backup tapes. A redundant site implies the use of identical equipment. Therefore, if your tapes are tested as valid at your facility, they would also be valid at the redundant site. However, a hot site is one that is supposed to be ready to activate at any moment, but it may not have identical equipment. It is most necessary to test the integrity of the restore process at hot sites.

53. **Answer: A.** Code injection infects processes in memory. After the computer is shut off (a dead acquisition), there is no guarantee of retrieving evidence of the attack. However, the options are maximized when there is a large swap space or memory and minimal RAM (although this can make performance very slow). In this case, memory continually pages out to the drive, and the chance of recovering memory state information is maximized. In a virtual environment, the computer's memory is still used, and a swap file still is accessed. The size of either is not implied just by use of the term "virtual machine."

54. **Answer: B.** The hot site, cold site, and redundant site all permit you to continue operations that are fully under your control. The reciprocal site involves handling your operations from within someone else's organization, which can lead to some unexpected difficulties. It is also very hard to enforce.

55. **Answer: D.** Software escrows provide for the storage of code that you have purchased. If future changes to that code are needed, and the company is no longer in existence, the software can be retrieved from the software escrow.

56. **Answer: A.** Electronic vaulting involves periodic bulk transfer of transactions completed. It's the most expeditious choice of the possible answers. Tape vaulting is more appropriate for backing up at the end of a period, such as a day or week. Remote journaling backs up only the fact that the transaction occurred, not the transaction itself. Tape rotation is performed when an organization is performing father and grandfather backups and needs to rotate a set of tapes offsite for disaster recovery.

57. **Answer: D.** With RAID 0+1 mirroring, the stripe set mitigates the risk of data unavailability due to a disk failure. The performance penalty from the mirror is reduced to the extent possible by striping the write operations across multiple drives. With RAID 0, read/write performance is enhanced with striping enabled, but the drawback is increased exposure to a head crash. Losing one of the disks of a stripe set results in the total loss of the striped drive. RAID 5 is the most commonly used form of RAID. RAID 5 stripes both data and parity information across three or more drives. The RAID 5 array is not destroyed from a single drive failure. It works best where performance is not critical and where there are few write operations. RAID 6 is designed to tolerate two simultaneous HDD failures yet requires a much more complex method of encoding. RAID 6 uses two drives for parity.

58. **Answer: B.** The best answer is B because it discusses training employees in how to respond to incidents, developing emergency procedures, reducing the impact of immediate dangers, and restoring critical systems. Answer A defines business continuity. Answer C defines only a small piece of business continuity. Answer D describes the business impact analysis.

59. **Answer: C.** In calculating the maximum tolerable downtime (MTD), the following times typically are used: critical: minutes to hours, urgent: 24 hours, important: 72 hours, normal: seven days.

60. **Answer: A.** RAID 0 offers enhanced read/write performance and is considered striping technology, but the drawback is increased exposure to a head crash. Losing one of the disks of a stripe set results in the total loss of the striped drive. RAID 5 is the most commonly used form of RAID. RAID 5 stripes both data and parity information across three or more drives. The RAID 5 array is not destroyed from a single drive failure. It works best where performance is not critical and where there are few write operations. RAID 6 is designed to tolerate two simultaneous HDD failures yet requires a much more complex method of encoding. RAID 6 uses two drives for parity. With RAID 0+1, mirroring the stripe set mitigates the risk of data unavailability due to a disk failure. The performance penalty from the mirror is reduced to the extent possible by striping the write operations across multiple drives.

61. **Answer: D.** Answer D describes business impact analysis. Answer A defines business continuity. Answer B discusses the disaster recovery process. Answer C defines only a small piece of business continuity.

62. **Answer: D.** In calculating the maximum tolerable downtime (MTD), the following times typically are used: critical: minutes to hours, urgent: 24 hours, important: 72 hours, normal: seven days.

63. **Answer: B.** Service level objective defines the level of service provided by alternate processes while primary processing is offline. This value should be determined by examining the minimum business need. Maximum acceptable outage is how long systems can be offline before causing damage. This value is required in creating recovery time objectives (RTOs) and is also known as maximum tolerable downtime (MTD). Maximum tolerable outage defines the maximum amount of time the organization can provide services at the alternate site. This value may be determined by items such as contractual values. Core processing is activities that are specifically required for critical processes and that produce revenue.

64. **Answer: A.** In calculating the maximum tolerable downtime (MTD), the following times typically are used: critical: minutes to hours, urgent: 24 hours, important: 72 hours, and normal: seven days.

65. **Answer: C.** RAID 6 is designed to tolerate two simultaneous HDD failures yet requires a much more complex method of encoding. RAID 6 uses two drives for parity. RAID 0 offers enhanced read/write performance and is considered striping technology, but the drawback is increased exposure to a head crash. Losing one of the disks of a stripe set results in the total loss of the striped drive. RAID 5 is the most commonly used form of RAID. RAID 5 stripes both data and parity information across three or more drives. The RAID 5 array is not destroyed from a single drive failure. It works best where performance is not critical and where there are few write operations. With RAID 0+1 mirroring, the stripe set mitigates the risk of data unavailability due to a disk failure. The performance penalty from the mirror is reduced to the extent possible by striping the write operations across multiple drives.

66. **Answer: A.** Maximum tolerable outage (MTO) defines the maximum amount of time the organization can provide services at the alternate site. This value may be determined by items such as contractual values. Service level objective defines the level of service provided by alternate processes while primary processing is offline. This value should be determined by examining the minimum business need. Maximum acceptable outage is how long systems can be offline before causing damage. This value is required in creating recovery time objectives (RTOs) and is also known as maximum tolerable downtime. Core processing is activities that are specifically required for critical processes and that produce revenue.

67. **Answer: A.** JBOD (Just a Bunch of Disks) allows users to combine multiple drives into one large drive. One of JBOD's only advantages is that in case of drive failure, only the data on the affected drive is lost. JBOD is not superior to RAID, is not faster than RAID, and offers no fault tolerance.

68. **Answer: C.** Critical processes that produce revenue would be considered a core activity. Answer A is incorrect because discretionary processes are considered nonessential. Answer B is incorrect because supporting processes require only minimum BCP services. Answer D does not specify a process but is a term used to describe how important the service or process is.

69. **Answer: C.** Tower of Hanoi uses five sets of tapes, each set labeled A through E. A simple tape scheme uses one tape for every day of the week and then repeats the next week. One tape can be for Mondays, one for Tuesdays, and so on. You add a set of new tapes each month and then archive the monthly sets. Grandfather, father, son uses four tapes for weekly backups, one tape for monthly backups, and four tapes for daily backups. Answer D does not describe a valid tape backup method.

70. **Answer: B.** RAID 5 is the most commonly used form of RAID. RAID 5 stripes both data and parity information across three or more drives. The RAID 5 array is not destroyed from a single drive failure and works best where performance is not critical and where there are few write operations. RAID 0 offers enhanced read/write performance and is considered striping technology, but the drawback is increased exposure to a head crash. Losing one of the disks of a stripe set results in the total loss of the striped drive. RAID 6 is designed to tolerate two simultaneous HDD failures yet

requires a much more complex method of encoding. RAID 6 uses two drives for parity. With RAID 0+1 mirroring, the stripe set mitigates the risk of data unavailability due to a disk failure. The performance penalty from the mirror is reduced to the extent possible by striping the write operations across multiple drives.

71. **Answer: B.** Grandfather, father, son uses four tapes for weekly backups, one tape for monthly backups, and four tapes for daily backups. A simple tape scheme uses one tape for every day of the week and then repeats the next week. One tape can be for Mondays, one for Tuesdays, and so on. You add a set of new tapes each month and then archive the monthly sets. Tower of Hanoi uses five sets of tapes, each set labeled A through E. Answer D does not describe a valid tape backup method.

72. **Answer: B.** A BIA is a process used to help business units understand the impact of a disruptive event. Part of that process is determining the maximum outage time before the company is permanently crippled. The other answers are part of the BCP process but not specifically part of the BIA portion.

73. **Answer: C.** Diverse routing is the practice of routing traffic through different cable facilities. Alternate routing is the ability to use another transmission line if the regular line is busy or unavailable.

74. **Answer: B.** You should perform drills with the plan. You should verify the plan details and who is in charge of the disaster recovery process. You also should keep a copy of the plan offsite. You should not place a copy of the plan on an open website because access to the plan should be controlled. Individuals with malicious intent could access the plans and use the information against the company.

75. **Answer: B.** A disaster recovery test is performed to see if the plan works and to determine as many unknowns as possible. Before the test, all necessary contingency arrangements should have been completed. The design of computer systems and software should conform to what has been laid out in the test plans. Procedures are in place that will facilitate recovery should a disaster occur.

76. **Answer: D.** The most visible way to demonstrate senior management's support and commitment to disaster recovery is to actually carry out the requisite disaster recovery testing. Testing verifies that the plan will actually work. Without testing, there is no demonstrated recovery.

77. **Answer: D.** A phone tree would be your best option. A phone tree contains a list of people and their phone numbers. In case of emergency, the phone tree can be activated. It starts dialing a prearranged list of numbers set up as a chain of calls. A phone tree can store many different types of messages so that each type of emergency has its own specific message. Software escrow is a form of insurance to protect companies in case a software vendor goes broke. Providing a website for employees to check would serve as a central point of communication, but this action would be passive in nature. If a disaster occurred at the facility in the middle of the night, employees would have no way to know that they should immediately check the website. Requiring employees to provide an emergency phone number is usually done more for the benefit of the employee than for the company. Should an accident happen, the company will know who to contact.

78. **Answer: D.** There is nothing like a power outage to make a business realize how critical clean, reliable power is. Without power, business cannot continue. The primary decision when determining if a generator should be purchased is the potential outage time. Electrical rates, cost of fuel, and the distance would not be primary factors in determining if a generator is needed.

79. **Answer: A.** Items that are considered vital meet the description of functions that are important and that can be performed by a backup manual process but not for a long period of time. Answer B is incorrect because it describes tasks that are important but that can be performed manually at a reasonable cost. Answer C is incorrect because critical is extremely important functions. Answer D is incorrect because driven by demand is not a valid functional label.

80. **Answer: B.** Equipment is not much good without the software to run on it. Part of a good disaster recovery plan should consist of ways to back up and restore software. Although backups can be stored onsite or offsite, it is most important to store offsite so that any disaster at the primary site will not leave the organization without data. Although temperature is a concern, 50 to 55 is not a defined range. Storing media at an employee's home is a serious problem. The media also should not be stored in the data center in a cabinet that is not fireproof.

81. **Answer: D.** Answer D is correct because all the backup media would be needed. When backing up, you have to choose either faster backup or longer restore. A full backup backs up all files, whether or not they have been modified. It removes the archive bit. An incremental backup backs up only those files that have been modified since the previous backup of any sort. It does not remove the archive bit. A differential backup backs up all files that have been modified since the last full backup. It does not remove the archive bit. Differential backups take longer to perform than incremental but can be restored quicker than an incremental.

82. **Answer: B.** The recovery point objective (RPO) defines how current the data must be, or how much data an organization can afford to lose. The greater the RPO, the more tolerant the process is to interruption. The service level agreement (SLA) specifies uptime from a service provider. Recovery time objective (RTO) specifies the maximum elapsed time to recover an application at an alternate site. The greater the RTO, the longer the process can take to be restored. Maximum tolerable downtime (MTD) is how long a business process can be stopped without causing financial harm to the business.

83. **Answer: C.** The recovery time objective (RTO) specifies the maximum elapsed time to recover an application at an alternate site. The shorter the RTO, the less time the process can take to be restored. A long RTO could use a cold site, whereas a shorter RTO would require a hot site. The service level agreement (SLA) specifies uptime from a service provider. The recovery point objective (RPO) defines how current the data must be, or how much data an organization can afford to lose. The greater the RPO, the more tolerant the process is to interruption. Maximum tolerable downtime (MTD) is how long a business process can be stopped without causing financial harm to the business.

84. **Answer: B.** Senior management is responsible for funding, initiating, and establishing the need for the BCP process. Some of the items the team are responsible for include testing, performing the BIA, and directing the planning, implementation, and testing process.

85. **Answer: C.** Answer C is correct because the full and last differential backup media would be needed. When backing up, you have to choose between faster backup and longer restore. A full backup backs up all files, regardless of whether they have been modified. It removes the archive bit. An incremental backup backs up only those files that have been modified since the previous backup of any sort. It does not remove the archive bit. A differential backup backs up all files that have been modified since the last full backup. It does not remove the archive bit. Differential backups take longer to perform than incremental but can be restored quicker than an incremental.

86. **Answer: C.** Recovery time objective (RTO) specifies the maximum elapsed time to recover an application at an alternate site. The greater the RTO, the longer the process can take to be restored. The service level agreement (SLA) specifies uptime from a service provider. The recovery point objective (RPO) defines how current the data must be, or how much data an organization can afford to lose. The greater the RPO, the more tolerant the process is to interruption. Maximum tolerable downtime (MTD) is how long a business process can be stopped without causing financial harm to the business.

87. **Answer: C.** The loss of competitive advantage would be considered a qualitative loss.

88. **Answer: B.** In this type of agreement, both parties agree to support each other in case of a disruptive event. A major outage could easily disable both companies, and their close location should be the number-one concern. All the other answers are valid concerns, but they are not the most critical.

89. **Answer: A.** A mutual aid agreement, also called a reciprocal agreement, is an arrangement with another company or organization that is in a similar industry and that has compatible systems. In this type of agreement, both parties agree to support each other in case of a disruptive event. Answer B is not another name for a mutual aid agreement. A hot site is designed to provide services after only a short outage. A hot site has equipment, communications, and everything that is needed to get the facility up in just a few minutes to hours. A redundant site is a fully redundant system.

90. **Answer: B.** Parallel processing of transactions to an alternate site is called remote journaling and is evidence that the transaction happened. The transfer of data to an offsite location is known as electronic vaulting. Duplicating database sets to multiple servers is database shadowing. Tape backup is a backup method that can be full, incremental, or differential.

91. **Answer: B.** Should a disaster occur, it will most likely be cost-prohibitive to attempt to recover to full capacity. Service level objectives are set to determine the required service levels to protect the business. Answers A and C are similar and generally refer to the time needed to get a service or department up and running. Answer D refers to the recovery point objective required to recover to and is mostly associated with data backup schedules and methods.

92. **Answer: C.** A simulation test would be best. With such a test the system may be tested on a simulated basis. This should be more accurate than either the checklist or structured walkthrough, because these are paper-based only. Warm test is not a valid test type. In the parallel test, some actual systems are indeed involved and run at the alternate site.

93. **Answer: B.** Parallel processing of transactions to an alternate site is known as remote journaling. The transfer of data to an offsite location is known as electronic vaulting. Duplicating database sets to multiple servers is database shadowing. Tape backup is a backup method that can be full, incremental, or differential.

94. **Answer: D.** Answer A best describes the location where the team lead should begin. A memorandum of understanding is a document that is maintained to specifically identify the people and their specific roles in a business continuity plan. Such documents must be monitored and controlled and tied to HR. That way, any change in employment can be reflected in the plan and will ensure that the people named are still operating in the planned capacity.

95. **Answer: C.** Duplicating database sets to multiple servers is database shadowing. The transfer of data to an offsite location is known as electronic vaulting. Parallel processing of transactions to an alternate site is known as remote journaling. Tape backup is a backup method that can be full, incremental, or differential.

96. **Answer: D.** After a disaster, when returning to the primary site, the order should be from least critical to most critical. Because services are already running at the backup site, it makes more sense to move small items back first to ensure that no unknown problems still exist that might cause interruptions to critical services.

97. **Answer: A.** When considering the RPO, redundant arrays, clustering, and journaling would all be faster than tape backup.

98. **Answer: D.** Although many individuals are involved in the DR/DCP plan, senior management is ultimately responsible for approval of the plan.

99. **Answer: B.** Although cold sites are cheaper than other recovery options, the cold site can require a month to prepare; therefore, answers A, C, and D are incorrect.

100. **Answer: False.** A full interruption is the most complete test. A parallel test is similar to a walk-through but actually starts operations at the alternative site. Operations of the new and old site may be run in parallel.

101. **Answer: True.** A hot site, warm site, and a cold site can all be offered by subscription service. The advantage of this option is that you are placing the responsibility of this service on someone else. The are several concerns: cost, time when the facility is available for testing, total number of subscribers.

102. **Answer: False.** A disaster is not over until operations have been returned to their normal location and function. While at an alternate site, a very large vulnerability exists, because any additional disaster could suspend operations.

103. **Answer: True.** The primary disadvantage of hot site recovery is cost. The hot site facility is ready to go. A hot site is fully configured and is equipped with the same system as the production network. Even though it can take over operations at a moment's notice, it is an expensive option.

104. The answers are as follows:

- **A.** Checklist: **3.**
- **B.** Structured walk-through: **5.**
- **C.** Simulation: **4.**
- **D.** Parallel: **2.**
- **E.** Full interruption: **1.**

Testing the disaster recovery plan is critical. Without performing a test, there is no way to know that the plan will work. Testing helps put more theoretical plans into reality. As a CISSP candidate, you should be aware of the different types of tests and how each is defined. Common test types include checklist, structured walk-through, simulation, parallel, and full interruption.

7

CHAPTER SEVEN

Legal, Regulations, Investigations, and Compliance

Security professionals are expected to understand how computer laws work, how investigations should be handled, and what is considered ethical behavior. As a CISSP, you will be required to sign a code of ethics confirming that you will always act in an ethical manner.

All security topics fall into one of three areas: prevention, detection, or response. This domain deals mainly with the final third of this security triad: response. How will you react when you realize that a computer crime has been committed? What will you do when you discover that a network intrusion has taken place? How will you handle potential computer evidence? Knowledge of these subjects is critical for successful mastery of this domain. The following list gives you some key areas to know:

- Ethics: due care/due diligence
- Intellectual property
- Incident response
- Forensics
- Evidence
- Laws

Quick Check

Practice Questions

1. What is *not* one of the three things that are needed to commit a computer crime?

   Quick Answer: **227**
   Detailed Answer: **228**

   ❍ **A.** Means
   ❍ **B.** Skill
   ❍ **C.** Motive
   ❍ **D.** Opportunity

2. The IAB (Internet Architecture Board) considers which of the following acts unethical?

   Quick Answer: **227**
   Detailed Answer: **228**

   ❍ **A.** Disrupting the intended use of the Internet
   ❍ **B.** Rerouting Internet traffic
   ❍ **C.** Writing articles about security exploits
   ❍ **D.** Developing security patches

3. What category of attack is characterized by the removal of small amounts of money over long periods of time?

   Quick Answer: **227**
   Detailed Answer: **228**

   ❍ **A.** Slicing attack
   ❍ **B.** Skimming attack
   ❍ **C.** Bologna attack
   ❍ **D.** Salami attack

4. You are assigned to a team that is investigating a computer crime. You are asked to make sure that the original data remains unchanged. Which of the following programs can be used to create a cryptographic checksum to verify the data's integrity?

   Quick Answer: **227**
   Detailed Answer: **228**

   ❍ **A.** PKZip
   ❍ **B.** MD5sum
   ❍ **C.** DES
   ❍ **D.** PGP

5. Paul is concerned about the proper disposal of old hard drives that contain propriety information. Which of the following techniques ensures that the data cannot be recovered?

   Quick Answer: **227**
   Detailed Answer: **228**

   ❍ **A.** Formatting
   ❍ **B.** FDISK
   ❍ **C.** Drive wiping
   ❍ **D.** Data parsing

Quick Check

6. Clement recently discovered that his grandmother's secret chocolate-chip cookie recipe was stolen and is being used by Mike to sell the exact same cookies at half the price. What intellectual property law has Mike broken?

Quick Answer: **227**
Detailed Answer: **228**

- ❍ **A.** Trademark
- ❍ **B.** Copyright
- ❍ **C.** Trade secret
- ❍ **D.** Patent

7. Which of the following is *not* one of the three categories of common law?

Quick Answer: **227**
Detailed Answer: **228**

- ❍ **A.** Criminal
- ❍ **B.** Civil
- ❍ **C.** Environmental
- ❍ **D.** Administrative

8. You are part of a study group that is preparing for the CISSP exam. Each group member must present a certain body of knowledge each week. You are asked to discuss the six categories of computer crimes as they are identified by ISC2. Which of the following is *not* one of those types of attacks?

Quick Answer: **227**
Detailed Answer: **228**

- ❍ **A.** Grudge attacks
- ❍ **B.** Financial attacks
- ❍ **C.** Malicious attacks
- ❍ **D.** Fun attacks

9. Brad overhears someone say that Bryce is planning to attack John's computer network. What type of evidence would a court consider this testimony?

Quick Answer: **227**
Detailed Answer: **228**

- ❍ **A.** Best evidence
- ❍ **B.** Hearsay
- ❍ **C.** Conclusive
- ❍ **D.** Admissible

10. Which of the following is *not* one of the three required actions that must be performed during a possible network intrusion?

Quick Answer: **227**
Detailed Answer: **229**

- ❍ **A.** Authenticate
- ❍ **B.** Document
- ❍ **C.** Acquire
- ❍ **D.** Analyze

Quick Check

11. What is the most important aspect of incident response?

Quick Answer: **227**
Detailed Answer: **229**

❍ **A.** A well-documented and approved response plan

❍ **B.** Honeypots

❍ **C.** Evidence handling

❍ **D.** Verification that no systems will be powered down until they are fully examined

12. A coworker is thinking about becoming CISSP certified and has questions about ethics and RFC 1087. Which of the following is *not* specified in RFC 1087?

Quick Answer: **227**
Detailed Answer: **229**

❍ **A.** Access to the Internet is a right that no individual should be denied.

❍ **B.** Negligence in conduct when performing activities on the Internet is unacceptable.

❍ **C.** It is unethical to disrupt the intended use of the Internet.

❍ **D.** The well-being of the Internet is the responsibility of all its users.

13. Louie is studying for his CISSP exam and comes to you with a question: What is the correct order of the items that make up the evidence life cycle? How will you answer him?

Quick Answer: **227**
Detailed Answer: **229**

❍ **A.** Collection, storage, analysis, presentation, and return to victim

❍ **B.** Seizure, storage, analysis, presentation, and return to victim

❍ **C.** Seizure, storage, validation, presentation, and return to victim

❍ **D.** Collection, analysis, storage, presentation, and return to victim

14. During a computer intrusion, an attacker typically attempts to cover his tracks. Which commonly known principle states that trace evidence will always remain?

Quick Answer: **227**
Detailed Answer: **229**

❍ **A.** Locard's principle

❍ **B.** Picard's principle

❍ **C.** Kruse's theory

❍ **D.** Gauntlett's theory

Quick Check

15. A local law firm, Dewey and Cheatem, has asked you to examine some potential computer evidence. Even though you have yet to examine the evidence, you are concerned. You were told that the evidence was misplaced, but it has been found on a table in the law firm's storage room. What potential rule has been broken?

Quick Answer: **227**
Detailed Answer: **229**

- ❍ **A.** Due process
- ❍ **B.** Chain of custody
- ❍ **C.** Habeas corpus
- ❍ **D.** Evidence objection

16. You are placed in charge of your company's new incident response team. Place the five steps of incident response in their proper order.

Quick Answer: **227**
Detailed Answer: **230**

- ❍ **A.** Identify, analyze, mitigate, investigate, and train
- ❍ **B.** Train, identify, analyze, mitigate, and investigate
- ❍ **C.** Identify, coordinate, mitigate, investigate, and educate
- ❍ **D.** Educate, identify, coordinate, mitigate, and investigate

17. Your boss has asked you to get a copy of SATAN to install on a networked computer. What is SATAN?

Quick Answer: **227**
Detailed Answer: **230**

- ❍ **A.** An incident response tool
- ❍ **B.** A network vulnerability scanner
- ❍ **C.** The first automated penetration testing tool
- ❍ **D.** A network sniffer

18. When a team is investigating a possible network intrusion, which of the following would be the best way for team members to communicate?

Quick Answer: **227**
Detailed Answer: **230**

- ❍ **A.** Email
- ❍ **B.** VoIP phones
- ❍ **C.** Instant Messenger
- ❍ **D.** Cell phone

19. Darla, your network support technician, comes to you with a question: What is Tripwire used for?

Quick Answer: **227**
Detailed Answer: **230**

- ❍ **A.** Tripwire is a host-based IDS.
- ❍ **B.** Tripwire is a signature-based IDS.
- ❍ **C.** Tripwire is a network-based IDS.
- ❍ **D.** Tripwire is a file integrity monitoring tool.

Quick Check

20. What is the name of the software that prevents users from seeing all items or directories on a computer, changes process output, and is most commonly found on a compromised UNIX/Linux computer?

Quick Answer: **227**
Detailed Answer: **230**

- ❍ **A.** Hidden file attributes
- ❍ **B.** File obscurity
- ❍ **C.** NTFS DataStreams
- ❍ **D.** Root kit

21. Ted's nighttime job at Stop-n-Shop gives him time to reprogram the cash register. Now each time he scans an item that costs 99 cents, the register shows the cost as 49 cents. Ted then pockets the remaining 50 cents. He figures that he will have stolen enough for a used car by the time summer is over. What type of hacking attack has Ted performed?

Quick Answer: **227**
Detailed Answer: **230**

- ❍ **A.** Privilege escalation
- ❍ **B.** Data diddling
- ❍ **C.** Tuple attack
- ❍ **D.** Salami

22. You have just found out that a company that wants you to consult for it has had its phone system hacked, and more than $5,000 worth of illegal phone calls have been made. What is the name for individuals who perform this type of activity?

Quick Answer: **227**
Detailed Answer: **230**

- ❍ **A.** Phreakers
- ❍ **B.** Script kiddies
- ❍ **C.** Hackers
- ❍ **D.** Crackers

23. Which of the following is *not* one of the primary categories of evidence that can be presented in a court of law?

Quick Answer: **227**
Detailed Answer: **230**

- ❍ **A.** Direct
- ❍ **B.** Indirect
- ❍ **C.** Real
- ❍ **D.** Demonstrative

24. Chain of custody includes which of the following?

Quick Answer: **227**
Detailed Answer: **230**

- ❍ **A.** Who, what, where, when, and how
- ❍ **B.** Who, when, why, how, motive, and where
- ❍ **C.** What, why, and how
- ❍ **D.** What, when, and where

Quick Check

25. What is criminal activity that is directly targeted against network devices called?

Quick Answer: **227**
Detailed Answer: **231**

- ❍ **A.** Computer crime
- ❍ **B.** Civil violations
- ❍ **C.** Criminal violations
- ❍ **D.** Illegal penetration testing

26. The 1996 U.S. Kennedy-Kassenbaum Act is also known by what other name?

Quick Answer: **227**
Detailed Answer: **231**

- ❍ **A.** HIPAA
- ❍ **B.** The 1996 Federal Privacy Act
- ❍ **C.** GASSP
- ❍ **D.** The 1996 U.S. National Information Infrastructure Protection Act

27. Fred is concerned that he may be called into civil court. Which of the following penalties can be levied against an individual found guilty in a civil case?

Quick Answer: **227**
Detailed Answer: **231**

- ❍ **A.** Imprisonment
- ❍ **B.** Fines
- ❍ **C.** Imprisonment and fines
- ❍ **D.** Community service

28. According to CERT, one of the key elements of establishing that a computer user has no right to privacy on a corporate computer includes which of the following?

Quick Answer: **227**
Detailed Answer: **231**

- ❍ **A.** Passwords
- ❍ **B.** Notification of privacy policy at the time of employment
- ❍ **C.** Login banners
- ❍ **D.** Verbal warnings

29. Which type of evidence is preferred in trials because it provides the most reliability and may include documents or contracts?

Quick Answer: **227**
Detailed Answer: **231**

- ❍ **A.** Direct evidence
- ❍ **B.** Collaborative evidence
- ❍ **C.** Secondary evidence
- ❍ **D.** Best evidence

Quick Check

30. Which of the following is considered a commercial application of steganography?

- ❍ **A.** Hashing
- ❍ **B.** Data diddling
- ❍ **C.** Digital watermarks
- ❍ **D.** XOR encryption

Quick Answer: **227**
Detailed Answer: **231**

31. Which type of evidence is based on information gathered from a witness's five senses?

- ❍ **A.** Direct evidence
- ❍ **B.** Collaborative evidence
- ❍ **C.** Secondary evidence
- ❍ **D.** Best evidence

Quick Answer: **227**
Detailed Answer: **231**

32. Enticement is best described by which of the following statements?

- ❍ **A.** It is not legal.
- ❍ **B.** It is legal.
- ❍ **C.** It is neither legal nor ethical.
- ❍ **D.** It is legal with a court order or warrant.

Quick Answer: **227**
Detailed Answer: **231**

33. Keyboard monitoring is an example of which of the following?

- ❍ **A.** Enticement
- ❍ **B.** Physical surveillance
- ❍ **C.** Entrapment
- ❍ **D.** Computer surveillance

Quick Answer: **227**
Detailed Answer: **231**

34. Fred has been asked to help examine a seized computer hard drive. He comes to you with a question. On most common disk systems, storage space is allocated in units called what?

- ❍ **A.** Bytes
- ❍ **B.** Bits
- ❍ **C.** Clusters
- ❍ **D.** Nibbles

Quick Answer: **227**
Detailed Answer: **231**

35. Mike has recently discovered that the material he wrote for a new book is being used by a competitor as a course manual. What law has the competitor potentially broken?

- ❍ **A.** Trademark
- ❍ **B.** Copyright
- ❍ **C.** Trade secret
- ❍ **D.** Patent

Quick Answer: **227**
Detailed Answer: **231**

Quick Check

36. You are placed in charge of a forensic investigation. Now that you have seized the suspect's computer, what should your next step be?

Quick Answer: **227**
Detailed Answer: **232**

❍ **A.** Create a logical copy

❍ **B.** Create cryptographic checksums of all files and folders

❍ **C.** Create a physical copy

❍ **D.** Examine the hard drive

37. Entrapment is best described by which of the following statements?

Quick Answer: **227**
Detailed Answer: **232**

❍ **A.** It is not legal.

❍ **B.** It is legal.

❍ **C.** It is neither legal nor ethical.

❍ **D.** It is legal with a court order or warrant.

38. Which of the following best describes file slack?

Quick Answer: **227**
Detailed Answer: **232**

❍ **A.** File slack is the free space remaining in a used cluster.

❍ **B.** File slack is the free space remaining on a hard drive.

❍ **C.** File slack is the free space remaining in a used byte.

❍ **D.** File slack is the space remaining when a file is erased.

39. You recently received a company-issued laptop that formerly belonged to another individual. While setting up your Documents folder, you notice remaining proprietary information from the former user. What does the ISC2 Code of Ethics direct you to do?

Quick Answer: **227**
Detailed Answer: **232**

❍ **A.** Leave the information, but make sure that it is backed up along with your data.

❍ **B.** Contact the individual about the information you found.

❍ **C.** Delete the information, and verify that it has been permanently removed.

❍ **D.** Inform your manager of your findings, and seek guidance.

40. Which of the following is *not* required of evidence for it to be admissible in court?

Quick Answer: **227**
Detailed Answer: **232**

❍ **A.** Reliable

❍ **B.** Sufficient

❍ **C.** Validated

❍ **D.** Relevant

Quick Check

41. Senior management and directors are expected to protect the company from network attacks or security breaches. What is this type of behavior called?

Quick Answer: **227**
Detailed Answer: **232**

- ❍ **A.** Due care
- ❍ **B.** In good faith
- ❍ **C.** Risk negligence
- ❍ **D.** Due prudence

42. Jack has decided to try his hand at phone hacking. He has built a box that simulates the sound of coins being dropped into a payphone. What is the device called?

Quick Answer: **227**
Detailed Answer: **232**

- ❍ **A.** A blue box
- ❍ **B.** A black box
- ❍ **C.** A red box
- ❍ **D.** A white box

43. Because of your recent good work in building the incident response team, you are asked to work with the newly created mobile sales force. Your success in this venture will certainly move you up the corporate ladder. You are asked to propose the best way to secure the data on the laptops that each salesperson will carry. Which of the following will you recommend?

Quick Answer: **227**
Detailed Answer: **232**

- ❍ **A.** Issue each salesperson a laptop locking cable.
- ❍ **B.** Use file encryption on the hard drives.
- ❍ **C.** Require each salesperson to VPN into the network remotely.
- ❍ **D.** Enforce the use of WEP for all wireless communication.

44. Financial institutions are most affected by which of the following laws?

Quick Answer: **227**
Detailed Answer: **232**

- ❍ **A.** Federal Privacy Act of 1974
- ❍ **B.** Gramm-Leach-Bliley Act of 1999
- ❍ **C.** HIPAA
- ❍ **D.** Interpol FRA

45. Employee monitoring through the use of CCTV is an example of which of the following?

Quick Answer: **227**
Detailed Answer: **233**

- ❍ **A.** Enticement
- ❍ **B.** Physical surveillance
- ❍ **C.** Entrapment
- ❍ **D.** Computer surveillance

Quick Check

46. Your consulting company is poised to gain a large defense contract. Your director wants you to learn more about your company's responsibility for security if the contract is approved. Which government entity is responsible for managing government systems that contain sensitive or classified information?

Quick Answer: 227
Detailed Answer: 233

❍ **A.** The FBI
❍ **B.** The NSA
❍ **C.** U.S. marshals
❍ **D.** NIST

47. Your director is so pleased about your prior findings that now she wants you to investigate who is responsible for managing government systems that *do not* contain sensitive or classified information. What will you tell her?

Quick Answer: 227
Detailed Answer: 233

❍ **A.** The FBI
❍ **B.** The NSA
❍ **C.** The Secret Service
❍ **D.** NIST

48. Your director also wants you to investigate who is responsible for investigating computer crimes within the U.S. Specifically, she wants to know which federal agencies are responsible for tracking and prosecuting individuals who deal in stolen passwords. What do you tell her?

Quick Answer: 227
Detailed Answer: 233

❍ **A.** The FBI
❍ **B.** The NSA
❍ **C.** The Secret Service and the NSA
❍ **D.** The FBI and the Secret Service

49. What did the 1987 Computer Security Act do?

Quick Answer: 227
Detailed Answer: 233

❍ **A.** It made it illegal for the government to eavesdrop on electronic communications without a warrant or court order.
❍ **B.** It required the U.S. government to conduct security-related training and identify federal systems that maintain sensitive information.
❍ **C.** It strengthened the penalties that an individual faces if caught eavesdropping on electronic communications without legal consent.
❍ **D.** It placed minimum requirements on private businesses for the practice of due diligence by requiring them to provide security-related training to all employees.

Quick Check

50. You are asked to authenticate a hard drive that was seized during an investigation. Your superiors want to make sure that subsequent copies are exact duplicates and that no changes occur to the data stored on the seized drive. Which of the following would be the best method of validating the data's integrity?

Quick Answer: **227**
Detailed Answer: **233**

❍ **A.** MD5

❍ **B.** SHA

❍ **C.** NTLM

❍ **D.** PGP

51. Which of the following is a computer-targeted crime?

Quick Answer: **227**
Detailed Answer: **233**

❍ **A.** DDoS

❍ **B.** Sharing child porn

❍ **C.** Browsing corporate secrets

❍ **D.** Hacktivism

52. When updating data contained in remote databases housed in your subsidiary locations in Europe, what additional international requirements might you have to abide by?

Quick Answer: **227**
Detailed Answer: **233**

❍ **A.** Safe Harbor

❍ **B.** European Commission's Directive on Data Protection

❍ **C.** Export Regulations Administration (EAR)

❍ **D.** Wassenaar Arrangement

53. Microsoft Corporation (microsoft.com) was permitted to force Mike Rowe to release the domain name he had set up to market his software products (MikeRoweSoft.com). On what grounds was Mike Rowe guilty?

Quick Answer: **227**
Detailed Answer: **233**

❍ **A.** Copyright violation

❍ **B.** Trade secret violation

❍ **C.** Trademark violation

❍ **D.** Patent infringement

54. When a company chooses to monitor its employees' email, what action must it take?

Quick Answer: **227**
Detailed Answer: **233**

❍ **A.** Spell out this policy in its Security Policy.

❍ **B.** Remind the employees in a warning banner.

❍ **C.** Provide periodic refresher training.

❍ **D.** All of the above.

Quick Check

55. Corporations must be able to prove in a court of law that they took reasonable care to protect their employees and their data from crime. What term describes this?

Quick Answer: **227**
Detailed Answer: **234**

- ❍ **A.** Prudent person
- ❍ **B.** Due diligence
- ❍ **C.** Safety net
- ❍ **D.** Due care

56. In a court of law, a case revolves around whether a particular license was signed by a particular person. Which evidence would be the best evidence to provide the court in this case?

Quick Answer: **227**
Detailed Answer: **234**

- ❍ **A.** A clear copy of a dated licensing agreement
- ❍ **B.** A witness who saw the license being signed
- ❍ **C.** A certificate awarded after the license was signed
- ❍ **D.** The tattered original document, lacking a date

57. A forensic copy of a suspect's server needs to be created as a what?

Quick Answer: **227**
Detailed Answer: **234**

- ❍ **A.** Bit stream copy
- ❍ **B.** Complete backup
- ❍ **C.** Archive copy
- ❍ **D.** Data dump

58. Many crimes that are known to have occurred are not reported to officials. This lack of reporting results in criminals not being prosecuted and keeps improved defensive measures from being developed. Which statement describes the most probable reason for a company's failure to report a crime?

Quick Answer: **227**
Detailed Answer: **234**

- ❍ **A.** Expected loss of revenue as soon as the computer is removed for the investigation
- ❍ **B.** Embarrassment and financial impact
- ❍ **C.** The belief that someone made a mistake that is unlikely to be repeated
- ❍ **D.** The desire to quietly study the activity without alerting the criminal

59. Which of the following is *not* one of the reasons that prosecuting international crime is difficult?

Quick Answer: **227**
Detailed Answer: **234**

- ❍ **A.** Lack of universal cooperation
- ❍ **B.** Low priority
- ❍ **C.** Ease of extradition
- ❍ **D.** Outdated laws and technology

Quick Check

60. Which of the following best describes the steps an organization takes to implement best security practices?

Quick Answer: **227**
Detailed Answer: **234**

- ❍ **A.** Certification
- ❍ **B.** Due care
- ❍ **C.** Accreditation
- ❍ **D.** Due diligence

61. What kind of oral or written evidence comes from an eyewitness account?

Quick Answer: **227**
Detailed Answer: **234**

- ❍ **A.** Secondary evidence
- ❍ **B.** Real evidence
- ❍ **C.** Direct evidence
- ❍ **D.** Demonstrative evidence

62. What kind of evidence can be a tangible object, tool, or property that was gathered from the crime scene?

Quick Answer: **227**
Detailed Answer: **234**

- ❍ **A.** Secondary evidence
- ❍ **B.** Real evidence
- ❍ **C.** Direct evidence
- ❍ **D.** Demonstrative evidence

63. How can the term "relevant" best be described?

Quick Answer: **227**
Detailed Answer: **234**

- ❍ **A.** An item that has substance or that can be treated as fact
- ❍ **B.** Reasonably proven
- ❍ **C.** Tends to prove or disprove facts that are important and material to the case
- ❍ **D.** Luring someone into creating additional evidence

64. Which of the following is not one of the commonly approved reasons that allow law enforcement to seize evidence?

Quick Answer: **227**
Detailed Answer: **234**

- ❍ **A.** Suspicion
- ❍ **B.** Search warrant
- ❍ **C.** Writ
- ❍ **D.** Extenuating circumstances

Quick Check

65. During the incident-handling process, it is critical to detect that a security breach has occurred. With this is mind, which of the following best describes an event?

Quick Answer: **227**
Detailed Answer: **234**

- ❍ **A.** A violation of security policy or law
- ❍ **B.** A noticeable occurrence
- ❍ **C.** A false negative trigger or event on an IDS
- ❍ **D.** A negative event on an IDS

66. You are asked to set up and configure an IDS. Which of the following is the worst state an IDS can operate in?

Quick Answer: **227**
Detailed Answer: **234**

- ❍ **A.** Positive
- ❍ **B.** False positive
- ❍ **C.** Negative
- ❍ **D.** False negative

67. The following statement can be found in which of the following ethical standards? "Act honorably, honestly, justly, responsibly, and legally."

Quick Answer: **227**
Detailed Answer: **235**

- ❍ **A.** RFC 1087
- ❍ **B.** ISC2 Code of Ethics
- ❍ **C.** The Computer Game Fallacy
- ❍ **D.** Generally Accepted Information Security Principles (GAISP)

68. The following statement can be found in which of the following ethical standards? "Wastes resources."

Quick Answer: **227**
Detailed Answer: **235**

- ❍ **A.** RFC 1087
- ❍ **B.** ISC2 Code of Ethics
- ❍ **C.** The Computer Game Fallacy
- ❍ **D.** Generally Accepted Information Security Principles (GAISP)

69. The following statement can be found in which of the following ethical standards? "Systems that are not protected are fair game to attack."

Quick Answer: **227**
Detailed Answer: **235**

- ❍ **A.** RFC 1087
- ❍ **B.** ISC2 Code of Ethics
- ❍ **C.** The Computer Game Fallacy
- ❍ **D.** Generally Accepted Information Security Principles (GAISP)

Quick Check

70. The following statement can be found in which of the following ethical standards? "Promote broad awareness of information security."

Quick Answer: **227**
Detailed Answer: **235**

- ❍ **A.** RFC 1087
- ❍ **B.** ISC2 Code of Ethics
- ❍ **C.** The Computer Game Fallacy
- ❍ **D.** Generally Accepted Information Security Principles (GAISP)

71. Which of the following best describes a logic bomb?

Quick Answer: **227**
Detailed Answer: **235**

- ❍ **A.** A program or portion of a program that remains inactive until a specific action occurs
- ❍ **B.** The action of removing fractions of a cent from each transaction
- ❍ **C.** A program or portion of a program that can round down a monetary value
- ❍ **D.** A security-breaking program that is disguised as something benign

72. What is another name for tort law?

Quick Answer: **227**
Detailed Answer: **235**

- ❍ **A.** Criminal law
- ❍ **B.** Civil law
- ❍ **C.** Administrative
- ❍ **D.** Regulatory

73. You are asked to help in a forensic investigation. Which of the following should you do first?

Quick Answer: **227**
Detailed Answer: **235**

- ❍ **A.** Copy the hard drive.
- ❍ **B.** Copy the USB thumb drive.
- ❍ **C.** Copy the contents of RAM memory.
- ❍ **D.** Clear the printer buffer.

74. As a forensic specialist, you are asked which of the following actions would most help with the admissibility of computer evidence.

Quick Answer: **227**
Detailed Answer: **235**

- ❍ **A.** Back up all computer files on the hard drive.
- ❍ **B.** Create a bit-level mirror image of the hard drive.
- ❍ **C.** Use the `copy` command to duplicate the hard drive.
- ❍ **D.** Reboot the hard drive with a write blocker before using a backup tool to logically copy all files.

Quick Check

75. What is the primary reason for the importance of the chain of custody?

Quick Answer: **227**
Detailed Answer: **235**

- ❍ **A.** It is used to account for everyone who had access to the evidence.
- ❍ **B.** It is used to prevent challenges from the defense.
- ❍ **C.** It is used to verify the admissibility and accuracy of the information contained within.
- ❍ **D.** It is used to verify the accuracy of the duplication process.

76. Who is responsible for PCI-DSS standards?

Quick Answer: **227**
Detailed Answer: **235**

- ❍ **A.** ISO
- ❍ **B.** EU
- ❍ **C.** U.S. Government
- ❍ **D.** Major credit-card companies

77. Which of the following protects the expression of ideas?

Quick Answer: **227**
Detailed Answer: **235**

- ❍ **A.** Patent
- ❍ **B.** Copyright
- ❍ **C.** Trademark
- ❍ **D.** Tradedress

78. Which of the following legal systems covers two or more legal systems?

Quick Answer: **227**
Detailed Answer: **235**

- ❍ **A.** Religious law
- ❍ **B.** Civil law
- ❍ **C.** Mixed law
- ❍ **D.** Dual law

79. Which of the following is the primary reason for chain of custody?

Quick Answer: **227**
Detailed Answer: **235**

- ❍ **A.** To prevent the defense from challenging
- ❍ **B.** To demonstrate it was properly controlled and handled
- ❍ **C.** To verify whether the copy that was used is admissible
- ❍ **D.** To verify changes to data

Quick Check

Practice Questions (Mix and Match)

80. Match each term with its definition.

A. Copyright: _____

B. Trademark: _____

C. Patent: _____

D. Trade secret: _____

1. A secret method or formula that requires a level of protection

2. Offered as an exclusive right by the government to protect inventions

3. An expression of words or ideas presented in a unique way

4. Distinctive in nature; can be a shape, color, symbol, or slogan

Quick Answer: **227**
Detailed Answer: **236**

Quick Check Answer Key

1. B
2. A
3. D
4. B
5. C
6. C
7. C
8. C
9. B
10. B
11. A
12. A
13. D
14. A
15. B
16. C
17. B
18. D
19. D
20. D
21. B
22. A
23. B
24. A
25. A
26. A
27. B
28. C
29. D
30. C
31. A
32. B
33. D
34. C
35. B
36. C
37. C
38. A
39. D
40. C
41. A
42. C
43. B
44. B
45. B
46. B
47. D
48. D
49. B
50. B
51. A
52. A
53. C
54. D
55. D
56. D
57. A
58. B
59. C
60. B
61. C
62. B
63. C
64. A
65. B
66. D
67. B
68. A
69. C
70. D
71. A
72. B
73. C
74. B
75. A
76. D
77. B
78. C
79. D
80. **A.** 3
B. 4
C. 2
D. 1

Answers and Explanations

1. **Answer: B.** Although skill may be useful to those attempting to commit a computer crime, means, motive, and opportunity are required. Ready-to-use programs can be downloaded from the Internet that allow any layman to launch an attack.

2. **Answer: A.** The IAB (Internet Activities Board) considers the following acts unethical:

   Gaining unauthorized access

   Disrupting the intended use of the Internet

   Wasting resources

   Destroying the integrity of computer-based information

   Being negligent when conducting Internet-based experiments

   Compromising privacy

3. **Answer: D.** A salami attack is characterized by the removal of very small amounts of money over a long period of time. This may be only fractions of a cent, but the idea is that the amount is so small that it goes unnoticed.

4. **Answer: B.** MD5sum can be used to verify data, to compare files, and to detect file corruption and tampering. Extremely fast and lightweight, it produces a 128-bit checksum.

5. **Answer: C.** Drive-wiping programs work by overwriting all addressable locations on the disk. Some programs even make several passes to further decrease the possibility of data recovery. What they provide for the individual who wants to dispose of unused drives is a verifiably clean medium. However, in the hands of a criminal, these programs offer the chance to destroy evidence. All other answers are incorrect because they do not adequately erase the data.

6. **Answer: C.** Organizations rely on proprietary information for their survival. This may include formulas, inventions, recipes, strategies, or processes. If this information is improperly disclosed, it could endanger the organization's financial capability to continue as a going concern. In other words, it could potentially cause a bankruptcy. If this information has been illegally acquired, the organization can seek protection and remedies under trade-secret laws.

7. **Answer: C.** The three categories of common law are criminal, civil, and administrative. Although there may be environmental laws, they would fall under the category of administrative law.

8. **Answer: C.** The CISSP CBK identifies six types of computer crimes:

   Grudge attacks

   Financial attacks

   Fun attacks

   Business attacks

   Military attacks

   Terrorist attacks

9. **Answer: B.** Hearsay evidence is defined as information that is not based on personal firsthand knowledge but was obtained through third parties. As such, it may not be

admissible in court. Best evidence is recorded, written, or photographed. Conclusive evidence is irrefutable. Admissible evidence is any evidence that can be allowed in court.

10. **Answer: B.** Although documentation is required, it is considered only a subsection of all three required actions that must be performed during an investigation:

    Acquisition: Evidence must be acquired in a forensically sound manner.

    Authentication: Any information or data that is recovered must be authenticated.

    Analysis: The evidence must be analyzed in a manner that is considered legal and that follows rules of procedure.

11. **Answer: A.** Although evidence handling and system verification are important parts of incident response, the most important aspect of incident response is a well-documented and approved response plan. Before an actual incident, an organization should know who will be involved, what steps should be performed, and how the individuals should respond based on the type of threat or attack. Honeypots are used before incident response as a means of detecting or containing malicious users.

12. **Answer: A.** Access to the Internet is not a right, but a privilege, and should be treated as such. You can read the complete RFC at www.faqs.org/rfcs/rfc1087.html.

13. **Answer: D.** Any type of evidence that is obtained from a possible crime must be handled under the strictest guidelines. The evidence life cycle is composed of the following five stages:

    Collection and identification

    Analysis

    Storage and preservation

    Presentation

    Return to the victim

14. **Answer: A.** Locard's exchange principle states that whenever two objects come into contact, a transfer of material will occur. The resulting trace evidence can be used to associate objects, individuals, or locations to a crime (see http://suite101.com/article/lockards-exchange-principle-a47558). Simply stated, no matter how hard someone tries to cover his or her tracks, some trace evidence always remains. The complexity of modern computers makes it almost impossible for suspects to erase all evidence of their activities. Although suspects can make recovery harder by deleting files and caches, some trace evidence always remains. During an investigation, slack space, cache, the registry, browser history, and the page files are just a few of the items that can be examined.

15. **Answer: B.** Chain of custody has been broken. The chain of custody is a critical component because the evidence it protects can be used in criminal court to convict persons of crimes or in civil court to punish them through monetary means. Therefore, evidence must always be handled in a careful manner to avoid allegations of tampering or misconduct. Someone must always have physical custody of the piece of evidence. Due process deals with the function of the legal process, habeas corpus deals with unlawful detention, and evidence objection is simply a distracter.

16. **Answer: C.** Five general steps outline the handling of an incident. The process starts at the point where the intrusion is detected:

    Identify the problem.

    Coordinate the response.

    Mitigate the damage.

    Investigate the root cause or culprit.

    Educate team members about avoiding future problems.

17. **Answer: B.** Although SATAN (Security Administrator's Tool for Analyzing Networks) was not the first vulnerability scanner, it was big news upon its release. It was developed by Dan Farmer and Wietse Venema in 1995 to help administrators find network vulnerabilities before attackers could do so.

18. **Answer: D.** Any type of communication method that uses the company's network may have been compromised. Therefore, during a possible network intrusion, the best form of communication is out-of-band communications. This includes cell phones, telephones, and pagers.

19. **Answer: D.** Tripwire is one of the most well-known tools available for detecting unauthorized alterations to OS system files and software. It functions by creating a known-state database of checksums for each file and executable. Then it periodically checks the known checksum against a newly generated one. Unlike an IDS, Tripwire can detect any change to any file. It is very useful during an incident response operation.

20. **Answer: D.** Root kits are software-based items that prevent users from seeing all items or directories on a computer. They are found in the UNIX/Linux and Windows environment. NTFS DataStreams are possible only in a Windows environment, hidden file attributes do not change program behavior, and file obscurity is a distracter.

21. **Answer: B.** Data diddling is the process of altering data or dollar amounts before or after they are entered into an application. This type of hacking attack can be prevented by using good accounting controls, auditing, or increased supervision. Privilege escalation is the process of making oneself administrator or root on a computer. There is no such thing as a tuple attack. A salami attack involves skimming small amounts of money or funds from an account with the hope that it will go unnoticed.

22. **Answer: A.** Hackers, crackers, and script kiddies are individuals who commit computer crimes. Phreaking predates hacking and is a classification of attack that deals specifically with phone fraud. One famous phreaker was John Draper, also known as Cap'n Crunch. The website http://en.wikipedia.org/wiki/Phreaking has a ton of interesting information.

23. **Answer: B.** The four types of evidence that can be presented in a court of law are direct, real, documentary, and demonstrative.

24. **Answer: A.** The chain of custody provides accountability and protection for the evidence to ensure that it has not been tampered with. The following five items are required for proper chain of custody: who discovered it; what the evidence is; where it is being stored and where it was found; when it was discovered, seized, or analyzed; and how it has been collected, stored, or transported.

25. **Answer: A.** Computer crime can be broadly defined as any criminal offense or activity that involves computers. It could be that the computer has been used to commit a crime or that the computer has been the target of a crime.

26. **Answer: A.** The 1996 U.S. Kennedy-Kassenbaum Act is also known as the Health Insurance and Portability Accountability Act (HIPAA). The Federal Privacy Act deals with the handling of personal information. GASSP (Generally Accepted Systems Security Principles) is not a law but an accepted group of security principles. The U.S. National Information Infrastructure Protection Act deals with the protection of confidentiality, integrity, and availability of data and networked systems.

27. **Answer: B.** The only penalty that can be awarded in a civil case is a fine.

28. **Answer: C.** CERT (Computer Emergency Response Team) recommends that corporations implement login banners that are displayed each time a computer user boots his or her computer. To read more about this, check out the CERT article at www.cert.org/advisories/CA-1992-19.html.

29. **Answer: D.** Best evidence is considered the most reliable in a court case. It includes documents, contracts, and legal papers. An example of direct evidence is evidence provided by a witness. Collaborative evidence supports a point or helps prove a theory. Secondary evidence includes copies of original documents or oral evidence provided by a witness.

30. **Answer: C.** The commercial application of steganography lies mainly in the use of digital watermarks. Digital watermarks act as a type of digital fingerprint and can verify proof of source. Individuals who own data or create original art want to protect their intellectual property. In cases of intellectual property theft, digital watermarks can be used to show proof of ownership.

31. **Answer: A.** An example of direct evidence is evidence provided by a witness. It could be something he saw, something he heard, or something he knows. Collaborative evidence supports a point or helps prove a theory. Secondary evidence includes copies of documents or oral evidence provided by a witness. Best evidence is considered the most reliable in a court case. It includes original documents, contracts, and legal papers.

32. **Answer: B.** Enticement is considered legal because it may lure someone into leaving some type of evidence after he or she has committed a crime. Entrapment is considered illegal and unethical because it may encourage someone to commit a crime that was not intended.

33. **Answer: D.** Keyboard monitoring is a type of computer surveillance. Before an organization decides to attempt this type of surveillance, it is critical that employees be informed that their computer activity may be monitored. Login banners are a good way to accomplish this legal notification.

34. **Answer: C.** The smallest unit of storage on a hard disk is known as a cluster or a logical unit of storage. Cluster size, as defined by Microsoft, is based on the drive's total capacity. As drive capacity increases, so does the cluster size. The other answers are incorrect because bits, bytes, and nibbles are all examples of binary notation.

35. **Answer: B.** A copyright is a protective measure that covers any published or unpublished literature, artistic work, or scientific work. This allows the creator of a work to enjoy protection of that work for a period of time. Usually, this includes the stipulation that the owner of the copyright is the only person who can legally profit from the

work, unless the owner gives express permission that a third party can use the work during that period. For example, the creator of a piece of software owns the copyright. Often, the creator can profit from this software by selling licenses to others as a means to allow them to legally use the software too. Essentially, this means that if you can see it, hear it, and/or touch it, it may be protected.

36. **Answer: C.** You need to create a physical copy. Programs that create a physical copy not only copy all the files and folders but literally duplicate all the information, down to the track, sector, and cluster of the original. Creating a logical copy consists of duplicating files and folders. This is the same process that occurs when you use any number of standard backup programs, such as Microsoft Backup or Norton Ghost. Files and folders are duplicated, but the information is not restored in the same location as the original, nor are the free space and slack space copied.

37. **Answer: C.** Entrapment is considered illegal and unethical in that it may encourage someone to commit a crime that was not intended (such as with honeypots). In contrast, enticement is considered legal because it may lure someone into leaving some type of evidence after the crime was committed.

38. **Answer: A.** When a computer writes files to the drive and the file size does not come out to be an even multiple of the cluster size, extra space must be used in the next cluster to hold the file. This cluster is only partially used. The remaining space in that cluster is called file slack. The file slack can hold information that can be important during an incident response investigation or forensic analysis.

39. **Answer: D.** The ISC2 Code of Ethics dictates that CISSP certified individuals should discourage unsafe and insecure practices. In this situation, inform management of your findings. If you are unauthorized to view such information, you should not back it up or keep a copy. Contacting the individual will not increase the likelihood that the problem will not happen in the future. Deleting the information only ignores the fact that there may be a security lapse or problem. You can view the complete Code of Ethics at https://www.isc2.org/cgi-bin/content.cgi?category=12#code.

40. **Answer: C.** For evidence to be admissible in court, it must meet three challenges: it must be reliable, it must be sufficient, and it must be relevant.

41. **Answer: A.** Due care is considered what a reasonable person or corporation would exercise under a given set of circumstances. Corporations that fail to practice due care in protecting the organization's network or information assets may open the organization to some legal liability.

42. **Answer: C.** A red box is a device that simulates the sound of coins being dropped in a payphone. Blue boxes simulate telephone tones, black boxes manipulate telephone line voltages, and white boxes turn a normal touch-tone keypad into a portable unit.

43. **Answer: B.** Using strong encryption on the hard drives is the best way to secure the data. Although locking cables may prevent the laptops from being removed from a hotel room or another location, they would not prevent someone from accessing the data. Neither would the use of WEP or the use of a VPN protect the data if someone could successfully gain physical access.

44. **Answer: B.** The Gramm-Leach-Bliley Act of 1999 requires financial institutions to develop privacy policies. The Federal Privacy Act of 1974 places limits on what type of

information the federal government can collect and disseminate about U.S. citizens. HIPAA (Health Insurance Portability and Accountability Act) is focused on the medical and health-care industry. There is no such thing as the Interpol FRA.

45. **Answer: B.** Physical surveillance can be hidden cameras, closed-circuit TVs, security cameras, hardware keyloggers, or security guards. The goal of physical surveillance is to capture evidence about a suspect's behavior or activities.

46. **Answer: B.** The National Security Agency (NSA) is responsible for all systems that maintain classified or sensitive information.

47. **Answer: D.** Although the National Security Agency is responsible for all systems that maintain classified or sensitive information, nonsensitive information systems are managed by NIST (the National Institute of Standards and Technology).

48. **Answer: D.** The FBI and the Secret Service are responsible for the tracking and apprehension of individuals dealing in stolen passwords. You can find more information at www.cybercrime.gov/reporting.htm.

49. **Answer: B.** The 1987 Computer Security Act required federal government agencies to conduct security-related training, identify sensitive systems, and develop plans to secure sensitive data that is stored on such systems. You can read more about this act at www.epic.org/crypto/csa/csa.html.

50. **Answer: B.** SHA-1 (SHA) creates a message digest that is 160 bits long, which is considered more robust than the 128-bit message digest created by MD5. NTLM and PGP are not hashing algorithms.

51. **Answer: A.** Computer-targeted crimes are ones that could not have been committed without the presence of a computer. DDoS differs from a regular DoS attack by using multiple zombie machines to attack your network. Answers B, C, and D are all crimes in which the computer is incidental to the crime (the crime can take place without the computer); they are called computer-assisted crimes. Hacktivism refers to hacking for a social cause or agenda (protesting).

52. **Answer: A.** The European Commission's Directive prevents the transfer of any personal data to non-European communities that do not comply with European standards for protecting privacy. The Safe Harbor agreement was created by the U.S. Department of Commerce working with the European Union. It establishes certification for companies that want to exchange data. EAR defines screening regulations for the U.S. The Wassenaar Arrangement regulates arms and dual-use goods but not data.

53. **Answer: C.** Mike Rowe was guilty of a trademark violation because of the possibility of confusion from hearing the name Microsoft versus MikeRoweSoft. A trademark is a name or symbol. Copyright protects original works. A trade secret is a proprietary intellectual property that gives a company its competitive advantage. A patent protects a process.

54. **Answer: D.** The company must be transparent about all policies that remove, or could invade, an employee's expected right to privacy. Furthermore, all employees of the company must be subjected to the same monitoring if monitoring is to be deployed. Simply identifying this as a policy is not enough. Neither are warning banners or training sufficient when done separately. All these items are required.

55. **Answer: D.** A company must show that it took due care. A prudent person is someone who supplies due care. Due diligence refers to performing proper research so that due care can be supplied. Safety net is a distracter.

56. **Answer: D.** The best evidence is an original document. All other answers are secondary evidence and is therefore are incorrect.

57. **Answer: A.** Forensic copies are bit stream copies that include files, slack space, and unallocated clusters.

58. **Answer: B.** There are many reasons why companies do not report security breeches. By and large the most common reason is embarrassment or financial impact. Although laws have changed that require most incidents to be reported, in the past this was not always the case, and some companies preferred to hide this information.

59. **Answer: C.** With computer crime being a global problem, you might think countries would work together to extradite computer criminals. But extradition is not easy. Answers A, B, and D are incorrect because lack of universal cooperation, low priority, and outdated laws and technology are all reasons why criminals are not brought to justice.

60. **Answer: B.** The steps an organization takes to implement best security practices are known as due care. Certification is the technical aspect of validating a process or procedure. Accreditation is management's acceptance of the certification process. Due diligence is known as prudent management and the execution of due care.

61. **Answer: C.** Direct evidence is evidence that is provided by oral or written statement. The witness provides this information by means of an eyewitness account. Secondary evidence is a copy or approved duplicate of evidence. Real evidence is evidence that speaks for itself. Demonstrative evidence is evidence that is provided by experts and can be considered opinions.

62. **Answer: B.** Real evidence can be a tangible object, tool, or property that was gathered from the crime scene. Secondary evidence is a copy or approved duplicate of evidence. Direct evidence is provided by oral or written statement; the witness provides this information by means of an eyewitness account. Demonstrative evidence is provided by experts and can be considered opinions.

63. **Answer: C.** "Relevant" can best be described as something that tends to prove or disprove facts that are important and material to the case. "Material" can best be described as having substance or capable of being treated as fact. "Reliable" can best be described as reasonably proven. "Enticement" can best be described as luring someone into creating additional evidence to help prosecute a crime.

64. **Answer: A.** Evidence typically can be seized for any of the following reasons: subpoena, search warrant, writ of possession, consensual, or extenuating circumstances. Suspicion is not a valid reason.

65. **Answer: B.** An event can best be described as a noticeable occurrence. An incident is an event that has been proven to violate security policy and/or law. A negative and a false negative would not set off an alarm and most likely would be undetectable.

66. **Answer: D.** The worst state an IDS can be in is a false negative, because this means an attack took place but the IDS did not detect it. A positive event means an attack took place and was detected. A false positive means no attack occurred but an alarm was triggered. A negative means no attack occurred and none was detected.

67. **Answer: B.** The ISC2 Code of Ethics lays out four items, one of which is to act honorably, honestly, justly, responsibly, and legally. This statement is not found in RFC 1087, Computer Game Fallacy, or GAISP.

68. **Answer: A.** RFC 1087 states the following as unethical and unacceptable any activity that purposely: Seeks to gain unauthorized access to the resources of the Internet, disrupts the intended use of the Internet, wastes resources (people, capacity, computers) through such actions, and destroys the integrity of computer-based information. These statements are not found in the ISC2 Code of Ethics, Computer Game Fallacy, or GAISP.

69. **Answer: C.** The Computer Game Fallacy is the belief that any computer system that is not protected is fair game. This statement is not found in RFC 1087, ISC2 Code of Ethics, or GAISP.

70. **Answer: D.** GAISP seeks to promote good security practices. This statement is not found in the Computer Game Fallacy, RFC 1087, or ISC2 Code of Ethics.

71. **Answer: A.** A logic bomb is a program or portion of one that remains inactive until a specific action occurs. The most commonly used value is a date. Answer B describes a salami attack. Answer C describes a rounding-down attack. Answer D describes a Trojan attack.

72. **Answer: B.** Tort law and civil law are the same thing. This type of law uses financial restitution to address the wrongs of the perpetrator. Criminal law uses jail time to punish the offender. Both administrative and regulatory law addresses regulatory standards that companies must adhere to.

73. **Answer: C.** During a forensic investigation, the analyst should always work from most volatile to least volatile. As such, the contents of memory should be copied first. The hard drive and thumb drive should be copied later. The printer buffer should not be cleared.

74. **Answer: B.** A bit-level copy of the hard drive is the best possible answer. A bit-level copy copies all files, along with drive slack and file slack. A logical copy, backup, or use of the `copy` command does not provide this ability and therefore does not make an exact duplicate.

75. **Answer: A.** The chain of custody is used to account for everyone who had access to the information or data. Chain of custody is important because it verifies that the information remains in an unchanged state. Its primary purpose is not to prevent challenges from the defense, verify admissibility, or verify the accuracy of the duplication process.

76. **Answer: D.** The major credit-card companies, such as MasterCard, Visa, and American Express, are responsible for PCI-DSS standards. It is not U.S.-specific, European-specific, or overseen by the ISO and the international PCI board. More than 70 companies are currently on the board.

77. **Answer: B.** Copyright covers the expression of ideas and not the ideas themselves; therefore, answers A, C, and D are incorrect.

78. **Answer: C.** A mixed law system is comprised of two or more legal systems. Answers A, B, and D are incorrect.

79. **Answer: B.** For evidence to be admissible in court, it needs to be shown that it was properly controlled and handled.

80. The answers are as follows:

A. Copyright: **3.**

B. Trademark: **4.**

C. Patent: **2.**

D. Trade secret: **1.**

A copyright is an expression of words or ideas presented in a unique way. A trademark is distinctive in nature and can be a shape, color, symbol, or slogan. A patent is offered as an exclusive right by the government to protect inventions. A trade secret is a secret method or formula that requires a level of protection.

CHAPTER EIGHT

Software Development Security

The Software Development Security domain is concerned with the security controls used by applications during their design, development, and use. Individuals studying this domain should understand the security and controls of application security, which includes the systems development process, application controls, and knowledge-based systems. Test candidates should also understand the concepts used to ensure data and application integrity. The following list gives you some specific areas of knowledge to be familiar with for the CISSP exam:

- SDLC (software development life cycle)
- Change (life cycle) management
- Database security
- Artificial Intelligence systems
- Mobile code
- Malware, viruses, and worms

Quick Check

Practice Questions

1. Which of the following is *not* a valid database management system model?

   Quick Answer: **259**
   Detailed Answer: **260**

   ❍ **A.** The hierarchical database management system
   ❍ **B.** The structured database management system
   ❍ **C.** The network database management system
   ❍ **D.** The relational database management system

2. During which stage of the software development life cycle should security be implemented?

   Quick Answer: **259**
   Detailed Answer: **260**

   ❍ **A.** Development
   ❍ **B.** Project initiation
   ❍ **C.** Deployment
   ❍ **D.** Installation

3. In which software development life cycle phase do the programmers and developers become deeply involved and do the majority of the work?

   Quick Answer: **259**
   Detailed Answer: **260**

   ❍ **A.** System Design Specifications
   ❍ **B.** Software Development
   ❍ **C.** Operation and Maintenance
   ❍ **D.** Functional Design Analysis and Planning

4. In the software development life cycle, what is used to maintain changes to development or production?

   Quick Answer: **259**
   Detailed Answer: **260**

   ❍ **A.** Certification
   ❍ **B.** Audit control team
   ❍ **C.** Manufacturing review board
   ❍ **D.** Change control

5. What is the most-used type of database management system?

   Quick Answer: **259**
   Detailed Answer: **260**

   ❍ **A.** The hierarchical database management system
   ❍ **B.** The structured database management system
   ❍ **C.** The network database management system
   ❍ **D.** The relational database management system

6. Place the software development life cycle phases in the proper order.

   Quick Answer: **259**
   Detailed Answer: **260**

   ❍ **A.** Initiation, software development, functional design analysis, operation, installation, disposal

Quick Check

❍ **B.** Initiation, software development, functional design analysis, installation, operation, disposal

❍ **C.** Initiation, functional design analysis, software development, installation, operation, disposal

❍ **D.** Initiation, functional design analysis, software development, operation, installation, disposal

7. Which of the following statements about Java applets is correct?

Quick Answer: **259**
Detailed Answer: **260**

❍ **A.** They are downloaded from a server.

❍ **B.** They are not restricted in computer memory.

❍ **C.** They are run from the browser.

❍ **D.** They are executed by your system.

8. Which of the following is a valid system development methodology?

Quick Answer: **259**
Detailed Answer: **260**

❍ **A.** The spring model

❍ **B.** The spiral model

❍ **C.** The production model

❍ **D.** The Gantt model

9. Which of the following best describes the Waterfall model?

Quick Answer: **259**
Detailed Answer: **260**

❍ **A.** The Waterfall model states that development is built one stage at a time, at which point the results flow to the next stage.

❍ **B.** The Waterfall model states that development should progress in a parallel fashion, with a strong change control process being used to validate the process.

❍ **C.** The Waterfall model states that the development process proceeds in a series of discrete steps, each completed before proceeding to the next.

❍ **D.** The Waterfall model states that all the various phases of software development should proceed at the same time.

10. Your friend is trying to learn more about databases and their structure. She wants to know what a tuple is.

Quick Answer: **259**
Detailed Answer: **260**

❍ **A.** A description of the structure of the database

❍ **B.** A “row” in a relational database that might be viewed as being similar to a “record” in a flat file

❍ **C.** An ordered set of values within a row in the database table

❍ **D.** Something that uniquely identifies each row in a table

Quick Check

11. Which of the software development life cycle phases is the point at which new systems need to be configured and steps need to be taken to make sure that security features are being used in the intended way?

   - ❍ **A.** System Design Specifications
   - ❍ **B.** Operation and Maintenance
   - ❍ **C.** Functional Design Analysis and Planning
   - ❍ **D.** Installation and Implementation

Quick Answer: **259**
Detailed Answer: **260**

12. Your CISSP study group has asked you to research information about databases. Specifically, they want you to describe what metadata is. What is your response?

   - ❍ **A.** Metadata is data that describes data.
   - ❍ **B.** Metadata is the data used in knowledge-based systems.
   - ❍ **C.** Metadata is used for fraud detection.
   - ❍ **D.** Metadata is the data used for metadictionaries.

Quick Answer: **259**
Detailed Answer: **261**

13. Jamie, your assistant, is taking some classes on database controls and security features. She wants to know what aggregation is. How will you answer her?

   - ❍ **A.** It is the process of combining data into large groups that can be used for data mining.
   - ❍ **B.** It is the process of combining security privileges to gain access to objects that would normally be beyond your level of rights.
   - ❍ **C.** It is the process of combining items of low sensitivity to produce an item of high sensitivity.
   - ❍ **D.** It is the process of combining several databases to view a virtual table.

Quick Answer: **259**
Detailed Answer: **261**

14. What term describes users' ability to infer or deduce information about data at sensitivity levels for which they do not have access privileges or rights?

   - ❍ **A.** Views
   - ❍ **B.** Inference
   - ❍ **C.** Channeled view
   - ❍ **D.** Presumption

Quick Answer: **259**
Detailed Answer: **261**

15. Which of the following best describes a database schema?

   - ❍ **A.** The structure of the database
   - ❍ **B.** The capability of different versions of the same information to exist at different classification levels within the database

Quick Answer: **259**
Detailed Answer: **261**

Quick Check

❍ **C.** An ordered set of values within a row in the database table

❍ **D.** Something that uniquely identifies each row in a table

16. Which type of malware is considered self-replicating?

❍ **A.** Boot sector

❍ **B.** Meme virus

❍ **C.** Script virus

❍ **D.** Worm

Quick Answer: **259**
Detailed Answer: **261**

17. Ashwin is building your company's new data warehouse. In a meeting, he said, "Data in the data warehouse needs to be normalized." What does this mean?

❍ **A.** Data is divided by a common value.

❍ **B.** Data is restricted to a range of values.

❍ **C.** Data is averaged.

❍ **D.** Redundant data is removed.

Quick Answer: **259**
Detailed Answer: **261**

18. Which of the following best describes the term "data dictionary"?

❍ **A.** A dictionary for programmers

❍ **B.** A database of databases

❍ **C.** A virtual table of the rows and tables from two or more combined databases

❍ **D.** A dictionary used within a database

Quick Answer: **259**
Detailed Answer: **261**

19. Which of the following best describes data mining?

❍ **A.** The use of data to analyze trends and support strategic decisions

❍ **B.** The use of data to determine how the information was collected and formatted

❍ **C.** The process of querying databases for metadata

❍ **D.** The process of adjusting the granularity of a database search

Quick Answer: **259**
Detailed Answer: **261**

20. Jerry has top-secret access to a database and can see that the USS *Yorktown* has left for Iraq. Ted has only public access to the same database. He can see that the ship has left port. However, the record shows that it is bound for Spain. What is this called?

❍ **A.** Polyinstantiation

❍ **B.** Tuple

❍ **C.** Schema

❍ **D.** Knowledgebase system

Quick Answer: **259**
Detailed Answer: **261**

Quick Check

21. Which of the software development life cycle phases is the point at which a project plan is developed, test schedules are assigned, and expectations of the product are outlined?

Quick Answer: 259
Detailed Answer: 261

❍ **A.** Software Development
❍ **B.** Functional Design Analysis and Planning
❍ **C.** Project Initiation
❍ **D.** System Design Specifications

22. Data checks and validity checks are examples of what type of application controls?

Quick Answer: 259
Detailed Answer: 261

❍ **A.** Preventive
❍ **B.** Constructive
❍ **C.** Detective
❍ **D.** Corrective

23. Which of the following is *not* a valid form of application control?

Quick Answer: 259
Detailed Answer: 261

❍ **A.** Preventive
❍ **B.** Constructive
❍ **C.** Detective
❍ **D.** Corrective

24. What document guarantees the quality of a service to a subscriber by a network service provider, setting standards on response times, available bandwidth, and system up times?

Quick Answer: 259
Detailed Answer: 261

❍ **A.** Service-level agreement
❍ **B.** Service agreement
❍ **C.** Business continuity agreement
❍ **D.** Business provider agreement

25. Which of the following is *not* one of the three main components of a SQL database?

Quick Answer: 259
Detailed Answer: 261

❍ **A.** Views
❍ **B.** Schemas
❍ **C.** Tables
❍ **D.** Object-oriented interfaces

26. Cyclic redundancy checks, structured walk-throughs, and hash totals are examples of what type of application controls?

Quick Answer: 259
Detailed Answer: 261

❍ **A.** Detective
❍ **B.** Preventive
❍ **C.** Error checking
❍ **D.** Parity

Quick Check

27. Christine has been alerted by her IDS that a web server on her network was attacked. While examining a trace of the ICMP traffic, she noticed that the attacker's packets were addressed to the network broadcast address and were spoofed to be from her web server. What type of attack has she been subjected to?

Quick Answer: 259
Detailed Answer: 262

❍ **A.** Smurf
❍ **B.** LAND
❍ **C.** Fraggle
❍ **D.** SYN flood

28. Which of the following best describes the OS protection mechanism that mediates all access that subjects have to objects to ensure that the subjects have the necessary rights to access the objects?

Quick Answer: 259
Detailed Answer: 262

❍ **A.** Accountability control
❍ **B.** Reference monitor
❍ **C.** Security kernel
❍ **D.** Security perimeter

29. Which of the following describes mobile code?

Quick Answer: 259
Detailed Answer: 262

❍ **A.** Code that can be used on a handheld device
❍ **B.** Code that can be used on several different platforms, such as Windows, Mac, and Linux
❍ **C.** Code that can be executed within a network browser
❍ **D.** A script that can be executed within an Office document

30. Black Hat Bob has just attacked Widget, Inc.'s network. Although the attack he perpetrated did not give him access to the company's network, it did prevent legitimate users from gaining access to network resources. What type of attack did he launch?

Quick Answer: 259
Detailed Answer: 262

❍ **A.** Spoofing
❍ **B.** TOC/TOU
❍ **C.** ICMP redirect
❍ **D.** DoS

31. Java-enabled web browsers allow Java code to be embedded in a web page, downloaded across the Net, and run on a local computer. This makes the security of the local computer a big concern. With this in mind, how does the Java runtime system ensure secure execution of the Java code?

Quick Answer: 259
Detailed Answer: 262

❍ **A.** Digital certificates
❍ **B.** Sandbox
❍ **C.** Applet boundaries
❍ **D.** Defense-in-depth

Quick Check

32. Chandra wants to learn more about the Software Capability Maturity Model. Help her put the five levels of this model in the proper order, from 1 to 5.

Quick Answer: **259**
Detailed Answer: **262**

- ❍ **A.** Initiating, defined, repeatable, optimizing, managed
- ❍ **B.** Initiating, defined, repeatable, managed, optimizing
- ❍ **C.** Initiating, repeatable, defined, managed, optimizing
- ❍ **D.** Initiating, repeatable, defined, optimizing, managed

33. Which of the following Software CMM levels is the step at which project management processes and practices are institutionalized and locked into place by policies, procedures, and guidelines?

Quick Answer: **259**
Detailed Answer: **262**

- ❍ **A.** Defined
- ❍ **B.** Repeatable
- ❍ **C.** Initiating
- ❍ **D.** Managed

34. Which of the following technologies establishes a trust relationship between the client and the server by using digital certificates to guarantee that the server is trusted?

Quick Answer: **259**
Detailed Answer: **262**

- ❍ **A.** ActiveX
- ❍ **B.** Java
- ❍ **C.** Proxy
- ❍ **D.** Agent

35. What is the process of cataloging all versions of a component configuration called?

Quick Answer: **259**
Detailed Answer: **262**

- ❍ **A.** The configuration library
- ❍ **B.** The component library
- ❍ **C.** The catalog database
- ❍ **D.** The software component library

36. Which of the following best describes a covert storage channel?

Quick Answer: **259**
Detailed Answer: **262**

- ❍ **A.** It is a communication channel that violates normal communication channels.
- ❍ **B.** It is a storage process that writes to storage in an unauthorized manner that typically is undetectable and written through an unsecure channel.
- ❍ **C.** It is a communication path that allows two processes to access the same storage and allows the contents to be read through a separate, less-secure channel.
- ❍ **D.** It is a storage process that requires the application of a root kit.

Quick Check

37. Which of the following is *not* one of the three ways in which inference can be achieved?

Quick Answer: **259**
Detailed Answer: **262**

- ❍ **A.** Preventive
- ❍ **B.** Deductive
- ❍ **C.** Abductive
- ❍ **D.** Statistical

38. Raj has been studying database security features. He reads that two control policies are used to protect relational databases. He remembers that one is MAC, but he has forgotten the second one. Which one is it?

Quick Answer: **259**
Detailed Answer: **263**

- ❍ **A.** PAC
- ❍ **B.** DAC
- ❍ **C.** SAC
- ❍ **D.** RBAC

39. Boyd just downloaded a game from a peer-to-peer network. Although the game seemed to install OK, his computer now is acting strangely. The mouse cursor moves by itself, URLs are opening on their own, and his web camera keeps turning itself on. What has happened?

Quick Answer: **259**
Detailed Answer: **263**

- ❍ **A.** A logic bomb was installed.
- ❍ **B.** A RAT (Remote-Access Trojan) was installed.
- ❍ **C.** A DDoS client was installed.
- ❍ **D.** An email virus was installed.

40. What is the goal of CRM?

Quick Answer: **259**
Detailed Answer: **263**

- ❍ **A.** To learn the behavior and buying habits of your customers
- ❍ **B.** To search for recurrences in data that can aid in making predictions about future events
- ❍ **C.** To uncover events that are interconnected
- ❍ **D.** To hunt for instances of events that are followed up by other events after a certain period

41. What technology is based on the methods by which the human brain is believed to work?

Quick Answer: **259**
Detailed Answer: **263**

- ❍ **A.** Neutron networks
- ❍ **B.** Fuzzy logic
- ❍ **C.** Neuron networks
- ❍ **D.** Neural technology

Quick Check

42. Now that your organization is preparing to retire its mainframe systems, you are asked to look at a distributed system as the replacement. What five requirements should a distributed system meet?

Quick Answer: **259**
Detailed Answer: **263**

- ❍ **A.** Interoperability, scalability, transparency, extensibility, control
- ❍ **B.** Interoperability, portability, transparency, extensibility, security
- ❍ **C.** Interoperability, portability, transparency, extensibility, control
- ❍ **D.** Interoperability, scalability, transparency, extensibility, security

43. George receives an email that did not come from the individual listed in the email. What is the process of changing email message names to look as though they came from someone else?

Quick Answer: **259**
Detailed Answer: **263**

- ❍ **A.** Spoofing
- ❍ **B.** Masquerading
- ❍ **C.** Relaying
- ❍ **D.** Redirecting

44. Raj is still studying database design and security. Can you tell him what cardinality means?

Quick Answer: **259**
Detailed Answer: **263**

- ❍ **A.** The number of rows in a relation
- ❍ **B.** The number of fields in a relation
- ❍ **C.** The number of attributes in a field
- ❍ **D.** The number of attributes in a relation

45. Wes asks you to help him prepare a practice test for your CISSP study group. Can you tell him which of the following relationships is incorrect?

Quick Answer: **259**
Detailed Answer: **263**

- ❍ **A.** Relation = table
- ❍ **B.** Record = attribute
- ❍ **C.** Tuple = row
- ❍ **D.** Attribute = column

46. Joey has been reading about databases and application security. He has asked you to define perturbation for him. Which of the following offers the best answer?

Quick Answer: **259**
Detailed Answer: **263**

- ❍ **A.** It is used to protect against polyinstantiation.
- ❍ **B.** It is a tool used to prevent aggregation.
- ❍ **C.** It is a tool used to aid in data mining.
- ❍ **D.** It is a tool used to fight inference attacks.

Quick Check

47. SubSeven and NetBus typically are placed in which of the following categories?

Quick Answer: **259**
Detailed Answer: **263**

❍ **A.** Virus
❍ **B.** Trapdoor
❍ **C.** Backdoor
❍ **D.** Malware

48. Jennifer's network has been hit by the following attack pattern: The attacker made many connection attempts to FTP. Each time, the handshake was not completed, and the source addresses were spoofed. The result was that legitimate users could not FTP to that computer. Which type of attack does this attack pattern match?

Quick Answer: **259**
Detailed Answer: **263**

❍ **A.** ACK attack
❍ **B.** Teardrop
❍ **C.** Fraggle
❍ **D.** SYN flood

49. What is the point in the software development life cycle phase at which information may need to be archived or discarded and a team may be assembled to examine ways to improve subsequent iterations of this or other products?

Quick Answer: **259**
Detailed Answer: **263**

❍ **A.** Revision and Replacement
❍ **B.** Functional Design Analysis and Planning
❍ **C.** Disposal and Postmortem Review
❍ **D.** System Design Specifications

50. Which type of virus can spread by multiple methods?

Quick Answer: **259**
Detailed Answer: **264**

❍ **A.** Multipartite
❍ **B.** Polymorphic
❍ **C.** Double partite
❍ **D.** Prolific

51. Polyinstantiation is a solution used by which of the following to remedy multiparty update conflicts?

Quick Answer: **259**
Detailed Answer: **264**

❍ **A.** Database locking
❍ **B.** SODA
❍ **C.** GREP
❍ **D.** Belief-based model

Quick Check

52. The following security labels exist on a network operating in a multilevel security mode:

Quick Answer: **259**
Detailed Answer: **264**

Label	Jack	John	File A	File B	File C	File D
Sensitivity	Top-Secret	Secret	Secret	Secret	Top-Secret	Top-Secret
Categories	North	East	East	East	East	North
	South	West		West		West
	East					
	West					

Jack edits file B and file C simultaneously and then saves both. Which files can John now access?

- ❍ **A.** Files A, B, C, and D
- ❍ **B.** Files A, B, and C
- ❍ **C.** Files A and B
- ❍ **D.** File A

53. Which generation of code development is most likely to focus on constraints?

Quick Answer: **259**
Detailed Answer: **264**

- ❍ **A.** Generation 5
- ❍ **B.** Generation 4
- ❍ **C.** Generation 3
- ❍ **D.** Generation 2

54. The network administrator has been analyzing network reports and is convinced that the network has been the victim of a SYN flooding DoS attack. What evidence might have been discovered that would support this conclusion?

Quick Answer: **259**
Detailed Answer: **264**

- ❍ **A.** Customers reporting that their connection requests were rerouted to a malicious web server
- ❍ **B.** The web server crashing with each request
- ❍ **C.** Excessive traffic on the front-end load-balancing servers
- ❍ **D.** IDS logs of incoming malformed packets

55. Which language, when used for development of your company's front-end application, results in a program that is least likely to have vulnerable code?

Quick Answer: **259**
Detailed Answer: **264**

- ❍ **A.** Machine code
- ❍ **B.** Assembler code
- ❍ **C.** C code
- ❍ **D.** SQL code

Quick Check

56. In your corporation, it is critical that the metadata surrounding business data be revealed to only the proper authorities, even though all employees require access to the business data. Access to the metadata is being controlled through the use of views so that only the appropriate authorities have deeper access. What is this technique called?

Quick Answer: 259
Detailed Answer: 264

❍ **A.** Encapsulation

❍ **B.** Polymorphism

❍ **C.** Instantiation

❍ **D.** Abstraction

57. To prevent covert channels via race conditions, it is critical that software modules be able to execute independently of each other. What is this called?

Quick Answer: 259
Detailed Answer: 264

❍ **A.** Low coupling and low cohesion

❍ **B.** Low coupling and high cohesion

❍ **C.** High coupling and low cohesion

❍ **D.** High coupling and high cohesion

58. Expert systems use forward and reverse chaining that is based on what?

Quick Answer: 259
Detailed Answer: 264

❍ **A.** The inference engine

❍ **B.** Certainty factors

❍ **C.** The rulebase

❍ **D.** Neural structures

59. What is the most common problem related to audit logs?

Quick Answer: 259
Detailed Answer: 264

❍ **A.** Audit logs can be examined only by auditors.

❍ **B.** Audit logs use parsing tools that distort the true record of events.

❍ **C.** Audit logs are not backed up.

❍ **D.** Audit logs are collected but not analyzed.

60. When you're dealing with mobile code and wireless devices, many security issues can arise. For example, when you're working with wireless devices that are using Wireless Application Protocol (WAP), which of the following is the primary security concern?

Quick Answer: 259
Detailed Answer: 265

❍ **A.** WAP is not a secure protocol.

❍ **B.** The web server that the wireless device is communicating with via SSL may have vulnerabilities.

❍ **C.** The wireless device may have vulnerabilities in its OS.

❍ **D.** The WAP gateway can be targeted by attackers.

Quick Check

61. Which generation(s) of code is/are most likely to focus on the logic of the algorithms?

Quick Answer: **259**
Detailed Answer: **265**

- ❍ **A.** Generation 5
- ❍ **B.** Generations 2, 3, and 4
- ❍ **C.** Generations 1 and 2
- ❍ **D.** Generations 1 and 5

62. Which type of database combines related records and fields into a logical tree structure?

Quick Answer: **259**
Detailed Answer: **265**

- ❍ **A.** Relational
- ❍ **B.** Hierarchical
- ❍ **C.** Object-oriented
- ❍ **D.** Network

63. What type of database is unique because it can have multiple records that can be either parent or child?

Quick Answer: **259**
Detailed Answer: **265**

- ❍ **A.** Relational
- ❍ **B.** Hierarchical
- ❍ **C.** Object-oriented
- ❍ **D.** Network

64. Your colleague wants to know when the best point within the software development life cycle (SDLC) is to create a list of potential security issues. What do you tell her?

Quick Answer: **259**
Detailed Answer: **265**

- ❍ **A.** Feasibility
- ❍ **B.** Development
- ❍ **C.** Design
- ❍ **D.** Requirements

65. Which of the following are correct?

Quick Answer: **259**
Detailed Answer: **265**

- **I.** The object linking and embedding database (OLE DB) is a replacement for open database connectivity (ODBC).
- **II.** ActiveX Data Objects (ADO) is an API that allows applications to access back-end database systems.
- **III.** Java Database Connectivity is a markup standard that is self-defining and provides a lot of flexibility in how data within the database is presented.
- **IV.** The data definition language (DDL) defines the structure and schema of the database.

Quick Check

- ❍ **A.** I and IV
- ❍ **B.** II, III, and IV
- ❍ **C.** I, II, III, and IV
- ❍ **D.** I, II, and IV

66. How can referential integrity best be defined?

Quick Answer: **259**
Detailed Answer: **265**

- ❍ **A.** Structural and semantic rules are enforced.
- ❍ **B.** Semantic rules are enforced.
- ❍ **C.** Structural rules are enforced.
- ❍ **D.** All foreign keys reference existing primary keys.

67. Lenny is trying to determine how much money a new employee makes. His job in HR allows him to see total payroll by department but not by person. The individual he is curious about just started a month ago, so Lenny simply compares that department's previous month's total salary to the current month's total salary. What has Lenny just done?

Quick Answer: **259**
Detailed Answer: **265**

- ❍ **A.** Enumeration
- ❍ **B.** An inference attack
- ❍ **C.** Polyinstantiation
- ❍ **D.** Online transaction processing (OLTP)

68. While browsing the company directory, you notice that your address is incorrect. To rectify the situation, you decide to modify the database that holds this information. Although the change seems to work, you notice later that the information has reverted to the previous, incorrect information. What do you believe is the source of the problem?

Quick Answer: **259**
Detailed Answer: **265**

- ❍ **A.** The user does not have modification rights.
- ❍ **B.** The schema does not allow changes from the user's machine.
- ❍ **C.** Someone in personnel has put a lock on the cell.
- ❍ **D.** Replication integrity is inaccurate due to mismatched times.

69. Knowledge discovery is also known as what?

Quick Answer: **259**
Detailed Answer: **266**

- ❍ **A.** Data warehousing
- ❍ **B.** Metadata
- ❍ **C.** Data mining
- ❍ **D.** Atomicity

Quick Check

70. Which of the following statements are true?

Quick Answer: **259**
Detailed Answer: **266**

I. Data definition language (DDL) allows users to make requests of the database.

II. Data manipulation language (DML) maintains the commands that enable a user to view, manipulate, and use the database.

III. Query language (QL) defines the structure and schema of the database. The structure could mean the table size, key placement, views, and data element relationship.

IV. The report generator creates printouts of data in a user-defined manner.

❍ **A.** I and II

❍ **B.** II and IV

❍ **C.** II, III, and IV

❍ **D.** I, II, III, and IV

71. Jim's new job at the headquarters of a major grocery store has him examining buyer trends. He uses the database to find a relationship between beer and diapers. He discovers that men over 20 are the primary buyers of these two items together after 10 p.m. What best describes Jim's actions?

Quick Answer: **259**
Detailed Answer: **266**

❍ **A.** Data warehousing

❍ **B.** Metadata

❍ **C.** Data mining

❍ **D.** Atomicity

72. Your application developer has created a new module for a customer-tracking system. This module will result in greater productivity. The application has been examined and tested by a second person in the development group. A summary of the test shows no problems. Based on the results, which of the following is not a recommended best practice?

Quick Answer: **259**
Detailed Answer: **266**

❍ **A.** The new code should be passed to quality assurance personnel so that they can certify the application.

❍ **B.** The application should be placed into operations and implemented.

❍ **C.** An accrediting official should wait for the results of certification.

❍ **D.** All changes must be logged in the change management database (CMDB).

Quick Check

73. Which of the following describes verification and validation?

Quick Answer: **259**
Detailed Answer: **266**

- ❍ **A.** Verification verifies that the product meets specifications. Validation is the completion of the certification and accreditation process.
- ❍ **B.** Verification measures how well the program or application solves a real-world problem. Validation verifies that the product meets specifications.
- ❍ **C.** Verification verifies that the product meets specifications. Validation measures how well the program or application solves a real-world problem.
- ❍ **D.** Verification verifies that the program or application meets certification requirements. Validation verifies that the product received accreditation.

74. You are assigned to modify an application to address a specific problem with the current release of the program. When the change is complete, you notice that other modules that should not have been affected appear to be nonfunctional. What do you believe is the cause?

Quick Answer: **259**
Detailed Answer: **266**

- ❍ **A.** The module has low cohesion.
- ❍ **B.** The module has high cohesion.
- ❍ **C.** The module is tightly coupled.
- ❍ **D.** The module is loosely coupled.

75. Jake has become concerned that a citizen programmer in the group has developed code for others in the department. What should be your primary concern?

Quick Answer: **259**
Detailed Answer: **266**

- ❍ **A.** That the programs are tested by others in the department
- ❍ **B.** That the programs have not been certified and verified
- ❍ **C.** That a copy of the code is held in a library
- ❍ **D.** That the code is adequately commented

76. Which of the following statements is most correct?

Quick Answer: **259**
Detailed Answer: **266**

- ❍ **A.** Relational database parents can have only one child.
- ❍ **B.** A relational database is designed so that a child can have only one parent.
- ❍ **C.** A hierarchical database is designed so that a parent can have only one child.
- ❍ **D.** A hierarchical database is designed so that a child can have only one parent.

Quick Check

77. What level of the capability maturity model features quantitative process improvement?

- ❍ **A.** Managed
- ❍ **B.** Defined
- ❍ **C.** Repeatable
- ❍ **D.** Optimized

Quick Answer: **259**
Detailed Answer: **266**

78. Your company has just signed a software escrow agreement. Which of the following best describes this document?

- ❍ **A.** An offsite backup
- ❍ **B.** A form of maintenance agreement
- ❍ **C.** A form of insurance
- ❍ **D.** A clustered software service

Quick Answer: **259**
Detailed Answer: **266**

79. With regard to database operations, canceling a set of changes and restoring the database to its prior state is called what?

- ❍ **A.** Savepoint
- ❍ **B.** Commit
- ❍ **C.** Rollback
- ❍ **D.** Audit point

Quick Answer: **259**
Detailed Answer: **267**

80. The capability maturity model features five maturity levels that begin with initial. What is the proper order of the remaining four levels?

- ❍ **A.** Repeatable, defined, managed, optimized
- ❍ **B.** Managed, repeatable, defined, optimized
- ❍ **C.** Repeatable, managed, defined, optimized
- ❍ **D.** Defined, optimized, repeatable, managed

Quick Answer: **259**
Detailed Answer: **267**

81. Data that describes other data is called what?

- ❍ **A.** Metadata
- ❍ **B.** Nonatomic data
- ❍ **C.** Data structure
- ❍ **D.** Transaction processing

Quick Answer: **259**
Detailed Answer: **267**

82. In which database model do you perceive the database as a set of tables that are composed of rows and columns?

- ❍ **A.** Hierarchical
- ❍ **B.** Network
- ❍ **C.** Relational
- ❍ **D.** Object

Quick Answer: **259**
Detailed Answer: **267**

Quick Check

83. With a relational database management system, you can constrain what a particular application or user sees by using what?

Quick Answer: **259**
Detailed Answer: **267**

- ❍ **A.** Schema
- ❍ **B.** Device media control language (DMCL)
- ❍ **C.** Data mine
- ❍ **D.** Database view

84. Security controls must be considered at which phases of the software life cycle?

Quick Answer: **259**
Detailed Answer: **267**

- ❍ **A.** Design analysis, software development, installation, and implementation
- ❍ **B.** Project initiation, software development, and operation maintenance
- ❍ **C.** Design specifications
- ❍ **D.** All of the above

85. The change control process is structured so that various steps must be completed to verify that no undocumented, unapproved, or untested changes are implemented. Which of the following is the final step?

Quick Answer: **259**
Detailed Answer: **267**

- ❍ **A.** Configure the hardware properly.
- ❍ **B.** Update documentation and manuals.
- ❍ **C.** Inform users of the change.
- ❍ **D.** Report the change to management.

86. You are asked to develop an advanced program that will interact with users. You are asked to look at knowledge-based systems. As such, expert systems use what type of information to make a decision?

Quick Answer: **259**
Detailed Answer: **267**

- ❍ **A.** `if...then` statements
- ❍ **B.** Weighted computations
- ❍ **C.** A process similar to that used by the human brain (reasoning)
- ❍ **D.** Weighted computations based on previous results

87. Which of the following is considered a middleware technology?

Quick Answer: **259**
Detailed Answer: **267**

- ❍ **A.** Atomicity
- ❍ **B.** OLE
- ❍ **C.** CORBA
- ❍ **D.** Object-oriented programming

Quick Check

88. The CMMI contains how many process areas?

Quick Answer: 259
Detailed Answer: 267

- ❍ **A.** 4
- ❍ **B.** 5
- ❍ **C.** 20
- ❍ **D.** 22

89. At which level of the CMM are processes likely to be variable (inconsistent) and depend heavily on institutional knowledge?

Quick Answer: 259
Detailed Answer: 268

- ❍ **A.** Level 1
- ❍ **B.** Level 2
- ❍ **C.** Level 3
- ❍ **D.** Level 4

90. When dealing with expert systems, which of the following are valid methods for reasoning when using inference rules?

Quick Answer: 259
Detailed Answer: 268

I. Forward chaining

II. Knowledge transparency

III. Backward chaining

IV. Knowledge representation

- ❍ **A.** II
- ❍ **B.** I and III
- ❍ **C.** I and IV
- ❍ **D.** I, II, III, and IV

91. Which of the following is a project-development method that uses pairs of programmers who work off of detailed specifications?

Quick Answer: 259
Detailed Answer: 268

- ❍ **A.** Waterfall
- ❍ **B.** Spiral
- ❍ **C.** Extreme
- ❍ **D.** RAD

92. Jake is using a commercial program that is free to use without pay with only limited functionality. This is most correctly called what?

Quick Answer: 259
Detailed Answer: 268

- ❍ **A.** Commercial software
- ❍ **B.** Freeware
- ❍ **C.** Shareware
- ❍ **D.** Crippleware

Quick Check

93. Which of the following can best be described as byte-code?

Quick Answer: 259
Detailed Answer: 268

- ❍ **A.** Java
- ❍ **B.** Assembly
- ❍ **C.** C language
- ❍ **D.** Fortran

94. Which of the following is an example of open vendor-neutral middleware?

Quick Answer: 259
Detailed Answer: 268

- ❍ **A.** OOA
- ❍ **B.** COM
- ❍ **C.** CORBA
- ❍ **D.** OOD

95. Which of the following allows objects written with different OOP languages to communicate?

Quick Answer: 259
Detailed Answer: 268

- ❍ **A.** OOA
- ❍ **B.** COM
- ❍ **C.** OOD
- ❍ **D.** CORBA

Practice Questions (True or False)

96. SQL is an example of a 4GL language.

Quick Answer: 259
Detailed Answer: 268

- ❍ True
- ❍ False

97. 5GL languages are designed to categorize assembly languages.

Quick Answer: 259
Detailed Answer: 268

- ❍ True
- ❍ False

98. The prototyping model is based on the concept that software development is evolutionary.

Quick Answer: 259
Detailed Answer: 268

- ❍ True
- ❍ False

99. Reengineering attempts to update software by reusing as many of the components as possible instead of designing an entirely new system. Reverse engineering is a technique that can be used to decrease development time by compiling existing code.

Quick Answer: 259
Detailed Answer: 268

- ❍ True
- ❍ False

Quick Check

100. Programmers should strive to develop modules that have high cohesion and low coupling.

❍ True

❍ False

Quick Answer: **259**
Detailed Answer: **268**

101. Entity relationship diagrams (ERDs) can be used to help define a data dictionary.

❍ True

❍ False

Quick Answer: **259**
Detailed Answer: **268**

102. Web-based application development (WBAD) is an application development technology that is used with technologies such as Extensible Markup Language (XML).

❍ True

❍ False

Quick Answer: **259**
Detailed Answer: **268**

103. Today, prototyping is rarely used because it costs development time and money.

❍ True

❍ False

Quick Answer: **259**
Detailed Answer: **269**

104. Zeroization is as effective as purging.

❍ True

❍ False

Quick Answer: **259**
Detailed Answer: **269**

Practice Questions (Mix and Match)

105. Match each virus term with its definition.

A. Stealth: _____

B. Meme: _____

C. Macro: _____

D. EICAR: _____

E. Encrypted virus: _____

1. Used by attacks such as "I love you" and Melissa

2. Can modify functionality, so detection is very difficult

3. Similar to a polymorphic virus but can change how the virus is stored on the disk

4. Used to verify the functionality of antivirus software

5. Somewhat like a chain letter or pyramid scheme

Quick Answer: **259**
Detailed Answer: **269**

Quick Check Answer Key

1. B
2. B
3. B
4. D
5. D
6. C
7. B
8. B
9. C
10. C
11. B
12. A
13. C
14. B
15. A
16. D
17. D
18. B
19. A
20. A
21. B
22. A
23. B
24. A
25. D
26. A
27. A
28. B
29. C
30. D
31. B
32. C
33. B
34. A
35. A
36. C
37. A
38. B
39. B
40. A
41. D
42. B
43. B
44. A
45. B
46. D
47. C
48. D
49. C
50. A
51. B
52. C
53. A
54. C
55. D
56. B
57. B
58. A
59. D
60. D
61. B
62. B
63. D
64. D
65. D
66. D
67. B
68. D
69. C
70. B
71. C
72. B
73. C
74. A
75. B
76. D
77. B
78. C
79. C
80. A
81. A
82. C
83. D
84. D
85. D
86. A
87. C
88. D
89. A
90. B
91. C
92. D
93. A
94. C
95. B
96. True
97. False
98. False
99. False
100. True
101. True
102. True
103. False
104. False
105. **A.** 2
    B. 5
    C. 1
    D. 4
    E. 3

Answers and Explanations

1. **Answer: B.** The structured database management system model is not a valid type. Four common database types are the hierarchical database management system, the object-oriented database management system, the network database management system, and the relational database management system.

2. **Answer: B.** Security should be implemented at the initiation of a project. When security is added during the project initiation phase, substantial amounts of money can be saved. Because the first phase is the project initiation phase, all other answers are incorrect.

3. **Answer: B.** Software Development is the point in the SDLC at which programmers and developers become deeply involved and provide the majority of the work.

4. **Answer: D.** Change control is used to maintain changes to development or production. Without it, control would become very difficult, because there would be no way to track changes that might affect the product's functionality or security.

5. **Answer: D.** The relational database management system is the most used type. It is structured such that the columns represent the variables and the rows contain the specific instance of data.

6. **Answer: C.** The complete list of software development life cycle phases is as follows:

   Project Initiation

   Functional Design Analysis and Planning

   System Design Specifications

   Software Development

   Installation and Implementation

   Operation and Maintenance

   Disposal

7. **Answer: B.** Java is downloaded from the server, executed by the browser, and run on your system. Java has limits placed on what it can do by means of a sandbox and was originally designed with restrictions on what could be done while loaded in memory. Originally their activities were restricted in memory and could not access certain parts of memory or access files or initiate network connections.

8. **Answer: B.** The spiral model is the only valid software development methodology listed. It was developed in 1988 at TRW.

9. **Answer: C.** The Waterfall model states that the development process proceeds in a series of discrete steps, each completed before proceeding to the next.

10. **Answer: C.** A tuple is an ordered set of values within a row in the database table.

11. **Answer: B.** The Operation and Maintenance phase of the SDLC is the point at which new systems need to be configured and steps need to be taken to make sure that no new vulnerabilities or security compromises take place. It is also at this step that if major changes are made to the system, network, or environment, the certification and accreditation process may need to be repeated.

12. **Answer: A.** Metadata is data about data that is used in data-mining and data-warehouse operations. Metadata is not used in knowledge-based systems, for fraud detection, or for data dictionaries.

13. **Answer: C.** Aggregation is the process of combining items of low sensitivity to produce an item of high sensitivity. It has the potential to be a rather large security risk.

14. **Answer: B.** Inference occurs when users can put together pieces of information at one security level to determine a fact that should be protected at a higher security level.

15. **Answer: A.** The schema is the structure of the database.

16. **Answer: D.** The greatest danger of worms is their capability to self-replicate. Left unchecked, this process can grow in volume to an astronomical amount. For example, a worm could send copies of itself to everyone listed in your email address book, and those recipients' computers would then do the same.

17. **Answer: D.** Normalization is the process of removing redundant data. It speeds the analysis process. Normalization is not the process of dividing by a common value, restricting to a range of values, or averaging the data.

18. **Answer: B.** A data dictionary contains a list of all database files. It also contains the number of records in each file and each field name and type.

19. **Answer: A.** Data mining is used to analyze trends and support strategic decisions. It enables complicated business processes to be understood and analyzed. This is achieved through the discovery of patterns in the data relating to the past behavior of business processes or subjects. These patterns can be used to improve the performance of a process by exploiting favorable patterns.

20. **Answer: A.** Polyinstantiation allows different versions of the same information to exist at different classification levels within a database. This permits a security model that can have multiple views of the same information, depending on your clearance level.

21. **Answer: B.** The Functional Design Analysis and Planning stage of the SDLC is the point at which a project plan is developed, test schedules are assigned, and expectations of the product are outlined.

22. **Answer: A.** Application controls are used to enforce an organization's security policy and procedures. Preventive application controls include data checks, validity checks, contingency planning, and backups. Answers C and D are incorrect because they are not controls, and answer B is a distracter.

23. **Answer: B.** The three valid types of application controls are preventive, corrective, and detective.

24. **Answer: A.** A service-level agreement is used to set the standards of service you expect to receive. It includes items such as response times, system utilization rates, the number of online users, available bandwidth, and system up times.

25. **Answer: D.** The three main components of SQL databases are schemas, tables, and views. Object-oriented interfaces are part of object-oriented database management systems.

26. **Answer: A.** Cyclic redundancy checks, structured walk-throughs, and hash totals are all examples of detective application controls. Application controls are used to enforce the organization's security policy and procedures. They can be preventive, detective, or corrective.

27. **Answer: A.** A smurf attack targets the network broadcast address and spoofs the source address to be from the computer to be attacked. The result is that the network amplifies the attack and floods the local device with the resulting broadcast traffic.

28. **Answer: B.** The reference monitor is the OS component that enforces access control and verifies that the user has the rights and privileges to access the object in question.

29. **Answer: C.** Mobile code is code that can be executed within a network browser. Applets are examples of mobile code. Mobile code is not used on a handheld device, nor is it a script that is executed in an Office document. And although mobile code may run on several different platforms, answer B is an incomplete answer.

30. **Answer: D.** A DoS (denial of service) attack does not give Black Hat Bob access to the network; it does, however, prevent others from gaining legitimate access. Spoofing is the act of pretending to be someone you are not. ICMP redirects can be used to route information to an alternative location. TOC/TOU attacks deal with the change of information between the time it was initially checked and the time it was used.

31. **Answer: B.** The sandbox is a set of security rules that are put in place to prevent Java from having unlimited access to memory and OS resources. It creates an environment in which there are strict limitations on what the Java code can request or do.

32. **Answer: C.** The Software Capability Maturity Model (CMM) was first developed in 1986 and is composed of the following five maturity levels:

    Initiating

    Repeatable

    Defined

    Managed

    Optimizing

33. **Answer: B.** The Software CMM is composed of five maturity levels. The Repeatable maturity level is the step at which project management processes and practices are institutionalized and locked in place by procedures, protocols, and guidelines.

34. **Answer: A.** ActiveX establishes a trust relationship between the client and server by using digital certificates to guarantee that the server is trusted. The shortcoming of ActiveX is that security is really left to the end user. Users are prompted if any problems are found with a certificate. Therefore, even if the certificate is invalid, a user can override good policy by simply accepting the possibly tainted code.

35. **Answer: A.** The configuration library is the process of cataloging all versions of a component configuration.

36. **Answer: C.** A covert storage channel is a communication path that writes to storage by one process and allows the contents to be read through another, less-secure channel. Answer A describes a covert channel. Answers B and D are distracters.

37. **Answer: A.** Inference occurs when a user with low-level access to data can use this access to infer information or knowledge that is not authorized. The three inference channels are deductive, abductive, and statistical.

38. **Answer: B.** Relational databases use one of two control policies to secure information on multilevel systems: MAC (mandatory access control) and DAC (discretionary access control). Answers A and C are distracters. RBAC (role-based access control) is not used in multilevel relational databases.

39. **Answer: B.** It is very likely that the game Boyd installed was bundled with a RAT (Remote-Access Trojan). The executable seems accessible, but after installation is performed, the Trojan program is loaded into the victim's computer. RATs can control programs because backdoors turn on hardware, open CD-ROM drives, and perform other malicious and ill-willed acts.

40. **Answer: A.** CRM (customer relationship management) is used in conjunction with data mining. The goal of CRM is to learn the behaviors of your customers. Businesses believe that by learning more about their customers, they can provide higher-quality customer service, increase revenues, and switch to more efficient sales techniques. Answer B describes forecasting, answer C describes associations, and answer D describes sequences.

41. **Answer: D.** Neural technology simulates the neural behavior of the human brain. The objective is for a computer to be able to learn to differentiate or model without formal analysis and detailed programming. These systems are targeted to be used in risk management, IDS, and forecasting. Fuzzy logic focuses on how humans think and is used in insurance and financial markets, where there is some uncertainty about the data. Answers A and C are distracters.

42. **Answer: B.** Interoperability, portability, transparency, extensibility, and security are the five requirements that all distributed systems should meet.

43. **Answer: B.** Masquerading is the act of changing email messages to look as though they came from someone else. Spoofing typically involves IP addresses. Relaying occurs when email is sent through an uninvolved third party. Redirecting is the process of sending data to a destination to which it may not have been addressed.

44. **Answer: A.** Cardinality is the number of rows in a relation.

45. **Answer: B.** Answers A, C, and D all represent a valid relationship. Answer B does not, because records are synonymous with rows and tuples, not attributes.

46. **Answer: D.** Perturbation is also called noise and is used as a tool to fight inference attacks. It works by infusing phony information into a database. The goal is to frustrate the attacker so that he or she will give up and move on to an easier target.

47. **Answer: C.** Backdoor programs include SubSeven, NetBus, Back Orifice, and Beast. These programs are characterized by their design. They use two separate components: a server, which is deployed to the victim, and a client, which the attacker uses to control the victim's computer.

48. **Answer: D.** A SYN attack is characterized by a series of TCP SYNs. Each SYN uses a small amount of memory. If the attacker sends enough of these spoofed SYN packets, the victim's machine fills up its queue and does not have adequate resources to respond to legitimate computers, denying other systems service from the victim's computer.

49. **Answer: C.** The Disposal and Postmortem Review phase of the SDLC is the point at which information may need to be archived or discarded. A postmortem team may be assembled to examine ways to improve subsequent iterations of this or other products.

50. **Answer: A.** Multipartite viruses can spread by many different methods. Polymorphic viruses can change themselves over time.

51. **Answer: B.** SODA (Secure Object-Oriented Database) allows the use of polyinstantiation as a solution to the multiparty update conflict. This problem is caused when users of various levels of clearance and sensitivity in a secure database system attempt to use the same information.

52. **Answer: C.** The suggestion here is that Jack somehow contaminated File B and caused it to be raised to a higher security level after he saved it. However, in Mandatory Access Control, a label cannot be changed after it is assigned (or it would be discretionary). John has access to files A and B based on his security clearance (sensitivity label) and need to know (categories) both before and after Jack's edit.

53. **Answer: A.** Fifth-generation languages (LISP, Prolog) are most focused on the logic of constraints. Fourth-generation (SQL, ColdFusion), third-generation (COBOL, Java), and second-generation (Assembly, Byte Code) are focused on the logic of algorithms.

54. **Answer: C.** SYN flooding is a resource attack on bandwidth. The attack does not involve malformed packets. The intent of the flood is to use up all the bandwidth so that legitimate incoming requests cannot be processed (not redirected). This flooding could result in excessive traffic on the front-end, load-balancing servers that seek to balance incoming requests between multiple back-end processing servers. Although crashing the server is not the ultimate goal of the attack, there is the possibility that this could occur.

55. **Answer: D.** The higher the level of language you use when programming, the less likely it is that the code will have unintended flaws that can be attacked. Instead of using C, you should use C++, but both of these are third-generation languages (3GL). SQL is a fourth-generation language (4GL).

56. **Answer: B.** Polymorphism is the ability to present data in a different light depending on the needs of the moment. Encapsulation is when an object has knowledge of functions and traits it requires so that other routines can access the object via standard function calls. Instantiation is the creation of an object based on its rule set. Abstraction refers to the suppression of unnecessary details but not the changing of details.

57. **Answer: B.** Low coupling means that the modules transfer data directly to each other without transferring data through a lot of other modules. High cohesion means that modules stand alone well by handling their own requirements and without calling other modules. High coupling and low cohesion are present when modules depend heavily on each other, leading to race conditions in which multiple modules could be vying for the same resource.

58. **Answer: A.** The inference engine creates the forward and reverse chains. Certainty factors reflect a confidence level that permits the chaining to occur. The rulebase describes what is known. Neural structures belong in artificial neural networks, not expert systems.

59. **Answer: D.** One of the most common problems with audit logs is that they are collected but not analyzed. Often, no one is interested in the audit logs until someone reports a problem. Even though it isn't a technical problem, this is an administrative and policy issue, because no analysis takes place. Answers A, B, and C are all important concerns but are not the most common problem.

60. **Answer: D.** The primary vulnerability is the WAP gateway. WAP requires some type of conversion, and this conversion is performed on the gateway. This means that, for a short period of time, the data is in a clear format while being converted from WAP to SSL, TLS, or another encrypted format. This makes the gateway an attractive target. Answers A, B, and C are incorrect because they do not represent the level of risk that the gateway does.

61. **Answer: B.** Fourth-generation (SQL, ColdFusion), third-generation (COBOL, Java), and second-generation (Assembly, Byte Code) are focused on the logic of algorithms. Fifth-generation languages (LISP, Prolog) are most focused on the logic of constraints. First-generation languages are written in machine language.

62. **Answer: B.** A hierarchical database combines related records and fields into a logical tree structure. A relational database uses columns and rows to organize the information. An object-oriented database is considered much more dynamic than earlier designs because it can handle not only data but also audio, images, and other file formats. A network database is unique in that it supports multiple parent or child records.

63. **Answer: D.** A network database is unique in that it supports multiple parent and child records. A relational database uses columns and rows to organize the information. A hierarchical database combines related records and fields into a logical tree structure. An object-oriented database is considered much more dynamic than earlier designs because it can handle not only data but also audio, images, and other file formats.

64. **Answer: D.** One of the primary reasons to use the SDLC is to build in security from the beginning. As such, security issues need to be identified as soon as possible. Although some issues can be worked out during feasibility, options are still open at that point, which makes final decisions impossible. Waiting until later to build in security simply adds to the cost.

65. **Answer: D.** Java Database Connectivity (JDC) is not a markup standard that is self-defining and provides a lot of flexibility in how data within the database is presented. JDC is an API communication mechanism for databases. Although it is true that the object linking and embedding database (OLE DB) is a replacement for open database connectivity (ODBC), ActiveX Data Objects (ADO) is an API that allows applications to access back-end database systems. The data definition language (DDL) defines the structure and schema of the database.

66. **Answer: D.** Referential integrity ensures that all foreign keys reference existing primary keys.

67. **Answer: B.** Inference is the ability to obtain privileged information that normally is unavailable. Enumeration is performed when the attacker gathers information about the network structure. It includes items such as what open shares and applications are available on a network. Polyinstantiation is the use of different information at different security levels. Online transaction processing is a mechanism used in databases to provide fault tolerance.

68. **Answer: D.** The most likely cause of the problem is invalid time synchronization. In a distributed environment, this can cause a server to overwrite newer data. If the change took a while to make, answer A cannot be correct. Answer B is incorrect because no change would be possible, even for a short period of time. Answer C is incorrect because it would be impossible for the user to make a change.

69. **Answer: C.** A knowledge discovery database (KDD) is also known as data mining. A data warehouse is used for data storage and can combine data from multiple sources. Metadata is used to discover the unseen relationships between data. Atomicity is used to divide works into units that are processed completely or not at all.

70. **Answer: B.** The correct statements are as follows: The data definition language (DDL) defines the structure and schema of the database. The data manipulation language (DML) contains all the commands that enable a user to manipulate, view, and use the database (view, add, modify, sort, and delete commands). The query language (QL) allows users to make requests of the database. The report generator creates printouts of data in a user-defined manner.

71. **Answer: C.** Jim is data mining—searching for unseen relationships. A data warehouse is used for data storage and can combine data from multiple sources. Metadata is used to discover the unseen relationships between data. Atomicity is used to divide work into units that are processed completely or not at all.

72. **Answer: B.** Before this significant change is made, the module should be technically tested (certification) and administratively approved (accreditation). Answers A, C, and D are all recommended best practices.

73. **Answer: C.** Verification verifies that the product meets specifications. Validation is the measurement of how well the program or application solves a real-world problem.

74. **Answer: A.** Cohesion and coupling are two items that need to be reviewed when creating code or modifying existing code. *Cohesion* is a module's ability to perform only a single precise task. *Coupling* refers to the amount of interaction. Both can have a significant effect on change management. Therefore, the goal is to work toward modules that have high cohesion and loose coupling.

75. **Answer: B.** Citizen (casual) programmers are people who can code but who do so from outside the SDLC process. The concern here is that they are writing programs and allowing others within the department to use them without any type of certification process. These programs have not been shown to work effectively or produce repeatable results. Lack of certification and review is a real problem. Answers A, C, and D are important, but they are not the primary concern.

76. **Answer: D.** A relational database is a two-dimensional table; this allows each table to contain unique rows, columns, and cells. Relational databases have advantages over hierarchical databases. One such advantage is that a number of different relations can be defined, including overcoming the limitation of hierarchical databases that allows a child to have only one parent. Answers A, B, and C are therefore incorrect.

77. **Answer: B.** The capability maturity model features five maturity levels that specify software development process maturity. These levels include initial, repeatable, defined, managed, and optimized. The defined level allows for quantitative process improvement.

78. **Answer: C.** Software escrow is a form of insurance. Suppose company A buys software from company B. Company A is concerned that company B may go broke. A copy of the software source code can be placed in a safe place so that company A can access and modify it in case company B goes bankrupt.

79. **Answer: C.** A commit completes the transaction. A savepoint is designed to allow the system to return to a certain point should an error occur. A rollback is similar, except that it is used when changes need to be canceled. An audit point is used as a control point to verify input, process, or output data.

80. **Answer: A.** The capability maturity model features five maturity levels that specify software development process maturity. These levels are initial, repeatable, defined, managed, and optimized.

81. **Answer: A.** Metadata is data that describes other data. Nonatomic data is a data value that consists of multiple data values. A data structure is a set of data in memory composed of fields. Transaction processing is a mode of computer operation.

82. **Answer: C.** Relational databases are two-dimensional tables; this allows each table to contain unique rows, columns, and cells. Hierarchical, network, and object do not meet these requirements.

83. **Answer: D.** A database view allows the database administrator to control what a specific user at a specific level of access can see. For example, an HR employee may be able to see department payroll totals but not individual employee salaries. A schema is the structure of the database. DMCL is unrelated to databases. Data mining is the process of analyzing metadata.

84. **Answer: D.** Security controls must be considered at all points of the SDLC process. To learn more about the software development life cycle, see NIST 800-14, "Generally Accepted Principles and Practices for Securing Information Technology Systems."

85. **Answer: D.** The change control process has the following steps: Make a formal request for a change, analyze the request, record the change request, submit the change request for approval, develop the change, and report the results to management.

86. **Answer: A.** Answers B, C, and D not fully define an expert system. An expert system is unique in that it contains a knowledge base of information and mathematical algorithms that use a series of `if...then` statements to infer facts from data.

87. **Answer: C.** Common Object Request Broker Architecture (CORBA) is vendor-independent middleware. Its purpose is to tie together different vendors' products so that they can seamlessly work together over distributed networks. Atomicity deals with the validity of database transactions. Object Linking and Embedding (OLE) is a proprietary system developed by Microsoft that allows applications to transfer and share information. Object-oriented programming is a modular form of programming.

88. **Answer: D.** The Capability Maturity Model (CMM) expired in 2007 and was replaced with the Capability Maturity Model Integration (CMMI) model. It features 22 process areas: causal analysis and resolution, configuration management, decision analysis and resolution, integrated project management, measurement and analysis, organizational innovation and deployment, organizational process definition, organizational process focus, organizational process performance, organizational training, project monitoring and control, project planning, process and product quality assurance, product integration, quantitative project management, requirements management, requirements development, risk management, supplier agreement management, technical solution, validation, and verification.

89. **Answer: A.** At level 1 of the CMM, processes likely to be variable (inconsistent) and depend heavily on institutional knowledge. At level 2, processes are seen as repeatable. At level 3, documented standards are put in place. At level 4, metrics and management standards are in place.

90. **Answer: B.** The two methods of reasoning when using inference rules are forward chaining and backward chaining. Knowledge transparency deals with knowledge representation.

91. **Answer: C.** Extreme programming, which is an off-shoot of agile, uses pairs of programmers who work from detailed specifications. Answer A is not correct because waterfall is a classical method. Answer B is not correct because spiral uses iterations that spiral out every 28 days. Answer D is not correct because RAD uses prototypes.

92. **Answer: D.** Crippleware, or trialware, is software that is partially functioning proprietary software that can be used without payment. Therefore, answers A, B, and C are incorrect.

93. **Answer: A.** Byte code, such as Java, serves as a type of intermediary code that must be converted to machine code before running.

94. **Answer: C.** CORBA is an open vendor-neutral middleware. Answers A, B, and D are incorrect because COM enables objects written in different languages to communicate, and OOA and OOD are software design methodologies.

95. **Answer: B.** COM enables objects written in different languages to communicate. Answers A, C, and D are incorrect because OOA and OOD are software design methodologies, and CORBA is vendor-neutral middleware.

96. **Answer: True.** SQL is a 4GL language. Others include CASE and Statistical Analysis System (SAS).

97. **Answer: False.** 5GL languages are designed to use knowledge-based systems to solve problems and use constraints instead of an algorithm.

98. **Answer: False.** The spiral model is the one that is based on the concept that software development is evolutionary.

99. **Answer: False.** It is true that reengineering attempts to update software by reusing as many of the components as possible instead of designing an entirely new system. However, reverse engineering is a technique that can be used to decrease development time by *decompiling* existing code. Reverse engineering has many legal issues and concerns.

100. **Answer: True.** Cohesion addresses the fact that a module can perform a single task with little input from other modules. Coupling is the measurement of the interconnecting between modules. Low coupling means that a change to one module should not affect another.

101. **Answer: True.** An ERD helps map the requirements and define the relationship between elements. The basic components of an ERD are an entity and a relationship. After a data dictionary is designed, the database schema can be developed.

102. **Answer: True.** WBAD offers standardized integration through the use of application development technologies such as XML. Its components include SOAP, WSDL, and UDDI.

103. Answer: False. Prototyping is still used. The advantage is that it can provide real savings in development time and costs.

104. Answer: False. Zeroization is the act of writing 0s, or a known pattern of bits, to media to make it difficult to recover the residual data. Purging makes data removal next to impossible. Therefore, purging is the higher level of data removal.

105. The answers are as follows:

A. Stealth: **2.**

B. Meme: **5.**

C. Macro: **1.**

D. EICAR: **4.**

E. Encrypted virus: **3.**

A stealth virus can modify functionality, so detection is very difficult. A meme is not a virus; it works like a chain letter. Its purpose is to forward the message from user to user, propagating the hoax. The "I love you" and Melissa viruses are examples of macro viruses. "I love you" was an active script that could infect via a number of vectors of systems running Microsoft Windows with Windows Scripting Host enabled. Melissa targeted Microsoft Office documents (specifically, Microsoft Word). These viruses target Office documents. The EICAR test is used to verify the functionality of antivirus software. It is basically a signature that all participating vendors recognize. Encrypted viruses are similar to polymorphic viruses but can change how they are stored on the disk. This form of malware can make use of a cryptographic key.

CHAPTER NINE

Information Security, Governance, and Risk Management

The Information Security Governance and Risk Management domain tests your knowledge of the items related to the triad of security: confidentiality, integrity, and availability (CIA). A large portion of this domain deals with risk management. There are many ways to manage risk; test candidates must be aware that risk assessment can be performed by quantitative, qualitative, or hybrid techniques. The CISSP also must understand security plans and procedures, implementing service-level agreements, and performing security assessments. Each of these items plays a role in managing the security of the organization's employees and assets. The following list gives you some key areas from security management that you need to be aware of for the CISSP exam:

- CIA (confidentiality, integrity, and availability)
- Roles and responsibilities
- Asset management
- Taxonomy: information classification
- Risk management: quantitative, qualitative, and hybrid
- Policies, procedures, standards, guidelines, baselines
- Knowledge transfer: awareness, training, education

Quick Check

Practice Questions

1. You have just won a contract for a small software development firm, which has asked you to perform a risk analysis. The firm provided you information on previous incidents and has a list of the known environmental threats of the geographic area. The firm's president believes that risk is something that can be eliminated. As a CISSP, how should you respond to this statement?

   ❍ **A.** Although it can be prohibitively expensive, risk can be eliminated.

   ❍ **B.** Risk can be reduced but cannot be eliminated.

   ❍ **C.** A qualitative risk analysis can eliminate risk.

   ❍ **D.** A quantitative risk assessment can eliminate risk.

Quick Answer: **292**
Detailed Answer: **293**

2. Which term describes the method of identifying vulnerabilities and threats and assessing the possible damage to determine where to implement security safeguards?

   ❍ **A.** Information management

   ❍ **B.** Risk analysis

   ❍ **C.** Countermeasure selection

   ❍ **D.** Classification controls

Quick Answer: **292**
Detailed Answer: **293**

3. Proper security management dictates separation of duties for all the following reasons except which one?

   ❍ **A.** It reduces the possibility of fraud.

   ❍ **B.** It reduces dependency on individual workers.

   ❍ **C.** It reduces the need for personnel.

   ❍ **D.** It provides integrity.

Quick Answer: **292**
Detailed Answer: **293**

4. As a potential CISSP, you need to know common RFCs and NIST standards. One such RFC is 2196. This IETF document provides basic guidance on security in a networked environment. What is the title of this document?

   ❍ **A.** "Ethics and the Internet"

   ❍ **B.** "Site Security Handbook"

   ❍ **C.** "Cracking and Hacking TCP/IP"

   ❍ **D.** "Security Policies and Procedures"

Quick Answer: **292**
Detailed Answer: **293**

Quick Check

5. Mr. Hunting, your former college math teacher, hears that you are studying for your CISSP exam and asks if you know the formula for total risk. What is the correct response?

Quick Answer: **292**
Detailed Answer: **293**

- ❍ **A.** Annual Loss Expectancy * Vulnerability = Total Risk
- ❍ **B.** Threat * Vulnerability * Asset Value = Total Risk
- ❍ **C.** Residual Risk / Asset Value * Vulnerability = Total Risk
- ❍ **D.** Asset Value / Residual Risk = Total Risk

6. What document gives detailed instructions on how to perform specific operations, providing a step-by-step guide?

Quick Answer: **292**
Detailed Answer: **293**

- ❍ **A.** Guidelines
- ❍ **B.** Policies
- ❍ **C.** Procedures
- ❍ **D.** Standards

7. Your CEO has hinted that security audits may be implemented next year. As a result, your director has become serious about performing some form of risk assessment. You are delegated the task of determining which type of risk assessment to perform. The director wants to learn more about the type of risk assessment that involves a team of internal business managers and technical staff. He does not want the assessment to place dollar amounts on identified risks. He wants the group to assign one of 26 common controls to each threat as it is identified. Which type of risk assessment does your manager want?

Quick Answer: **292**
Detailed Answer: **293**

- ❍ **A.** Delphi
- ❍ **B.** Delegated
- ❍ **C.** Quantitative
- ❍ **D.** FRAP

8. Which of the following is a document that is considered high level in that it defines formal rules by which employees of the organization must abide?

Quick Answer: **292**
Detailed Answer: **293**

- ❍ **A.** Guidelines
- ❍ **B.** Policies
- ❍ **C.** Standards
- ❍ **D.** Procedures

9. As part of the pending risk assessment, your corporation wants to perform a threat analysis. What are the primary types of threats?

Quick Answer: **292**
Detailed Answer: **293**

- ❍ **A.** Environmental and accidental
- ❍ **B.** Destructive and passive
- ❍ **C.** Natural and planned
- ❍ **D.** Man-made and natural

Quick Check

10. What document is similar to a standard but provides only broad guidance and recommendations?

Quick Answer: **292**
Detailed Answer: **293**

- ❍ **A.** Policies
- ❍ **B.** Guidelines
- ❍ **C.** Procedures
- ❍ **D.** Baselines

11. You are asked to speak at the next staff meeting. Your director wants you to discuss why risk analysis is important. What will you say?

Quick Answer: **292**
Detailed Answer: **293**

- ❍ **A.** Risk analysis is something every company should perform to demonstrate that it is in control of its assets, resources, and destiny.
- ❍ **B.** Risk analysis is important because it is required before an organization can sell stock by means of an IPO.
- ❍ **C.** Risk analysis is important because it demonstrates profitability.
- ❍ **D.** Risk analysis is important because it helps ensure that your company will survive an audit.

12. One of your coworkers, who knows that you are studying for your CISSP exam, comes to you with the following question: What is a cost-benefit analysis? How will you answer?

Quick Answer: **292**
Detailed Answer: **294**

- ❍ **A.** A cost-benefit analysis should identify safeguards that offer the maximum amount of protection for the minimum cost.
- ❍ **B.** A cost-benefit analysis should identify targets that have been identified as low risk.
- ❍ **C.** A cost-benefit analysis should identify safeguards that are easy to implement for the protection of low-value targets.
- ❍ **D.** A cost-benefit analysis should identify safeguards that offer the minimum amount of protection for the maximum cost.

13. Which of the following is used to verify a user's identity?

Quick Answer: **292**
Detailed Answer: **294**

- ❍ **A.** Authorization
- ❍ **B.** Identification
- ❍ **C.** Authentication
- ❍ **D.** Accountability

Quick Check

14. Your consulting firm has won a contract for a small, yet growing, technology firm. The CEO has wisely decided that the firm's proprietary technology is worth protecting. Which of the following is *not* a reason why this organization should develop information classification?

Quick Answer: **292**
Detailed Answer: **294**

❍ **A.** Information classification should be implemented to demonstrate the organization's commitment to good security practices.

❍ **B.** Information classification should be implemented to ensure successful prosecution of intellectual property violators.

❍ **C.** Information classification identifies which level of protection should be applied to the organization's data.

❍ **D.** Information classification should be implemented to meet regulatory and industry standards.

15. Your administrative assistant has started an online risk assessment certificate program. She has a question: What primary security concept defines the rights and privileges of a validated user? What will your answer be?

Quick Answer: **292**
Detailed Answer: **294**

❍ **A.** Authorization

❍ **B.** Identification

❍ **C.** Authentication

❍ **D.** Accountability

16. Which of the following can be used to protect confidentiality?

Quick Answer: **292**
Detailed Answer: **294**

❍ **A.** CCTV

❍ **B.** Encryption

❍ **C.** Checksums

❍ **D.** RAID

17. Your company has brought in a group of contract programmers. Although management feels it is important to track these users' activities, they also want to make sure that any changes to program code or data can be tied to a specific individual. Which of the following best describes the means by which an individual cannot deny having performed an action or caused an event?

Quick Answer: **292**
Detailed Answer: **294**

❍ **A.** Identification

❍ **B.** Auditing

❍ **C.** Logging

❍ **D.** Nonrepudiation

Quick Check

18. Which of the following can be used to protect integrity?

- ❍ **A.** CCTV
- ❍ **B.** Encryption
- ❍ **C.** Checksums
- ❍ **D.** RAID

Quick Answer: **292**
Detailed Answer: **294**

19. Christine has been given network access to pilot engineering design documents. Although she can view the documents, she cannot print them or make changes. Which of the following does she lack?

- ❍ **A.** Identification
- ❍ **B.** Authorization
- ❍ **C.** Authentication
- ❍ **D.** Validation

Quick Answer: **292**
Detailed Answer: **294**

20. Which of the following can be used to provide accountability?

- ❍ **A.** CCTV
- ❍ **B.** RAID
- ❍ **C.** Checksums
- ❍ **D.** Symmetric encryption

Quick Answer: **292**
Detailed Answer: **294**

21. CISSP candidates are required to understand change control management and data classification. Which data classifications are valid for marking documents that have gone through change control?

- ❍ **A.** Residential and government
- ❍ **B.** Government and commercial
- ❍ **C.** Commercial and private
- ❍ **D.** International and national

Quick Answer: **292**
Detailed Answer: **294**

22. Which of the following can be used to protect availability?

- ❍ **A.** RAID
- ❍ **B.** Encryption
- ❍ **C.** Checksums
- ❍ **D.** CCTV

Quick Answer: **292**
Detailed Answer: **294**

23. Which data classification method uses labels such as confidential, private, and sensitive?

- ❍ **A.** Government
- ❍ **B.** IP SEC
- ❍ **C.** Commercial
- ❍ **D.** PUB SEC

Quick Answer: **292**
Detailed Answer: **295**

Quick Check

24. Your team has worked several weeks designing a network for a new overseas facility. The design includes a border router with web and email services behind it. This is followed up by a stateful inspection firewall. The servers inside the network have been configured to NSA secure standards, and each workstation uses biometric authentication. What type of security is being described?

- ❍ **A.** Single-layered defense
- ❍ **B.** Defense-in-depth
- ❍ **C.** Principle of least privilege
- ❍ **D.** Defense-in-parallel

Quick Answer: **292**
Detailed Answer: **295**

25. Which data classification method uses labels such as confidential, sensitive but unclassified, and unclassified?

- ❍ **A.** Government
- ❍ **B.** IP SEC
- ❍ **C.** Commercial
- ❍ **D.** PUB SEC

Quick Answer: **292**
Detailed Answer: **295**

26. You are an advisory board member for a local nonprofit organization. Because your fellow board members know of your expertise in security, they approach you with the following question: Who is ultimately responsible for information security? How will you answer them?

- ❍ **A.** Information custodians
- ❍ **B.** Users
- ❍ **C.** Managers
- ❍ **D.** Senior management

Quick Answer: **292**
Detailed Answer: **295**

27. Barry, your CTO, has asked you to design the security model for the San Diego site. Which security model would you *not* recommend?

- ❍ **A.** Layered
- ❍ **B.** Default open
- ❍ **C.** Defense-in-depth
- ❍ **D.** Default closed

Quick Answer: **292**
Detailed Answer: **295**

28. What is the correct order for the following items?

- ❍ **A.** Identify, authorize, authenticate
- ❍ **B.** Authenticate, authorize, identify
- ❍ **C.** Authorize, authenticate, identify
- ❍ **D.** Identify, authenticate, authorize

Quick Answer: **292**
Detailed Answer: **295**

Quick Check

29. What is ARO?

Quick Answer: **292**
Detailed Answer: **295**

❍ **A.** Average Risk Occurrence

❍ **B.** Annual Risk Occurrence

❍ **C.** Annualized Rate of Occurrence

❍ **D.** Annualized Risk Outage

30. Which of the following does *not* require prior employee notification?

Quick Answer: **292**
Detailed Answer: **295**

❍ **A.** Monitoring emails

❍ **B.** Monitoring unsuccessful login attempts

❍ **C.** Monitoring voice communications

❍ **D.** Monitoring web traffic

31. Your intern comes to you with the following question about your company's change control board: What is *not* one of the primary reasons why a change control board is needed? How do you answer?

Quick Answer: **292**
Detailed Answer: **295**

❍ **A.** Change control is needed so that all changes can be controlled.

❍ **B.** Change control is needed so that changes can be made quickly.

❍ **C.** Change control is needed so that the impact of new changes can be studied.

❍ **D.** Change control is needed so that changes can be reversed.

32. Which of the following should be performed in conjunction with a termination?

Quick Answer: **292**
Detailed Answer: **295**

❍ **A.** Exit interview

❍ **B.** Potential limitation of computer access

❍ **C.** Prior notice of termination

❍ **D.** Adequate private time to say good-bye to friends and coworkers

33. Based on the CBK, what is the highest level of government data classification?

Quick Answer: **292**
Detailed Answer: **295**

❍ **A.** Confidential

❍ **B.** Secret

❍ **C.** Sensitive

❍ **D.** Top secret

Quick Check

34. Your manager is concerned about a new piece of software being developed by a contractor. Your manager wants you to verify that no means of unauthenticated access is left in the finished product. What is another name for a method of unauthenticated access into a program?

❍ **A.** Covert wrapper

❍ **B.** Slip

❍ **C.** Wrapper

❍ **D.** Backdoor

Quick Answer: **292**
Detailed Answer: **296**

35. Which of the following is the lowest level of private-sector data classification?

❍ **A.** Public

❍ **B.** Secret

❍ **C.** Unclassified

❍ **D.** Sensitive but unclassified

Quick Answer: **292**
Detailed Answer: **296**

36. Whose role is to examine security policies and procedures and provide reports to senior management about the effectiveness of security controls?

❍ **A.** Infosec security officer

❍ **B.** Auditor

❍ **C.** Users

❍ **D.** Data owners

Quick Answer: **292**
Detailed Answer: **296**

37. What is the process of determining the level of risk at which the organization can operate and function effectively?

❍ **A.** Risk acceptance

❍ **B.** Risk mitigation

❍ **C.** Risk transference

❍ **D.** Risk reduction

Quick Answer: **292**
Detailed Answer: **296**

38. Who has the functional responsibility of security?

❍ **A.** Infosec security officer

❍ **B.** Auditor

❍ **C.** Users

❍ **D.** Data owners

Quick Answer: **292**
Detailed Answer: **296**

Quick Check

39. James, the summer intern, asks if you can show him how to calculate ALE. What do you tell him?

Quick Answer: **292**
Detailed Answer: **296**

❍ **A.** Annualized Rate of Occurrence (ARO) / Single Loss Expectancy (SLE) = ALE

❍ **B.** Single Loss Expectancy (SLE) * Annualized Rate of Occurrence (ARO) = ALE

❍ **C.** Total Risk (TR) * Annualized Rate of Occurrence (ARO) = ALE

❍ **D.** Residual Risk (RR) / Asset Value (AV) * Vulnerability (V) = ALE

40. What is the lowest level of government data classification?

Quick Answer: **292**
Detailed Answer: **296**

❍ **A.** Public

❍ **B.** Unclassified

❍ **C.** Secret

❍ **D.** Sensitive but unclassified

41. Which of the following is *not* an acceptable response to risk?

Quick Answer: **292**
Detailed Answer: **296**

❍ **A.** Acceptance

❍ **B.** Displacement

❍ **C.** Reduction

❍ **D.** Transference

42. You are an advisory board member for a local nonprofit organization. The organization has been given a new server, and members plan to use it to connect their 20 client computers to the Internet for email access. Currently, none of these computers has antivirus software installed. Your research indicates that there is a 90% chance that these systems will become infected after email is in use. There's a good chance that a virus could bring down the network for an entire day. The nonprofit's 10 paid employees make about $12 an hour. A local vendor has offered to sell 20 copies of antivirus software to the nonprofit organization for $500. The nonprofit wants to know what the ALE for this proposed change would be. Assuming that employees work an eight-hour day, how will you answer?

Quick Answer: **292**
Detailed Answer: **296**

❍ **A.** $120

❍ **B.** $500

❍ **C.** $720

❍ **D.** $864

Quick Check

43. The nonprofit organization that you are an advisory board member of decides to go forward with the proposed Internet and email connectivity project. The CEO wants like to know how much money, if any, will be saved through the purchase of antivirus software. Here are the projected details:

Quick Answer: 292
Detailed Answer: 296

20 computers are connected to the Internet.

There's a 90% probability of virus infection.

Ten paid employees make $12 an hour.

A successful virus outage could bring down the network for an entire day.

20 copies of antivirus software will cost the nonprofit $500.

- ❍ **A.** $0
- ❍ **B.** $364
- ❍ **C.** $960
- ❍ **D.** $1,290

44. Which of the following describes the process of revealing only external properties to other components?

Quick Answer: 292
Detailed Answer: 296

- ❍ **A.** Encryption
- ❍ **B.** Abstraction
- ❍ **C.** Obfuscation
- ❍ **D.** Data hiding

45. Which of the following is the highest level of private-sector (commercial) data classification?

Quick Answer: 292
Detailed Answer: 297

- ❍ **A.** Proprietary
- ❍ **B.** Classified
- ❍ **C.** Secret
- ❍ **D.** Confidential

46. Which of the following is used to segregate details to focus on only one particular piece or item?

Quick Answer: 292
Detailed Answer: 297

- ❍ **A.** Encryption
- ❍ **B.** Abstraction
- ❍ **C.** Obfuscation
- ❍ **D.** Data hiding

Quick Check

47. The nonprofit organization that you are an advisory board member of wants you to apply the principles of qualitative risk analysis to the organization. How do you accomplish this task?

Quick Answer: **292**
Detailed Answer: **297**

❍ **A.** (1) Assign a dollar value to the risk, (2) assign a value to the potential loss, (3) perform an ALE calculation to see whether a potential safeguard is worth the cost.

❍ **B.** (1) Develop attack scenarios, (2) assign a dollar value to each potential loss, (3) rank the results by dollar value, placing the highest loss values first.

❍ **C.** (1) Measure possible risk, (2) measure the costs associated with protecting the assets, (3) rank the resulting risk and the importance of the asset.

❍ **D.** (1) Develop risk scenarios, (2) analyze each scenario to determine the outcome, (3) rank the resulting risk and the importance of the asset.

48. According to NIST Special Publication (SP) 800-27, what should be an organization's goal in regard to risk?

Quick Answer: **292**
Detailed Answer: **297**

❍ **A.** Only when there is no other option should an organization accept risk.

❍ **B.** Risk should be reduced to an acceptable level.

❍ **C.** Risk should be eliminated.

❍ **D.** Notable risks should be reevaluated at least every three years.

49. Your director has asked you to implement a security awareness program. When considering a security awareness program, which of the following is not correct?

Quick Answer: **292**
Detailed Answer: **297**

❍ **A.** A security awareness program improves awareness of security policies and procedures.

❍ **B.** A security awareness program should run continuously and visibly reprimand those who are in noncompliance.

❍ **C.** A security awareness program helps employees understand the need to protect company assets.

❍ **D.** A security awareness program teaches employees how to perform their jobs more securely.

50. The nonprofit organization that you are an advisory board member of wants you to evaluate the organization's security policy. Those at the organization believe that encryption should be used on their network now that it is connected to the Internet. Primarily, they are concerned that malicious hackers may be able to tap into their systems and steal donor information and demographic data. Based on

Quick Answer: **292**
Detailed Answer: **297**

the principles of risk management, what should your decision to use encryption be based on? Choose the most correct answer.

❍ **A.** If the network is vulnerable, systems should be implemented to protect the data.

❍ **B.** If the network is vulnerable, the cost of protecting the system should be weighed against the costs associated with such a disclosure.

❍ **C.** If the network is vulnerable, systems should be implemented to protect the data, regardless of the cost.

❍ **D.** Because it is a nonprofit organization, the probability of attack is not as great; therefore, the risk should be accepted or transferred through the use of insurance.

51. Data abstraction is a practical necessity at what TCSEC layer?

Quick Answer: **292**
Detailed Answer: **297**

❍ **A.** B3

❍ **B.** D1

❍ **C.** D2

❍ **D.** F

52. You work for a company that has a large web-based storefront. Recently, a vulnerability was discovered in the application's front-end software. If this vulnerability is exploited, your company's database could be breached. Any breach would mean the loss of competitive customer account information. Although no credit card information is on file, any pilfered information would result in the demise of your corporation. This website provides $500,000 profit monthly. A new commercial application for your line of business is available for $2 million. Your current application's vendor is writing a patch to make available a workaround product that costs $20,000. Your insurance company will not cover any damages that occur under your current configuration. For an added fee of $1,000 a day, it will cover the patched configuration. For no added cost, it will cover all losses if you acquired the new commercial application. Meanwhile, your company has already spent $1.5 million writing your own replacement application. This application is undergoing a parallel test and is scheduled to be released in two more months. Which course of action should you recommend to your company?

Quick Answer: **292**
Detailed Answer: **297**

❍ **A.** Shut down the portal until your team has finished the replacement product.

❍ **B.** Acquire the patch and workaround product, and use them until your replacement product is available.

❍ **C.** Buy the new commercial product.

❍ **D.** Accept the risk, stay in production, and push the programming team to finish early.

Quick Check

53. Which term refers to a prudent person who implements controls to behave responsibly when caring for data entrusted to him or her?

- ❍ **A.** Due care
- ❍ **B.** Due diligence
- ❍ **C.** Legally liable
- ❍ **D.** Culpable

Quick Answer: **292**
Detailed Answer: **297**

54. Replace the italic words in the following sentence with the terms commonly used when discussing risk management: A software product used by your company includes an unknown *weakness*. This *risk* can lead to an exploit from the Internet and enable a malicious hacker to *access* your customer's credit cards.

- ❍ **A.** Vulnerability, exposure, target
- ❍ **B.** Exposure, vulnerability, threat
- ❍ **C.** Vulnerability, threat, expose
- ❍ **D.** Exposure, threat, destroy

Quick Answer: **292**
Detailed Answer: **298**

55. Place the following steps of the life cycle of a security program in sequential order.

- ❍ **A.** Monitor, implement, organize, operate, evaluate
- ❍ **B.** Monitor, organize, implement, evaluate, operate
- ❍ **C.** Organize, implement, operate, monitor, evaluate
- ❍ **D.** Monitor, organize, evaluate, implement, operate

Quick Answer: **292**
Detailed Answer: **298**

56. Who is responsible for the security of data?

- ❍ **A.** The data's custodian
- ❍ **B.** The company's owner
- ❍ **C.** The computer's owner
- ❍ **D.** The data's owner

Quick Answer: **292**
Detailed Answer: **298**

57. What formula identifies residual risk?

- ❍ **A.** Annual Loss Expectancy (ALE) * Control Gap
- ❍ **B.** (Threat * Vulnerability) * Control Gap
- ❍ **C.** (Threat * Vulnerability) – Countermeasures
- ❍ **D.** Annual Loss Expectancy (ALE) * Threat

Quick Answer: **292**
Detailed Answer: **298**

Quick Check

58. Information security seeks to protect a triad of principles. Which of the following is not included in that triad?

Quick Answer: 292
Detailed Answer: 298

- ❍ **A.** Authorization
- ❍ **B.** Integrity
- ❍ **C.** Confidentiality
- ❍ **D.** Availability

59. With regard to the classification of information, the levels of sensitivity used by the U.S. military include all the following except which one?

Quick Answer: 292
Detailed Answer: 298

- ❍ **A.** Unclassified
- ❍ **B.** Controlled
- ❍ **C.** Confidential
- ❍ **D.** Secret

60. What does a company practice by developing and implementing security policies, procedures, and standards?

Quick Answer: 292
Detailed Answer: 298

- ❍ **A.** Due care
- ❍ **B.** Risk assessment
- ❍ **C.** Due diligence
- ❍ **D.** Security classification

61. Which of the following terms is *not* related to quantitative risk analysis?

Quick Answer: 292
Detailed Answer: 298

- ❍ **A.** Exposure Factor (EF)
- ❍ **B.** Annualized Rate of Occurrence (ARO)
- ❍ **C.** Annual Risk Acceptance (ARA)
- ❍ **D.** Single Loss Expectancy (SLE)

62. Which of the following is not part of the commercial information classification system?

Quick Answer: 292
Detailed Answer: 298

- ❍ **A.** Confidential
- ❍ **B.** Private
- ❍ **C.** Sensitive
- ❍ **D.** Unclassified

Quick Check

63. As part of the risk assessment team, you are asked to describe which of the following is a flaw, loophole, oversight, or error that makes your company susceptible to attack or damage. What is your answer?

- ❍ **A.** Risk
- ❍ **B.** Vulnerability
- ❍ **C.** Threat
- ❍ **D.** Exploit

Quick Answer: **292**
Detailed Answer: **298**

64. Place the following terms in the most logical order.

- ❍ **A.** Asset valuation, threat analysis, control analysis, mitigation, policy creation, awareness
- ❍ **B.** Threat analysis, control recommendation, asset valuation, mitigation
- ❍ **C.** Policy creation, risk mitigation, control evaluation, training
- ❍ **D.** Build, acquire, test, create, control, assess

Quick Answer: **292**
Detailed Answer: **298**

65. The result of a recent risk assessment has led to the upgrade of the organization's firewall. Which risk control most closely fits this response?

- ❍ **A.** Transfer the risk
- ❍ **B.** Mitigate the risk
- ❍ **C.** Accept the risk
- ❍ **D.** Ignore the risk

Quick Answer: **292**
Detailed Answer: **298**

66. What was one of the first documents that had the goal of harmonizing security criteria internationally?

- ❍ **A.** TCSEC
- ❍ **B.** ITSEC
- ❍ **C.** Common Criteria
- ❍ **D.** BS 7799

Quick Answer: **292**
Detailed Answer: **299**

67. Quantitative risk assessments seek to perform all the following except which one?

- ❍ **A.** Assign dollar values to defined risks
- ❍ **B.** Use questioners and interviews to determine high-risk items
- ❍ **C.** Use mathematical formulas
- ❍ **D.** Determine tangible values

Quick Answer: **292**
Detailed Answer: **299**

Quick Check

68. You are asked to calculate the Annual Loss Expectancy (ALE) for a new IT asset where the Annualized Rate of Occurrence is 60%. If the Asset Value is $500 and the Single Loss Expectancy (SLE) is $450, what is the Exposure Factor (EF)?

Quick Answer: 292
Detailed Answer: 299

- ❍ **A.** 50%
- ❍ **B.** 90%
- ❍ **C.** $50
- ❍ **D.** $270

69. You are called back to do more calculations for a pending risk assessment, because the company has gathered additional information. If the Asset Value is now $1,000, what will the ALE be with an SLE of $800 and an ARO of twice yearly?

Quick Answer: 292
Detailed Answer: 299

- ❍ **A.** $1,200
- ❍ **B.** $.80
- ❍ **C.** $400
- ❍ **D.** $1,600

70. Your final risk-assessment task is to provide your manager with a quick assessment on a new asset. To do so, you are given the following information. Can you calculate the ALE?

Quick Answer: 292
Detailed Answer: 299

Single Loss Expectancy = $2,500

Exposure Factor = .9

Annualized Rate of Occurrence = .4

Residual Risk = $30

- ❍ **A.** $900.00
- ❍ **B.** $2,100.50
- ❍ **C.** $1,000.00
- ❍ **D.** $1,800.27

71. Place the following risk assessment steps in order, from last to first.

Quick Answer: 292
Detailed Answer: 299

I. Derive annual loss potential
II. Assign value to assets
III. Reduce, transfer, or avoid the risk
IV. Estimate potential loss
V. Perform a threat analysis

- ❍ **A.** II, III, I, V, IV
- ❍ **B.** III, IV, V, I, II
- ❍ **C.** III, I, V, IV, II
- ❍ **D.** II, IV, I, V, III

Quick Check

72. What kind of qualitative risk assessment features anonymous feedback?

Quick Answer: **292**
Detailed Answer: **299**

- ❍ **A.** Facilitated Risk Assessment Process (FRAP)
- ❍ **B.** Delphi
- ❍ **C.** Focus groups
- ❍ **D.** Storyboarding

73. What element of the risk assessment process denotes the percentage of risk that a company would suffer if an asset were compromised by a realized risk?

Quick Answer: **292**
Detailed Answer: **299**

- ❍ **A.** Vulnerability
- ❍ **B.** Risk
- ❍ **C.** Exposure factor
- ❍ **D.** Threat

74. You are asked to work with your manager to develop new security objectives. Which of these would be considered very short-term in nature?

Quick Answer: **292**
Detailed Answer: **299**

- ❍ **A.** Tactical
- ❍ **B.** Operational
- ❍ **C.** Weekly
- ❍ **D.** Strategic

75. Which form of risk assessment takes the most time, and why?

Quick Answer: **292**
Detailed Answer: **299**

- ❍ **A.** Qualitative, because it is so objective
- ❍ **B.** Quantitative, because even with tools for automation, a large amount of data must be gathered
- ❍ **C.** Qualitative, because even with tools for automation, a large amount of data must be gathered
- ❍ **D.** Quantitative, because the approval time typically is very lengthy

76. The NSA's Infosec Security Assessment (IAM) is a good example of a qualitative risk-assessment methodology. As such, which of the following statements is least correct?

Quick Answer: **292**
Detailed Answer: **299**

- ❍ **A.** It may not provide the type of input that senior management finds easiest to work with.
- ❍ **B.** It can be completed quickly.
- ❍ **C.** It uses impact attributes that are based on confidentiality, integrity, and availability.
- ❍ **D.** It features a good method of performing numeric calculations such as ALE and ARO.

Quick Check

77. What term best describes something that is an instance of being vulnerable to losses from a threat?

Quick Answer: **292**
Detailed Answer: **299**

- ❍ **A.** Vulnerability
- ❍ **B.** Risk
- ❍ **C.** Exposure
- ❍ **D.** Threat

78. Which of the following statements is incorrect?

Quick Answer: **292**
Detailed Answer: **299**

- ❍ **A.** Procedures are a high-level document.
- ❍ **B.** Standards detail how to perform tasks in a uniform way.
- ❍ **C.** Guidelines offer recommended actions.
- ❍ **D.** Policies are strategic in nature.

79. How do you find out what level of risk the enterprise can safely tolerate and still continue to function effectively?

Quick Answer: **292**
Detailed Answer: **299**

- ❍ **A.** Risk assessment
- ❍ **B.** Risk elimination
- ❍ **C.** Risk mitigation
- ❍ **D.** Risk reduction

80. How is SLE determined?

Quick Answer: **292**
Detailed Answer: **299**

- ❍ **A.** By multiplying the Asset Value by the Annualized Rate of Occurrence
- ❍ **B.** By dividing the Exposure Factor by the Asset Value
- ❍ **C.** By multiplying the Asset Value by the amount vulnerable or exposed
- ❍ **D.** By dividing the Asset Value by the Asset Cost

81. What was the original name of ISO 27002?

Quick Answer: **292**
Detailed Answer: **299**

- ❍ **A.** ISO 27000
- ❍ **B.** ISO 17799
- ❍ **C.** BS 1769
- ❍ **D.** TCSEC

82. OCTAVE is designed to act as a framework to support risk analysis. How many phases are in the OCTAVE framework?

Quick Answer: **292**
Detailed Answer: **300**

- ❍ **A.** 1
- ❍ **B.** 2
- ❍ **C.** 3
- ❍ **D.** 4

Quick Check

83. You are asked to review some existing security documentation. Which of the following documents could best be described as discretionary and not mandatory?

Quick Answer: 292
Detailed Answer: 300

❍ A. Policy
❍ B. Guideline
❍ C. Procedure
❍ D. Standard

84. You are asked to calculate the total cost of ownership (TCO). Which of the following does TCO *not* include?

Quick Answer: 292
Detailed Answer: 300

❍ A. Asset cost
❍ B. Replacement cost
❍ C. Maintenance cost
❍ D. Vendor support cost

85. You have several clients throughout the U.S. for which you are assigned to manage risk. One client is in D.C., another is in San Jose, and a third is in Boston. Use the following scale to assess the quantitative risk-impact score for Boston.

Quick Answer: 292
Detailed Answer: 300

Location	Threat	Vulnerability
D.C.	4	2
San Jose	3	1
Boston	2	2

❍ A. A score of eight
❍ B. A score of zero
❍ C. A score of four
❍ D. A score of three

Practice Questions (True or False)

86. Standards define compulsory requirements.

Quick Answer: 292
Detailed Answer: 300

❍ True
❍ False

87. A parallel run is an example of a change management technique.

Quick Answer: 292
Detailed Answer: 300

❍ True
❍ False

88. Labels are a requirement of TCSEC C-level security.

Quick Answer: 292
Detailed Answer: 300

❍ True
❍ False

Quick Check

89. Tangible values are all that need to be examined when performing an asset evaluation.

- ❍ True
- ❍ False

Quick Answer: **292**
Detailed Answer: **300**

90. A policy is a management-driven objective.

- ❍ True
- ❍ False

Quick Answer: **292**
Detailed Answer: **300**

91. The security officer is ultimately responsible for security.

- ❍ True
- ❍ False

Quick Answer: **292**
Detailed Answer: **300**

92. The risk analysis team should be composed of people from security management.

- ❍ True
- ❍ False

Quick Answer: **292**
Detailed Answer: **300**

93. The asset owner is responsible for the security controls that are designed to protect the asset.

- ❍ True
- ❍ False

Quick Answer: **292**
Detailed Answer: **300**

94. Application error is one type of risk that the organization should be concerned about.

- ❍ True
- ❍ False

Quick Answer: **292**
Detailed Answer: **300**

Practice Questions (Mix and Match)

95. Match each risk assessment formula with its definition.

A. Asset Value: _____

B. Exposure Factor: _____

C. Annual Loss Expectancy: _____

D. Annualized Rate of Occurrence: _____

E. Single Loss Expectancy: _____

1. Percentage of asset loss caused by the identified threat
2. The average expected loss per year
3. Expressed as Asset Value ($) * Exposure Factor
4. The total worth of the item being assessed
5. How many times a threat will occur within a year

Quick Answer: **292**
Detailed Answer: **300**

Quick Check Answer Key

1. B
2. B
3. C
4. B
5. B
6. C
7. D
8. B
9. D
10. B
11. A
12. A
13. C
14. B
15. A
16. B
17. D
18. C
19. B
20. A
21. B
22. A
23. C
24. B
25. A
26. D
27. B
28. D
29. C
30. B
31. B
32. A
33. D
34. D
35. A
36. B
37. B
38. A
39. B
40. B
41. B
42. D
43. B
44. D
45. D
46. B
47. D
48. B
49. B
50. B
51. A
52. B
53. A
54. C
55. C
56. D
57. A
58. A
59. B
60. A
61. C
62. D
63. B
64. A
65. B
66. B
67. B
68. B
69. D
70. C
71. C
72. B
73. C
74. B
75. B
76. D
77. C
78. A
79. C
80. C
81. B
82. C
83. B
84. B
85. C
86. True
87. True
88. False
89. False
90. True
91. False
92. False
93. True
94. True
95. **A.** 4
    B. 1
    C. 2
    D. 5
    E. 3

Answers and Explanations

1. **Answer: B.** Risk can be reduced, rejected, transferred, or accepted, but it can never be eliminated. Companies must decide how much risk they can live with, the value of the asset they are protecting, and how to best protect this asset.

2. **Answer: B.** Risk analysis is the method of identifying vulnerabilities and threats and assessing the possible damage to determine where to implement security safeguards. Information management is a general term and is unrelated to the risk management process. Countermeasure selection comes after the risk-management process, as do classification controls.

3. **Answer: C.** Separation of duties provides security by ensuring that no one individual has complete control over any one process or activity. It provides for the reduction of fraud and reduces the dependency on individual workers.

4. **Answer: B.** RFC 2196 is the "Site Security Handbook," which deals with security policy. "Ethics and the Internet" is RFC 1087. There are no RFCs for "Cracking and Hacking TCP/IP" or "Security Policies and Procedures."

5. **Answer: B.** The formula for total risk is Threat * Vulnerability * Asset Value = Total Risk.

6. **Answer: C.** Procedures are detailed in that they give the operator explicit instructions on how to perform specific operations, providing a step-by-step guide. Policies, guidelines, and standards are all higher-level documents.

7. **Answer: D.** Facilitated Risk Analysis Process (FRAP) is designed to be performed by a team of business managers and technical staff from within the organization. The team's goal is to brainstorm and identify risk. As the FRAP team identifies risk, they apply a group of 26 common controls designed to categorize each type of risk. Delphi requires answers to be submitted in written form. Delegated is not a valid form of risk assessment. Quantitative risk assessment seeks to apply an objective numeric value.

8. **Answer: B.** Policies are high-level documents that outline in a very broad sense what employees can and cannot do. For example, an organization may issue a policy that no unauthorized individuals are allowed in the facility. How this policy would be carried out would be left up to the appropriate lower-level documents, such as a procedure on access control.

9. **Answer: D.** A threat is something that is a source of danger. Threats can be natural or man-made.

10. **Answer: B.** Guidelines are general rules and recommendations to employees and staff. This is an example of a guideline: "Consoto Corp. believes that job rotation is an important part of security; therefore, it is recommended that employees be rotated within their departments at least twice a year."

11. **Answer: A.** Risk analysis is something that every company should perform—not only to demonstrate that it is in control of its assets, resources, and destiny, but also as an act of due diligence.

12. **Answer: A.** The cost-benefit analysis is an important step of the risk analysis process, because it helps you identify safeguards that offer the maximum amount of protection for the minimum cost.

13. **Answer: C.** Authentication is the manner in which a user is validated. It is typically performed by means of passwords, tokens, or biometrics. Authorization relates to what a particular user is allowed to do. Identification does not equate to authentication. Accountability is tied to audit trails and logging, because it is a way to track compliance and system misuse.

14. **Answer: B.** Information classification demonstrates the commitment to good security practices, helps identify what information is worth protecting, and should be pursued to meet all federal, state, local or industry regulations. Information classification may not help prosecute intellectual property violators located in third-world countries, because enforcement laws are inconsistent.

15. **Answer: A.** Authorization defines what a user can and cannot do. Identification is how the user claims his or her identity. Authentication is the manner in which a user is validated. Accountability is tied to audit trails and logging, because it is a way to track compliance and system misuse.

16. **Answer: B.** Confidentiality ensures that data in storage or in transit is not exposed to unauthorized individuals. Loss of confidentiality can be intentional or caused by human error. Encryption of data can help ensure confidentiality. CCTV can be used for accountability, checksums guarantee integrity, and RAID helps protect availability.

17. **Answer: D.** Nonrepudiation is used to verify that an individual has performed an action or event. Transaction logs, digital certificates, and access control mechanisms are some of the ways in which nonrepudiation can be established.

18. **Answer: C.** The fundamentals of security are based on CIA (confidentiality, integrity, and availability). Checksums guarantee the integrity of data. CCTV can be used for accountability. Encryption of data can help ensure confidentiality. RAID can be used to make sure that data and resources are available as needed.

19. **Answer: B.** Although you may be identified and authenticated into a computer system or network, that does not mean you are authorized or that an item is required to do your job functions. Authorization is more of a gray area because each user typically is limited in his or her rights and privileges within the network. Working under the *principle of least privilege*, a user should have no more access than what is required. Therefore, although Christine may need access to the engineering documents, she does not have the right to print or make changes to them.

20. **Answer: A.** CCTV (closed-circuit TV) can be used for accountability because employees can be monitored and recorded to verify their actions and location.

21. **Answer: B.** Two commonly used schemes are government and commercial (business). Each uses various labels, such as top-secret, secret, private, and confidential, to identify the handling and value of the information to the organization.

22. **Answer: A.** RAID (redundant array of inexpensive disks) is an excellent tool to make sure that data is available when needed.

23. **Answer: C.** The commercial form of data classification uses four levels to classify data: confidential, private, sensitive, and public. Answers B and D are distracters because there are no such classifications. Answer A is incorrect because that data classification uses levels such as top-secret.

24. **Answer: B.** The methodology of defense-in-depth is one of layered security. Its goal is to layer defense in such a way as to present many barriers to a potential intruder. Even if one device or layer is overcome, the attacker still must defeat many other hurdles. Single-layered defense and defense-in-parallel are incorrect because they are the opposite of what is described. The principle of least privilege relates to what privileges and access a user is given.

25. **Answer: A.** The U.S. government form of data classification has five levels: top-secret, secret, confidential, sensitive but unclassified, and unclassified. Answers B and D are distracters because there are no such classifications.

26. **Answer: D.** Although workers or information custodians may be charged with the day-to-day responsibility of information security, ultimately senior management is responsible. If any loss of CIA occurs, management can be held responsible and liable for lack of due care.

27. **Answer: B.** Actually, there are only two basic security design models: default open and default closed. The best approach is default closed. This means that all resources and applications should be disabled by default. Only those needed by employees to perform their jobs should be activated.

28. **Answer: D.** The only correct answer is to identify the user, authenticate the user into the system, and then authorize the user to perform essential activity.

29. **Answer: C.** Annualized Rate of Occurrence (ARO) is an estimate of how many times in one year a threat or negative event will occur.

30. **Answer: B.** It is best to inform employees through policy and procedure that their email, voice communications, and Internet activity may be monitored. It is generally agreed that event and audit functions, such as failed logins, do not require employee notification.

31. **Answer: B.** A change control board can serve a very useful role by ensuring that changes can be controlled, new changes can be studied, and detrimental changes can be reversed. Changes should not be made quickly without the knowledge of all responsible parties.

32. **Answer: A.** Terminated employees should be given an exit interview. They should be reminded of any NDAs or other agreements they signed at hiring, computer privileges should be removed, passwords should be changed, and the terminated employees should be monitored while still in the facility.

33. **Answer: D.** Top-secret is the highest level of U.S. government data classification. Secret is the level below it. Both confidential and sensitive are part of the private-sector (business) data classification scheme.

34. **Answer: D.** A backdoor is sometimes built into a program at its inception. It allows a programmer to debug and test the application without performing a full authentication. It is important that these be removed from the program before it leaves beta status. A wrapper is a program used to conceal a Trojan. Slip and covert wrapper are distracters.

35. **Answer: A.** The private-sector (business) data classification scheme has four levels, of which the lowest is public. The other three answers are part of the U.S. government's data classification scheme.

36. **Answer: B.** Auditors are responsible for reviewing what policies and procedures have been developed. They must also verify employee compliance and report their findings to senior management so that they can determine whether the stated goal of their security system is working.

37. **Answer: B.** Risk mitigation is the process of determining the level of risk at which the organization can operate and function effectively. Risk acceptance is the act of accepting risk. Risk transference is the act of moving the risk to another party, typically an insurance company. Risk reduction is the act of working toward reducing risk in the organization.

38. **Answer: A.** The infosec security officer is delegated the responsibility of implementing and maintaining security by the organization's senior-level management. Auditors are responsible for policy review. Users are responsible for complying with policy while performing day-to-day tasks. Data owners are responsible for the policy's accuracy and integrity.

39. **Answer: B.** Annual Loss Expectancy (ALE) is Single Loss Expectancy (SLE) * Annualized Rate of Occurrence (ARO). Therefore, ALE is the annual financial loss the organization can expect from any one particular threat.

40. **Answer: B.** Unclassified is the lowest level of the U.S. government's data classification scheme.

41. **Answer: B.** You cannot displace risk; it may be only accepted, reduced, or transferred.

42. **Answer: D.** Here is the formula for the Annual Loss Expectancy:

    ALE = ARO * SLE, or .9 * 960 = $864

    Annualized Rate of Occurrence is 90%, or .9

    Single Loss Expectancy is ($12 per hour * 8 hours) * 10 employees = $960

    Therefore, the nonprofit could expect to lose $864 by not using antivirus software.

43. **Answer: B.** Annual Loss Expectancy is calculated this way:

    ARO * SLE, or .9 * 960 = $864

    The annual savings is the ALE minus the cost of the deterrent, or $864 – $500 = $364.

    Therefore, the nonprofit organization would save $364 by purchasing the antivirus software.

44. **Answer: D.** Data hiding is the process of revealing only external properties to other components. Data hiding can be accomplished through a layering or encapsulation process or by preventing an application from accessing hardware directly. Encryption is the process of turning data into an unintelligible form. Abstraction is used to remove complexity. Obfuscation is to make something unclear or unnecessarily complicated.

45. **Answer: D.** The highest level of private-sector (business) data classification is confidential. This is followed by private, sensitive, and public. Secret is part of the government data classification. Classified and proprietary are not part of either data classification.

46. **Answer: B.** Abstraction is used to remove complexity and distill data to its essentials. Encryption is the process of turning data into an unintelligible form. Obfuscation is to make something unclear or unnecessarily complicated. Data hiding is the process of only revealing to other components their external properties.

47. **Answer: D.** Qualitative risk analysis is unlike quantitative analysis in that it is not based on the dollar value of the possible loss. Qualitative risk analysis ranks threats on a scale to evaluate their risks and possible adverse effects. The process of performing qualitative risk analysis involves experience and judgment.

48. **Answer: B.** NIST Special Publication (SP) 800-27 (http://csrc.nist.gov/publications/nistpubs/800-27A/SP800-27-RevA.pdf) defines 33 security principles. Principle 5 states that risk should be reduced to a level that is acceptable to the organization.

49. **Answer: B.** According to NIST Special Publication (SP) 800-12 (http://csrc.nist.gov/publications/nistpubs/800-12/handbook.pdf), security awareness programs should raise employees' security awareness, teach them secure practices, and help them understand the need to safeguard company assets. Security awareness programs typically are more effective if they are of short duration and reward individuals for good behavior.

50. **Answer: B.** The principle of risk management requires the examination of vulnerabilities and the associated costs to mitigate them. It is very likely that the cost of protection may outweigh the value of the asset. Whereas some risk assessments use dollar amounts (quantitative) to value the assets, others use numeric values (qualitative) or ratings based on breaches of confidentiality, integrity, and availability to measure value.

51. **Answer: A.** TCSEC (Trusted Computer System Evaluation Criteria) is a set of criteria used to evaluate security functionality and assurance. It separates these categories into various levels ranging from D (minimal protection) to C (discretionary access policy), B (mandatory access policy), and A (formally proven security). Level B is composed of three sublayers: B1, B2, and B3. Data abstraction is required at the B3 security domain level.

52. **Answer: B.** This scenario could leave you vulnerable to attack. You must take all the figures at face value, and remember that you don't deploy a cure that costs more than you stand to lose. Your product is two months out. Shutting down the portal will cost you $1 million in profit, and the fickle customers who will not return. If you buy the competing commercial product, you will have spent $2 million and lost your $1.5 million development costs. Accepting the patched scenario with increased insurance premium will cost $80,000, and doing nothing puts your entire business at risk, with no coverage by your insurance company.

53. **Answer: A.** No one can prevent all potential for risk, but by acting prudently and with due care, you can minimize mishaps. Due diligence is due care over time. As such, this involves not just implementing controls but maintaining them over time. Liability has to do with what you are responsible for. Culpable means that someone is deserving of blame.

54. **Answer: C.** Vulnerabilities are weaknesses in design or implementation. Threat refers to the risk associated with someone breaching your security by use of an exploit. Exposure refers to what part of your company can be seen after a vulnerability has been exploited.

55. **Answer: C.** A security program has a full life cycle that permits continuous improvement. Starting with organizing, it then implements, operates, monitors, and evaluates performance to feed back into any necessary organization restructuring. This starts the process over again.

56. **Answer: D.** Although it could be said that senior management is ultimately responsible, day-to-day responsibility falls on the data's owner. The data's owner is responsible for the security of that data, not the custodian or computer owner.

57. **Answer: A.** Residual risk is usually quantitatively defined by the equation (Threats * Vulnerabilities * Asset Value) * Control Gap, or by (Threats, Vulnerabilities, and Asset Value) – Countermeasures. However, your quantitative formula for Annual Loss Expectancy (ALE) is Asset Value * Exposure Factor (EF) * Annualized Rate of Occurrence (ARO). This refers to your threats, vulnerabilities, and asset value as an annualized value.

58. **Answer: A.** The security triad addresses Confidentiality, Integrity, and Availability. The CIA triad is sometimes called the AIC triad, but both refer to the same three items.

59. **Answer: B.** The levels of the U.S. military data classification are top-secret, secret, confidential, sensitive but unclassified, and unclassified. Controlled is not a valid level of this model.

60. **Answer: A.** Due care is the act of acting reasonable and prudent. A risk assessment is the process of assessing risk. This is most commonly done by quantitative or qualitative means. Due diligence is due care over time. As such, this would not be just implementing controls, but maintaining them over time. Security classification is performed to place a value on documents and to help transmit that to users of such documents.

61. **Answer: C.** Annual Risk Acceptance (ARA) is not a term used with quantitative risk assessment. Quantitative risk assessment is the act of determining what threats your organization faces, analyzing your vulnerabilities to these threats, and then determining how you will deal with the risk. It functions by using dollar amounts and formulas such as SLE, ARO, AV, and ALE.

62. **Answer: D.** Levels of the public (business) information classification system are confidential, private, sensitive, and public. Unclassified is part of the U.S. military data classification system.

63. **Answer: B.** Vulnerability is a flaw, loophole, oversight, or error that makes the organization susceptible to attack or damage. Risk is the probability of adverse effects. A threat is the possibility that a vulnerability can be exploited. An exploit is the code or mechanism through which an attack occurs.

64. **Answer: A.** The correct answer is asset valuation, threat analysis, control analysis, mitigation, policy creation, awareness.

65. **Answer: B.** There are several ways to deal with risk: risk rejection, risk transference, risk acceptance, and risk mitigation. Upgrading a firewall is an example of risk mitigation.

66. **Answer: B.** Information Technology Security Evaluation Criteria (ITSEC) was developed by the Europeans. It was one of the first documents that had the goal of harmonizing security criteria internationally.

67. **Answer: B.** Quantitative risk assessment seeks to assign dollar values, uses mathematical formulas, and seeks to determine tangible values. However, it does not use questioners or interviews. Those techniques are used by qualitative assessment.

68. **Answer: B.** The needed formula is AV * EF = SLE, or 450/500 = .90, or 90%.

69. **Answer: D.** The formula needed to solve this equation is SLE * ARO = ALE, or 800 * 2 = $1,600.

70. **Answer: C.** SLE * ARO = ALE, or $2,500 * .4 = $1,000.

71. **Answer: C.** The question asks you to list these in reverse order. However, the correct forward order is assign value to assets; estimate potential loss per threat; perform a threat analysis; derive annual loss potential; and reduce, transfer, or avoid the risk.

72. **Answer: B.** The Delphi technique features anonymous feedback. FRAP, focus groups, and storyboarding do not.

73. **Answer: C.** The exposure factor is an element of the risk assessment process that denotes the percentage of risk that a company would suffer if an asset were compromised by a realized risk. A vulnerability is a flaw, loophole, oversight, or error that makes the organization susceptible to attack or damage. Risk is the probability of adverse effects. A threat is the possibility that a vulnerability can be exploited.

74. **Answer: B.** There are three ways to look at planning, which range from very short-term to long-term: operational, tactical, and strategic. Operational plans are considered short-term.

75. **Answer: B.** Quantitative takes the most time. Qualitative assessments can be performed very quickly.

76. **Answer: D.** The NSA IAM is a qualitative risk assessment methodology. It can be completed quickly and uses CIA as impact attributes. Although this makes the process move quickly, it does not provide numeric feedback. It does not use ALE, SLE, or ARO. Those are all features of quantitative assessments.

77. **Answer: C.** An exposure is an instance of being exposed to losses from a threat. A vulnerability is a flaw, loophole, oversight, or error that makes the organization susceptible to attack or damage. Risk is the probability of adverse effects. A threat is the possibility that a vulnerability can be exploited.

78. **Answer: A.** Procedures are not high-level documents; policies are.

79. **Answer: C.** Risk mitigation is the level of risk the enterprise can safely tolerate and still continue to function effectively.

80. **Answer: C.** SLE = Asset Value (AV) * Exposure Factor (EF).

81. **Answer: B.** The question asks you what the original name of ISO 27002 was. Answer B is correct, because ISO 177799 is part of a series of documents designed to support the auditing and control function of the organization.

82. **Answer: C.** OCTAVE is just one of the frameworks for which a CISSP should have a basic understanding; another is PCI. The OCTAVE framework is comprised of three phases, which include (1) identifying assets and threats, (2) identifying vulnerabilities and potential safeguards, and (3) conducting a risk analysis.

83. **Answer: B.** Guidelines are recommendations and are considered discretionary, whereas policies, procedures, and standards are all considered mandatory documents.

84. **Answer: B.** Several things are needed to calculate total cost of ownership (TCO). These can include asset cost, maintenance cost, and vendor support cost; however, the replacement cost is not one of those items.

85. **Answer: C.** Answer C is correct. To calculate the quantitative score, multiply the threat by the vulnerability (2 * 2 = 4).

86. **Answer: True.** Standards are much more specific than policies. Standards are tactical documents because they lay out specific steps or processes required to meet a certain requirement. For example, a standard may set a mandatory requirement that all email communication is encrypted.

87. **Answer: True.** There are several ways to handle change management, such as phased, hard, and parallel.

88. **Answer: False.** Although the Orange Book (TCSEC) controls can be used to reduce risk, only levels B1 and greater require labels.

89. **Answer: False.** Both tangible and intangible values should be examined. For example, how do they affect the buyer or consumer of the product or service?

90. **Answer: True.** Policies are high-level documents that are implemented by management.

91. **Answer: False.** Ultimately, senior management is responsible for security.

92. **Answer: False.** The risk analysis team should be made up of individuals from throughout the organization.

93. **Answer: True.** The asset owner is responsible and as such should have a voice in what controls are needed and implemented.

94. **Answer: True.** Application errors are just one of the risks that the risk assessment team should examine. Others include human, equipment, data loss, and malicious attacks.

95. The answers are as follows:

    A. Asset Value: **4.**

    B. Exposure Factor: **1.**

    C. Annual Loss Expectancy: **2.**

    D. Annualized Rate of Occurrence: **5.**

    E. Single Loss Expectancy: **3.**

    The asset value is the total worth of the item being assessed. The exposure factor is the percentage of asset loss caused by identified threats. The annual loss expectancy is the average loss per year. The annualized rate of occurrence is how many times a threat will occur within a year. The single loss expectancy is the amount that is lost every time the threat is realized. This is expressed as Asset Value ($) * Exposure Factor.

10

CHAPTER TEN

Security Operations

The Security Operations domain examines the items that are used on a day-to-day basis to keep a network up and running in a secure state. Therefore, topics from virus control to personnel management, security auditing, audit trails, and backup are introduced. Some of these items are expanded on within other domains because, in the end, all security topics are interrelated. The following list gives some key areas of knowledge that you need to master for this part of the CISSP exam:

- ▶ Change control and configuration management
- ▶ Dual control, separation of duties, rotation of duties
- ▶ Vulnerability assessment and pen-testing
- ▶ Asset management and control from creation to destruction

Quick Check

Practice Questions

1. Attackers are always looking for ways to identify systems. One such method is to send a TCP SYN to a targeted port. What would an attacker expect to receive in response to indicate an open port?

   ❍ **A.** SYN
   ❍ **B.** SYN ACK
   ❍ **C.** ACK
   ❍ **D.** ACK FIN

Quick Answer: **322**
Detailed Answer: **323**

2. Which of the following is an example of a directive control?

   ❍ **A.** Policies
   ❍ **B.** Data validation
   ❍ **C.** Job rotation
   ❍ **D.** Fault-tolerant systems

Quick Answer: **322**
Detailed Answer: **323**

3. Brad uses Telnet to connect to several open ports on a victim computer and capture the banner information. What is the purpose of his activity?

   ❍ **A.** Scanning
   ❍ **B.** Fingerprinting
   ❍ **C.** Attempting a DoS
   ❍ **D.** Privilege escalation

Quick Answer: **322**
Detailed Answer: **323**

4. An access-control matrix can be used to associate permissions of a subject to an object. Permissions can be tied to a lattice of control. If the lattice of control for Cindy and Bob is read and read/write, which of the following is true?

Subject	Procedure A	File X	File Y
Cindy	No access	Execute	No access
Bob	No access	Read	No access
Alice	Read	Read/write	No access

   ❍ **A.** Bob will be able to read File X.
   ❍ **B.** Bob has full control of File X.
   ❍ **C.** Bob cannot access File X.
   ❍ **D.** Alice has full access on File Y.

Quick Answer: **322**
Detailed Answer: **323**

Quick Check

5. The attacker waits until his victim establishes a connection to the organization's FTP server. Then, he executes a program that allows him to take over the established session. What type of attack has taken place?

Quick Answer: **322**
Detailed Answer: **323**

❍ **A.** Password attack
❍ **B.** Spoofing
❍ **C.** Session hijack
❍ **D.** ARP redirection

6. Which of the following represents an auditing best practice?

Quick Answer: **322**
Detailed Answer: **323**

❍ **A.** Audit all successful events.
❍ **B.** Write the audit logs to a sequential access device.
❍ **C.** To prevent the loss of data, overwrite existing audit logs if they become full.
❍ **D.** Configure systems to shut down if the audit logs become full.

7. Which form of information gathering is considered very low tech but can enable attackers to gather usernames, passwords, account information, customer information, and more?

Quick Answer: **322**
Detailed Answer: **323**

❍ **A.** Fingerprinting
❍ **B.** Scavenging
❍ **C.** Port scanning
❍ **D.** Dumpster diving

8. You ask your new intern to harden a system that will be used as a web server. Which of the following is the best way to perform this process?

Quick Answer: **322**
Detailed Answer: **323**

❍ **A.** Install the OS and software, configure IP routing, connect the system to the Internet and download patches and fixes, configure packet filtering, test the system, and phase the system into operation.
❍ **B.** Install the OS and software, configure IP routing, configure packet filtering, connect the system to the Internet and download patches and fixes, test the system, and phase the system into operation.
❍ **C.** Install the OS and software, download patches and fixes, configure IP routing, configure packet filtering, test the system, and connect the system to the Internet.
❍ **D.** Install the OS and software, configure IP routing, configure packet filtering, connect the system to the Internet, and test the system.

Quick Check

9. Widget, Inc., is preparing to implement auditing. To meet this goal, Elaine has been asked to review all company security policies and examine the types of normal activity on the network. What has she been asked to do?

Quick Answer: **322**
Detailed Answer: **323**

- ❍ **A.** Look for vulnerabilities
- ❍ **B.** Develop a baseline
- ❍ **C.** Determine network utilization
- ❍ **D.** Search for security violations

10. Omar has installed a root kit on a networked Linux computer. What is its purpose?

Quick Answer: **322**
Detailed Answer: **324**

- ❍ **A.** To serve as a backdoor
- ❍ **B.** For administrative control
- ❍ **C.** For penetration testing
- ❍ **D.** For vulnerability mapping

11. Which of the following does JBOD *not* provide?

Quick Answer: **322**
Detailed Answer: **324**

- ❍ **A.** Reuse of existing drives
- ❍ **B.** Large logical drives
- ❍ **C.** Fault tolerance
- ❍ **D.** Loss of only the data on a failed drive

12. Which of the following will system auditing most likely cause?

Quick Answer: **322**
Detailed Answer: **324**

- ❍ **A.** Available bandwidth will increase, because all processing is taking place internally.
- ❍ **B.** Depending on what and how much auditing is being performed, system performance may degrade.
- ❍ **C.** System performance may actually increase as logged items are processed in parallel with normal activities.
- ❍ **D.** Available bandwidth will decrease because all logged items are being processed over the network.

13. Albert's new position includes responsibility for the day-to-day security of the network. The previous employee who held this job configured the network to be default open. Now, Albert has decided that he should go through critical systems, reload the OS, and verify that unneeded programs and services are not installed. What is Albert doing?

Quick Answer: **322**
Detailed Answer: **324**

- ❍ **A.** Vulnerability scanning
- ❍ **B.** Hardening
- ❍ **C.** Bastioning
- ❍ **D.** Configuring the devices to the principle of full privilege

Quick Check

14. Which of the following is *not* one of the three protection control types?

Quick Answer: **322**
Detailed Answer: **324**

- ❍ **A.** Corrective
- ❍ **B.** Recovery
- ❍ **C.** Response
- ❍ **D.** Deterrent

15. You are hired by a small software firm to test its security systems and to look for potential ways to bypass authentication controls on Linux servers. You are asked to see whether it is possible to get root access on the Apache web server. What type of testing have you been hired to do?

Quick Answer: **322**
Detailed Answer: **324**

- ❍ **A.** Vulnerability
- ❍ **B.** Penetration
- ❍ **C.** Scanning
- ❍ **D.** Mapping

16. Which type of protection control is used to discourage violations?

Quick Answer: **322**
Detailed Answer: **324**

- ❍ **A.** Security
- ❍ **B.** Recovery
- ❍ **C.** Response
- ❍ **D.** Deterrent

17. James works for a software development company. He is worried about the reassignment of magnetic media that may contain sensitive information. Which of the following is the best solution for media reassignment?

Quick Answer: **322**
Detailed Answer: **324**

- ❍ **A.** Formatting
- ❍ **B.** Degaussing
- ❍ **C.** Delete *.*
- ❍ **D.** Security guidelines

18. Mingo has been asked to get a quote for a new security fence and lights to be placed around the perimeter of a remote manufacturing site. He comes to you and asks why the company is spending funds for this project. How should you answer?

Quick Answer: **322**
Detailed Answer: **324**

- ❍ **A.** To deter intruders
- ❍ **B.** To protect the assets and the organization's facility
- ❍ **C.** To monitor employee ingress and egress on the organization's property
- ❍ **D.** To protect employee safety and welfare

Quick Check

19. Background checks are an important part of operations security. Which of the following groups should be carefully inspected?

Quick Answer: **322**
Detailed Answer: **324**

❍ **A.** External vendors

❍ **B.** Cleaning crews

❍ **C.** Operators

❍ **D.** Temporary staff

20. Danny has been investigating the purchase of a new operations security software package. One vendor asked him about clipping levels. What are clipping levels used for?

Quick Answer: **322**
Detailed Answer: **324**

❍ **A.** To reduce the amount of data to be evaluated

❍ **B.** To set password length and maximum age

❍ **C.** To set local and remote login attempts

❍ **D.** To configure SNMP traps

21. Which type of protection control is used to reduce risks associated with attacks?

Quick Answer: **322**
Detailed Answer: **324**

❍ **A.** Corrective

❍ **B.** Recovery

❍ **C.** Response

❍ **D.** Deterrent

22. Which of the following offers the best approach to making sure that an organization has uninterrupted access to data?

Quick Answer: **322**
Detailed Answer: **324**

❍ **A.** Electronic vaulting

❍ **B.** Hot-swappable drives

❍ **C.** RAID

❍ **D.** Backup

23. Your consulting firm has been asked to help a medium-sized firm secure its servers and domain controllers. Which of the following is *not* a requirement for a secure computing room?

Quick Answer: **322**
Detailed Answer: **325**

❍ **A.** Controlled access

❍ **B.** Dropped ceilings

❍ **C.** Raised floors

❍ **D.** Log files or CCTV to verify who enters or leaves the room

Quick Check

24. Albert is continuing his process of OS hardening. Because he usually does not work with Linux, he comes to you with a question: On Windows machines you find network "services" running. What are such network applications called in Linux? What do you tell him?

❍ **A.** Services
❍ **B.** Applets
❍ **C.** Daemons
❍ **D.** PIDs

Quick Answer: **322**
Detailed Answer: **325**

25. Jeff has discovered some strange chalk markings outside the front door of his business. He has also noticed that people with laptops have been hanging around since the markings were made. What has Jeff discovered?

❍ **A.** Graffiti
❍ **B.** War driving
❍ **C.** Vulnerability marking
❍ **D.** War chalking

Quick Answer: **322**
Detailed Answer: **325**

26. Which RAID level indicates just striping across multiple disks at a byte level?

❍ **A.** 0
❍ **B.** 1
❍ **C.** 2
❍ **D.** 3

Quick Answer: **322**
Detailed Answer: **325**

27. You are asked to develop the air-conditioning system for the new data center. Which of the following is the optimum design?

❍ **A.** Negative ventilation
❍ **B.** Ionized ventilation
❍ **C.** Positive ventilation
❍ **D.** Neutral ventilation

Quick Answer: **322**
Detailed Answer: **325**

28. Because your boss has been pleased with the progress you have made on the design on the new data center, he has given you additional responsibility for the fire suppression system. Which of the following fire suppression systems does *not* leave water standing in a pipe and activates only when a fire is detected?

❍ **A.** Deluge
❍ **B.** Dry pipe
❍ **C.** Controlled
❍ **D.** Post-action

Quick Answer: **322**
Detailed Answer: **325**

Quick Check

29. Data center doors should *not* have which characteristic?

Quick Answer: **322**
Detailed Answer: **325**

- ❍ **A.** Solid-core construction
- ❍ **B.** Hinges on the outside
- ❍ **C.** Keypad locks
- ❍ **D.** Hinges on the inside

30. Which RAID level indicates byte-level parity?

Quick Answer: **322**
Detailed Answer: **326**

- ❍ **A.** 1
- ❍ **B.** 2
- ❍ **C.** 3
- ❍ **D.** 4

31. Contingency management does *not* include which of the following?

Quick Answer: **322**
Detailed Answer: **326**

- ❍ **A.** Maintaining continuity of operations
- ❍ **B.** Establishing actions to be taken after an incident
- ❍ **C.** Performing verification of IDSs
- ❍ **D.** Ensuring the availability of critical systems

32. Which of the following best describes a contingency plan?

Quick Answer: **322**
Detailed Answer: **326**

- ❍ **A.** The process of controlling modifications to system hardware or software
- ❍ **B.** Documented actions for items such as emergency response and backup operations
- ❍ **C.** Maintaining essential information system services after a major outage
- ❍ **D.** The process of backing up, copying, and storing critical information

33. Which type of operations security control gives the IS department enough time to audit an individual's activities and may deter him or her from performing prohibited acts?

Quick Answer: **322**
Detailed Answer: **326**

- ❍ **A.** Terminations
- ❍ **B.** Mandatory vacations
- ❍ **C.** Background checks
- ❍ **D.** Change control management

Quick Check

34. Which of the following best describes configuration management?

Quick Answer: **322**
Detailed Answer: **326**

- ❍ **A.** The process of controlling modifications to system hardware or software
- ❍ **B.** Documented actions for items such as emergency response and backup operations
- ❍ **C.** Maintaining essential information system services after a major outage
- ❍ **D.** The process of backing up, copying, and storing critical information

35. Which RAID level indicates block-level parity?

Quick Answer: **322**
Detailed Answer: **326**

- ❍ **A.** 1
- ❍ **B.** 2
- ❍ **C.** 3
- ❍ **D.** 4

36. Dot.Com Investment, Inc., has decided that its policies need to ensure that no one person can act alone to make a financial distribution or disbursement of funds. Which of the following has the company implemented?

Quick Answer: **322**
Detailed Answer: **327**

- ❍ **A.** Separation of duties
- ❍ **B.** Job rotation
- ❍ **C.** Mandatory vacations
- ❍ **D.** Job classification

37. Alice is concerned about keeping the network free of computer viruses. Without implementing new technical controls, which of the following is one of the most effective means to prevent the spread of viruses?

Quick Answer: **322**
Detailed Answer: **327**

- ❍ **A.** Employee training
- ❍ **B.** Network design
- ❍ **C.** Advise users to respond to spam, requesting that their addresses no longer be used or solicited
- ❍ **D.** Egress filtering

38. Potential employees typically should not have which of the following performed?

Quick Answer: **322**
Detailed Answer: **327**

- ❍ **A.** Background checks
- ❍ **B.** Reference checks
- ❍ **C.** Credit status checks
- ❍ **D.** Education claim checks

Quick Check

39. Jane is researching the distribution and spread of computer viruses. Which of the following is the most common means of transmitting computer viruses?

Quick Answer: **322**
Detailed Answer: **327**

- ❍ **A.** Hacker programs
- ❍ **B.** Email
- ❍ **C.** Illegal software
- ❍ **D.** Peer-to-peer networks

40. Which RAID level combines striping and mirroring?

Quick Answer: **322**
Detailed Answer: **327**

- ❍ **A.** 7
- ❍ **B.** 8
- ❍ **C.** 9
- ❍ **D.** 10

41. From a security perspective, which of the following is the most important portion of media control labeling?

Quick Answer: **322**
Detailed Answer: **327**

- ❍ **A.** The date of creation
- ❍ **B.** The volume name and version
- ❍ **C.** The classification
- ❍ **D.** The individual who created it

42. Which protocol do clients use to download emails to their local computer from server-based inboxes?

Quick Answer: **322**
Detailed Answer: **327**

- ❍ **A.** SMTP
- ❍ **B.** SNMP
- ❍ **C.** IMAP
- ❍ **D.** POP3

43. As network defenses become more robust, what attack methodology can best be used to supersede these barriers?

Quick Answer: **322**
Detailed Answer: **327**

- ❍ **A.** Session hijacking
- ❍ **B.** Social engineering
- ❍ **C.** Web exploits
- ❍ **D.** Vulnerability tools

Quick Check

44. You are contacted by a rather large ISP. The ISP has accused you of sending its customers large amounts of spam. What is the most likely explanation for this occurrence?

❍ **A.** SMTP has been left enabled.

❍ **B.** POP3 has been left enabled.

❍ **C.** Relaying has been left enabled.

❍ **D.** Your IMAP server has been hacked.

Quick Answer: **322**
Detailed Answer: **327**

45. You are asked to work on a contract with a new client. Your company is concerned about security and wants to select a stronger encryption algorithm. What document needs to be modified to define the specifications for this new algorithm?

❍ **A.** Policies

❍ **B.** Standards

❍ **C.** Procedures

❍ **D.** Baselines

Quick Answer: **322**
Detailed Answer: **328**

46. What term describes information that may remain on computer media after it has been erased?

❍ **A.** Shadowing

❍ **B.** Data remanence

❍ **C.** Mirroring

❍ **D.** Ghosting

Quick Answer: **322**
Detailed Answer: **328**

47. The TCSEC defines several levels of assurance requirements for secure computer operations. Which of the following is *not* one of those levels of assurance?

❍ **A.** Trusted recovery

❍ **B.** System integrity

❍ **C.** Trusted facility management

❍ **D.** Confidential operations

Quick Answer: **322**
Detailed Answer: **328**

48. Trusted facility management is a TCSEC assurance requirement for secure systems. As such, which class must support separation of operator and system administrator roles?

❍ **A.** A1

❍ **B.** A2

❍ **C.** B1

❍ **D.** B2

Quick Answer: **322**
Detailed Answer: **328**

Quick Check

49. Your CISSP study group has asked you to research IPL vulnerabilities. What does IPL stand for, and how is it used?

Quick Answer: **322**
Detailed Answer: **328**

❍ **A.** Internet protocol loss, DoS

❍ **B.** Initial program load, startup

❍ **C.** Internet post lag, web-based vulnerability

❍ **D.** Initial process location, buffer overflows

50. Black Hat Bob has placed a sniffer on the network and is attempting to perform traffic analysis. Which of the following is *not* an effective countermeasure against traffic analysis?

Quick Answer: **322**
Detailed Answer: **328**

❍ **A.** Packet padding

❍ **B.** Noise transmission

❍ **C.** Covert channel analysis

❍ **D.** ARP redirection

51. During orientation training at your new company, you ask if you are allowed to sell your vacation time back to the company. You are informed that not only must you take your vacation, but you also must take it in one block, and that other employees are already trained to rotate in and assume your job during your absence. Why would the company refuse to buy back your vacation?

Quick Answer: **322**
Detailed Answer: **328**

❍ **A.** To ensure survival. A company is weakened if it relies too heavily on one employee.

❍ **B.** To receive industry certification. When employees have multiple skill sets, a company can be certified under ISO 27001:2005.

❍ **C.** To minimize fraud. Fraudulent activities can more easily be detected when employees are rotated periodically.

❍ **D.** To lower healthcare costs. Health insurance providers are rewarding companies that encourage preventive healthcare, such as mandatory vacations.

52. The server crashed overnight and rebooted itself. What is this type of recovery called?

Quick Answer: **322**
Detailed Answer: **328**

❍ **A.** System cold start

❍ **B.** Emergency system restart

❍ **C.** System reboot

❍ **D.** System hard boot

Quick Check

53. A maintenance hook is found during a parallel test of your new product. The programming team is small, and the programmer is available and can quickly take out the maintenance hook so that testing can continue. What action should you take?

Quick Answer: **322**
Detailed Answer: **328**

- ❍ **A.** Permit the code change, and then update the change control documentation as soon as possible.
- ❍ **B.** Delay the modification until the change control documentation can be submitted, processed, and approved.
- ❍ **C.** Permit the code change. Because the product has not yet been released to production, change control has not been initiated.
- ❍ **D.** Prevent any changes, because the maintenance hook will be a feature of the new product.

54. Which new method of clearing a hard drive provides the greatest level of assurance that previously stored data is irretrievable?

Quick Answer: **322**
Detailed Answer: **328**

- ❍ **A.** Zeroing method
- ❍ **B.** Gutmann method
- ❍ **C.** Wiping method
- ❍ **D.** All of the above provide the same level of assurance

55. What is the most common cause of loss of intellectual property?

Quick Answer: **322**
Detailed Answer: **329**

- ❍ **A.** Virus
- ❍ **B.** Espionage
- ❍ **C.** Pirating
- ❍ **D.** Negligence

56. Which RAID configuration has a single point of failure?

Quick Answer: **322**
Detailed Answer: **329**

- ❍ **A.** RAID 0
- ❍ **B.** RAID 1
- ❍ **C.** RAID 5
- ❍ **D.** RAID 10

57. What are two current email attacks that a security professional needs to be aware of?

Quick Answer: **322**
Detailed Answer: **329**

- ❍ **A.** Phishing and pharming
- ❍ **B.** Spear phishing and phreaking
- ❍ **C.** Phishing and Pwn 2 Own
- ❍ **D.** Spear phishing and whaling

Quick Check

58. Who would you recommend to your company as someone who can perform penetration testing?

Quick Answer: **322**
Detailed Answer: **329**

- ❍ **A.** Script kiddie
- ❍ **B.** Cracker
- ❍ **C.** Hacker
- ❍ **D.** Pharmer

59. What is the most important security concern when reviewing the use of USB memory sticks?

Quick Answer: **322**
Detailed Answer: **329**

- ❍ **A.** They might not be compatible with all systems.
- ❍ **B.** They might lose information or become corrupted.
- ❍ **C.** Memory sticks can copy a large amount of data.
- ❍ **D.** Memory sticks' contents cannot be backed up.

60. Several coworkers are installing an IDS, and you are asked to make an initial review. One of the installers asks you which of the following is the worst condition for an IDS. What is your response?

Quick Answer: **322**
Detailed Answer: **329**

- ❍ **A.** Positive
- ❍ **B.** Negative
- ❍ **C.** False positive
- ❍ **D.** False negative

61. Trusted recovery is defined in Common Criteria. Which is not one of the trusted recovery mechanisms listed in Common Criteria?

Quick Answer: **322**
Detailed Answer: **329**

- ❍ **A.** Manual recovery
- ❍ **B.** Automated recovery
- ❍ **C.** Automated recovery with due loss
- ❍ **D.** Automated recovery without undue loss

62. A trusted recovery solution requires proactive work. What are the primary components?

Quick Answer: **322**
Detailed Answer: **329**

- ❍ **A.** Failure preparation and system recovery
- ❍ **B.** Failure preparation and system backup
- ❍ **C.** Backup, recovery, and repair
- ❍ **D.** Failure preparation and failure detection

Quick Check

63. Which of the following best defines privileged functions?

Quick Answer: **322**
Detailed Answer: **329**

- ❍ **A.** Activities performed by individuals in the security management group
- ❍ **B.** Activities that require an elevated level of access
- ❍ **C.** Activities that are performed in a secure setting
- ❍ **D.** Activities assigned to all security personnel

64. Clair tries to log in to her account three times. On the third attempt, she receives a message that the account has been suspended. Which of the following best describes what has occurred?

Quick Answer: **322**
Detailed Answer: **329**

- ❍ **A.** Clair has been reported for a security violation.
- ❍ **B.** Clair passed the clipping level.
- ❍ **C.** Clair attempted to access a privileged control.
- ❍ **D.** Clair is forgetful.

65. Your organization is concerned about emanation security. Therefore, security management has installed copper mesh in the facility's outer walls and ceiling. What is the primary purpose of this activity?

Quick Answer: **322**
Detailed Answer: **329**

- ❍ **A.** To increase the range of the company's wireless system
- ❍ **B.** To decrease interference from neighboring wireless systems
- ❍ **C.** To design a white-noise enclosure
- ❍ **D.** To implement a control zone

66. Which of the following is the best example of a compensating administrative control?

Quick Answer: **322**
Detailed Answer: **330**

- ❍ **A.** Disaster recovery plan
- ❍ **B.** Warning banner
- ❍ **C.** Supervision
- ❍ **D.** IDS

67. Your organization has set up an email relay agent that does not require authentication. What is the result of this action?

Quick Answer: **322**
Detailed Answer: **330**

- ❍ **A.** Your company is more secure against email spam and spoofing.
- ❍ **B.** Third parties can relay email through your email server.
- ❍ **C.** Users at home can read their work email.
- ❍ **D.** Email can be used in the organization's VPN.

Quick Check

68. What do you call the activity of looking at responses to active probes to services such as ICMP and TCP to examine subtle changes in how the protocol stack has been implemented?

- ❍ **A.** OS fingerprinting
- ❍ **B.** Active OS fingerprinting
- ❍ **C.** Passive OS fingerprinting
- ❍ **D.** Scanning

Quick Answer: **322**
Detailed Answer: **330**

69. Troy is concerned about an existing connection being taken over. He has been reading about a person or process pretending to be another person or process. What is this called?

- ❍ **A.** Spoofing
- ❍ **B.** Sniffing
- ❍ **C.** Hijacking
- ❍ **D.** Trojan

Quick Answer: **322**
Detailed Answer: **330**

70. Which of the following is a valid defense against Van Eck phreaking?

- ❍ **A.** Secure fax systems
- ❍ **B.** TEMPEST
- ❍ **C.** Performing social engineering training
- ❍ **D.** Securing PBX systems

Quick Answer: **322**
Detailed Answer: **330**

71. Which of the following is the best example of a recovery administrative control?

- ❍ **A.** Disaster recovery plan
- ❍ **B.** Rebuilding after a disaster
- ❍ **C.** Supervision
- ❍ **D.** IDS

Quick Answer: **322**
Detailed Answer: **330**

72. When discussing operation controls, which control is the best example of providing confidentiality protection?

- ❍ **A.** Rotation of duties
- ❍ **B.** Separation of duties
- ❍ **C.** Dual control
- ❍ **D.** Quality assurance

Quick Answer: **322**
Detailed Answer: **330**

73. A team is performing a penetration test for your company. You have concerns as you review the penetration test company's insurance. A coworker tells you that someone was injured when

Quick Answer: **322**
Detailed Answer: **330**

Quick Check

an automated navigation system failed during what turned out to be a test on a system that was not supposed to be part of the security assessment. What document was not defined and understood that could have prevented this problem?

❍ **A.** Rules of engagement

❍ **B.** Insurance requirements

❍ **C.** Work proposal

❍ **D.** Capability reports

74. The authentication control module has just been reset to trigger an alert to the administrator after only three failed login attempts. What is this an example of?

Quick Answer: **322**
Detailed Answer: **330**

❍ **A.** A physical control

❍ **B.** A clipping level

❍ **C.** An IDS sensor

❍ **D.** A security control

75. Which of the following best describes changes to hacking tools over the last few years?

Quick Answer: **322**
Detailed Answer: **331**

❍ **A.** Hacking tools require less technical skill to use.

❍ **B.** Hacking tools are more advanced and require less skill.

❍ **C.** Hacking tools are more advanced but require that the user understand computer languages and how to compile code.

❍ **D.** Hacking tools are becoming more advanced.

76. Which storage technology offers no increase in speed or fault tolerance but does allow someone to make use of older hard drives by combining them into one massive array?

Quick Answer: **322**
Detailed Answer: **331**

❍ **A.** Redundant array of independent tapes (RAIT)

❍ **B.** Just a bunch of disks (JBOD)

❍ **C.** Massive array of inactive disks (MAID)

❍ **D.** Redundant array of inexpensive disks (RAID 1)

77. Which of the following best describes grid computing?

Quick Answer: **322**
Detailed Answer: **331**

❍ **A.** Grid computers have a high level of trust.

❍ **B.** It is a fault-tolerant technology similar to redundant servers that features central control.

❍ **C.** It features a distributed control mechanism.

❍ **D.** It is well suited for applications that require secrecy.

Quick Check

78. Which method of data erasure magnetically scrambles the patterns on a hard drive so that it is unrecoverable?

Quick Answer: **322**
Detailed Answer: **331**

- ❍ **A.** Zeroization
- ❍ **B.** Degaussing
- ❍ **C.** Shredding
- ❍ **D.** Drive wiping

79. What type of attack uses a number of computers with different network addresses to target and exhaust all the available ports of an organization's web servers?

Quick Answer: **322**
Detailed Answer: **331**

- ❍ **A.** Spoofing
- ❍ **B.** Denial of service
- ❍ **C.** Distributed denial of service
- ❍ **D.** Mail bombing

80. While SMTP is the protocol of choice for sending email, two other popular protocols can be used to receive email. By default, what port numbers are used for POP3 and IMAP?

Quick Answer: **322**
Detailed Answer: **331**

- ❍ **A.** 110, 143
- ❍ **B.** 110, 25
- ❍ **C.** 443, 111
- ❍ **D.** 134, 110

81. Company A is asked to implement a backup plan that can be used to restore data after a disaster or incident that results in a loss of data. Company B is asked to examine what methods of data destruction are acceptable when old hard drives are retired and no longer needed. If you were asked to assist company B, which of the following methods would you recommend as being the best choice of data destruction regardless of whether the data was kept onsite or offsite?

Quick Answer: **322**
Detailed Answer: **331**

- ❍ **A.** Manual erase of all files
- ❍ **B.** Formatting
- ❍ **C.** Zeroization
- ❍ **D.** Seven pass drive wipe

Quick Check

82. Modern organizations need the capability to track assets, control change, and manage risk. Which of the following is least likely to have to go through the change-management process?

Quick Answer: **322**
Detailed Answer: **331**

- ❍ **A.** An update to the disaster recovery plan
- ❍ **B.** Antivirus update
- ❍ **C.** An upgrade of the PBX to a VoIP system
- ❍ **D.** Production code update

83. Your company decides to implement BYOD and allow individuals on your team to bring their own devices to work. Which of the following would be a top security concern?

Quick Answer: **322**
Detailed Answer: **331**

- ❍ **A.** Connectivity
- ❍ **B.** Policy
- ❍ **C.** Antivirus requirement
- ❍ **D.** Network storage

84. During a penetration test, you discover a vulnerability on dynamically generated web pages that enables attackers to input malicious script into the page by hiding it within legitimate requests. What is the name of this exploit?

Quick Answer: **322**
Detailed Answer: **331**

- ❍ **A.** Cross-site scripting
- ❍ **B.** SQL injection
- ❍ **C.** LDAP injection
- ❍ **D.** Buffer overflow

85. Because of an unfilled position in the quality-assurance department, management decides to allow programmers to review and update their own code. One of the programmers is upset because of a poor performance review, and he has altered the payroll program so that if he is fired, the application will print random numbers on all employees' paychecks. Setting aside the operational security issues, which of the following is the most correct match?

Quick Answer: **322**
Detailed Answer: **332**

- ❍ **A.** Salami attack
- ❍ **B.** Incremental attack
- ❍ **C.** Buffer overflow
- ❍ **D.** Logic bomb

Quick Check

Practice Questions (True or False)

86. In applications where data is regularly active, massive array of inactive disks (MAID) would be a good storage option.

❍ True

❍ False

Quick Answer: **322**
Detailed Answer: **332**

87. The big advantage of IMAP over SMTP is that it lets users read messages without automatically downloading them to their systems.

❍ True

❍ False

Quick Answer: **322**
Detailed Answer: **332**

88. Organizations should allow mail relaying so that mail can be forwarded to the proper end user.

❍ True

❍ False

Quick Answer: **322**
Detailed Answer: **332**

89. A smurf attack uses ICMP and forged ping traffic.

❍ True

❍ False

Quick Answer: **322**
Detailed Answer: **332**

90. When a double-blind penetration test is performed, the assessment team members know all the details of the network, and the organization does not know the security assessment is being performed.

❍ True

❍ False

Quick Answer: **322**
Detailed Answer: **332**

91. Purging is the term used to describe a system's RAM being cleared.

❍ True

❍ False

Quick Answer: **322**
Detailed Answer: **332**

92. Job rotation is performed primarily to prevent burnout in employees.

❍ True

❍ False

Quick Answer: **322**
Detailed Answer: **332**

93. A CCTV system is an example of a preventive control.

❍ True

❍ False

Quick Answer: **322**
Detailed Answer: **332**

94. RAID 1 is the most expensive per megabyte.

❍ True

❍ False

Quick Answer: **322**
Detailed Answer: **332**

Quick Check

Practice Questions (Mix and Match)

95. Match each attack with how often it should be performed:

Quick Answer: 322
Detailed Answer: 332

A. Antivirus updates: _____

B. Intrusion detection: _____

C. Penetration testing: _____

D. Disaster recovery testing: _____

E. Vulnerability scanning: _____

1. At least once a year

2. Continuously

3. Daily or as required

4. Weekly or bi-monthly

5. Quarterly

96. Place the appropriate RAID level number next to its description:

Quick Answer: 322
Detailed Answer: 333

Letter	RAID Level	Description
A		Striping and mirroring
B		Interleave parity
C		Mirroring
D		Block-level parity
E		Hamming code parity
F		Striping
G		Byte-level parity

Quick Check Answer Key

1. B
2. A
3. B
4. A
5. C
6. B
7. D
8. C
9. B
10. A
11. C
12. B
13. B
14. C
15. B
16. D
17. B
18. D
19. B
20. A
21. A
22. C
23. B
24. C
25. D
26. A
27. C
28. B
29. B
30. C
31. C
32. B
33. B
34. A
35. D
36. A
37. A
38. C
39. B
40. D
41. C
42. D
43. B
44. C
45. B
46. B
47. D
48. D
49. B
50. D
51. C
52. B
53. A
54. B
55. D
56. A
57. D
58. C
59. C
60. D
61. C
62. A
63. B
64. B
65. D
66. C
67. B
68. B
69. A
70. B
71. A
72. B
73. A
74. B
75. B
76. B
77. C
78. B
79. C
80. A
81. D
82. B
83. B
84. A
85. D
86. False
87. True
88. False
89. True
90. False
91. False
92. False
93. True
94. True
95. **A.** 3
   B. 2
   C. 1
   D. 5
   E. 4
96. **A.** RAID 10
   B. RAID 5
   C. RAID 1
   D. RAID 4
   E. RAID 5
   F. RAID 0
   G. RAID 3

Answers and Explanations

1. **Answer: B.** TCP is a connection-oriented protocol. As such, it attempts to complete a three-step handshake at the beginning of a communication session. The three steps are as follows:

   SYN

   SYN ACK

   ACK
2. **Answer: A.** Policies, standards, guidelines, procedures, and regulations are all examples of directive controls.
3. **Answer: B.** Fingerprinting is the act of service and OS identification. Fingerprinting allows an attacker to formulate a plan of system attack. Scanning is the act of identifying open ports. DoS is a denial of service. Privilege escalation requires an active connection or system access.
4. **Answer: A.** Under the rules of the lattice of control, the subject is allowed to access an object only if the security level of the subject is greater than or equal to that of the object. A lattice is an upper and lower bound of access. Answers B and C are incorrect because the specified options are outside the bounds of what a normal user can change. Answer D is incorrect because Alice has no access to File Y.
5. **Answer: C.** A session hijack is the process of taking over an established legitimate session. This type of attack gives an attacker an authenticated connection into a network.
6. **Answer: B.** The primary purpose of auditing is to hold individuals accountable for their actions. Hackers and other wrongdoers often attempt to cover their tracks by removing evidence of their activities from the audit log. This is why it is important to write the audit logs to a sequential access device. This could be a CD-ROM, DVD, tape drive, or even a line printer. This ensures that the evidence will be available for later review. Although auditing all successful events is possible, it would place an increased load on the system. Overwriting existing audit logs as they become full could erase valuable information. Configuring systems to shut down if the audit logs become full would allow the hacker or wrongdoer to stage a DoS attack. Loggable items should be chosen carefully.
7. **Answer: D.** Although dumpster diving is considered very low-tech, it can be a very successful way to gather information about an organization and its customers. The best defense against dumpster diving is to make sure that all sensitive information is cross-shredded and properly destroyed before being disposed of.
8. **Answer: C.** This is the proper order: install the OS and software, download patches and fixes, configure IP routing, configure packet filtering, test the system, and connect the system to the Internet. Not until the system is fully hardened and configured should it be connected to the Internet.
9. **Answer: B.** Before you can determine what inappropriate activity is, you must determine what is appropriate. This process is known as baselining, and it involves the following two tasks:

   Analysis of company policy: This helps determine what constitutes a potential security incident or event within your organization.

   Examination of current network and system activity: Reviewing audit logs gives you a better understanding of normal usage patterns and what should and should not be happening.

10. **Answer: A.** Root kits are additional programs that may take the place of legitimate programs (such as ls, cat, and pwd in UNIX and Linux). They can give attackers unauthenticated access. After one of these programs has been installed, the attacker can return to the computer later and access it without providing login credentials or without going through any type of authentication process.

11. **Answer: C.** JBOD (Just a Bunch of Disks) does not provide redundancy or fault tolerance. It does allow for reuse of existing drives and larger logical drives. If a failure of one drive occurs, only data on that drive is lost.

12. **Answer: B.** Auditing can cause a decrease in system performance because of the amount of system resources being used. Logged items may or may not be logged remotely. If so, additional bandwidth would be used, but system performance would still be affected.

13. **Answer: B.** Hardening is the process of identifying what a specific machine will be used for and removing or disabling all system components, programs, and services that are not necessary for that function. This vastly increases the system's security.

14. **Answer: C.** No category of protection control type is known as response.

15. **Answer: B.** Penetration testing is the process of testing a network's defenses and attempting to bypass its security controls. The goal is to understand the organization's vulnerability to attack. These types of tests are performed with written consent of the network's owner and may be attempted by internal employees or external consultants. One good source for learning more about penetration testing is www.isecom.org/research/osstmm.html.

16. **Answer: D.** Deterrent controls are used to discourage security violations.

17. **Answer: B.** Although setting up guidelines, deleting, and formatting data are good starting points for ensuring the removal of sensitive data, the best solution is degaussing the media.

18. **Answer: D.** Employee safety and welfare should always be the driving force of any security measure. Well-lit, secured areas provide an additional level of protection for employees entering and leaving the area. Secondary benefits are protecting company assets and deterring intrusion or hostile acts.

19. **Answer: B.** Individuals working on cleaning crews should be carefully inspected, because they typically have access to all areas of an organization's facility.

20. **Answer: A.** Setting clipping levels refers to determining the trip point at which activity is logged or flagged. For example, a clipping level of three failed remote login attempts may be set before the failed login attempt is recorded as a violation. This also prevents brute-force attacks. This reduces the amount of data to be evaluated and makes it easier to search for true anomalies.

21. **Answer: A.** Corrective controls are a type of protection control used to reduce or eliminate risks associated with attacks.

22. **Answer: C.** RAID (redundant array of independent disks) provides fault tolerance against hard drive crashes. Electronic vaulting enables you to restore vital business data from anywhere across your enterprise, anytime you need it. Hot-swappable drives allow you to replace defective drives without rebooting but may not prevent downtime. Backups let you restore lost or damaged data.

23. **Answer: B.** Controlled access, log files, and raised floors are just a few of the items that should be built into a secure computing room. It should not have dropped ceilings or hollow-core doors, because these items make it easier for attackers to bypass operations security.

24. **Answer: C.** Daemons are processes or applications that run on UNIX or Linux computer systems that provide network services. A network application in the Windows world is called a service. An applet is a program designed to be executed from within another application. A PID is a process ID. Even though these concepts might not be covered on the exam, they still are important for you to understand.

25. **Answer: D.** War chalking is the process of identifying a wireless network. It originated from hobo code of the 1930s and 1940s. Sometime around 2002, it began being applied to wireless networks. Common war chalking symbols include a closed circle to indicate a closed network, two back-to-back half circles to identify an open network, and a circle with a W in it to indicate a network with WEP encryption.

26. **Answer: A.** RAID (redundant array of independent disks) is a technology that employs two or more drives in combination for fault tolerance and performance. Striping improves performance but does not provide fault tolerance. The more common levels of RAID are as follows:

    0: Striping

    1: Mirroring

    2: Hamming code parity

    3: Byte-level parity

    4: Block-level parity

    5: Interleave parity

    7: Single virtual disk

    10: Striping and mirroring combined

27. **Answer: C.** Data centers should be positively ventilated by design. This means that the positive pressure acts as an effective means of ensuring that contaminants do not enter the room through small cracks or openings. This design pushes air outward toward doorways and other access points within the room. The idea is to keep harmful contaminants away from sensitive equipment. When more than one server room is used, the most critical should be the most highly pressurized.

28. **Answer: B.** There are four main types of fire suppression systems:

    A wet pipe system, which is always full of water.

    A dry pipe, which contains compressed air. When a fire is sensed, the air escapes and the pipes fill with water, which is subsequently discharged into the area.

    A deluge system, which uses large pipes and can significantly soak an area with a large volume of water.

    A preaction system, which is a combination of a dry pipe and a wet pipe system.

    There is no post-action type of fire suppression system.

29. **Answer: B.** Data center doors should not be hinged to the outside, because anyone could remove the hinge pins and gain easy access.

30. **Answer: C.** RAID (redundant array of independent disks) is a technology that employs two or more drives in combination for fault tolerance and performance. Byte-level parity reserves one dedicated disk for error correction data. This provides good performance and some level of fault tolerance. Other levels of RAID are as follows:

    0: Striping

    1: Mirroring

    2: Hamming code parity

    3: Byte-level parity

    4: Block-level parity

    5: Interleave parity

    7: Single virtual disk

    10: Striping and mirroring combined

31. **Answer: C.** Although IDSs can help you detect security breaches, they are not part of contingency management. Contingency management includes establishing actions to be taken before, during, and after an incident; verifying documentation and test procedures; and ensuring the availability of critical systems.

32. **Answer: B.** The goal of contingency planning is to document the required actions for items such as emergency response or backup operations. Its goal is to mitigate business risks due to a mission-critical functional failure caused by any internal or external means. None of the other items describes a contingency plan.

33. **Answer: B.** Mandatory vacations give the IS department enough time to audit an individual's activities and may deter that person from performing prohibited acts. The idea is that the employee will not be allowed to work or access the network while on vacation. Terminations usually are reserved as a last resort. Background checks help validate potential employees. Change control management is used to control hardware and software processes that are used in the production environment.

34. **Answer: A.** Configuration management is the process of controlling modifications to system hardware or software. Its goal is to maintain control of system processes and to protect against improper modification.

35. **Answer: D.** RAID (redundant array of independent disks) is a technology that employs two or more drives in combination for fault tolerance and performance. Block-level parity RAID requires a minimum of three drives to implement. Other levels of RAID are as follows:

    0: Striping

    1: Mirroring

    2: Hamming code parity

    3: Byte-level parity

    4: Block-level parity

    5: Interleave parity

    7: Single virtual disk

    10: Striping and mirroring combined

36. **Answer: A.** Separation of duties is the principle that one person acting alone should not be able to compromise an organization's security in any way. Job rotation and mandatory vacations are two ways in which this principle can be enforced.

37. **Answer: A.** The most effective nontechnical control of computer viruses is through employee education. Advising users to respond to spam not only will increase the amount of mail received, but also could increase their risk of infection from computer viruses.

38. **Answer: C.** Background checks, reference checks, and education claim checks are three items that should be verified. Depending on the job, verifying credit status could be considered out of bounds.

39. **Answer: B.** Most computer viruses are transmitted through email. According to experts at Panda Software, nearly 80% of computer virus infections come through email venues.

40. **Answer: D.** RAID (redundant array of independent disks) is a technology that employs two or more drives in combination for fault tolerance and performance. RAID Level 10 combines mirroring and striping. It requires a minimum of four drives to implement but has higher fault tolerance than RAID 0. Other levels of RAID are as follows:

    0: Striping

    1: Mirroring

    2: Hamming code parity

    3: Byte-level parity

    4: Block-level parity

    5: Interleave parity

    7: Single virtual disk

    10: Striping and mirroring combined

41. **Answer: C.** The classification of the data is the most important aspect, because it can tell people how the data should be handled. Media control labeling includes the date of creation, the volume name and version, the classification, the individual who created it, and the retention period.

42. **Answer: D.** POP3 (Post Office Protocol Version 3) is a widely used protocol that allows clients to retrieve their emails from server-based inboxes. SMTP is an email transport protocol. SNMP is used for network management. IMAP typically leaves messages on the server.

43. **Answer: B.** Social engineering is an attacker's manipulation of individuals and the natural human tendency to trust. This art of deception is used to obtain information that will allow unauthorized access to networks, systems, or privileged information.

44. **Answer: C.** The most likely explanation of this occurrence is that a mail relay has been left enabled. Spammers find open relays by port scanning wide ranges of IP addresses. After spammers find a mail server, they attempt to use it to send mail to a third party. If successful, they use this system to spew their junk email. This widely used technique allows spammers to hide their true IP address and victimize an innocent third party.

45. **Answer: B.** In real life, it is potentially likely that several of these documents may need to be modified. Standards are the document that requires immediate action. Policies are tied to basic requirements. Procedures are step-by-step instructions. Baselines define the acceptable risk levels.

46. **Answer: B.** Data remanence is information that may remain on computer media after it has been erased. Mirroring refers to RAID, ghosting relates to the duplication of drives, and shadowing is a distracter.

47. **Answer: D.** The TCSEC (Trusted Computer System Evaluation Criteria), also known as the Orange Book, defines several levels of assurance requirements for secure computer operations. Confidential operations is not a valid level. The valid levels of operational assurance specified in TCSEC are

    System architecture

    System integrity

    Covert channel analysis

    Trusted facility management

    Trusted recovery

48. **Answer: D.** B2 systems must support separate operator and system administrator roles. TCSEC requirements for separation of operator and system administrator roles are closely tied to the concept of least privilege, because TCSEC sets controls on what various individuals can do.

49. **Answer: B.** IPL (initial program load) signifies the start of a system. It is important because an operator may boot the device into a nonnetworked configuration or from a CD, a USB, or even a floppy disk to hijack or bypass normal security measures.

50. **Answer: D.** Packet padding, noise transmission, and covert channels are considered effective countermeasures against traffic analysis. Attackers use ARP redirection to redirect traffic on switched networks.

51. **Answer: C.** Mandatory vacations and job rotation help identify fraud. ISO 27001:2005 certification is awarded for quality information security management systems and requires more checks than just demonstrated fraud controls.

52. **Answer: B.** Rebooting after the system has failed is called an emergency system restart. A system cold start occurs when the computer is powered on (not a reboot). A system reboot occurs when the system is shut down gracefully and allowed to reboot. The phrase "system hard boot" is a distracter.

53. **Answer: A.** A maintenance hook is a backdoor into an application that is sometimes used during the development process. These hooks need to be removed before a product is released. A parallel test is performed on a product that is deemed ready to release. This hook needs to be removed as soon as possible, and then the change control documentation needs to be completed to record the change in the software's operation.

54. **Answer: B.** Answers A, B, and C are all techniques for clearing a drive. The correct answer is the Gutmann Method. Neither zeroing (writing all 0s to the drive) nor wiping suggests a number of repeat passes. Although the Gutmann method (35 wipes) is considered excessive with today's technology even by Peter Gutmann ("Data

Remanence in Semiconductor Devices"), it would provide greater assurance than a single pass with 0s or a wipe. The Department of Defense discusses different requirements for secure wiping of media in DoD 5220.22.

55. **Answer: D.** Negligence is the number-one cause of data loss.

56. **Answer: A.** A RAID 0 involves data striping only; there is no redundancy. RAID 1 is mirroring. RAID 5 uses interleaved parity, where the parity is written to all drives. RAID 10 is a combination of RAID 0 and RAID 1 and can recover from multiple drive failures.

57. **Answer: D.** Phishing, spear phishing, and whaling refer to email hacks that seek to get a victim to click a link that leads to loss of information. Spear phishing is when a group or person has been specifically targeted. Whaling is when the person is highly visible and/or important to society. Pharming does not involve email; it involves redirecting traffic to a malicious site. Pwn 2 Own is a competition at CANSECWEST that challenges participants to find weaknesses in popular PC operating systems.

58. **Answer: C.** Ethical hackers are trained security professionals who can look for weaknesses in your IT structure. Script kiddies are people who play with downloadable free tools. They often can cause more damage than benefit from their testing. A cracker is a malicious hacker. Pharmer is a distracter.

59. **Answer: C.** Memory sticks can copy and hold large amounts of information. This presents a security risk, because someone can easily place one of these devices in his pocket and carry the information out of the company. Although answers A, B, and D are important, they are not the most important security concern.

60. **Answer: D.** The worst state for an IDS is a false negative. A false negative means that an event occurred but no alarm was triggered.

61. **Answer: C.** The concept behind trusted recovery is that a trusted system should be able to recover from a failure. Trusted recovery is defined in Common Criteria. The three specified types are manual recovery, automated recovery, and automated recovery without undue loss.

62. **Answer: A.** Failure preparation and system recovery are the two main components of trusted recovery. Failure preparation means that adequate backups have been created and are also periodically tested. System recovery is the act of restoration.

63. **Answer: B.** Privileged functions are activities and duties that require special access or elevated levels of control within a trusted environment. Answer A is incorrect because not all activities performed by the security management group are privileged functions. Answer C is incorrect because privileged activities may not always be performed in a secure setting. Answer D is incorrect because just because someone is in the security management group does not mean he or she will perform privileged functions.

64. **Answer: B.** When Clair attempted to log in to her account three times and failed, she reached the clipping level. This caused her account to be suspended. A clipping level is just one of the operation controls an organization can use. Others include mandatory vacations, rotation of duties, and dual controls.

65. **Answer: D.** Installing copper mesh in the facility's outer walls and ceiling is a control against emanation signal leakage. This is a follow-up to an earlier technology known as TEMPEST. Whereas TEMPEST hardened the device, control zones harden the facility.

66. **Answer: C.** Supervision is the best example of a compensating administrative control. Answer A is an example of an administrative recovery control. Answer B is an example of a technical deterrent. Answer D is an example of a technical detective.

67. **Answer: B.** An email relay means that third parties can relay email through your email server. This is considered an undesirable situation because malicious individuals may attempt to use your company to forward their spam. Answer A is incorrect because the company is now less secure, not more secure. Answer C is incorrect because this has nothing to do with users reading their work email at home. Answer D is incorrect because a mail relay is not related to a VPN.

68. **Answer: B.** OS fingerprinting involves looking at responses to active probes to services such as ICMP and TCP to examine subtle changes in the ways in which the protocol stack has been implemented. Two types of fingerprinting exist. The most accurate answer is active, because traffic is being injected into the network and directed toward specific hosts. Passive fingerprinting simply listens to traffic, whereas port scanning looks for specific services running on a host.

69. **Answer: A.** Spoofing is the act of one person or process pretending to be another person or process. Sniffing is to passively intercept data. Hijacking is taking over an existing connection. In a hijacking attack, the attacker is waiting for the victim to connect to a service, and then the attacker takes control. A Trojan is a piece of software that appears to be legitimate but is not, and it contains malicious code.

70. **Answer: B.** Van Eck phreaking is the practice of detecting EMI and wireless signals from CRTs and other electronic equipment with the objective of decoding and revealing the information. TEMPEST was the original technology used to try to deter this type of attack.

71. **Answer: A.** A disaster recovery plan is an example of an administrative recovery control. Answer B is an example of a physical recovery. Answer C is an example of a compensating administrative control. Answer D is an example of a technical detective.

72. **Answer: B.** Separation of duties requires two separate individuals to perform a task. Consider the last time you were at the grocery store and a cost override was needed at the cash register. Most likely the store manager was required to complete this activity; it could not be performed by the cashier. Answers A, C, and D are good controls, but they do not address confidentiality.

73. **Answer: A.** Before a penetration test is performed, several things are of great importance. One is that a signed agreement should be in place before any testing begins. Second, this agreement should very clearly lay out the rules of engagement. The rules of engagement should address what tests are to be performed, what systems are to be tested, and what are acceptable test techniques. Anytime a penetration test is performed, there is always the risk that something can go wrong, but controls can be put in place to mitigate such risks. OSSTMM is a good example of a penetration test methodology. See www.isecom.org/research/osstmm.html.

74. **Answer: B.** A clipping level is a threshold of activity and as such must be exceeded before an alarm or alert is set. It is designed to separate events from incidents. Someone attempting to log in and failing one time is an event. Someone trying to log in 50 times at midnight and failing is an incident. A clipping level is an example of a technical control, not a physical control. An IDS sensor is used to capture events for an IDS. Capturing failed logins is a security control, but this is not the most complete answer.

75. **Answer: B.** Hacking tools are changing. Although the last several years have seen a great increase in hacking tools, the tools themselves have become much more sophisticated and capable. Most of these, such as Metasploit, are easy to use and require very limited technical skills.

76. **Answer: B.** JBOD offers little except the ability to reuse older disks by combining them into one massive drive. JBOD offers no speed improvements and no fault tolerance. Its only advantage is that if one drive dies, you lose only the data on that drive. RAIT can be compared to RAID, but it uses tape drives. MAID is kept inactive until it is used; it can be used for backup or other operations. RAID 1 is disk mirroring and offers fault tolerance.

77. **Answer: C.** Grid computing is similar to clustering but is not the same. Clustering offers a high level of trust, centralized control, and a fault-tolerant technology. Grid computing does not have centralized control; systems can come and go as they please. They can be added on an as-needed basis and could be systems that are used for other purposes. SETI at home is an example. Because of this, grid computing should not be used for highly sensitive projects, because the information may be exposed.

78. **Answer: B.** Degaussing is a method of magnetically scrambling the patterns on a hard drive so that they are unrecoverable. Degaussing, which can be performed by either AC or DC current, creates a large magnetic field. The result is that the information is practically unrecoverable. Zeroization works by zeroing all data on the drive. The pattern of 1s and 0s used makes it very difficult to recover the data. Shredding is a form of physical destruction. As such, it is impossible to recover the information. High-security information stored on disk drives usually is destroyed using this method. Drive wiping is similar to zeroization in that a pattern of 1s and 0s is written to the drive. These passes of 1s and 0s may be done three times, seven times, or more.

79. **Answer: C.** A distributed denial of service uses two or more compromised computers to target and disable a victim's availability. Spoofing is the act of pretending to be a person or process. A denial of service originates from one computer. A mail bomb is used to fill up a victim's email account.

80. **Answer: A.** POP3 uses TCP port 110, and IMAP uses TCP port 143.

81. **Answer: D.** A seven pass drive wipe is the best choice of all the options shown. Answers A, B, and C would not sufficiently remove sensitive information.

82. **Answer: B.** Antivirus would be the least likely to require a review by change management. Answers A. C, and D are incorrect because changes to the recovery plan, upgrading a PBX, and changes to production code are all normally items that would require an update.

82. **Answer: B.** Policy is the most important item because there needs to be a specific policy that governs personal devices connected to the corporate network. Answers A, C, and D are incorrect because the policy would specify connectivity, antivirus protection, and shared network storage.

84. **Answer: A.** Cross site scripting (XSS) occurs when dynamic websites rely on user input; a malicious user can input malicious script into the page by hiding it within legitimate requests. Common exploitations include search engine boxes, online forums, and blogs. Answers B, C, and D do not describe an XSS attack.

85. **Answer: D.** Answers A, B, and C are incorrect because only a logic bomb can be described as a modification of code designed to launch at a specific event.

86. **Answer: False.** The real advantage of MAID is that it reduces power requirements and increases drive life in applications where the data is not accessed frequently.

87. **Answer: True.** IMAP lets users read their messages without automatically downloading them to their systems. POP does not offer that ability. POP can create real problems for mobile users because all their mail ends up being downloaded onto a single device—a laptop, desktop, or mobile device.

88. **Answer: False.** Although the name may sound like something that the company would want to allow, this is not the case. Mail relaying allows someone from outside the organization to send mail through the company's email system. Spammers use this technique to hide their true address and cause the mail relay agent to suffer the blocks that result from being the spam agent.

89. **Answer: True.** A smurf attack works by sending a spoofed ping to all hosts on a network. The reply is spoofed to the victim, and the victim is flooded with ICMP ping traffic.

90. **Answer: False.** When a double-blind assessment is performed, the insiders do not know the time or place of the penetration test. The team performing the assessment has only basic knowledge of the network, such as an IP address range.

91. **Answer: False.** Purging describes clearing hard drives, CDs, DVDs, and other media so that it is next to impossible to recover the information. Common methods used include drive wiping, degaussing, and physical destruction.

92. **Answer: False.** Although keeping employees happy is always important, job rotation is primarily performed to ensure that more than one person can perform a job and uncover fraudulent activities.

93. **Answer: True.** A CCTV system can help prevent problems because individuals may see they are being recorded. A CCTV can also be used as a detective control.

94. **Answer: True.** RAID 1 is the most expensive per byte of data because data is written to two drives, each an exact copy of the other.

95. The answers are as follows:

    A. Antivirus updates: **3.** Daily or as required

    B. Intrusion detection: **2.** Continuously

    C. Penetration testing: **1.** At least once a year

    D. Disaster recovery testing: **5.** Quarterly

    E. Vulnerability scanning: **4.** Weekly or bi-monthly

96. The answers are as follows:

Letter	RAID Level	Description
A	**RAID 10**	Striping and mirroring
B	**RAID 5**	Interleave parity
C	**RAID 1**	Mirroring
D	**RAID 4**	Block-level parity
E	**RAID 2**	Hamming code parity
F	**RAID 0**	Striping
G	**RAID 3**	Byte-level parity

Safari Books Online

FREE Online Edition

Your purchase of *CISSP Practice Questions Exam Cram* includes access to a free online edition for 45 days through the **Safari Books Online** subscription service. Nearly every Pearson IT Certification book is available online through **Safari Books Online**, along with thousands of books and videos from publishers such as Addison-Wesley Professional, Cisco Press, Exam Cram, IBM Press, O'Reilly Media, Prentice Hall, Que, Sams, and VMware Press.

Safari Books Online is a digital library providing searchable, on-demand access to thousand of technology, digital media, and professional development books and videos from leading publishers. With one monthly or yearly subscription price, you get unlimited access to learnin tools and information on topics including mobile app and software development, tips and trick on using your favorite gadgets, networking, project management, graphic design, and much more.

Activate your FREE Online Edition at informit.com/safarifree

STEP 1: Enter the coupon code: NYZYKCB

STEP 2: New Safari users, complete the brief registration form. Safari subscribers, just log in.

If you have difficulty registering on Safari or accessing the online edition, please e-mail customer-service@safaribooksonline.com